Adult lives

A life course perspective

Adult lives

A life course perspective

Edited by Jeanne Katz, Sheila Peace and Sue Spurr

The Open University

First published in 2012 by

The Policy Press, University of Bristol, Fourth Floor, Beacon House,
Queen's Road, Bristol BS8 1QU, UK

www.policypress.co.uk

in association with

The Open University, Walton Hall, Milton Keynes, MK7 6AA, United
Kingdom

www.open.ac.uk

British Library Cataloguing in Publication Data
A catalogue record for this book is available from the British Library.

Library of Congress Cataloging-in-Publication Data
A catalog record for this book has been requested.

ISBN 978 1 44730 043 4 paperback
ISBN 978 1 44730 044 1 hardcover

Text design by The Policy Press, Bristol.
Cover design by Qube Design Associates, Bristol.
Front cover: image kindly supplied by Amy H. Peace Buzzard.
Printed and bound in Great Britain by Hobbs, Southampton.
The Policy Press uses environmentally responsible print
partners.

FSC
www.fsc.org
MIX
Paper from
responsible sources
FSC® C020438

Contents

Acknowledgements

Every effort has been made to trace the copyright holders, but if any have been inadvertently overlooked the publishers will be pleased to make the necessary arrangements at the first opportunity. Grateful acknowledgement is made to the following sources for permission to reproduce material in this book.

Part I Contextualising adulthood

Real voice I.1   Extract from *The Diving Bell and the Butterfly* (1998) London: Fourth Estate Ltd.

Chapter 1   Extract from V.L. Bengtson, G.H. Elder Jr., and N.M. Putney, 'The life course perspective on ageing: Linked lives, timing, and history' in M.L. Johnson (ed.) *The Cambridge Handbook of Age and Ageing* (2005), Cambridge: Cambridge University Press, © Cambridge University Press, reproduced with permission.

Chapter 3   Extract from D. Phillips, *Quality of Life: Concept, policy and practice*, © 2006, London: Routledge. Reproduced by permission of Taylor & Francis Books UK.

Chapter 4   Extract from A. Bowling, *Ageing Well: Quality of life in old age*, ©2005, Buckingham: Open University Press. Reproduced with the kind permission of Open University Press. All rights reserved.

Chapter 5   Extract from *Sociology of Health and Illness* (1982) vol. 4, no. 2, pp. 167–82 (Wiley).

Chapter 6   Extract from T.C. Harrison and A. Stuifbergen, 'A hermeneutic phenomenological analysis of aging with a childhood onset disability', *Health Care for Women International* (2005) vol. 26, no. 8, pp. 731–47 (Routledge), reprinted by permission of the publisher (Taylor & Francis Group, http://www.informaworld.com).

Chapter 7   Extract from *Ageing, Health and Care* (2010), Bristol: The Policy Press.

Chapter 8   Extract reproduced by permission of SAGE Publications, London, Los Angeles, New Delhi and Singapore, from Bond, J., Peace, S., Dittmann-Kohli, F. and Westerhoff, G.J. (eds) *Ageing in Society: European perspectives on gerontology* (© 2007) London: Sage Publications.

Chapter 9   Extract from T. Kitwood, *Dementia Reconsidered: The person comes first*, ©1997, Buckingham: Open University Press. Reproduced with the kind permission of Open University Press. All rights reserved.

Chapter 11   Extract from *Disability: A life course approach* (2003) Cambridge: Polity Press.

Chapter 12   Extract from C. Bigby (2004) *Ageing with a Lifelong Disability: A guide to practice, program and policy issues for human services professionals*, London and Philadelphia: Jessica Kingsley Publishers. Reproduced with kind permission of Jessica Kingsley Publishers.

Part II Transforming adulthood

Part III Understanding adulthood

Chapter 36   Extract from A. Gallagher and N. Sykes, 'A little bit of heaven for a
              few? A case analysis', *Ethics and Social Welfare* (2008) vol. 2, no. 3,
              pp. 299–307, reprinted by permission of the publisher (Taylor &
              Francis Group, http://www.informaworld.com).
Chapter 37   Extract from J. Mason, 'Mixing methods in a qualitatively driven way',
              Qualitative Research, vol. 6, no. 1, pp. 9–25, copyright © 2006 by Sage
              Publications. Reprinted by permission of SAGE.
Chapter 39   Extract from *BMJ* (2008) vol. 337, pp. 687–9.
Chapter 40   Extract from R. Jones and R. Ward, *LGBT Issues: Looking beyond
              categories* (2010) Edinburgh: Dunedin Academic Press, reproduced
              with permission.
Chapter 42   Extract from *Journal of Advanced Nursing* (2010) vol. 66, no. 9,
              pp. 1968–79 (Wiley).
Chapter 43   Extract from *BMJ* (2009) vol. 339, pp. 737–9.
Real voice III.1 Extract from *Keeper* (2009) London: Short Books.

Introduction

Jeanne Katz, Sheila Peace and Sue Spurr

Adult lives: A life course perspective brings together chapters and 'real voices' written from many different perspectives. The title *Adult lives* defines the nature of the narrative succinctly, as our concern moves beyond just one aspect of ageing that could encompass old age and the multidisciplinary focus of gerontology to a broader definition that takes on board a life course perspective and addresses the diversity of all adulthood.

In taking a life course perspective, the aim is to understand how those living and working together in an ageing society interrelate. Today global and personal ageing are intertwined. It is estimated that during 2014 the number of people over the age of 65 living in the UK will overtake the number under the age of 16 (Jeavans, 2004), and that by 2034, 5 per cent of the population will be aged 85 or over (ONS, 2010), 2.5 times more than in 2009. The proportion of people between young adulthood and the 'third age' (over 60) has also grown in relation to children and young people in western industrialised societies. These adult lives are defined by the experience of history, are structurally specific and draw on different interpersonal resources. Experiences of the life course alter as different cohorts move through time, and debates continue over changing attitudes and wishes. There is a need to recognise the impact of both the past and present on future adult lives.

While some chapters focus on later life, the aim is to centre on issues that will interest a wide audience. This collection offers the opportunity to generate ideas between people of different generations and cohorts, and across people with different roles within society, whether as spouses, siblings, parents, children, carers, practitioners, relatives or friends. In terms of policy and practice the collection will be of specific interest to those working in health, social care and housing as well as in many allied areas.

It is for these reasons that there are two different forms of content: a concern to hear real voices, and chosen chapters that are either newly commissioned for this reader or have already been published. In bringing together this combination of readings the aim is to focus on the breadth of everyday living and the existing range of scholarship. You will find that the real voices come at the beginning or end of each part of the selected readings, where we hear the stories of a partner whose spouse has experienced a stroke; a daughter-in-law whose mother-in-law experiences dementia; a couple who are living with the experience of mental health problems. These real voices are central to this reader, adding reality to more structured research and discussion.

The selected content considers the individual – their biological, social and psychological character – as well as the society in which they live. It reviews and offers a critique of this duality, exploring and positioning personal lives. In addition it seeks to identify a number of structural, practical, ethical and political dimensions of the societal infrastructure for supporting adults throughout their lives. To capture and structure this diversity of readings they have been grouped into three parts that focus on contextualising, transforming and understanding adulthood, which are broadly outlined as follows.

Part I: Contextualising adulthood

An understanding of adulthood is addressed through different aspects of the life course that recognise the significance of diversity within ageing, and where the context of ageing is identified as biological, social and environmental. A focus on individual lives considers the implications of physical ageing for functioning and participating in society. While the complexity of personal relationships demonstrates levels of interdependence, the many contexts in which people live situate their lives. Here the implications for the individual and their social networks of both social inclusion and exclusion are also explored.

Part II: Transforming adulthood

A human rights perspective is the common theme for grounding policy and practice that influences and supports adult lives. This is especially true for those dependent on health, social care and accommodation where practices such as partnership working, assessment and safeguarding are fundamental. The impact of globalisation is also addressed and varied examples bring new perspectives from across the world.

Part III: Understanding adulthood

The final part of the reader returns to a wider understanding of adulthood that can be gained first, through considering the ethical principles that may guide relationships and second, by examining how research evidence interprets adult life and interacts with practice and policy. In particular it addresses the value of qualitative and multi-method approaches to research in unpacking the complexity of life as seen in the real voices which illuminate the text throughout.

★★★★★★★★★★★★

The chapters in this book are not intended to provide a comprehensive overview of adulthood, ageing or the life course. Clearly there are many other readings that, space permitting, would have equally enhanced this reader. Nonetheless, we believe that this particular collection will encourage critical thinking and bring together a more integrated way of considering adult lives across the life course.

References

Jeavans, C. (2004) 'Welcome to the ageing future', BBC News, 29 November (http://newsvote.bbc.co.uk/mpapps/pagetools/print/news.bbc.co.uk/1/hi/uk/4012797.stm).

ONS (Office for National Statistics) (2010) 'Ageing: fastest increase in the "oldest old"', 24 June (www.statistics.gov.uk/cci/nugget.asp?id=949).

PART I

Contextualising adulthood

Introduction

The first part of this reader, divided into three sections, draws our attention to the experience and context of adult lives. In recognising not only the central tenets of biography that encompass the biological, social and psychological characteristics of the individual, it also situates this experience in both everyday and exceptional environments where personal social capital can be tested, enabled or excluded.

In thinking about adulthood and ageing, 21st-century researchers and practitioners refer to concepts of quality of life and the life course that underpin this section. Both these concepts are contested and interpreted in different ways and the chapters here provide theoretical, research-based and practical illustrations. In their influential chapter, **Vern Bengston and colleagues** set the scene. They explain that only in the mid-20th century did researchers take on board Wright Mills' (1959) view of the integral relationship between history and biography with implications for quality of life that paved the way for a different approach to research which really recognised individuals' perspectives. Presenting a detailed discussion of the principles underlying a life course perspective, they explain why the traditional life cycle approach is no longer appropriate for 21st-century adults living during rapid social change. But in ageing populations do people think ahead to plan for later life? **Rebecca Jones** explores whether and how people imagine themselves as old, and why this is important from a biographical point of view as well as in terms of planning for a future quality of life.

Underlining one of the themes of this reader, that 'quality of life must start with the individual, her or his own feelings, thoughts and emotions', **David Phillips** emphasises the centrality of human autonomy. He suggests that any inclusive theory or conceptualisation of quality of life must acknowledge how individuals view their own lives and seek to develop mastery that can give satisfaction and/or pleasure. However, measuring quality of life is complex, particularly as subjective and objective well-being are not necessarily related. **Ann Bowling**, a widely recognised author in this field, notes that formerly, there were widespread assumptions that measurement of quality of life in old age was impossible. Similarly

1

to Phillips, she notes that quality of life is not only a contested topic, but different forms of measurement suggest different priorities. Nevertheless, through combining the results of quantitative and qualitative research, her data suggest some patterns in the stated priorities of older people in relation to quality of life, including: psychological well-being, good health, good relationships and being active socially. However, she cautions against making assumptions that these are universal beliefs, noting substantial differences for some sizeable minorities with diverse lifestyles or with very different life experiences.

The quality of life and health of those with lifelong or disabling conditions is explored in separate chapters, one by **Michael Bury** and the other by **Tracie Harrison** and **Alexa Stuifbergen**. Bury's seminal paper on biographical disruption uses the example of rheumatoid arthritis to address interruptions in life and to illustrate how different people perceive the illness, drawing on different personal resources, both cognitive and material, to manage and justify their positions as well as explain the disease. In the case of women who since childhood have lived their lives with the ravages of polio, Harrison and Stuifbergen argue that they endeavoured to normalise and 'pushed their bodies and dismissed their physical decline as long as possible' in order to try to accommodate the contemporary cultural norms for women. This work positions the person as engaged and capable of experiencing different levels of well-being. In these chapters the life trajectory of each individual is guided by the experience of their own personal biological profile, and a focus on health and well-being forms the basis of the next section, which explores in greater detail the epidemiological, social and psychological factors influencing quality of life.

Section Two begins with an extract from **Christina Victor**'s book *Ageing, health and care*, considering the social implications of health differences. She describes the link between health and mortality, and why socioeconomic status has usually been associated with health outcomes, recognising that the association of status with the labour market raises gender differences. Social class or social position is also associated with longevity as well as the health experiences of older people, but does not tell us about their quality of life, nor is this a good explanatory variable for the health experiences and life expectancy of minority ethnic groups. Moving from the statistical and social to the psychological, **Alfons Marcoen and colleagues** provide an overview of psycho-gerontological research and theories. They foreground what happens psychologically when people age, focusing not only on losses and deficits, but on the creative opportunities to sustain and develop a positive sense of self. Such recognition of self is also central to the next chapter that collates some subsections from *Dementia reconsidered* by the late **Tom Kitwood**. Kitwood pioneered positive images of treatment of those with dementia. He recognised how possibly due to fear, many cultures condoned the depersonalisation and dehumanisation of those with serious disabilities, particularly people with dementia. He developed the concept of personhood, and person–centred care, ensuring that it not only reflected current scientific knowledge, but also care practice. But person–centred care for frail older people, as argued by **Mike Nolan and Serena Allan**, while acknowledging the importance of the self, does not take into account the reciprocity involved in all aspects of care, and based on Nolan et al's (2006) Senses Framework, they suggest instead 'relationship–centred care' and demonstrate how this works in practice.

Chapters from **Mark Priestley** and **Christine Bigby** conclude this section on individual ageing and social relationships by focusing on some of the complexities of ageing with disabilities. Priestley unpacks the 'accepted' notions of adulthood and the life course, and the underlying assumption that help with daily living does not apply to people as adults. He argues that as a consequence of this widely held belief, disabled people are infantilised, assumed to be either dependent cross–generationally or institutionalised, and presumed unable to 'exercise their adult rights and responsibilities'. Bigby also acknowledges the disabling environment, but suggests a strategy for developing 'formalised' informal support for people with intellectual disabilities, especially in later life. Networks are (built and) lost increasingly during the life course for people with intellectual disabilities as their situation means they often lack opportunities to establish relationships. She proposes that formal services facilitate opportunities for meeting new people in order to foster, develop and maintain strong relationships to enhance their quality of care and social well-being over their life course.

The context of adult lives forms the last section of Part I. While **Sheila Peace and colleagues** are concerned with the relationship between the person and their environment in later life, theoretical perspectives relating to issues such as press-competence can be used across the life course. Here they explore how and why this has come to be used in environmental gerontology, considering how a particular environment can be enabling, or disabling, for people with different levels of competence or motivation. In explaining 'place theory and dementia concepts' they express the hope that environmental (re)design will improve quality of life for those with limited personal resources and/or cognitive capacity. Building on the person–environment fit, **Caroline Holland and Sheila Peace**, in the subsequent chapter, suggest that the life course is a helpful organising concept for situating the adult in relation to their accommodation across the life course. They argue that this approach facilitates comparisons between the causes and effects of relocation. They also raise issues about the potential of assistive technologies to enhance the lives of older people, in some cases facilitating 'staying put', and in the following chapter **Caroline Holland** explains further why it is important to both understand older people's current relationship with technologies, and to involve them in design. She chronicles how older people when younger embraced new innovations, but now may feel left behind and disempowered by the rapid development of technologies; to a degree, they are socially excluded.

The issue of social exclusion is a powerful theme in this reader, applicable to a variety of contexts and environments, and is therefore the subject of the next three chapters, which focus on different interpretations of 'community'. The first two chapters explore specific types of social exclusion. **Barbara Glover**, in discussing the position of older and disabled prisoners, illustrates how despite specific legislation prison accommodation does not accommodate the increasing limitations of prisoners as they age. Her research elucidates the extent to which these older prisoners are physically and emotionally excluded from functioning, for example, being able to undertake conventional personal care. Likewise, **Josie Tetley**, in moving us from accommodation to community, describes a second 'invisible' group of older people, that of the Black and African Caribbean population living in the north of England. Her sample were drawn exclusively from those who were known to a centre that catered exclusively for their community; however, like the older prisoners, they too had difficulty in having their specific needs addressed, as a result of local services not understanding how they wanted these met, and their interpretation of what was on offer. The essence of these pieces can be tested against the edited chapter from **Daniel Dorling's** influential book, *Injustice,* which concludes this section where he presents a historical overview of different forms of social exclusion in affluent societies. He explains how concepts of well-being related to finances have developed over the past century, exploring ways in which poverty is measured, looking not only at specific indicators but also at personal meaning that can vary across affluent nations.

References

Nolan, M.R., Brown, J., Davies, S., Nolan, J. and Keady, J. (2006) *The Senses Framework: Improving care for older people through a relationship-centred approach,* Getting Research into Practice (GRIP) Series, No 2, Sheffield: University of Sheffield.

Wright Mills, C. (1959) *The sociological imagination,* Oxford: Oxford University Press.

The Turnip
Jean-Dominique Bauby

Extract from *The Diving Bell and The Butterfly* (1998) London: Fourth Estate Ltd.

ON 8 JUNE it will be six months since my new life began. Your letters are piling up on the dresser, your drawings on my wall, and since I cannot hope to answer each one of you I have decided to issue these *samizdat* bulletins to report on my life, my progress and my hopes. At first I refused to believe that anything serious had happened. In my semi-conscious state following the coma, I thought I would shortly be back in my Paris stamping-grounds, with just a couple of canes to help me along.'

Those were the first words of the first mailing of my monthly letter from Berck, which I decided in late spring to send to my friends and associates. Addressed to some sixty people, that first bulletin created a mild stir and repaired some of the damage caused by rumour. The city, that monster with a hundred mouths and a thousand ears, which knows nothing but says everything, had written me off. At the Cafe de Flore, one of those base camps of Parisian snobbery which send up rumours like flights of carrier pigeons, some close friends of mine overheard a conversation at the next table. The gossipers were as greedy as vultures who have just discovered a disembowelled antelope. 'Did you know that Bauby is now a total vegetable?' said one. 'Yes, I heard. A complete vegetable,' came the reply. The word 'vegetable' must have tasted sweet on the know-it-all's tongue, for it came up several times between mouthfuls of Welsh rarebit. The tone of voice left no doubt that henceforth I belonged on a vegetable stall and not to the human race. France was at peace. One couldn't shoot the bearers of bad news. Instead I would have to rely on myself if I wanted to prove that my IQ was still higher than a turnip's.

Thus was born a collective correspondence which keeps me in touch with those I love. And my hubris has had gratifying results. Apart from an irrecoverable few who maintain a stubborn silence, everybody now understands that he can join me in my cocoon, even if sometimes the cocoon takes me into unexplored territory.

I receive remarkable letters. They are opened for me, unfolded and spread out before my eyes, in a daily ritual that gives the arrival of the post the character of a hushed and holy ceremony. I carefully read each letter myself. Some of them are serious in tone, discussing the meaning of life, invoking the supremacy of the soul, the mystery of every existence. And by a curious reversal, the people who focus most closely on these fundamental questions tend to be people I had known only superficially. Their small talk had masked hidden depths. Had I been blind and deaf. or does it take the glare of disaster to show a person's true nature?

Other letters simply relate the small events that punctuate the passage of time: roses picked at dusk, the laziness of a rainy Sunday, a child crying himself to sleep. Capturing the moment, these small slices of life, these small gusts of happiness, move me more deeply than all the rest. A couple of lines or eight pages, a Middle Eastern stamp or a suburban postmark ... I hoard all these letters like treasure. One day I hope to fasten them end to end in a half-mile streamer, to float in the wind like a banner raised to the glory of friendship.

It will keep the vultures at bay.

SECTION ONE

Quality of life and the life course

1

The life course perspective on ageing: Linked lives, timing, and history

Vern L. Bengtson, Glen H. Elder, Jr., and Norella M. Putney

Only in the last few decades have researchers in ageing recognized the importance of larger social and historical contexts for understanding the health and wellbeing of individuals across the lifespan. Prior to the mid 1960s, the study of human lives was exceedingly rare in sociology and psychology, especially in relation to sociohistorical context (Elder, 1998). Most human development research was characterized by a life cycle approach, one of the oldest accounts of how lives and families are organized over time. The life cycle provided a useful way of thinking about the intergenerational patterning of lives, and their sequence of role transitions, such as marriage and childbearing. The duration of inter-generational cycles, however, varies greatly, depending on the timing of marriage and childbearing. The greater the time spread between the generations, the more diverse the individual's historical experience. In addition the life cycle does not represent contemporary patterns of divorce and remarriage or childbearing outside of marriage. And it does not apply to the never married or non-parents. While the concept of life cycle provided an account of role sequences and linked lives, it did not locate people according to their life stage or historical context.

In the 1960s and 1970s, the life cycle approach began to converge with a new awareness of the multiple meanings of age. Age orders social roles and new events, but it also orders people through birth year and birth cohorts. Chronological age refers to stage in the developmental ageing process. These new ways of thinking about age included an emphasis on subjective experiences with society's age structures and the individual's own construction of the lifecourse, as expressed particularly in the pioneering work of Bernice Neugarten (Neugarten and Datan, 1973). Age distinctions were required to place families in history and to mark the transitions of adult life. Since the mid 1980s, inquiry into the continuity and change of human lives in relation to interpersonal, structural, and historical forces has grown exponentially (Elder, 2003; Elder and Johnson, 2001). Lifecourse studies have become integral to social scientific research on ageing.

The lifecourse perspective

The lifecourse as concept and theoretical orientation

The 'lifecourse' is conceptualized as a sequence of age-linked transitions that are embedded in social institutions and history. As a theoretical orientation, the lifecourse perspective sensitizes researchers to the fundamental importance of historical conditions and change for understanding individual development and family life. It establishes a common field of inquiry by defining a framework that guides research in terms of problem identification and formulation, variable selection and rationales, and strategies of design and analysis. The institutional structuring of lives is at the core of lifecourse analysis (Mortimer and Shanahan, 2003). Institutional contexts – the family, schools, work and labor markets, church, government – define both the normative pathways of social roles, including key transitions, and the psychological, behavioral, and health-related trajectories of persons as they move through them.

Age, in its various meanings, serves as the analytic link between changing lives, changing family relations, and changing historical contexts. Families are age-differentiated, especially because generational position defines an individual's place in the extended family structure and shapes identities, roles, and responsibilities. At the same time, families are age-integrated in that individuals of varying, ages and cohorts are joined together and family-related roles and activities extend across life even as specific roles and activities shift up the generational ladder over time (Settersten, 2003). Within pluralistic contemporary societies, lifecourse trajectories and transitions display considerable variability. Yet despite this variability, continuity remains a predominant feature of individual psychological and behavioral trajectories. Multigenerational families as well display considerable continuity over time.

Principles of the lifecourse

Five principles define the lifecourse perspective.

First is the principle of 'linked lives,' which emphasizes the interconnectedness of lives, particularly as linked across the generations by bonds of kinship. Lives are embedded in relationships with people and are influenced by them. They are linked over time in relation to changing times, places, and social institutions. Economic declines can have reverberating effects on the multiple and interlocking pathways of family members. For example, a mother's entry into the labor force can alleviate her family's financial troubles and contribute to her children's educational attainment, but it may also change the routines of family life or the balance of power in her marital relationship. Likewise, the plans of grandparents for retirement can be changed when adult children and grandchildren return home and need their support.

The second lifecourse principle pertains to historical time and place, emphasizing the importance of social and historical context in shaping individual lives. Large events such as depressions and wars, or the relative tranquillity or turbulence of a historical period, shape individual psychology, family interactions, and world views. Such historical events and conditions create the opportunities and constraints that circumscribe choices and behaviors and can change the direction of lives. Follow-up studies of children who grew up during the Depression show that sociohistorical events (such as the Second World War and the US government's G.I. Bill) sometimes mitigated the negative effects of economic deprivation in childhood, opening up educational and career opportunities in young adulthood (Elder 1987). Social change can also reduce options, as occurred in the economic restructuring of the 1980s and 1990s.

The third principle emphasizes the importance of transitions and their timing relative to the social contexts in which individuals make choices (Bengtson and Allen, 1993; Elder, 1995); the developmental antecedents and consequences of life transitions, events, and behavior patterns vary according to their timing in a person's life. There can be a 'best fit' in the timing of individual development and family life stage, and their temporal convergence with structural and historically created opportunities (Elder et al., 2003). For example, all age cohorts were confronted by the social upheavals of the late 1960s and 1970s, but at different stages in their lifecourse which presented different options and adaptive pressures. Biographical and historical timing had consequences for their demographic behavior, occupational outcomes, and psychological wellbeing (Putney and Bengtson, 2003). The pace of biographical, institutional, and historical change are characteristically asynchronous, producing structural or cultural lags. These disjunctures create tensions in individual lives, but they can also provide the impetus for change.

The fourth principle concerns agency and the idea that planfulness and effort can affect life outcomes. Lifecourse theory recognizes that individuals are active agents in the construction of their lives. They make choices within the opportunities and constraints provided by family background, stage in the lifecourse, structural arrangements, and historical conditions [...].

The fifth principle centers on the idea that ageing and human development are life-long processes, and the relationships, events, and behaviors of earlier life stages have consequences for later life relationships, statuses, and wellbeing. For example, longitudinal research has shown that the nurturing affirmation of children by parents contributes to higher self-esteem in adulthood (Roberts and Bengtson, 1996). Personal change and continuity are represented by concepts of lifespan development, such as cumulative advantage and disadvantage and self-identity.

Generations, cohorts, and social change

[...] The concept of 'generation', most commonly used as a kinship term denoting position in the biological line of descent, does not easily index historical location or processes. This is because differences in childbearing patterns and the temporal gap between generations vary between families. In this sense, generations and age groups are not equivalent.

To understand the diverse pathways of individuals and families over the last half-century requires that they be situated in historical context. Analytically, this can be accomplished through the concept of 'age cohort'. Cohort implies the intersection of historical influence as indexed by birth year, and individual development or maturation. Birth cohorts share a social and cultural history, experiencing events and cultural moods when they are at the same stage of life. Characteristics of a birth cohort and events that the cohort experiences combine to affect members in distinctive ways, influencing their attitudes, behaviors, and outcomes across the entire lifecourse. Economic and political conditions leave lasting marks on those born in different historical periods. For women, the interaction of biology and biography with prevailing gender role norms and structural constraints has profoundly shaped their lives, but it has done so in historically specific ways, depending on their cohort membership. There is much variability within cohorts as well; members can be distinguished by class, gender, race, or their age when confronted by different socioeconomic events and conditions.

Cohort effects refer to the impact of historical events and structural arrangements on members of a given cohort as they grow older. However, such effects are not one-way; ageing cohorts in turn affect social structures (Riley et al., 1994). The responses of one cohort to historical experiences often become normative patterns, affecting later born cohorts (Alwin and McCammon, 2003).

Age cohorts operate as forces of social change. 'Generational turnover', or cohort succession, is often cited as a significant source of population change in attitudes and behaviors, as new cohorts bring their unique orientations into the population (Ryder, 1965). The cohort perspective suggests that historical conditions leave an indelible imprint on the attitudes of young adults at a time when they are most susceptible to absorbing the social values of the period, a phenomenon known as the 'impressionable youth' hypothesis (Alwin et al., 1991; Alwin and Krosnick, 1991; Clausen, 1993; Elder, 1994). Crucial to this argument is the way personal biography aligns with historical contingencies to produce sharp and durable variations across cohorts.

Paradoxically, societies can change both because individuals change (intracohort or aging effects) and because they remain stable or unchanged after an early period of socialization. Change occurs through cohort succession, where earlier born cohorts with certain values and characteristics are replaced by younger cohorts with different values and characteristics (Alwin and McCammon, 2003). This set of mechanisms is referred to as the Age–Period–Cohort model of social change because these mechanisms encapsulate the influence of ageing, time period and cohort membership on social change. The impact of a historical event on a cohort may be decomposed into a main effect (that which affects other cohorts similarly), and a unique effect (that which affects the cohort particularly). In addition, the strength or direction of change due to ageing may be conditioned on the unique historical location of each cohort.

De-institutionalization of the lifecourse

The structure of the lifecourse is closely linked to work life transitions. Across the first half of the twentieth century, these transitions became increasingly segmented into three distinct periods, reflecting an age-differentiated lifecourse (Riley et al., 1994): preparation for work when young (education); work, during the middle years; and retirement from work in late midlife (Kohli, 1986). In the last few decades, however, there are signs that age structuring in education and work may be loosening a de-institutionalization, or destandardization, of the lifecourse (Heinz, 2003). These changes in the 'expected' lifecourse have implications for the study of lives and multigenerational families. Lifecourse patterns once thought fairly stable have become more fluid. They have shifted across different spheres – education, work, retirement, family – for successive cohorts of men and women, for subgroups (especially by race and social class), and across cultures.

Individuals can now move between areas and simultaneously pursue education, work, and leisure experiences throughout life, rather than being restricted to one or the other in different stages of life. In the area of work, there are indications that patterned 'career' trajectories are giving way to increasing individualization (Heinz, 2003). Heinz argues that in post-industrial society there is an increasing emphasis upon personal decisions and responsibility in the shaping of work life, and a corresponding decline of normative age-markers for the timing and sequencing of labor market participation, and the timing of retirement. Paid work remains the foundation of the lifecourse, but continuous careers and stable employment are less certain because of more turbulent and globalized labor markets. At the beginning of the millennium, workers are increasingly 'on their own', assuming greater responsibility for the timing of transitions, the time spent in school and work, the construction of their own pathways through the employment system, and ultimately the adequacy of provisions in retirement.

[...]

Conclusion

How does one make sense of the complex connections that link the course of an individual's life within the context of broader social influences, such as family and society? What are the effects of social change on the experiences and direction of human lives, and on the processes of ageing itself? Such questions have long puzzled developmental theorists who have sought to understand the complex interplay of environmental and biological forces in human development (Baltes, 1997; Bronfenbrenner, 1979, 1989). It was not until the 1960s that family and ageing researchers interested in the study of lives began to pay heed to Mills' (1959) central insight that history shapes, and is shaped by, biography. A convergence of influences required new ways of looking at how people lived their lives – understandings that far exceeded the reach of traditional life cycle approaches. Several important trends of the twentieth century account for this dramatic change in research focus and energy: the maturation of early child development samples; the rapidity of social change: the changing age structure of society, particularly the ageing of the populations; and the dramatic growth of longitudinal research over the last few decades.

Since the 1960s, the lifecourse approach itself has been shaped by studies of the social world, its constraints, options, and social change. As a theoretical orientation, the lifecourse perspective orients research as to how lives are socially organized in biological, social, and historical time and guides explanations of how the resulting social pattern affects the way individuals think, feel, and act, as they age over time. Their proper study challenges us to take all life stages into account through linked lives across generations, from infancy to the grandparents of old age. This approach is particularly relevant today, where the rapid growth of the oldest segments of society lends greater significance to problems of the aged. Lifecourse studies are helping to locate people in a matrix of age-graded, family relationships and to place families in the social structures, cultures, and populations of time and place. These studies have brought time and temporality to an understanding of individual lives, families, and ageing.

References

Alwin, D. F., and J. A. Krosnick (1991) "Aging, cohorts, and the stability of socio-political orientations over the life span," *American Journal of Sociology*, 97 (1): 169–95.

Alwin, D. F., and R. J. McCammon (2003) "Generations, cohorts and social change." In J.T. Mortimer and M. J. Shanahan, eds., *Handbook of the life course.* New York: Kluwer Academic/Plenum Press, pp. 3–19.

Alwin, D. F., Cohen, R., and T. Newcomb (1991) *Political attitudes over the life span: the Bennington women after 50 years.* Madison, Wis.: University of Wisconsin Press.

Baltes, P. B. (1997) "The role of modelling processes in personality development." In *The young child: reviews of research.* Washington, D.C.: National Association for the Education of Young Children.

Bengtson, V. L., and K. Allen (1993) "The life course perspective applied to families over time." In P. Boss, W. Doherty, R. La Rosa, W. Schumm, and S. Steinmetz, eds., *Sourcebook of family theories and methods: a contextual approach.* New York: Kluwer Academic/Plenum Press, pp. 469–98.

Bronfenbrenner, U. (1979) *The ecology of human development.* Cambridge, Mass.: Harvard University Press.

Bronfenbrenner, U. (1989) "Ecological systems theory." In R. Vasta, ed., *Annuals of child development,* Vol. VI. Greenwich, Conn.: JAI Press.

Clausen, J.A. (1993) *American lives.* New York: Free Press.

Conger, R. D., and G. H. Elder, eds. (1994) *Families in troubled times. Adapting to change in rural America.* New York: Aldine de Gruyter.

Elder, G. H., Jr. (1987) "War mobilization and the life course: a cohort of World War II veterans," *Sociological Forum,* 2 (3): 449–72.

Elder, G.H., Jr. (1994) "Time, human agency, and social change: perspectives on the life course," *Social Psychology Quarterly,* 57: 4–15.

Elder, G. H., Jr. (1995) "The life course paradigm: social change and individual development". In P. Moen, G. H. Elder, Jr., and K. Luscher, eds., *Examining lives in context: perspectives on the ecology of human development*, pp. 101–39.

Elder, G.H., Jr. (1998) "Life course and human development." In W. Damon, ed., *Handbook of child psychology*. New York: Wiley, pp. 939–91.

Elder, G.H., Jr. (2003) "Generations and the life course: their interdependence." Keynote paper presented at the annual meeting of the International Sociological Association, Taipei, Taiwan, March.

Elder, G. H., Jr., and M. K. Johnson (2001) "The life course and aging: challenges, lessons, and new directions." In R.A. Settersten, J., ed., *Invitation to the life course: toward new understandings of later life*. Amityville, N.Y.: Baywood, pp. 49–81.

Elder, G. H., Jr., Johnson, M. K., and R. Crosnoe (2003) "The emergence and development of life course theory." In J. T. Mortimer and M. J. Shanahan, eds., Handbook of the life course. New York: Kluwer Academic/Plenum Press, pp. 3–19.

Heinz, W. R. (2003) "From work trajectories to negotiated careers: the contingent work life course." In J. T. Mortimer and M. J. Shanahan, eds., *Handbook of the life course*. New York: Kluwer Academic/Plenum Press, pp. 185–204.

Kohli, M. (1986) "The world we forgot: a historical review of the life course." In V. W Marshall, ed., *Later life: the social psychology of aging*. Beverly Hills, Calif.: Sage, pp. 271–303.

Mills, C. W. (1959) *The sociological imagination*. New York: Oxford University Press.

Mortimer, J.T. and M.J. Shanahan, eds. (2003) "Preface." In J.T. Mortimer and M.J. Shanahan, eds., *Handbook of the life course*. New York: Kluwer Academic/Plenum Press, pp. xi–xvi.

Neugarten, B. L., and N. Datan (1973) "Sociological perspectives on the life cycle." In P. B. Baltes and K.W. Schaie, eds., *Life-span developmental psychology: personality and socialization*. New York: Academic Press, pp. 53–69.

Putney, N. M., and V. L. Bengtson (2003) "Intergenerational relations in changing times." In J.T. Mortimer and M.J. Shanahan, eds., *Handbook of the life course*. New York: Kluwer Academic/Plenum Press, pp. 149–64.

Riley, M.W., Kahn, R. L., and A. Finer, eds. (1994) *Age and structural lag*. New York: Wiley.

Roberts, R. E. L., and V. L. Bengtson (1996) "Affective ties to parents in early adulthood and self-esteem across 20 years," *Social Psychology Quarterly*, 59: 96–106.

Roberts, R. E. L., and V. L. Bengtson (1999) "The social psychology of values: effects of individual development, social change, and family transmission over the life span." In C. D. Riff and V. W. Marshall, eds., *The self and society in aging processes*. New York: Springer, pp. 453–82.

Ryder, N. B. (1965) "The cohort as a concept in the study of social change," *American Sociological Review*, 30: 843–61.

Settersten, R. A., Jr. (2003) "Age structuring and the rhythm of the life course." In J. T. Mortimer and M. J. Shanahan, eds., *Handbook of the life course*. New York: Kluwer Academic/Plenum Press, pp. 81–98.

2

Imagining old age

Rebecca L. Jones

Introduction

> 'I hardly ever think about getting old and how long my life
> will be because it depresses me. Not to mention the fact that I
> see it as a waste of time. Why think about when I'm going to
> die while I'm still in my prime of living? I should be thinking
> about today and not tomorrow.' (research participant, quoted in
> Altpeter and Marshall, 2003, p 748)

At one level, we all know that, unless we die 'young', we will all grow 'old'
eventually. A life course runs from birth to death and, for most people, this
will include a stage of being 'old'. But somehow, it seems hard for many
people to believe that they will ever really be old themselves.

We might expect that people who are 'middle-aged' or 'older' would
have less difficulty imagining what life will be like when they are old
than people who are currently 'young', since their own old age is less
distant. Certainly we know that younger people often have particularly
negative and homogenised visions of old age (Scott et al, 1998; Mosher-
Ashley and Ball, 1999; Kimuna et al, 2005; Phoenix and Sparkes, 2006,
2007), and we might expect this to mean that younger people would have
greater difficulty in imagining being old themselves. However, it is well
documented that even people who would usually by categorised as 'old'
or 'older' on the basis of their chronological age often speak as if they are
not themselves old (Bultena and Powers, 1978), as, for example, when
a 90-year-old describes a 70-year-old as an 'old dear' (Jones, 2006). The
difficulty of imagining yourself as old extends across the life course.

In UK English there are significant differences between the adjectives
'old' and 'older'. 'Old' is an absolute, whereas 'older' is relative to something
else, often another person. The term 'older person' is generally considered
to be more polite than the term 'old person', but some people argue that
we should reclaim 'old' as part of a wider project of not denying ageing.
This topic is debated by Andrews (1999, 2000), Bytheway (2000) and

Gibson (2000). This chapter focuses particularly on people imagining themselves to be 'old' rather than merely 'older'.

Some of the explanations that gerontologists and other scholars have given for why people often find it hard to imagine being old are examined first. The chapter then asks why it matters that people should be able to imagine their own old age. Finally, some techniques are considered that could be used by researchers and other people if they want to encourage people to think about their own old age.

Why might imagining old age be difficult?

Many gerontologists and other scholars have argued that modern UK society is ageist (Butler, 1969; Macdonald and Rich, 1984; Bytheway and Johnson, 1990; Bytheway, 1995, 2005; Copper, 1997). By this they generally mean that people who are categorised as 'old' or 'older' are systematically undervalued and discriminated against. If people generally fear and devalue old age, it is perhaps not surprising if they don't want to put themselves in the category 'old person', even in their imagination.

Many people associate growing old with bodily decline and a loss of sexual attractiveness, particularly for women (Sontag, 1978). Since we live in a culture which places a high value on youthful types of health and sexual attractiveness, it is understandable if people don't want to be associated with the opposite (Heilbrun, 1997).

Some gerontologists have argued that many people think of old people as being so different from themselves that becoming old involves losing your true self. Featherstone and Hepworth (1989, 1991) identified a common trope of a 'mask of ageing': someone in middle age or later life looking at themselves in the mirror and feeling as if the mask of an old person had appeared on top of their true face. This suggests that their true self is not their older self, further supporting the idea that people might find it hard to imagine their own ageing because of their fear of being old.

More philosophically, Adam (forthcoming, 2012) has argued that imagining growing older involves imagining the future, and that can be difficult at both personal and wider societal levels. Of particular relevance here is Adam's discussion of two of the ways in which people sometimes imagine the future, which she names 'future as fate' and 'future as fortune'.

By 'future as fate' she means the belief that the future has been pre-determined by gods or ancestors. Adam characterises this approach as one that was prevalent in pre-modern societies, but you can still see remnants of this idea in the way that some people talk about the future. People sometimes say things like 'well, what will be, will be' or 'it's in the lap of the gods'. While someone saying that might not actually believe that the shape of their own old age is pre-determined by God (although they might do), phrases like this suggest a feeling that there is little you can do to affect what happens. This suggests one reason why people might not want to imagine their own ageing – if there's nothing you can do about it, there's not much point thinking about it, your task is just to wait for it to unfold and perhaps to make the best of what occurs.

By 'future as fortune' Adam means the belief that people can shape their future through their present acts. They can make rational plans to optimise the future that then arises. This might suggest that people would find it easier to imagine their own ageing, if they feel that they can affect it through their own actions. However, Adam draws attention to the way that this view of the future means that it is much more uncertain than 'future as fate'. When societies are changing very fast, as in the UK in the 21st century, it can be much harder to be sure that your actions now will have the outcomes you want in the future. For example, in the 1990s and early 2000s in the UK some people thought that the best way to provide income for their own later old age was to take out mortgages to buy properties that they then rented out to other people (buy-to-let). Since the property downturn around 2007, many of those people have found themselves in negative equity with houses they cannot sell. Thus, their plans for financing their retirement have not come to fruition. Experiences such as this can make the future feel very uncertain to some people. This might contribute to reluctance to imagine their personal future.

Some people might find it particularly difficult to imagine their own old age if they have little contact with older people. For example, Phoenix and Sparkes (2006) found that young people often base their ideas about their own ageing on what they see of their parents and grandparents, although some people lack contact with their birth family because of adoption or family break-up. Other people, such as lesbian, gay and bisexual people, may not expect their older relatives' lifestyles to bear much resemblance to their own later life (Goltz, 2008). With the decline of all-age institutions such as party-political groups and churches and other faith organisations, many people are argued to be living more age-segregated lives (Uhlenberg and de Jong Gierveld, 2004). This may mean that younger people have fewer opportunities to get to know older people well, which may increase ageism and the view of older people as very different (Hagestad and Uhlenberg, 2005). This, in turn, may make it more difficult for people to imagine that they will ever be old themselves.

Some researchers have found that it is particularly difficult to enable people to think *realistically* about their own old age. People tend to either imagine terrible pessimistic stereotypes of abusive or negligent care in residential homes, or overly optimistic visions of a life of leisure and international travel (Bulbeck, 2005; Patterson et al, 2009). While some older people undoubtedly do suffer terrible abuse and neglect, and others, particularly those with considerable wealth, do enjoy 'the golden years', most people's experiences are somewhere on the continuum between these two extremes.

Why does it matter?

If imagining your own old age can be so difficult, should we even bother to attempt it? Why does it matter that people should be able to imagine it?

While people find it hard to imagine that they will ever really be old, it is also clear that many younger people worry in a general way about growing older (Neikrug, 2003), and some even expect old age to be miserable (Lacey et al, 2006). Lacey et al argue that this expectation can lead to poor decision making in the present because a future aged self is not valued: if you can't really imagine that you will ever be old, there is no point taking actions now that will protect your future old self. This is argued to be one contributory factor in some behaviours which have negative effects in the long term, such as smoking – if people do not expect to live long, and are not invested in making their future life happy, there is less reason to defer current gratifications (Goltz, 2008).

Lacey et al (2006) and Neikrug (2003) also argue that younger people's failure to imagine that they will ever be old themselves reinforces ageism, intergenerational conflict and misunderstanding. If you do not really believe that you will ever be old yourself, it is harder to treat the older people you meet as if they are real and complex individuals like yourself.

At a collective and societal level, people's failure to imagine their own ageing might be argued to contribute to some of the problems that arise for some older people, such as the lack of high-quality, affordable care for frail older people. Pickard (forthcoming, 2012) draws attention to the likely future lack of informal carers for older people, due to demographic changes; she argues that this has received insufficient policy attention. Many surveys have found that people underestimate the cost of care in later life. For example, a Department of Health survey in 2009 found that 51 per cent of people estimated the cost of residential care in old age at less than £10,000 – the average is actually £30,000 (Bowcott, 2009). It seems possible that some of this systematic underestimation arises from people's unwillingness to think about their own old age in realistic and concrete ways.

What might help people to imagine their own old age?

Many people have an interest in helping people to imagine their own old age. Campaigning organisations working to improve the position of older people in society, such as Age UK, might want to do this in order to reduce ageism and the view of old people as very different from younger people. Health practitioners might want to do so in order to help people change health behaviours which have serious long-term effects, such as smoking or eating too much salt. This final section focuses on the techniques that researchers, such as gerontologists, might find useful when investigating this topic.

If, as has been argued above, one reason that people are reluctant to imagine their own ageing is because they imagine that old age is always a time of decline and difficulty, presenting information which counters this view would be beneficial. In my own research I used just two key statistics: that only about 5 per cent of people aged 75-85 in the UK live in care homes and only 22 per cent of those aged 85+ (*The Scottish Government, 2004*); pensioners are also less likely to live in low-income households than any other group apart from couples with no children (www.poverty.org. uk/64/index.shtml). While researchers bear a responsibility not to paint an over-rosy view of old age (for example, the statistics on income are much less good for some groups of older people, such as single women), I found that introducing just a few more positive representations of later life seemed to enable people to move on from pessimistic visions of old age (Jones, 2011). Other sources of positive but realistic visions of old age include those found in *Growing old disgracefully* (The Hen Co-op, 1993).

Altpeter and Marshall (2003), Tiemann and Stone (1992) and Phoenix (forthcoming, 2012) all recommend asking concrete questions about the future, not general ones. Phoenix suggests questions such as 'Think about yourself in 30 years time – where are you? What are you doing? What do you look like? What does a typical day involve?'. Tiemann and Stone suggest some even more specific questions such as 'What kind of clothes do you wear?' and 'Where is your family?' (1992, p 646). People could also be asked about hobbies and interests they might have taken up or still be pursuing, and about how they might work around any losses of physical function they experience. Such specific questions help to move people from the vastness of trying to imagine a whole future to the much more manageable task of imagining one particular aspect of it. Likewise, encouraging research participants to talk about older people they do know, and how they want their own life to be different or similar, can be helpful.

Phoenix (forthcoming, 2012) recommends facilitating encounters between younger and older people as part of the research process, especially when both groups share characteristics and interests. In one study, she showed younger athletes a short film of older bodybuilders talking about the role of bodybuilding in their lives. She found this a much more successful way of enabling younger people to imagine themselves as older than when she attempted to get them to imagine being old without such a stimulus.

Several researchers report that creative and visual methods can be particularly helpful. Phoenix (forthcoming, 2012) argues that both asking people to contribute images that represent their ideas about their own ageing and showing them non-stereotyped images of later life are fruitful. Masters and Holley (2006) used a 'future-self worksheet' into which undergraduates pasted or drew images to imagine their own later life in five specified domains (physical self, environment/residence, social world, financial support and psychological/spiritual self). Goltz (2008) used a range of creative methods, including drama, poetry and song-writing, to enable his participants to envisage a wide range of non-traditional futures. I have found that, more simply, asking people to draw pictures that represent themselves in later life can also work well (Jones, 2011).

Conclusion

While in this chapter I have argued that enabling people to imagine growing old is both necessary and possible, a note of caution should be sounded as to the agenda and motivations of those urging such imaginings, and the specific focus they suggest for those imaginings. Ekerdt draws our attention to the ways in which 'retirement is colonising adulthood' as a combination of voices, including those arising from changes to pension provision, 'urge adults to undertake a life-long project of retirement preparation' (Ekerdt, 2004, p 4). He argues that focusing too much on retirement can have a variety of negative consequences, such as making an artificial and unhelpful distinction between retired and working people; creating unrealistic expectations about lifestyles after retirement, especially as people age into old age; implying that the point of work is solely to enable a financially comfortable retirement; and suggesting that financial circumstances are the most important factor in a happy old age. While my focus in this chapter has been on a wider issue than retirement planning, I, too, could perhaps be accused of over-emphasising the significance of imagining one's old age, since my professional interests as a gerontologist are served by arguing for its importance.

References

Adam, B. (forthcoming, 2012) 'Future matters for ageing research', in R.L. Jones and J. Bornat (eds) *Imagining futures*, London/Milton Keynes: Centre for Policy on Ageing/The Open University.

Altpeter, M. and Marshall, V.W. (2003) 'Making aging "real" for undergraduates', *Educational Gerontology*, vol 29, no 9, p 739.

Andrews, M. (1999) 'The seductiveness of agelessness', *Ageing & Society*, vol 19, pp 301-18.

Andrews, M. (2000) 'Ageful and proud', *Ageing & Society*, vol 20, pp 791-5.

Bowcott, O. (2009) 'Andy Burnham: Britain faces elderly care "timebomb"', *The Guardian*, 18 September.

Bulbeck, C. (2005) 'Schemes and dreams: young Australians imagine their future', *Hecate*, vol 31, no 1, pp 73-84.

Bultena, G.L. and Powers, E.A. (1978) 'Denial of ageing: age identification and reference group orientation', *Journal of Gerontology*, vol 33, pp 748-54.

Butler, R.N. (1969) 'Age-ism: another form of bigotry', *The Gerontologist*, vol 9, pp 243-6.

Bytheway, B. (1995) *Ageism*, Buckingham: Open University Press.

Bytheway, B. (2000) 'Youthfulness and agelessness: a comment', *Ageing & Society*, vol 20, pp 781-9.

Bytheway, B. (2005) 'Ageism and age categorisation', *Journal of Social Issues*, vol 61, no 2, pp 361-74.

Bytheway, B. and Johnson, J. (1990) 'On defining ageism', *Critical Social Policy*, vol 27, pp 27-39.

Copper, B. (1997) 'The view from over the hill', in M. Pearsall (ed) *The other within us: Feminist explorations of women and aging*, Boulder, CO: Westview Press, pp 121–34.

Ekerdt, D.J. (2004) 'Born to retire: the foreshortened life course', *The Gerontologist*, vol 44, no 1, pp 3-9.

Featherstone, M. and Hepworth, M. (1989) 'Ageing and old age: reflections on the postmodern life course', in B. Bytheway, T. Keil, P. Allatt and A. Bryman (eds) *Becoming and being old: Sociological approaches to later life*, London: Sage Publications, pp 143-57.

Featherstone, M. and Hepworth, M. (1991) 'The mask of ageing and the postmodern life course', in M. Featherstone, M. Hepworth and B.S. Turner (eds) *The body: Social process and cultural theory*, London: Sage Publications, pp 371-89.

Gibson, H.B. (2000) 'It keeps us young', *Ageing & Society*, vol 20, pp 773-9.

Goltz, D. (2008) 'Investigating queer future meanings: destructive perceptions of "the harder path"', *Qualitative Inquiry*, vol 15, no 3, pp 561-86.

Hagestad, G.O. and Uhlenberg, P. (2005) 'The social separation of old and young: a root of ageism', *Journal of Social Issues*, vol 61, no 2, pp 343-60.

Heilbrun, C.G. (1997) *The last gift of time: Life beyond sixty*, New York: The Dial Press.

Hen Co-op, The (1993) *Growing old disgracefully: New ideas for getting the most out of life*, London: Piatkus.

Jones, R.L. (2006) '"Older people" talking as if they are not older people: positioning theory as an explanation', *Journal of Aging Studies*, vol 20, no 1, pp 93-106.

Jones, R.L. (2011) 'Imagining bisexual futures: positive, non-normative later life', *Journal of Bisexuality*, vol 11, no 2, pp 245–70.

Kimuna, S.R., Knox, D. and Zusman, M. (2005) 'College students' perceptions about older people and aging', *Educational Gerontology*, vol 31, no 7, pp 563-72.

Lacey, H.P., Smith, D.L. and Ubel, P.A. (2006) 'Hope I die before I get old: mispredicting happiness across the adult lifespan', *Journal of Happiness Studies*, vol 7, pp 167-82.

Macdonald, B. and Rich, C. (1984) *Look me in the eye: Old women, aging and ageism*, London: The Women's Press.

Masters, J.L. and Holley, L.M. (2006) 'A glimpse of life at 67: the modified future-self worksheet', *Educational Gerontology*, vol 32, no 4, pp 261-9.

Mosher-Ashley, P.M. and Ball, P. (1999) 'Attitudes of college students toward elderly persons and their perceptions of themselves at age 75', *Educational Gerontology*, vol 25, no 1, pp 89-102.

Neikrug, S.M. (2003) 'Worrying about a frightening old age', *Aging and Mental Health*, vol 7, no 5, pp 326-33.

Patterson, L.G., Forbes, K.E. and Peace, R.M. (2009) 'Happy, stable and contented: accomplished ageing in the imagined futures of young New Zealanders', *Ageing & Society*, vol 29, no 3, pp 431-54.

Phoenix, C. (forthcoming, 2012) '"Erm, I don't know.... It's not something that I really think about": facing the fear in research on ageing', in R.L. Jones and J. Bornat (eds) *Imagining futures*, London/Milton Keynes: Centre for Policy on Ageing/The Open University.

Phoenix, C. and Sparkes, A.C. (2006) 'Keeping it in the family: narrative maps of ageing and young athletes' perceptions of their futures', *Ageing & Society*, vol 26, pp 631-48.

Phoenix, C. and Sparkes, A.C. (2007) 'Sporting bodies, ageing, narrative mapping and young team athletes: an analysis of possible selves', *Sport, Education and Society*, vol 12, no 1, pp 1-17.

Pickard, L. (forthcoming, 2012) 'Researching the future with survey data: projections of family care for older people', in R.L. Jones and J. Bornat (eds) *Imagining futures*, London/Milton Keynes: Centre for Policy on Ageing/The Open University.

Scott, T., Minichiello, V. and Browning, C. (1998) 'Secondary school students' knowledge of and attitudes towards older people: does an education intervention programme make a difference?', *Ageing and Society*, vol 18, pp 167-83.

Scottish Government, The (2004) 'Older people in Scotland: Results from the Scottish Household Survey 1999–2002', Edinburgh: The Scottish Government (www.scotland.gov.uk/Publications/2004/05/19405/37644).

Sontag, S. (1978) 'The double standard of ageing', in V. Carver and P. Liddiard (eds) *An ageing population: A reader and sourcebook*, Sevenoaks: Hodder & Stoughton in association with The Open University Press, pp 72-80.

Tiemann, K.A. and Stone, M.D. (1992) 'Projective aging: an engaging technique for teaching issues in growing older', *Educational Gerontology*, vol 18, pp 645-9.

Uhlenberg, P. and de Jong Gierveld, J. (2004) 'Age-segregation in later life: an examination of personal networks', *Ageing & Society*, vol 24, no 1, pp 5-28.

3

Quality of life

David Phillips

A first view of quality of life

'Quality of life' is one of those popular phrases we see and hear
with increasing frequency. For example, at the individual level it is a
commonplace in professional discussions about disability and serious
illness, and at the collective level it is given serious attention in social
policy debates, and is a stock-in-trade for EU policymakers (Noll, 2002).
Unfortunately, though, it is used so often, and in so many different contexts
for so many different purposes, that it is difficult to pin down an agreed
meaning. The problem is exacerbated by its use by different academic
disciplines, each with differing traditions.

At first sight, quality of life is a simple, straightforward construct. Most
of us have a reasonably clear idea of what sorts of things would enhance
our own individual quality of life (and probably the quality of life of other
individuals too), for example, higher pay; longer holidays; more satisfaction
in our working lives; time to pursue enjoyable and satisfying leisure pursuits;
emotional fulfilment in our relationships; and having a long healthy and
happy life – all lived within a safe, caring and supportive local community.
Similarly, there is little dispute about some of the factors which enhance
collective quality of life – of communities, societies, and indeed, globally.
On most people's lists these would include: a peaceful, noncoercive and
congenial social environment; social norms of interpersonal respect; a
sustainable and pollution-free physical environment; and, perhaps slightly
more controversially, collectively resourced provision of education of
children up to a reasonable level of literacy and numeracy; and adequate
physical, economic and nutritional resources for everyone.

But the problems, disagreements and even contradictions start to
emerge as we move from the general, rather vague, warm and fuzzy
vision of quality of life through to more specific definitions. To give some
simple examples [...] are the objective aspects of quality of life, including

income and longevity, more important than its subjective elements, such as happiness and emotional fulfilment? And, second, at the subjective level, how do we measure the difference in quality of life between, on the one hand, someone who is happy but leads a pleasure-seeking life, making less of themselves than they could do and, on the other, a person who fulfils their human capabilities, seeks enlightenment rather than pleasure, has a satisfying life but is perhaps less happy than their more hedonistic counterpart? Does the happier or the more enlightened person have a higher level of subjective well-being and how does this translate into comparing the quality of their lives? These questions are as old as intellectual thought itself.

[...]

SWB: Subjective Wellbeing

The more information that becomes available on SWB, the more perplexing this construct appears to be. First, it is clear that genetics, personality and 'homeostasis' are extremely important to SWB. It seems very likely that some people are born cheerful and others are born miserable and that they will mostly stay that way throughout their lives: certainly they may have major ups and downs, particularly if they have a financial windfall or suffer a serious disability, but in the long run their SWB will probably revert to their personal norm. On the other hand, though, people's SWB – and indeed the SWB of *peoples,* that is, whole nations – is vulnerable to dramatic decline if there is a long-term downturn in national fortunes, through political disintegration or national financial collapse.

Second, it is clear that money is – under differing circumstances – both completely irrelevant and extremely important. At the national level it seems to be irrelevant in relation to economic growth (and even doubling or more of national income) in nations that are already rich. People's expectations seem to rise in line with economic growth so that, as national income rises, the population expects more and more in order merely to remain as happy as it was before. Thus, the objective benefits of increased national wealth, in terms of longevity, reduced infant mortality, better infrastructure, etc, do not translate into higher national levels of subjective well-being. At individual level, it looks like materialists, in other words, people with an excessive love for money or rather for the things that money can buy, find themselves still wanting more, no matter how much they have and thus never increasing their long-term SWB, even though they will get short-term increases. Here the hedonic treadmill is in operation at both the macro and micro levels.

On the other hand, for poor countries and more generally, for poor people whose basic needs have not yet been fully met, then an increase in income will almost certainly translate into a substantive enhancement of SWB. There is a clear relationship here between an increase in absolute income and an increase in SWB. The other circumstance where it is likely that there will be an increase in SWB consequent to an increase in income at above basic needs level, is where the increase in income is relative. If one group gets an increase in money and their peers do not, then the former will feel, and will be, relatively as well as absolutely, better off. This largely explains the small but significant correlations between income and SWB within developed nations.

Third, it seems clear that the best way for a person to enhance their SWB is to enter – and stay in – a long-term emotionally satisfying relationship. If they are also employed and well educated, this will be a bonus.

What, then, are the policy implications for enhancing people's subjective wellbeing? In relation to people as individuals, and leaving aside the spectre of genetic engineering, it seems that it is important for governments to provide opportunities for education and employment and to facilitate and nurture long-term emotional relationships through family and tax laws. In this context Argyle (1999) comments that governments should place less emphasis on raising incomes, except among the very poor, and more emphasis should be placed on employment. Similarly, Diener and Lucas (1999) say that if they want to enhance people's quality of life, then governments need to focus less on people's subjective well-being and more on their objective well-being.

Therefore, it is clear that in policy terms there is not a lot that governments can do directly to enhance SWB. It looks like their best policy option, ironically, is to strive instead to enhance objective well-being irrespective of any direct impact on SWB. Ironically, though, perhaps the most direct government policy impact on SWB is at a very abstract level through nurturing the fabric of society itself through actively promoting national trust, social inclusion and social cohesion. [...]

The next task now is to move from happiness, satisfaction and subjective well-being towards a more holistic approach to quality of life.

From subjective well-being to quality of life

SWB has been seen to have it strengths and its limitations. Perhaps the greatest strength of any approach to subjective well-being is that it pays serious attention to people's happiness and life satisfaction. Happiness may not be enough as a measure of quality of life. [...] But even though SWB cannot be a sufficient criterion of quality of life, any measure of quality of life that took no account at all of whether a person was miserable or dissatisfied would surely be lacking an important dimension. It is clear, though, that there is more to quality of life than just subjective attributes such as happiness or satisfaction. There are objective qualities too, and some of these, such as sufficient nutrition, a non-hazardous environment, and a long and healthy life are universally, or virtually universally uncontroversial as components of quality of life. This section starts with subjective notions of quality of life, and broadens them, first, from the hedonic to the eudaimonic within an essentially subjectivist framework and then from subjective to objective, but always with a view to people's own conceptions of what is good for their quality of life, as well as incorporating the views of academics and other 'experts'.

Hedonic and eudaimonic approaches to SWB

Two broadly differing traditions in subjective approaches to quality of life have been identified in the literature: hedonic and eudaimonic (Diener and Suh, 1999; Ryan and Deci, 2001). The hedonic tradition stresses the nobility of the individual, with an emphasis upon personal freedom, self-preservation and self-enhancement, and is derived from a philosophical tradition encompassing Hobbes, Locke and Rousseau. This tradition relates specifically to subjective well-being and is the starting point for hedonistic psychology with its emphasis on the integrity of individuals' personal judgements about the good and bad elements of their lives, the attainment of pleasure and the avoidance of pain.

The eudaimonic tradition stretches even further back, to the Aristotelian conception of 'the good life', of moderation, reason and justice, and it focuses on meaning, self-realisation and the actualisation of human potential. Here well-being is defined in terms of the degree to which a person is 'flourishing' or 'fully functioning'. Diener and Suh (1999) include in this tradition teachings of St Thomas Aquinas on the importance of virtue and personal salvation and they trace the pedigree of this school of thought back as far as Confucianism with its emphasis on scholarship and duty in relationships.

Ryan and Deci (2001) claim that the philosophical basis for the eudaimonic approach is derived from Aristotle's dismissal of hedonism as vulgar and from his search for higher values. They make the point that pleasure and happiness are not always the same as, or even necessarily related to, well-being. They cite Waterman (1993) as saying that eudaimonia occurs when people's life activities are most congruent or meshing with deeply held values and are holistically or fully engaged, a state Waterman called *personal expressiveness*. Unlike hedonic measures (which are intrinsically linked to desire fulfilment), personal expressiveness is strongly related to personal growth and development and to the realisation of one's true potential. [...]

Following on from Waterman's initiative, Ryff and Keyes (1995) introduce the construct of *psychological well-being* which taps into six aspects of human actualisation: autonomy; personal growth; self-acceptance; life purpose; mastery; and positive relatedness. Within the same tradition, Ryan and Deci (2001) have developed *self-determination theory* which attempts to specify both what it means to 'actualise the self and how that can be accomplished. Self-determination theory posits three basic psychological needs: autonomy; competence; and relatedness.

According to self-determination theory, satisfaction of basic psychological needs normally promotes hedonic as well as eudaimonic well-being. Therefore, it uses measures of SWB along with assessments of self-actualisation, vitality and mental health 'in an effort to assess well-being conceived of as healthy, congruent and vital functioning' (Ryan and Deci, 2001: 147). Ryan and Deci conclude from an extensive literature review that it is most appropriate to conceive of well-being as a multidimensional phenomenon including aspects of both hedonic and eudaimonic well-being, while taking into account that there are tensions and divergences between these two features.

A major empirical study undertaken by Ann Bowling (1995) supports Ryan and Deci's self-determination theory and casts light on the potential balance between its hedonic and eudaimonic components. She ascertained the views of the most important experts of all: members of the general public – the people who make judgements about their own quality of life. Bowling undertook a study of the factors that people think are central to their own quality of life by asking open-ended questions about what was important in their lives. Given the overall findings noted above, it is perhaps not surprising that people ranked their relationship with family or relatives most highly. This was followed by their own health, then health of other significant person(s) in their lives. The item that came fourth in importance covered finances and standard of living. It is perhaps surprising that this item came so low in the list but it is interesting to note that it was the one most often cited in the first five choices overall, even though it was not cited as the most important.

It is significant that health, both their own and of their loved ones, came so high in this list. [...] It is also interesting that money, which is central to utilitarian, hedonic approaches to quality of life, was ranked as less important not only than close relationships but also than the wellbeing of family and friends – both of these probably having more affinity with eudaimonic aspects of quality of life, and the latter definitely being 'other-regarding' rather than (or as well as) self-centred in nature.

Staying with the subjective perspective on quality of life, Rapley (2003: 50) summarises the key characteristics of what he refers to as several widely accepted definitions of quality of life: 'All specify that QOL is an *individual psychological* perception of the material reality of aspects of the world' (italics in original). So this perspective is firmly embedded in individuals' psychological perceptions rather than in the independent objective reality of their existence. The perspective he starts from is the definition given by the influential World Health Organization Quality of Life (WHOQOL) Group:

> [Quality of life] is an individual's perception of their position in life in the context of the culture and value systems in which they live and in relation to their goals, expectations, values and concerns ... incorporating ... physical health, psychological state, level of independence, social relations, personal beliefs and their relationship to salient features of the environment ... quality of life refers to a subjective evaluation which is embedded in a cultural, social and environmental context. (1995: 1403)

Relevant to both Rapley's overview and the WHO definition is another British empirical study complementary to Bowling's, but focusing on perceptions of this environmental context. Rogerson et al. (1996) undertook a nationwide survey of public opinion about environmental issues having a major impact on people's quality of life. The researchers again here did not rely on their own definitions but asked respondents to select and rank the important elements. According to Rogerson et al. (1996: 38), they are as follows:

- crime, both violent and non-violent;
- health services;
- the environment, including pollution, access to scenic areas and the climate;
- housing (cost of owner-occupied and private rented housing and quality of public rented housing);
- racial harmony;
- educational facilities;
- employment prospects, including wage levels and time spent travelling to work;
- unemployment levels;

■ cost of living;

■ shopping, sports and leisure facilities.

Their results echo Bowling's in the sense that financial issues are not at the top of the list and health provision is seen as of very high importance. It is not surprising that concern about crime comes first but it is perhaps less predictable that the environment comes higher than housing or education. [...]

The approach taken by Bowling and Rogerson et al., in consulting people about what they see as being most important to their quality of life, is an important development away from the internal world of subjective well-being itself while still keeping individuals' agency, integrity and autonomy in a central position. [...]

This was a way of classifying quality of life is not entirely uncontroversial. [...] Some commentators have no place at all for subjective well-being in their conceptualisations of quality of life (let alone, locality-based formulations of SWB) and it is noted in the following section that there can be tensions and even contradictions between a person's subjective and objective well-being.

Although Rapley (2003) espouses an overtly locally-oriented subjectively defined approach to quality of life, he accepts too that quality oflife usually also refers to normative expectations of what citizens should reasonably be able to expect from their lives. In this context he refers to Cummins' (1997) contention that subjective and objective approaches to quality of life are both essential but that they are often poorly related to each other (Rapley, 2003: 30). To demonstrate this, he constructs a taxonomy that contrasts subjective well-being and objective living conditions. This is presented in Table 3.1, along with labels added here in italics.

Two of the cells are uncontroversial, intuitively obvious and straightforward: well-being and deprivation, or the happy rich and the unhappy poor. Within this straightforward view of the world the aim of policy for maximising the good life is to move people from the latter to the former cell. At first sight, the other two cells look like oddities, possibly self-contradictory. [...]

Table 3.1 Subjective well-being and objective living conditions

Objective living conditions	Subjective well-being	
	Good	Bad
Good	Well-being *The happy rich*	Dissonance *The unhappy rich*
Bad	Adaptation The happy poor	Deprivation The unhappy poor

Source: Adapted from Rapley (2003: 31)

The judgement of Argyle (1999: 357) on the happy poor is forceful: 'their apparent satisfaction with their lot has been interpreted as a state of adaptation and learned helplessness produced by long experience of being unable to do anything about it'. It is certainly the case that Argyle's judgement is correct for very large numbers of people in the most utmost and indefensible states of deprivation for whom it is imperative that steps be taken to ameliorate their objective circumstances.

However, above the level of meeting basic, or perhaps intermediate, needs it is important not to throw out the quality of life baby along with the 'adaptation' bathwater. There is a real danger of privileging objective, material conditions at the expense of the 'heavyweight', though nonetheless subjective, values of eudaimonic quality of life and thus fighting an inappropriate battle against the circumstances of an at present deeply satisfied group among the 'happy poor' which might lead inexorably to them falling into the worse quality of life situation of being among the 'unhappy rich'. Here the essential thing is to ensure that no-one falls beneath the threshold of an unacceptable objective standard of living.

It is at this point in the discussion that it becomes clear that the straightforward taxonomy which dichotomises SWB versus objective living conditions is only of limited usefulness and that it is necessary to move to a more sophisticated model. This process has already commenced with the expanding of SWB from its hedonic base through to a eudaimonic perspective that in one sense remains at the subjective level because it still entirely concerns features internal to people's minds. In other words, it does not include external objective and material features that affect their lives. On the other hand, though, it goes beyond their actual affect and satisfaction and desires and moves towards what their desires would be if they fully conformed to self-realisation and the actualisation of human potential. So, from a eudaimonic perspective, the subjective part of the taxonomy can be seen as including autonomy, competence and relatedness as well as the hedonic features of positive affect, negative affect and life satisfaction.

[…]

Conclusion

A fundamental theme of this chapter is that quality of life must start with the individual, her or his own feelings, thoughts and emotions. It is a tenant of this chapter that any rounded and comprehensive theory or conceptualisation of quality of life, whether at individual, community or societal level, must take account of individuals' own judgements about their own lives. Omitting or devaluing such a perspective denies the importance of human autonomy, which is arguably central to the notion of humanity itself.

Such an approach, highly principled and person-centred though it is, is not without its problems. It is clear that there is no necessary relationship between subjective and objective well-being, for example, the massive increases in income accruing to developed countries over the past half-century have not led to corresponding increases in subjective well-being. In addition, there are strong genetic causes for differences in SWB between people. Perhaps most important from a moral perspective is the issue of adaptation or false consciousness among individuals and groups who suffer high levels of deprivation but also report high levels of SWB – the 'happy poor'. It is another tenet of this chapter that the quality of life of people in such circumstances must encompass more than the success of their adaptive responses to adversity – it is that adversity itself which needs to be ameliorated.

[…]

References

Argyle, M. (1996) Subjective well-being, in Offer, A. (ed.) *In pursuit of the Quality of Life,* Oxford, Oxford University Press.

Bowling, A. (1995) What things are important in people's lives? A survey of the public's judgements to inform scales of health related quality of life, *Social Science and Medicine*, 41, 1, 447-62.

Cummins, R. (1997) *The Comprehensive Quality of Life Scale: Intellectual Disability Fifth Edition,* Toorak, Deakin University School of Psychology.

Deiner, E. and Lucas, R. (1999) Personality and subjective well-being, in Kahneman, D., Deiner, E. and Schwarz, N. (eds) *Well-Being: The Foundations of Hedonic Psychology*, New York, Sage.

Deiner, E. and Suh, E. (1999) National differences in subjective well-being, in Kahneman, D., Deiner, E. and Schwarz, N. (eds) *Well-Being: The Foundations of Hedonic Psychology*, New York, Sage.

Noll, H. (2002) Towards a European system of social indicators: theoretical framework and system architecture, *Social Indicators Research*, 58, 47-87.

Rapley, M. (2003) *Quality of Life Research: A Critical Introduction,* London, Sage.

Rogerson, R., Findlay, A., Paddison, R. and Morris, A. (1996) Class, consumption and quality of life, *Progress in Planning*, 45, 1-66.

Ryan, R. and Deci, E. (2001) On happiness and human potentials: a review of research on hedonic and eudaimonic well-being, *Annual Review of Psychology*, 52, 141-66.

Ryff, C. and Keyes, C. (1995) The structure of psychological well-being revisited, *Journal of Personality and Social Psychology,* 69, 719-27.

Waterman, A. (1993) Two concepts of happiness: contrasts of personal expressiveness and hedonic enjoyment, *Journal of Personality and Social Psychology,* 64, 678-91.

WHOQOL Group (1995) The World Health Organisation Quality of Life Assessment (WHOQOL): position paper from the World Health Organisation, *Social Science and Medicine,* 41, 1403-9.

4

Implications for ageing well in the twenty-first century

Ann Bowling

[...]

Despite early research by social gerontologists on constituents of Quality of Life (QoL), the factors which influence QoL in older age have remained largely theoretical. Doubt has even been raised about whether such a complex construct can be defined and measured at all. However, results from the survey of people aged 65 and over living at home in Britain, which are presented here, indicate that older people were able to define what is good and bad QoL, and to suggest ways in which this could be enhanced both for themselves and for other people their age.

Summary of main findings

The results of this research indicate that, in general, life in older age can be described positively for most people, with the majority reporting their QoL to be good, and, for most, these ratings were unchanged, or had improved, at follow-up. Most respondents also rated their mental and physical health positively, were actively engaged in social activities and felt supported. At follow-up, the main change mentioned by respondents was their declining health. They also reported many good things that they enjoyed about growing older, including their independence and freedom, although the worst things about growing older included worsening health and consequent loss of independence.

Comparisons of the results with the author's earlier work indicates that older and younger adults' general perspectives of QoL are similar (Bowling 1995a, 1995b, 1996), but older people simply have more life challenges (e.g. risk of declining health, bereavement, loss of mobility, reduced income) which affect their priorities. As some respondents indicated, they felt like young people inside. Also consistent with this earlier research, men and women, and people in different older age groups emphasized different themes, in reflection of their traditional roles in life and differing priorities.

The main independent indicators of self-rated good QoL at baseline in the regression model, and which explained 26.70% of the variance in QoL ratings (which is sizeable on subjective topics) were: making (downward) social comparisons between oneself and others who were worse-off; having an optimistic outlook; having good health and physical functioning; having more social activities, frequent social contacts and support; not feeling lonely; having good local facilities; and feeling safe in one's area of residence (see Box 4.1 for summary).

Box 4.1: Summary of the regression modelling

The main, independent predictors of self- rated QoL in the regression model were:

▶ people's standards of social comparison and expectations in life - making downward social comparisons with those worse off,

▶ a sense of optimism and belief that 'all will be well in the end' rather than a tendency to think the worst;

▶ having good health and physical functioning;

▶ engaging in a large number of social activities, frequent social contacts, feeling helped and supported, not feeling lonely

▶ living in a neighbourhood with good community facilities and services, including transport;

▶ feeling safe in one's neighbourhood;

▶ self-efficacy, and having a sense of control over one's life, lost significance in the model, but was possibly a mediating variable.

These factors contributed more to perceived QoL than objective socioeconomic indicators such as education, social class, income or home ownership. This supports earlier research showing that subjective indicators were more predictive than objective socioeconomic indicators of self-rated QoL (Zizzi et al. 1998; Bowling and Windsor 2001).

The main lay themes, which people believed formed the foundations for a good QoL, which emerged from both the open-ended survey responses and the in-depth, follow-up interviews, overlapped considerably. They supported the results of the regression model, but with the addition of two other key factors: the importance of the perception of having an adequate income, and of retaining independence and control over one's life. The key determinants of QoL which emerged from both of these interview methods are shown in Box 4.2.

Box 4.2: Lay models of quality of life identified by the open-ended survey questions and in-depth interviews

Older people's views of quality of life were:

▸ having good social relationships with family, friends and neighbours;
▸ participating in social and voluntary activities, and individual interests;
▸ having good health and functional ability;
▸ living in a good home and neighbourhood;
▸ having a positive outlook and psychological well-being;
▸ having an adequate income;
▸ maintaining independence and control over one's life.

All respondents expressed a wide range of more personal reasons about why the QoL themes they mentioned were important to them. Each set of the lay themes, which were derived from the two different methods used, overlapped considerably. The main difference was that the in-depth interview approach allowed ample time to explore QoL and so most themes were mentioned by most respondents. This was in contrast to the semi-structured interviews, which imposed greater time constraints on the interview due to the length of the questionnaire, and thus people mentioned fewer themes each. Hence, although there was the danger of bias from response shift between the two interviews (adjustment of expectations over time, leading to different ratings of life), which could have affected the comparisons between the datasets, this did not appear to have been over-influential in this study. In sum, the comparison of results from the triangulated approach indicated that overall QoL is built on a series of interrelated drivers (main themes), while individuals may' emphasize varying constituent parts (sub-themes).

The results of the quantitative analyses, then, were remarkably consistent with lay views. But the exceptions were that both income and perceived self-efficacy lost statistical significance in the regression model, which assessed independent predictors of QoL. In contrast, these aspects of life (having enough money, retaining independence and control) were emphasized as important in the lay models derived from both the in-depth and semi-structured interviews. The implication is that, as people themselves say that these areas are important for QoL, better indicators of them are needed, and they need encompassing within a model of QoL.

Self-efficacy is a theoretically important concept in this context (Baltes and Baltes 1990b; Blazer 2002), and was found to be associated with better psychological and physical health and social resources. However, it was influenced by socioeconomic position, suggesting there were social structure barriers to its development. It is possible that the measure of self-efficacy was mediating between variables in the regression model of QoL. For example, the effect of self efficacy on QoL may have been partly mediated by functional status which did retain significance in the final model. Improved measurement, relevant to older people, is probably required – the measure of self-efficacy used was not designed specifically for use with older people. And, in relation to income, it is possible that in older age, when incomes are more levelled due to people's reliance mainly on pensions (although a wide range of annual income still exists), objective indicators of financial status are less sensitive than perceived financial circumstances. This finding has implications for the design of measurement instruments (Le. it is important to tap perceptions).

Combining both the quantitative and more qualitative approaches, then, this study suggests that the main building blocks, or drivers, of QoL in older age can be summarized as follows:

- having an optimistic outlook and psychological well-being, especially in relation to making downward rather than unrealistic upward social comparisons;
- having good health and physical functioning;
- having good social relationships, preventing loneliness, and feeling helped and supported;
- maintaining social roles, especially engaging in a large number of social activities, including voluntary work, and having individual interests;
- living in a neighbourhood with good community facilities and services, including access to affordable transport, and feeling safe in one's neighbourhood;
- having an adequate income;
- maintaining a sense of independence and control over one's life.

Respondents often commented on the multifaceted nature of QoL, and the interdependency of its components. For example, retaining one's independence and social participation were often described as being dependent on retaining good health and an adequate financial situation, as well as access to transport. These can also be influenced by social and community resources, as well as one's psychological characteristics. Overall, this research showed that most respondents enjoyed the flexibility of retirement, and freedom from the time constraints of paid work, but these could only be really enjoyed if relatively good health was maintained, if people had enough money and lived in areas which facilitated social relationships, neighbourliness, activity and mobility. Greater recognition is needed in definitions of QoL, and its measurement, that influencing variables include people's own characteristics and circumstances, their individual interpretations and priorities, and the dynamic interplay between people and their surrounding social structures in a changing society. Thus, broad, rather than single-model theoretical approaches are needed in order to understand the experience of ageing, and QoL in older age.

The positive circumstances and attitudes of older people, and the identification of a common core of values for QoL, however, should not deflect attention from the negative circumstances and attitudes of sizeable minorities, and society's responsibility towards them, or obscure the diversity of older people. While there was considerable consensus on the main constituents of what gave life quality, different priorities emerged depending on whether people were questioned about the good or bad areas of life quality, priorities and suggestions for improvements. For example, while having good social relationships was the most commonly mentioned constituent that gave people's lives quality, poor health, living in poor housing and neighbourhoods and not having enough money were the most often mentioned things that took quality away. And both health and money were the most often mentioned as the most important areas of quality of life overall. Having health, followed by having enough money, were the most often mentioned areas when people were asked about what single thing would improve the quality of their own lives. However, finance, *followed* by health, was most often mentioned as the single thing that would improve the lives of other people their age. The descriptive analyses also indicated, in particular, that, not only were incomes often very low, for many there was also a feeling of not being safe walking alone outdoors at night and, although ratings of the facilities in neighbourhoods were generally positive, poorer ratings were given overall to local social and leisure facilities, facilities for people aged 65+, transport and closeness to shops. These are essential elements of social capital which enable social participation and involvement in communities. There were also differences in the QoL themes mentioned by men and women, and by people in younger and older age groups. For example, [...] women were more likely than men to mention home and neighbourhood, social relationships and social activities as giving their life quality, whereas men were more likely to mention finances and independence, perhaps reflecting traditional gender role divisions. People aged 75+ were more likely than younger respondents to mention health, home and neighbourhood as giving life quality.

Further comment about the contribution of psychological outlook is needed. Relative deprivation theory holds that happiness, well-being and QoL partly depend on what people have relative to a norm, which is affected by what others have. If people make downward social comparisons of themselves and their circumstances with others who are worse off than them, they are likely to be happier and more satisfied with their situation than people who make upward comparisons with people who are better off. [...]

Those who made downward social comparisons with those who were worse off had better psychological health (GHQ scores). However, the data also showed that those on the lowest incomes were most likely to make upward comparisons. Inevitably, those on the lowest incomes may find downward comparisons more difficult, and downward comparisons may be an unrealistic suggestion for some groups. But despite their relatively low incomes, only a minority of respondents felt that they were worse off than they had expected to be, and many had optimistic outlooks on life. This is likely to partly reflect low expectations and their standards for making social comparisons. As the subject for comparison was often a hypothetical group ('i.e. people my own age'), low expectations of older age contributed to their perceptions. While positive psychology might encourage people to make downward social comparisons for their enhanced well-being, they should not be encouraged to have unrealistically low expectations which can only disadvantage their experiences and achievements throughout life. Higher expectations would be productive if they led to a more demanding public. For example, this could be to the benefit of older people if it resulted in less age discrimination in society (e.g. in access to appropriate health services) (Bowling 1999, 2002; Bowling et al. 2001; Bond et al. 2003).

Traditional sociological theory holds that well-being depends on one's socioeconomic position in society. It has been argued that, for those in disadvantaged social positions, including those in retirement and older age groups, this status adds to their sense of powerlessness and loss of control (Phillipson 1987; Fennell et al. 1988). Less than half of the respondents in the QoL survey felt they had a lot of control over their lives, although just under two-thirds scored middle to high for self-efficacy overall. As pointed out above, self-efficacy was found to be influenced by socioeconomic position. People with the highest socioeconomic status (with the highest level of education, the highest incomes, in the highest social classes, and those who are home owners) were advantaged by being more likely to have the highest self-efficacy. Similarly, the direction of social comparisons was affected by level of income. Thus, there are likely to be socioeconomic barriers to the promotion of psychological resources in individuals. There is evidence from other studies that one's outlook is associated with the place occupied in the status hierarchy (Marmot 2004). This is an issue that has been neglected by positive psychologists.

[…]

Can people build up their psychological resources? As one grows older the need to be strong increases in the face of adversity and loss. […] The employment of psychological resources is important for success when facing the dynamic between life's challenges and depleting reserves. The use of self-enhancing social comparisons (e.g. when in poor health) has been suggested as one strategy for maintaining self-esteem and well-being (Ryff 1999). Another is the use of 'selective optimization with compensation' (Baltes and Baltes 1990b). For example, when selected activities have to be discarded (e.g. due to ill-health or bereavement) strategies need to be activated in order to find new ones and to maximize the chances of maintaining reserves. There is some supportive evidence that these strategies are associated with higher levels of life satisfaction and QoL, (Freund and Baltes 1998).

Older people interviewed for this survey demonstrated considerable coping skills when faced with declining health, lower income and the loss of spouses, relatives and friends through death. People spoke of their own personalities, attitudes and philosophies on life as affecting their QoL, as these influenced their interpretation of their current circumstances and past life events. Their coping strategies were said to include acceptance of life, making downward social comparisons, 'feeling lucky' and having an optimistic outlook. Some spoke of actively 'making their own QoL' by 'keeping busy' and seeking out social and leisure activities which gave them satisfaction, and of finding new activities when they were no longer able to continue with usual interests due to ill-health. Social comparisons and expectations, and level of optimism, were among the main independent predictors of perceived QoL in the regression model, although self-efficacy (self-mastery) did not retain significance in the final model.

There is an increasing popular literature on the self-promotion of psychological well-being. Positive affect (e.g. feeling hopeful about the future, being self-confident, having enjoyment of life – see Ostir et al. 2004) is widely recognized as having protective benefits against poor health and physical functioning, including reduction of risk of medical events such as stroke and myocardial infarction (Segerstrom et al. 1998; Ostir et al. 2000, 2001a, 2001b).

In this study, positive outlook was associated with better psychological health and with good QoL. Positive psychologists, reminiscent of positive-thinking movements, believe that optimism can be learned, and that having a happy outlook can be cultivated. Avoidance of focusing on negative thoughts is argued to be insufficient alone to promote a positive mood – positive thoughts are also needed, Seligman (2004) argued that one has to identify and use one's signature strengths and traits (e.g. kindness, originality, humour, optimism, generosity) to be happy, and that once people are aware of these they find life more gratifying and develop natural buffers against stress and life events. It should be remembered, however, that getting people to 'cheer up' is not easily achieved in real life. Moreover, it has been postulated that there is a dispositional effect on perceived QoL. [...] Lykken and Tellegen (1996) argued, on the basis of their twin studies, that up to around half of the variance in well-being was associated with genetic variation rather than social circumstances, which potentially limits suggestions for self-development. However, this remains an unresolved issue.

The QoL themes which emerged from this research are all areas relevant to health and social policy, and where targets for action and audit could be set. This research illustrated the interdependency of different areas of life. Public policy departments tend to regard their own areas in isolation of others, while the promotion of well-being requires that interdependencies and knock-on effects are understood and taken into account. Age Concern England's (2003) policy report on the findings of this survey emphasized the need for local and central government to undertake several approaches. These included the need to assess the impact on the QoL of older people of current government policies and programmes on pensions, health services and neighbourhood renewal and action; to develop the capacity of older people themselves and encourage their involvement in community consultation processes; to support the voluntary sector in its promotion of social inclusion and social relationships among this group; and to encourage the social inclusion of older people by tackling barriers to participation which include age discrimination as well as problems of taxation and insurance.

Finally, the next generations of older and retired people, including those born between 1945 and 1965, are likely to be more radical than the current generation, and become major campaigning groups. The 17 million people in Britain who grew up with peace movements, the women's liberation movement, anti-racism, environmentalism and in the vanguard of the sexual revolution are approaching retirement. They have been the first generation to grow up in a strong consumer-oriented society and have been led to expect the satisfaction of their needs. In fact, because of their vast numbers, the next generation of older people is likely to be more economically and politically powerful than the current one. They are anticipated to be more demanding, active, liberal in attitude and have higher expectations of life (Huber and Skidmore 2003; Harkin and Huber 2004). On the basis of consumer research in Britain and the USA, and focus group interviews in England, Harkin and Huber (2004) reported that the baby boomers were refusing to age in a stereotypical manner, and saw retirement as a time for adventurous travel. Scales and Scase (2000) also reported that people currently aged in their 50s have active and hedonistic views of their retirement. This generation is particularly likely to promote active ageing more vigorously than any other preceding it. While it has been argued that governments ignore them at their peril, it is, as yet, unknown whether this particular generation will use their voting power to promote their own interests or push for wider social change (Huber and Skidmore 2003).

References

Age Concern England (2003) *Adding Quality to Quantity: Older People's Views on Quality of Life and its Enhancement*, compiled by A. Bowling and C Kennelly. London: Age Concern England.

Baltes, P.B. and Baltes, M.M. (1990b) Psychosocial perspectives on successful aging: the model of selective optimisation with compensation, in P.B. Baltes and M.M. Baltes (eds) *Successful Aging: Perspectives from the Behavioural Sciences*. New York: Cambridge University Press.

Blazer, D. (2002) Self-efficacy and depression in late life: a primary prevention proposal, *Ageing and Mental Health*, 6: 315-24.

Bond, M., Bowling, A., McKee, D. et al (2003) Is age a predicator of access to cardiac services? *Journal of Health Services Research and Policy*, 8: 40-7.

Bowling, A. (1995a) What things are important in people's lives? *Social Science and Medicine*, 41: 1447-62.

Bowling, A. (1995b) The most important things in life: comparisons between older and younger population age groups by gender, *International Journal of Health Sciences*, 6; 169-75.

Bowling, A. (1996) The effects of illness on quality of life, *Journal of Epidemiology and Community Health*, 50; 149-55.

Bowling, A. (1999) Ageism in cardiology, *British Medical Journal*, 319: 1353-5.

Bowling, A. (2001) *Measuring Disease: A Review of Disease Specific Measurement Scales*, 2nd edn. Buckingham: Open University Press.

Bowling. A. (2002) An 'inverse satisfaction' law? Why don't older patients criticise health services? Speaker's corner, *Journal of Epidemiology and Community Health*, 56: 482.

Bowling, A. and Ebrahim, S. (2001) Glossaries in public health: older people, *Journal of Epidemiology and Community Health*, 55: 223-6.

Bowling, A. and Windsor, J. (2001) Towards the good life: a population survey of dimensions of quality of life, *Journal of Happiness Studies*, 2: 55-81.

Bowling, A., Bond, M., McKee, D. et al (2001) Equity in access to exercise tolerance testing, coronary angiography, and coronary artery bypass grafting by age, sex and clinical indications, *Heart*, 85: 680–6.

Fennell, D., Phillipson, C., and Evers, H. (1998) *The Sociology of Old Age*. Milton Keynes: Open University Press.

Freund, A.M. and Baltes, P.B. (1998) Selection, optimization, and compensation as strategies of life management: correlations with subjective indicators of successful aging, *Psychology and Aging*, 13: 531-43.

Harkin, J. and Huber, J. (2004) *Eternal Youths: How the Baby Boomers are Having Their Time Again*. London: DEMOS.

Huber, J. and Skidmore, P. (2003) *The New Old: Why the Baby Boomers Won't Be Pensioned Off*. London: DEMOS.

Lykken, D. and Tellegen, A. (1996) Happiness is a stochastic phenomenon, *Psychological Science*, 7: 186-9.

Marmot, M. (2004) *Status Syndrome*. London: Bloomsbury.

Ostir, G.V., Markides, K.S., Black, S.A. and Goodwin, J.S. (2000) Emotional well-being predicts subsequent functional independence and survival, *Journal of the American Geriatric Society*, 48: 473-8.

Ostir, G.V. Markides, K.S., Black, S.A. and Goodwin, J.S. (2001a) The association between emotional well-being and the incidence of stroke in older adults, *Psychosomatic Medicine*, 63: 210-15.

Ostir, G.V., Oeek, M.K., Markides, K,S, and Goodwin, J.S, (2001b) The association of emotional well-being on future risk of myocardial infarction in older adults, *Primary Psychiatry*, 8: 34-8 .

Ostir, G.V., Ottenbacher, J.K, and Markides, K.S. (2004) Onset of frailty in older adults and the protective role of positive affect, *Psychology and Aging*, 19: 402-8.

Perls, T.T. and Silver, M.H. (1999) *Living to 100: Lessons in Living to Your Maximum Potential at Any Age*. New York: Basic Books.

Phillipson, C. (1987) The transition to retirement, in G. Cohen (ed.) *Social Change in the Life Course*. London: Tavistock.

Research into Ageing (2004) *How to Thrive Past 55*. London: Research into Ageing.

Ryff, C.D. (1999) Psychology and aging, in W. Hazzard, J. Blass, W. Ettinger, J. Halter and J. Ouslander (eds) *Principles of Geriatric Medicine and Gerontology*, 4th edn. New York: McGraw-Hill.

Scales, J. and Scase, R. (2000) *Fit and Fifty: A Report Prepared for the Economic and Social Research Council*. Essex: Institute for Social and Economic Research, University of Essex and the University of Kent at Canterbury.

Seligman, M. (2004) *Authentic Happiness: Using the New Potential for Lasting Fulfilment*. New York: Free Press.

Wilkinson, R. (1996) *Unhealthy Societies – The Afflictions of Inequality*. London: Routledge.

Zizzi, A., Barry, M.M. and Cochrane, R. (1998) A mediation model of quality of life for individuals with severe mental health problems, *Psychological Medicine*, 28: 1221–30.

5

Chronic illness as biographical disruption

Michael Bury

Extract from *Sociology of Health and Illness* (1982) vol. 4, no. 2, pp. 167–82.

Introduction

The purpose of this paper is to explore a limited range of theoretical and empirical issues thrown up by the study of chronic illness. It focuses on a field study of rheumatoid arthritis carried out by the author between 1976 and 1979 in the north-west of England. The data reported here were gathered by semi-structured interviews with a series of thirty patients being referred, for the first time, to an outpatient rheumatology clinic. These individuals comprised twenty-five women and five men (the disease has a four times higher prevalence among women than among men). The majority of the women were aged between 25 and 54, two being under 24 and six being over 55 years of age. The five men were aged between 45 and 64. Fifteen of the women worked, either part-time or full-time. All but one were working-class women, with jobs such as machine operator, school kitchen worker, bakery worker and punch-card operator. All but three respondents were married with families, often including young children.

[…] The aim was to concentrate on those with an emerging illness at the earliest possible point, to explore the problems of recognition and changes in life situation and relationships occasioned by the development of the illness. I therefore relied on the identification of probable rheumatoid arthritis patients by a consultant rheumatologist, based on referral letters from a general practitioner. In all but one case a definite diagnosis was subsequently confirmed. The interviews were conducted once at home before attending the clinic, and again after the first two consultations. In addition, observations in the clinic setting were possible, providing informal conversations with respondents and other patients.

Chronic illness as a disruptive event

[…] The perspective to be developed here is that of chronic illness as a major kind of disruptive experience, or, using Giddens's (1979) term,' critical situation'. Giddens makes the point that 'we can learn a good deal about day-to-day situations in routine settings from analysing circumstances in which those settings are radically disturbed' (p. 123).

[…] My contention is that illness, and especially chronic illness, is precisely that kind of experience where the structures of everyday life and the forms of knowledge which underpin them are disrupted. Chronic illness involves a recognition of the worlds of pain and suffering, possibly even of death, which are normally only seen as distant possibilities or the plight of others. In addition, it brings individuals, their families, and wider social networks face to face with the character of their relationships in stark form, disrupting normal rules of reciprocity and mutual support. The growing dependency involved in chronic illness is a major issue here. Further, the expectations and plans that individuals hold for the future have to be re-examined. Thus, I …maintain that the development of a chronic illness like rheumatoid arthritis is most usefully regarded as a 'critical situation', a form of biographical disruption, not only as a way of describing what happens, but also to provide a more explicit analytic focus.

…I wish to link three aspects of disruption to the unfolding of a chronic illness. First, there is the disruption of taken for granted assumptions and behaviours; the breaching of common-sense boundaries… This 'what is going on here' stage involves attention to bodily states not usually brought into consciousness and decisions about seeking help. Second, there are more profound disruptions in explanatory systems normally used by people, such that a fundamental re-thinking of the person's biography and self-concept is involved. Third, there is the response to disruption involving the mobilisation of resources, in facing an altered situation.

Onset and the problem of recognition

[…] One of the most important features of chronic illness is its insidious onset. Non-communicable diseases do not 'break-out' they 'creep-up'. Davis (1963) indicates how the transition from trivial symptoms to a developing and persisting disability has an impact on those concerned. It involves the initiation into a new social arena where common-sense guidelines are no longer sufficient… Even in the case of heart attacks people report finding themselves in a critical situation of great uncertainty, where they may have little or no idea of what is happening to them.

[…]

The emergence of rheumatoid arthritis is an experience unlikely to involve others until a relatively late stage. The role of significant others in recognition is limited and it is possible for some, though not all, patients to hide their symptoms or disguise their effects for long periods. …Even having been referred to a specialist clinic (often some months after onset), some were still hiding their illness from their family. Indeed, two women used the interview situation to help reveal to their spouses the seriousness of their condition. Clearly, where symptoms of a condition coincide with those widely distributed in a population (in this case aches and pains) the processes of recognition and of legitimating the illness are particularly problematic.

As the symptoms persisted the probability of some kind of arthritis or rheumatism suggested itself, or was suggested by others… There is rarely anything in the individual's biography which provides an immediate basis for recognition of the illness *as* illness […]

The significance of age requires underlining. The image of arthritis as a disease of the elderly is common. On the one hand it makes the possibility of a straightforward process of recognition remote. Arthritis was seen, initially,… as a 'wear and tear' disease, a consequence of becoming old with inevitable disabling consequences, particularly expressed in fears of seizing-up and becoming crippled. Individuals, even in their forties and fifties, did not think of arthritis as occurring in the way experienced, and this was even more true for the women in their twenties. The emergence of the condition implied a 'premature ageing' for the individual (Singer 1974). As such, it marked a biographical shift from a perceived normal trajectory through relatively predictable chronological steps, to one fundamentally abnormal and inwardly damaging. The relationship of 'internal and external reality' was upset.

Commonsense assumptions lose their grip and yet alternative explanations do not readily present themselves. The individual is unsure about whether and how to disclose the illness, both to significant others and to outsiders, such as the general practitioner. But for those who decide to consult a logic is set in motion, although the course of referral is rarely a smooth one. […] Finally, sometimes after considerable delay, referral to the rheumatology out- patient clinic occurred.

This marked the end of the initial stage. Such referral was often treated with relief – suggesting as it did that the individual was 'going to get sorted out'. The relief was, however, more than simply that of coping with functional problems and growing pain and discomfort. It was also a sign that the individual was justified in presenting their symptoms and that their behaviour in general was warranted. The prospect of official recognition and treatment therefore had a range of expectations attached to it.

Emerging disability and the problem of uncertainty

The place of uncertainty in the experience of illness, and especially chronic illness, is widely recognised (Davis 1960, Wiener 1975). This involves both uncertain knowledge about the impact and course of the condition and of appropriate behaviour in the face of its effects. In the case of rheumatoid arthritis the emergence of obvious signs of disability, … can become overriding. In some instances respondents were simply 'taken over' by the disease.[…] Whilst the tolerance of others in such a situation will be tested, the individual can elicit or try to insist on the legitimacy of his actions. But this legitimacy raises a new set of problems, involving a re-evaluation of the relationship between the now-visible disease and selfhood. It is in this context that medical knowledge takes on particular importance.

Access to medical knowledge, at least in the case of physical illness, offers an opportunity to conceptualise the disease as separate from the individual's self.[…] The objectivity of disease provides, through medical science, a socially legitimate basis both for deviant behaviour and clinical intervention. Assertions that scientific objectivity acts as an ideological force frequently fail to address this question of legitimacy. To be able to hold the disease 'at a distance', as it were, assists the claim that one is a victim of external forces. To do anything less is to accept fully the burden of responsibility.

However,… a strict separation of disease and self (for that matter disease and social relationships in general) is precarious. The experience of the patients in this study underlined the uneasy balance which is struck between seeing the condition as an outside force and yet feeling its invasion of all aspects of life. Thus, patients approached the specialist with mixed feelings. On the one hand, they wanted definite knowledge of their physical state and its causes, and yet felt, realistically, that there was a limited amount which the doctors could do in effecting a cure. They expected their drugs to be changed or 'sorted out', but often added that the main issue was still going to be learning to live with it. Medical intervention was, therefore, regarded at the same time as both important and limited.

[…]

Not only this, but individuals also face the limits of medical knowledge and treatment regimens. […] Thus, whilst the diagnosis of the disease provides something firm to relate to, and to explain to others, the actual nature of the disease remains elusive and the treatments empirical.

[…]

The realisation that medical knowledge is incomplete, and that treatment is based on practical trial and error, throws individuals back on their own stock of knowledge and biographical experience. The search for a more

comprehensive level of explanation, a more certain basis of coping with
the illness is often a long and profound one. Comaroff and Maguire (1981),
following Durkheim's views on the role of science, indicate the need to
complete knowledge gained from specialist sources; a need to tie in formal
knowledge with the person's total biography.

[...]

Chronic illness and the mobilisation of resources

...Attempts to impose meaning on threatening and seemingly arbitrary
events, such as the appearance of rheumatoid arthritis, involve an
examination of the constellation of familial and biographical experiences.
In addition, the individual is inevitably drawn into rearranging his or her
wider personal and community involvements. The presence or absence of a
supportive social network may make a significant difference in the course
of disablement. [...]

The disruption of friendship and community involvement arises not
only because of functional limitations (for example restrictions in mobility,
problems of fatigue) but also because of the embarrassment which such
disabilities create. Maintaining normal activities, for example being able to
sit in one position for a long period of time at a cinema, or maintaining
normal appearances in a social gathering at a club or pub, have to become
deliberately conscious activities, and thus frustrating and tiring. In the end
the effort simply does not seem worth it. The erstwhile taken-for-granted
world of everyday life becomes a burden of conscious and deliberate
action. The simplest outing becomes a major occasion of planning and
expedition. Thus, the handicaps of social isolation and dependency which
flow from these disruptions in social intercourse are not simply derived
from the ability or inability to carry out tasks and activities. Individuals
begin to restrict their terrain to local and familiar territory where they are
least likely to be exposed to the gaze and questions of acquaintances and
strangers (Goffman, 1968, Barker and Bury, 1978).

[...] Strauss (1975) has pointed out that withdrawal from social
relationships and growing social isolation are major features of chronic
illness. In the early stages of a disease one of the most difficult areas of
maintaining normal relationships, and mobilising resources, especially
among younger sufferers, is at work. Two women with jobs which involved
the continuous use of their hands exemplified the problems. One felt that
her workmates had little sympathy and that she could demand no special
consideration. As was common among the study group, she was reluctant
to do so anyway in case she drew unwelcome attention to herself and her

work. She was under pressure to keep pace with the speed of work and she constantly worried about the loss of her job.

[…]

Departing from behaviour which is deemed appropriate carries its own specific disadvantages and thus is avoided as far as possible. Much depends on the degree of flexibility which both formal institutions and informal relationships are prepared to allow.

[…]

Occupation and social class are, of course, closely related although their relationship in illness is a complex matter. The importance of social class for my discussion lies in the variable distribution of resources in society and thus the ability of individuals from different social strata to compensate for the effects of disability and thus offset economic and other handicaps. However, the picture is not always straightforward.

[…]

Discussion and concluding remarks

In describing the experience of the onset and development of rheumatoid arthritis I have tried to suggest a perspective which conceptualises chronic illness as a particular kind of disruptive experience. This disruption throws into relief the cognitive and material resources available to individuals. It displays the key forms which explanations of pain and suffering in illness take in modern society, the continuity and discontinuity of professional and lay modes of thought and the sources of variability in experience arising from the influence of structural constraints over the ability to adapt.

Under normal conditions the relationship between self and others is a precarious enterprise, characterised as it is in contemporary settings by high degrees of self-reflection, individualism and the manipulation of appearances (Berger et al, 1974). This precariousness is held in check by a wide range of 'cognitive packages' available to individuals and groups, each of which is more or less successful in structuring and maintaining meaning. In so far as it is possible to identify dominant motifs, those which resonate strongly with scientific and technical imperatives are likely to be the most influential. Not surprisingly, therefore, medical knowledge and medical practice have become central features in modern society

However, knowledge and practice are not necessarily perceived in the same light. Treatments are often empirical in character and patients may feel let down by the limits of medical intervention and technology, or indeed by a realisation of the limits of medical knowledge itself. But my study provides no ground for assuming that these problems indicate any generalised disillusionment with medicine as a system of knowledge and explanation.

Indeed, the reverse may be the case; criticism directed at poor communication by doctors, or inappropriate treatment and advice, contrasting with the high expectations held of medicine. [...]

Medical conceptions of chronic organic disease and its causation are not regarded as illegitimate 'reifications' from a lay point of view. They provide an objective fixed point on a terrain of uncertainty. The problem, however, is that such knowledge itself often turns out to be ambiguous and limited. Rheumatoid arthritis thus appears as a definite entity, yet its implications for the future are uncertain. Such knowledge is incomplete and has to be supplemented by, and set against, a body of knowledge and meaning drawn from the individual's own biography. The search for the cause of the illness,.... is at one and the same time a search for its meaning. The separation of cause and meaning has an important but limited place in lay thought. [...]

Important though the place of medicine is in facilitating and constraining the adaptation of individuals (and those with whom they live and work) to the presence of chronic illness, this is clearly not the only, or necessarily the most important, issue. I have also tried to show that disruptions in biography are, at one and the same time, disruptions of social relationships and the ability to mobilise material resources. To be sure, medical knowledge and lay knowledge about disease and illness enter these fields, but it is clear that the warrantability of a person's changed behaviour, through chronic illness, is determined by many other factors. We know relatively little about the 'limits of tolerance' within families and workplaces, and how they vary between different social groups and settings. The disruption of reciprocity, the problems in legitimating changed behaviour and the overall effects of stigma associated with chronic illness all affect the individual's ability to mobilise resources to advantage. Conversely, the variability in resources between different social groups affect the processes mentioned here. As Illsley (1980) has pointed out, the processes involved in the interaction between wider social structures and the experiences of ill-health, within specific cultural and familial contexts, are still poorly understood. The perspectives of biographical disruption and the interplay of lay and professional modes of thought are offered here as a contribution to tackling that problem.

References

Barker, J. and Bury, M.R. (1978), 'Mobility and the elderly: a community challenge', in V. Carver and P. Liddiard (eds), *An Ageing Population*, Hodder and Stoughton, Sevenoaks.

Berger, P., Berger, B. and Kellner, H. (1974), *The Homeless Mind,* Penguin, Harmondsworth.

Comaroff, J. and Maguire, P. (1981), 'Ambiguity and the search for meaning: childhood leukaemia in the modern clinical context'. *Social Science and Medicine*, vol. 15B, pp. 115–23.

Davis, F. (1960), 'Uncertainty in medical prognosis clinical and functional', *American Journal of Sociology*, vol. 66, pp. 41–7.

Davis, F. (1963), *Passage through Crisis: Polio Victims and their Families*, Bobbs–Merrill, Indianapolis.

Giddens, A. (1979), *Central Problems in Social Theory,* Macmillan, London.

Goffman, E. (1968), *Stigma: Notes on the Management of Spoiled Identity,* Penguin, Harmondsworth.

Illsley, R. (1980), *Professional or Public Health?* Nuffield Provincial Hospitals Trust, London.

Singer, E (1974) 'Premature social ageing: the social psychological consequences of a chronic illness', *Social Science and Medicine*, vol. 18, pp. 143–51.

Strauss, A.L. (1975), *Chronic Illness and the Quality of Life*, Mosby, St Louis.

Weiner, C. (1975) 'The burden of rheumatoid arthritis: tolerating the uncertainty', *Social Science and Medicine*, vol. 9, pp 97–104.

6

Aging with a childhood onset disability

Tracie C. Harrison and Alexa Stuifbergen

Extract from T.C. Harrison and A. Stuifbergen, 'A hermeneutic phenomenological analysis of aging with a childhood onset disability', *Health Care for Women International* (2005) vol. 26, no. 8, pp. 731–47 (Routledge), reprinted by permission of the publisher (Taylor & Francis Group, http://www.informaworld.com).

There is growing concern about how women who have lived from childhood to late adulthood with impairment are aging (Campbell, 1994; Harrison, 2004). The concern is not without reason. Aging with a disability from early to late life is an increasingly common phenomenon. [...] Moreover, for those with impairments, the likelihood of comorbid and secondary conditions increases with age, thereby adding to the complexity and cost of their health care needs.

[...]

Methodology

We conducted this study[1] in order to explore the meaning of aging for women with childhood onset disability. The central guiding question was, "What is the meaning of aging for women with childhood onset disabilities?" This question was answered with a qualitative design that consisted of interviews, field notes, life course charts, and specified demographic information. The methodology chosen to guide the study was hermeneutic phenomenology.

[...]

Results

The women's experiences were interpreted based upon their life course narratives. Common themes were analyzed within childhood (0 to 12 years), adolescence (13 to 22 years), young adulthood (23 to 34 years), middle adulthood (35 to 54 years), and later adulthood or now (55 to 65 years).

---

[1] This qualitative study explored the experiences of 25 women who developed impairments due to paralytic polio during childhood.

Childhood

Disrupted normalcy

Despite the young age at which they were infected, most women remembered "getting polio." They lost control of their bodies. One woman could only move her thumb, while another could move only from the left elbow down. They felt hot with pain in their heads, throats, necks, or backs. Polio disrupted the ability of the self to will the body to action, it disrupted the usual sensory input to and from the body, and, subsequently, it disrupted the subjective interpretation of the self as it existed in the world. The women recalled how a childhood viral infection left them irrevocably altered. The childhood theme of disrupted normalcy was broken into two subthemes: the abrupt loss and constructing the altered body.

The abrupt loss

The women told of their initial treatment for polio as an abrupt loss. It involved a short illness that left them suddenly paralyzed. In response, life moved unexpectedly quickly and without explanation. They were sent to a physician for a spinal tap to diagnose poliomyelitis, which frightened them as much their symptoms. After the procedure, all but one of the women were taken from their families and placed in isolation where further treatment for their bodies was initiated.

During the time of the initial treatment the women described feeling isolated, uninformed, naive, afraid, sad, or all of these. Their bodies were the focus of care, and they experienced increasing amounts of unfamiliar stimuli, which the conscious self could not understand. [...]

Constructing the altered body

After the initial treatment for polio, the majority continued to receive long-term therapy. Some were discharged to rehabilitation centers for extended care. Others left the hospital for home unable to walk, crawling, or being carried by parents. Keeping the muscles stretched, which was usually done by mothers, and learning to walk were priorities.

Typically, the women mentioned various corrective surgeries to improve the function of a particular extremity, such as the hand or foot. Other surgeries attempted to balance the individual's physical growth. Deborah, who contracted polio at 3 months of age, described six childhood orthopedic surgeries. She stated, "One of the surgeries was to stop the growth of this (left) leg so that this (right) leg could catch up. But they let me go home and I had a growth spurt. So I ended up with my right leg longer than my left. Can't win for losing." The majority of surgeries were done to correct an abnormal curvature of the spine, which often required multiple surgeries and body casts for as long as 6 months.

Living with the altered body

Living with the altered body details the childhood recognition of being different in appearance and ability. They became conscious of an altered experience, different from others without impairments. As they compared one limb with the other or compared their bodies with those of siblings or peers, the differences were notable. [...] They all noted the differences in their bodies' appearance and ability.

The women recalled that as children with altered bodied and altered physical abilities, their experience of the world was altered. Their place in the world was considered special, whether they were being included or excluded. Some could not run during childhood games, while others could not trust people to be consistently kind. The women knew that what made them different included more than appearance and ability. The difference they experienced included a way of being in the world. Kathy, who had polio at age 12, described her experience in elementary school, where she was taken, put in a chair, and left until she was picked up. She said, "A lot of children were afraid. I was never cruelly treated. I wasn't other than looked at, of course. But, nobody was ever malicious. I was in my own world."

[...] Over time, the women began to see themselves as "different limitations that you know of as yourself." The self and the limitations were part of being in the world as themselves – the body and the limits were all part of the child.

Adolescence

Conscious of the body's improvement

The women continued with their long-term therapy through most of their early teens, but by the time they entered into their early twenties many performed activities for themselves for the first time, such as feeding themselves or dressing. They also lost their leg and back braces. The braces were tight and restrictive. Not wearing them liberated the women mentally. They were still impaired but less likely to feel disabled. This also meant they could wear the shoes and clothes that other girls were wearing. By losing their braces they lost symbols of disability.

Willing the body to achieve potential

As adolescents, the women were able to do more with their bodies and were conscious of using their bodies to achieve their will. Women who were carried or required assistance to transfer from place to place as children were able to walk on their own as adolescents. Others who were wheelchair bound were able to sit up without braces supporting their bodies. They were still limited, but they were able to use their increased abilities along with strategies and devices to perform activities, which meant they could influence their futures. Although unsure of their potential for careers, marriages, children, or all of these, many found themselves eventually doing those things. In fact, the majority went to college, married, and had a family. Others chose different paths. Regardless of the path they took, it was during the adolescent years that they realized they could use their bodies to influence their lives.

Knowing and showing the body's limits

[…]
The women discussed issues of hiding the impaired body most frequently when describing their adolescent years. Since their experiences continued to indicate some level of disability, many were faced with letting others know in social situations. A high value on appearance was reported during the adolescent years. Many feared they would be shunned by others due to their appearance.

Young adulthood

Reinforcing the will to achieve

During young adulthood, the women wanted to show that their physical differences did not prevent them from leading full lives as women, and their growing independence fed their motivation to achieve more. They described themselves as being more comfortable with their bodies. Their discomforts were less severe than in previous years. They had become adept at using and controlling their bodies, even as sexual and reproductive issues arose. As they perceived themselves as capable, their impairments were less meaningful in defining who they were as women. They knew their limits and considered them as they lived their lives, but they were determined to show that they were able to meet goals. They wanted to show that they could do many of the things that women without disabilities could or could not do. Elizabeth, who had polio at 6 months, stated that she did not take a job for a charity because she had to say she was disabled to sell products. She said, "You didn't bring up your handicap or use it as a crutch to throw it out there in front of people. So, therefore, I didn't do it. I wanted to make it on my own in what I considered a normal environment." It was during this time that the women achieved increasing levels of independence and enjoyed adventures.

Conquering problems

As women became more independent, they became more personally ambitious, which increased their expectations of their bodies at the same time it made them less sensitive to sensory input from their bodies. Once the women were aware that problems were occurring, they responded with strategies to either dismiss or overcome them. [...]

Middle adulthood

Willed to success but pushed to decline

It was during middle adulthood that many of the women began to achieve success in their lives and careers, but they had pushed their bodies to decline in order to achieve success. The demands of family and work continued, and the rewards they received through their achievements reinforced their need to push their bodies further. Over time, their ability to push their bodies to accommodate their will was disrupted, their senses were inundated with pain and fatigue, and their emotions were labile. This was the time of further injury and of other health problems such as hypertension, diabetes, and pneumonia. This theme was represented with two subthemes: achieving success and pushing the declining body.

Achieving success

During middle adulthood, the women achieved success in their lives for different reasons and in different ways. Women, such as Alita and Lena, focused on community service, as well as career success. One woman dedicated herself to her career as a social worker with multiple community projects; others measured their success in their lifestyles or in their families' cohesion. No matter the reason for their achievements or the way they defined their achievements, the achievements fed their will to do more. The women were fulfilled through achievement; they were gaining accolades for their achievements that many women without disabilities were not gaining.

Pushing the declining body

Over time, the women continued to push their bodies until they reached a critical point in their ability to cognitively and emotionally process the changes. They kept doing activities even after their bodies tired out, but the women tried to keep pushing. Deborah confirmed this: "Then my health really started going down because I was pushing myself too much. Well, I was working long hours and not really catching up in my rest and I was ignoring it." Some women reported a sense of urgency during this time: "I felt an urgency in the good times to do everything that I could do because I wasn't sure when the next bad time was going to come up."

[...]

The breaking point

The women eventually realized they had overlooked their bodies' needs. Typically, the women sensed increasing problems with their bodies but were not aware of what to do about them. This changed when the women stopped many activities of their daily lives so they could become attentive to their bodies' needs; they could not achieve their will without their bodies. They recognized that their bodies were instrumental in their lives. Beatrice stated, "Well, it pretty well gets to the point you just can't. When you can't walk from one room to the next, you can't. You break in a sweat. You just can't."

The women responded to their bodies' needs by decreasing their organized social activities, increasing the help they received from others, increasing their use of assistive devices, and seeking help from post-polio groups and specialists. Eventually many retired from work. These responses were gradual and did not occur without consideration. For instance, the question of whether to retire to prevent further decline was not an easy decision. Many debated the impact of the decision. If they retired at an early age, would they have enough money to live on into the future? Were they of the appropriate social age to leave the workplace? Would they miss the social interaction? Could they continue to work and take care of themselves? These were among the most common questions they asked themselves.

Threats from increasing dependency

After the women responded to their bodies' needs by decreasing many activities that supported their sense of self and by using assistive devices, their self-perceptions were threatened. When the women donned their braces and other devices, they again donned their childhood symbols of disabilities. It threatened their sense of independence and present identity. They did not want to be redefined as dependent, ill, or sick women. Moreover, it threatened their future because it left them questioning who they would become and how they would be treated. They did not want anyone to feel sorry for them. Lena, who contracted polio at age 10 years, said, "I've never liked it when everybody would treat me special just because I'm here [wheelchair]. No, if I don't feel sorry for myself, then nobody is going to. I have no use for you. I'm sorry. Go feel sorry for somebody else or feel sorry for yourself."

Later adulthood or now

Integrating needs

As the women discussed their current lives, they focused on the needs of their bodies as well as the needs of the self. The ability and need to focus on both their bodies and their personal will was a key aspect of the wisdom they accumulated with age. Their bodies were experiencing pain, fatigue, balance problems, and breathing difficulties, which demanded that they direct their attention to the physical aspects of being alive. They also enjoyed life by using their bodies for simple pleasures. For example, Charlotte would go to a church made of logs so she could touch and smell the logs.

[...]

Preserving the body

To survive, the women stated they could no longer push their bodies. The women no longer saw physical improvement as possible as in their youth; therefore, they used strategies to preserve their bodies, such as being organized and conserving their physical energy. Being organized was important because energy could be preserved if things were found easily or were within easy reach. The women also conserved their energy by planning activities. It did not mean they could not do anything. It meant that they had to choose what they wanted to do and plan that activity so that it did not cause harm to their bodies. Conserving to preserve the body also meant that the women rested when their bodies felt tired. This would allow them to continue either later in that day or the next day without feeling pain. If they did not rest, they could be debilitated for several days.

Conflicts between self and body

Over time, the women experienced further physical decline, which created a conflict regarding the best health strategies. For many, physical changes with age were negative, and they debated their decisions to preserve their bodies with rest. For instance, weight gain was a problem. It did not look good to them, and it made using their bodies more difficult. Moreover, the conflict between the self and the body continued when the women felt surges of energy. The energy was deceiving because the women could feel the energy in their minds, but it would not last, or it would cause pain if they tried to physically respond to it by being more physically active.

When last interviewed, the women were conflicted about the best way to care for themselves. They wanted to maintain function with age. They attempted to preserve the function they had, and they perceived decline despite their attempts. They believed, however, that their bodies declined at a slower rate when they rested more frequently than if they continued to push themselves. In response, three attempted exercise in ways that did not cause pain or fatigue. Another started a high protein diet. Others were reluctant to seek help for their bodies. After all, few health care providers knew of polio; they found few whose advice they would take. They needed health care providers to acknowledge and understand them as polio survivors.

Discussion

In this life course qualitative study we provide evidence for the assertion that functional decline with age for women with disabilities may not be a purely biological necessity (Stuifbergen & Becker, 2001); behavioral components, influenced by psychological, social, and cultural circumstances, may influence the rate and timing of decline. In other words, the environmental demands on them were perceived by the women to have affected their health decisions. For example, the women grew up in an environment where they were encouraged to be independent, where their bodies were reconstructed with a goal of normalcy, and where they were determined never to be treated as naive uninformed objects again. Subsequently, the women grew up with a strong desire to be self-sufficient. Over time, their will to achieve motivated them to continue despite any physical consequences. Moreover, the women pushed themselves to fulfil multiple roles in order to be women in society while ignoring or being unable to attend to their health.

[...]

We believe an important finding was that, over time, the women realized that they needed to incorporate the physical needs of their bodies with their desire to achieve success as women within their environments. At this critical point, they began to change their behaviors to enjoy life while responding to their bodies' needs. Regretfully, this wisdom was gained at a time when physical decline seemed inevitable to them.

Age influenced the way the women adapted to their disability. Their impairments varied in severity and in the impact they had at various points. Yet their response to the impairment changed in many common ways over the years. Personal and social views of their age influenced their reaction and the reaction of others to their impairments. For example, the women were encouraged to be independent as children. They pushed themselves to normalize and limit the impact of impairment upon their young adult lives; however, their ability to push themselves had limits as they aged. Although the women were no longer treated as naive, uniformed objects in their later adulthoods, their experiences in their youth influenced their reactions to the needs of their aging bodies. When they were faced, once again, with the need for braces and other assistive devices they were developmentally displaced; they were confronted with childhood symbols of disability that threatened the adult identities they had worked to create.

[…] Moreover, the impairments that threatened their independence were experienced over the life course, which became more threatening as they aged due to worsening symptoms and decreased energy to cope with increasing demands. After years managing their impairments, the women recognized that in mid-to later life their bodies were responding and healing slowly. This meant that they had to focus most of their attention on their bodies' changes. This was not socially supported; they lived within a society unprepared to give them early retirement with extensive health care needs. The women with polio were also combating the threat of reliving what that they had overcome – being vulnerable, marginalized, and naive objects of medical treatment.

[…]

In conclusion, living in the world was an embodied experience for the women, and their impairments impacted the choices they made. As women, they journeyed through life in their bodies, which were impaired due to the effects of polio from a young age. From this perspective, the women saw their bodies from a continuum of abilities, which changed for them as it does for many. Their disabilities, however, constrained or narrowed their choices at a very early age. Despite the constraints, they pushed to achieve their goals as women within society. Regretfully, many suffered the consequences of pushing beyond what was physically sustainable and socially supported.

References

Campbell, M.L. (1994). *Later life effects of early life disability: Comparisons of age-matched controls on indicators of physical, psychological and social status*. Final report. Washington, DC: Rehabilitation Research and Training Center on Aging. The National Institute on Disability & Rehabilitation, Department of Education.

Harrison, T. (2004). Women aging with childhood onset disability: A holistic approach using the life course paradigm. *Journal of Holistic Nursing, 21*(3), 242–259.

Stuifbergen, A. and Becker, H. (2001). Health promotion practices in women with multiple sclerosis. *Physical Medicine and Rehabilitation Clinics of North America, 12*(1), 9–22.

SECTION TWO

Individual ageing and social relationships

7

Health and mortality

Christina R. Victor

Extract from *Ageing, Health and Care* (2010) Bristol: The Policy Press.

[...]

Describing and analysing the health of older people: patterns of mortality

During 2008, there were 509,000 deaths registered in England and Wales, of which 266,000 (52%) were males and 243,000 were females, compared with 551,585 in 1901. This serves to re-emphasise the substantial decrease in death rates that there has been in Britain over the last century. The vast majority of deaths registered in 2008 were accounted for by older people: deaths at age 65 and over accounted for 83% of the total and those aged 85 and over accounted for 35% of the total (a total of 182,000). 'Premature' mortality, deaths between the ages of 16 and 64 are increasingly rare from a population perspective, accounting for 16% of deaths with deaths in childhood accounting for 1%. Victor (2005) has drawn attention to the changing age profile of mortality and this trend is continuing, with mortality being increasingly prevalent in the later phases of the lifecourse. In 1901 in England and Wales, some 40% of all deaths were accounted for by children aged 0-14, with a further 44% accounted for by those aged 65 and over. While there may be some inaccuracies in this mortality age profile because birth registration only became a legal requirement in 1841 and potentially there could be some doubts about the true ages of this over-65 group, it is unlikely to radically distort the distribution. Indeed, if there is any error it is likely to overestimate the number of deaths of people aged 65 and over. This elegantly illustrates how reductions in deaths and death rates in infancy and childhood have served to change the distribution of death within society and the whole way that we as a society think about death. Perhaps the increasing prevalence of death in the later phases of life, rather than it being more equally distributed across the lifecourse, has contributed to the development of negative stereotypes of old age. One conclusion we can draw from the previous analysis is that the bulk of societies' health problems (as measured by mortality) are experienced by older people, and that at a population level, ill-health is comparatively rare among the rest of the population. Thus, in terms of 'health needs' we could argue that it is older people who demonstrate the 'greatest needs' and that they should form the focus of health service expenditure and activities.

[...] Using data for 2005, Table 7.1 shows that the pattern of mortality across the population demonstrates a classic J-shaped distribution. The first year of life is clearly relatively hazardous as mortality rates are (relatively) high at about 5 per 1,000 live births but then decrease and are low at less than 1 per 1,000 population until about the age of 45 from when mortality rates increase by a factor of three for each 10-year age grouping (see Table 7.1). Manton (1986, 1999) suggests that the pattern of mortality in mid and later life (that is, post 45 years) is influenced by two interacting sets of factors: senescence (or the rate of 'natural ageing') and the distribution of risk factors for specific diseases such as heart disease or cancer within populations, for example the prevalence of smoking, obesity, lack of exercise or environmental/occupational health hazards. However, it is not clear from such aggregate-level data as to the relative contribution of these differing (or complementary) explanatory frameworks or whether they operate differentially within age, gender, class and ethnicity subgroups. However, this identification of behavioural and lifestyle factors in

Table 7.1: Death rates by age and gender, England and Wales, 2005

Age	Rate per 1,000		
	M	F	M/F ratio
Under 1	6.0	4.0	1.5
1-4	0.2	0.2	1.0
5-9	0.1	0.1	1.0
10-14	0.1	0.1	1.0
15-19	0.4	0.2	2.0
20-24	0.6	0.3	2.0
25-34	0.8	0.4	2.0
35-44	1.5	0.9	1.6
45-54	3.6	2.4	1.5
55-64	8.9	5.6	1.5
65-74	24.0	15.4	1.5
75-84	67.4	48.1	1.4
85+	171.6	152.7	1.1
All ages	9.9	9.3	1.1

Source: ONS (2006, table 4)

explaining the patterns of mortality in later life suggests that senescence and/or genetic heritage offer only a partial explanation for observed patterns of health in later life. This also offers up the possibility that, if behavioural/lifestyle factors are important in influencing the pattern of mortality in later life, then this distribution may change as younger age groups, with different risk profiles, move into old age.

Another key trend is evident from Table 7.1 and that is the higher death rates demonstrated by men as compared with women. At all ages, men demonstrate mortality rates that are higher than their female counterparts. This excess is especially prominent for the 15-34 age groups (although the rates are low in both groups and absolute numbers are small). For those aged between 65 and 84 years, the male mortality rate excess is in the order of 50%, with this differential decreasing to 10% for the over-85 age group. Thus, a key finding from the analysis of mortality data is that men have worse health than women and that the very young and the very old experience the highest (relative) mortality rates and thus the worst health.

As well as age and gender there are other sociodemographic factors that shape and contextualise our lives and which are associated with the distribution of health and illness within contemporary society. Marmot (2008) demonstrates very powerfully that profound inequalities in health remain a feature of the global landscape and social class-based inequalities are a pervasive and stubborn feature of British society although Wilkinson and Pickett (2009) argue that inequalities in health, and other social outcomes, are neither universal nor inevitable. Social class within the UK context is usually operationalised in terms of the classification of occupations – a system first reported nationally in 1911 and which has become an established component of British social research. Thus, there is a well-established body of empirical work demonstrating how socioeconomic status is associated with health outcomes, especially infant mortality, premature mortality and expectation of life and the probability of reaching old age (see DH, 2009). The Black Report on health inequalities (Black, 1980) is an exemplar of this approach, carefully enumerating how occupationally-based measures of social class are very strongly linked with health and other aspects of life chances such as educational achievement. As well as documenting the link between class and mortality, there is also a body of work examining whether social class gradients in mortality in the UK are increasing, decreasing or remaining stable (see Mitchell et al, 2000; Davey Smith et al, 2002; Ramsay et al, 2008). However, the focus in much of this work has been on socioeconomic differentials in premature adult mortality/infant mortality. Socioeconomic differentials in mortality in later life have been the subject of much less attention although, as we can see, these now account for almost all of the deaths in the UK. We suggest that part of this (relative) neglect reflects the problems involved in attributing a 'social class' location to those who are no longer part of the labour force (see Grundy and Holt, 2001; Bowling, 2004). Which is the best measure of socioeconomic position to use in studies with older people? Within the UK, Grundy and Holt (2001) suggest that deprivation indicators should be paired with either class (as measured by occupation) or educational qualifications. Applying an occupationally based class typology to older women is problematic given that many may not have worked in the formal labour market or only in a very limited way. This latter issue may become less problematic as future cohorts of older women are likely to have had higher rates of, and longer engagement with, the formal labour market. Whether the type of often part-time work that many women participate in 'accurately' reflects their class position or is adequately dealt with by this type of typology is another issue. Thus, there has been a search for other indicators to use to profile what might be broadly termed 'social position' such as housing tenure or education. In addition, there has been, until fairly recently, an implicit and perhaps uncritical assumption that 'older people' can be conceptualised as a single homogeneous social category. The use of categories such as '65 years and older' in reports and policy documents inadvertently (perhaps) created an impression that this population subgroup did not demonstrate the socially based differentials in terms of age, gender and class so characteristic of the rest of British society. Given the pervasive effect of social class on a whole swathe of life chances in Britain, it seems highly unlikely that such differentials will disappear on entering old age. However, applying a social class or social status attributional system to older people is not a new issue. Albrecht (1951) raised these issues in her studies of changes in social status across the lifecourse and accurately profiling the social position of older people remains a challenge for social researchers: a challenge that is compounded when we want to make comparisons either over time or across different societies.

What, if any, is the evidence for class-based differentials in mortality being continued into later life? Using a variety of differing datasets such as 'routine' mortality data or the follow-up of specific cohorts, evidence that class-based inequalities persist into later life is robust. The precise extent of the differential is variable, reflecting the influence of the original data sources and the way that social position is defined (see Avlund et al, 2003). Nazroo et al (2009), analysing deaths reported for ELSA participants, demonstrated inequalities in mortality for both men and women aged over 50 using three measures of 'class': occupational class, educational qualifications and wealth. The mortality differentials in old age reported by Nazroo et al (2009) are not trivial. For men aged 60-74, death rates for those with a degree were (approximately) 40% lower than those without

any educational qualification; managerial and professional workers had
mortality rates that were 43% lower than their counterparts from manual
jobs and those in the highest wealth quintile (top 20%) had a mortality rate
that was a third (36%) that of the poorest group. These were reduced but
still evident for males aged 75 and over where the mortality differential
between the educational groupings was 32%; 22% for the class-based
typology and 45% for the wealth categories. Given the established problems
of employing these typologies to women, can we determine class-based
health inequalities in later life? Looking first at the 60–74 age group,
Nazroo et al (2009) reported mortality differentials of 63% for education
43% for social class and 84% for wealth compared with differentials of
40% for education, 32% for class and 43% for wealth for women aged
75 and over. Again, while the size of some of these differentials may be
influenced by small cell counts, we cannot attribute all of these differentials
to artefact or measurement error. So while differentials may decrease
across old age they remain present even at the oldest age groups (see also
Victor, 1991; Jyhlä and Luukkaala, 2006). The indicators used as measures
of socioeconomic position are to some degree context specific. It remains
to be seen whether the utility of specific measures varies as new cohorts,
with differing experiences of education, occupational histories and housing
markets, enter old age.

[...]

The probability of reaching 'old age' is also linked to social class (Table
7.2). There is a seven-year differential in life expectancy at birth for men
(80 years versus 73 years) and women (85 years versus 78 years) between
the top and bottom of the class hierarchy. For those who reach the age
of 65 years, there is then a four-year differential in further expectation of
life across the class hierarchy. So not only is there a differential by social
class in the chances of reaching 65 years, there is also a further differential
in life expectancy from this age onwards. Increases in life expectancy at
birth/age 65 since 1972 have served to maintain class differentials and not
reduced them. In combination with the data on mortality, the expectation
of life data confirm that there is, within contemporary Britain, a significant
health divide based around class in terms of achieving old age and in the
amount of life to be enjoyed once having achieved old age, and there is
no evidence to indicate that these differentials have decreased over the last
three decades.

Thus, in terms of mortality, social class exerts a strong influence on the
chances of reaching old age and on the health experience of older people.
These data also demonstrate that health gains, as reflected in a variety

Table 7.2: Life expectancy by social class, England and Wales, 1972-2005

Males				
Social class	Birth		Age 65+	
	1971	2005	1971	2005
1	71.9	80.0	14.0	18.3
2	71.9	79.4	13.3	18.0
3 non-manual	69.5	78.4	12.6	17.4
3 manual	70.0	76.5	12.2	16.3
4	68.3	75.7	12.2	15.7
5	66.5	72.7	11.6	14.1
All non-manual	71.2	79.2	13.9	17.6
All manual	69.1	75.9	12.1	15.9
All classes	69.3	77.0	12.3	16.6

Females				
Social class	Birth		Age 65+	
	1971	2005	1971	2005
1	79.0	85.1	19.1	22.0
2	71.1	83.2	17.2	21.0
3 non-manual	78.3	82.4	17.9	19.9
3 manual	75.2	80.5	16.4	18.7
4	75.3	79.9	16.9	18.9
5	74.2	78.1	16.6	17.7
All non-manual	77.7	82.9	17.5	20.5
All manual	75.2	80.0	16.6	18.6
All classes	75.3	81.1	16.3	19.4

Source: ONS (2008, tables 1 and 3)

of different measures including expectation of life, are rarely equitably distributed across the population. Here we can see that those from the most privileged occupational classes are the most likely to benefit from increased life expectancy. These data eloquently and succinctly demonstrate the enormous influence that social economic status has on the health experience of older people and, by extension, other aspects of later life. While there are no comparable data on ethnicity, it seems highly unlikely that increases in life expectancy, improved mortality and probability of surviving to reach 'old age' will have been shared equally across the major ethnic groups. However, the use of life expectancy as a measure is limited as it tells us nothing about the quality or health status of these lives.

[...]

Social class, age and gender are established dimensions of social differentiation within British society. Ethnicity is a newly-emerging and developing source of health inequality, reflecting the changing nature of our population as we embrace ethnicity and cultural diversity. One of the key changes in the nature of old age in Britain is the 'ageing' of our migrant communities. There are still comparatively few older people who are drawn from the migrant communities who moved to the UK between 1948 and the 1980s. Infant mortality data are published for minority ethnic communities within the UK and hint at the types of differentials that (probably) characterise later life. In 2007, the infant mortality rate for children born to 'White British' parents was 4.5 per 1,000 compared with over 9 per 1,000 for several minority ethnic communities (9.8 per 1,000 for the Caribbean community; 9.6 for the Pakistani community; 6.0 for the African community; 5.8 for the Indian community; and 4.0 for the Bangladeshi community). Thus, with the exception of the Bangladeshi community, infant mortality rates are between 30 and 100% higher among minority ethnic communities compared with the general population. Are these mortality differentials maintained across the lifecourse and into later life? There are very well-established mortality differentials by race in the US and between ethnic groups in some European states (see, for example, Bos et al, 2004) but, as Jarman and Aylin (2004) observe, until ethnicity is accurately and completely recorded on death certificates in the UK we can only speculate as to the range and direction of inequalities in adult death rates between and within ethnic groups in the UK.

[...]

Key points

In this chapter we have seen that virtually all health problems – as measured by mortality [...] – demonstrate an age-related increase. [...]

We have found that [...] mortality rates are higher for men than for women [...]. Social class or social position more broadly, exerts a powerful influence on the experience of health in later life. Consistently, where data are available, older people from the least privileged backgrounds are less likely to reach old age, [...]. We have very limited evidence about ethnicity but it seems reasonable to speculate that members of minority ethnic communities probably experience worse health in old age than the rest of the population. Thus, we can conclude that factors other than biology are important in influencing the pattern of disease in old age.

[...]

Bibliography

Albrecht, R. (1951) 'The social roles of older people', *Journal of Gerontology*, 6(2), 138-45.

Avlund, K., Holstein, B., Osler, M., Damsgaard, T., Holm-Pedersen, P. and Rasmussen, N. (2003) Social position and health in old age: the relevance of different indicators of social position. *Scandinavian Journal of Public Health*, 31(2), 126-36.

Black, D. (chair) (1980) *Inequalities in health*. London: HMSO.

Bos, V., Kunst, A.E., Keij-Deerenberg, I.M., Garssen, J. and Mackenbach, J.P. (2004) Ethnic inequalities in age- and cause-specific mortality in The Netherlands. *International Journal of Epidemiology*, 33, 1112-19.

Bowling, A. (2004) Socioeconomic differentials in mortality among older people. *Journal of Epidemiology and Community Health*, 58, 438-40.

Davey Smith, G., Dorling, D., Mitchell, R. and Shaw, M. (2002) Health inequalities in Britain: continuing increases up to the end of the 20th century. *Journal of Epidemiology and Community Health*, 56, 434-5.

DH (2009) *Government response to the Health Select Committee report on health inequalities*. London: The Stationery Office (available at www.dh.gov.uk/prod_consum_dh/groups/dh_digitalassets/documents/digitalasset/dh_099782.pdf).

Grundy, E. and Holt, G. (2001) The socioeconomic status of older adults: how should we measure it in studies of health inequalities? *Journal of Epidemiology and Community Health*, 55, 895-904.

Jarman, B. and Aylin, P. (2004) Death rates in England and Wales and the United States: variation with age, sex, and race. *British Medical Journal*, 329, 1367-7.

Jylhä, M. and Luukkaala, T. (2006) Social determinants of mortality in the oldest-old: social class and individual way-of-life. In Robine, J.-M., Crimmins, E., Horiuchi, S. and Yi, Z. (eds) *Human longevity, individual life duration, and the growth of the oldest-old population*. Dordrecht: Springer.

Manton, K.G. (1986) Cause specific mortality patterns among the oldest old: multiple cause of death trends 1968 to 1980. *Journal of Gerontology*, 41(2), 282-9.

Manton, K. (1999) Dynamic paradigms for human mortality and ageing, *Journal of Gerontology: Biological Sciences*, 54A, B247-B254.

Marmot, M. (chair) (2008) *Closing the gap in a generation*. Report of the WHO Commission on Social Determinants of Health. Geneva: World Health Organization (available at www.who.int/social_determinants/en/).

Mitchell, R., Dorling, D. and Shaw, M. (2000) *Inequalities in life and death: What if Britain were more equal?* York: Joseph Rowntree Foundation.

Nazroo, J., Goodman, J., Marmot, M. and Blundell, R. (2009) *Inequalities in health in an aging population: Patterns, causes and consequences.* London: ESRC (www.esrcsocietytoday.ac.uk/esrcinfocentre/viewawardpage.aspx?awardnumber=RES-000-23-0590).

Ramsay, S.E., Morris, R.W., Lennon, L.T., Wannamethee, S.G. and Whincup, P.H. (2008) Are social inequalities in mortality in Britain narrowing? Time trends from 1978 to 2005 in a population-based study of older men. *Journal of Epidemiology and Community Health,* 62, 75-80.

Victor, C.R. (1991) Continuity or change: inequalities in health in later life. *Ageing and Society,* 11, 23-39.

Victor, C.R. (2005) *The social context of ageing.* London: Routledge.

Wilkinson, R. and Pickett, K. (2009) *The spirit level: Why more equal societies almost always do better.* London: Allen Lane.

8

Psychological ageing

Alfons Marcoen, Peter G. Coleman and Ann O'Hanlon

Extract reproduced by permission of SAGE Publications, London, Los Angeles, New Delhi and Singapore, from Bond, J., Peace, S., Dittmann-Kohli, F. and Westerhoff, G.J. (eds) *Ageing in Society: European perspectives on gerontology* (© 2007) London: Sage Publications.

[…]

Main domains of research

The domain of psychological ageing research is actually a fabric of rather loosely linked theories and empirical investigations on age-related changes of different psychological functions and attributes in late adulthood and old age. Cognitive ageing continues to dominate the study of the psychology of ageing. In recent years notable advances have been made in other previously neglected fields, particularly within the interrelated areas of emotion, motivation and personality. Though much of the work in these fields remains at the exploratory stage, it hold the potential of a major contribution to ageing studies. We shall consider each of these three research areas in turn, after we discuss cognitive ageing.

Cognitive ageing

Development and ageing of memory and psychometric intelligence in late adulthood and old age were the focus of numerous investigations. […]

Subjective beliefs

Older people seldom report cognitive growth. On the contrary, memory complaints, doubts about one's abilities to adapt to new technologies, and the expectation of further decline are only a few examples of the perceived association between ageing and cognitive decline. Age-related changes in cognitive functioning are generally investigated in a perspective of losses rather than gains. […]

A gains perspective on cognitive ageing: post-formal thinking and wisdom

In the overall picture of cognitive ageing, references to losses predominate. Research on the positive gain of wisdom, for instance, has been described as one of the 'least studied' (Sternberg, 1990, p. ix) and 'long neglected' (Birren and Fisher, 1990, p. 317) of all psychological constructs. The scarcity of research in this area is due to a more immediate concern to identify and offset deficits and declines. Nevertheless, recently, researchers have sought to define and measure cognitive gains in later adulthood.

[...]

Research on wisdom has many theoretical and applied benefits reasons, not least its association with a range of positive attributes and experiences including greater autonomy and psychological mindedness (Wink and Helson, 1997), better psychological health (Erikson et al., 1986; Wink and Helson, 1997) and greater success in dealing with life's challenges (Kramer, 2000). The judgements made in wise decisions can facilitate a more harmonious world.

Yet defining wisdom is not easy and there is much debate about its associated components. Early research examined the characteristics people associate with wisdom or wise people. In one such study, Holliday and Chandler (1986) asked 150 participants (age range 22–86 years) to generate descriptors of wise people, as well as shrewd, perceptive, intelligent, spiritual and foolish people. They found that wisdom was defined in terms of learning from experience, being open-minded and knowledgeable, being of an older age, and having the ability to consider different perspectives. Additional components identified to date include greater awareness and empathy with others, and greater insight into human experiences and human potentials. The occurrence of wisdom is also believed to necessitate an awareness of conflict and ambiguity (Sternberg, 200 I), greater use of humour (Taranto, 1989), greater openness to experiences (Wink and Helson, 1997; Staudinger et al., 1997) and the ability to successfully regulate emotions (Kramer, 1990). [...]

The above characteristics might suggest that wisdom occurs only rarely. This was disputed by Randall and Kenyon (2001), who used biographical interviews to explore wisdom as being more broadly and regularly manifested in the lives of 'ordinary people'. The dimensions of wisdom they delineated include cognitive, practical/experimental, interpersonal, ethical/moral, and spiritual/mystical. In documenting 'narrative wisdom', they argue that wisdom can be discovered in all our lives, by exploring the lives we have lived, the challenges that have been addressed and the choices that were made.

Reflective practices can be central to the process of knowledge accumulation. It is only by engaging in reflective thinking and by looking at experiences and phenomena from different perspectives that the cognitive and knowledge-based aspects of wisdom can occur. Through a process of reflexivity, people are more likely to see reality without the Occurrence of distortions, and increase the probability of gaining true insight about people and experiences.

[...]

Emotions and ageing

Psycho-gerontology, like psychology in general, has not given anything like equivalent attention to emotional compared with cognitive functioning. This reflects in part a western bias towards defining humans in terms of their thinking and reasoning abilities. Feelings tend to be regarded as part of the lower animal order, often looked down upon as vestiges of patterns of action that once were useful in our evolution but are no longer so. Yet in fact it is the partnership of our emotions with our rational faculties that distinguishes us as higher animate beings. It has taken a different, more respectful, attitude to emotions, stimulated especially by the work of ethologists, to realise that they are centrally important in human and animal behaviour. Emotions are our way of responding to situations where we are not sure how we should respond. Humans, as well as animals, are not automata. They often find themselves in situations where they lack appropriate patterns of behaviour, when they are not fully adapted to an environment that has changed, or when no habit or instinct fits a situation. Emotions are important at such junctures because they prompt us towards certain types of action when perhaps we should do something but lack already established modes of action (Oatley and Jenkins, 1996).

Psychologists who work in this field employ the concepts of 'primary' and 'secondary' emotions. The primary emotion systems are born with us and relate to action systems that are triggered by events we experience in relation to our goals: thus, happiness at the achievement of goals, sadness at their loss, anger at frustration of a plan to reach a goal, and anxiety because of a conflict between goals, including the important goal of self-preservation. Secondary emotions, such as embarrassment, guilt and pride, arise early in life as children develop complex forms of representation of the world around and of an inner world of mental states shared with others.

In striking contrast to the general picture of decline which the study of cognitive ageing presents, older people by and large impress by their ability to master their negative emotions and present a positive face to the world. Many commentators start from the so-called 'paradox' of late-life well-being (Westerhof et al., 2003). Whereas ill-health, disability, bereavement, loss of expectations and the many other social disadvantages that often characterise late life are associated with diminished morale and life satisfaction at younger stages of life, older individuals display much higher levels of well-being than one might expect on the grounds of these general associations alone. Clearly people as they age acquire a certain emotional resilience, ways of coping with loss that younger people in general lack. As will be stressed again further on, it is important not to over-generalise these differences; not all older people display equivalent levels of resilience.

Investigations of emotions by means of self-report assessments have indicated a systematic decline in negative emotions with age while positive emotions appear to remain fairly constant (Charles et al., 2001; Dittmann-Kohli et al., 2001; Labouvie-Vief and Medler, 2002). Older people are less likely to use immature defences, are better able to control emotions, and show generally less reactivity and lower arousal. Socio-emotional selectivity theory developed by Carstensen and colleagues (Carstensen et al., 1999; Carstensen et al., 2003) explains this bias towards positive images in terms of older individuals' greater emphasis on maintaining the positives in their lives in the light of their limited time expectation. As a result they are less interested in the more time-demanding task of identifying and removing threats in the future which may never materialise for them.

However, this generalisation is dependent on the context. Where older people are dealing with familiar situations and can rely on well-rehearsed solutions to emotional problems they appear less reactive than younger people; but where they are dealing with novel and demanding situations older people may experience greater levels of disturbance (Labouvie-Vief, 2005). Consistent with socioemotional selectivity theory, they also function better in situations that are personally relevant to them (Rahhal et al., 2002). Thus older people's continued positive emotional functioning may depend on control of demands put upon them by the environment (Labouvie-Vief and Marquez Gonzales, 2004).

Motivation and ageing

Theories of developmental changes in motivation in adulthood have typically emphasised two basic needs, variously worded (Bakan, 1966; Bode, 2003):

- 'agency', 'power' or 'mastery'
- 'communion', 'intimacy' or 'belonging'

These developments are often depicted as having a gendered character, with older men learning to display more 'feminine' motivations and older women more 'masculine' motivations. Greater relatedness can compensate for men's loss of competence, whereas women's often late-won independence is something they may safeguard strongly. The resultant greater androgynous character of later life is claimed to be advantageous to both men and women. Although the evidence for such theories in modern societies as opposed to traditional societies (Gutmann, 1987) is slight – a recent representative Dutch study found no decrease in gender differences with age (Westerhof and Bode, 2006) – they continue to have appeal to those searching for greater purpose and meaning in the experience of ageing.

New impetus has recently been given to research on ageing and motivation by Deci and Ryan's (2000) examination of the concept of psychological need, and their specification of competence, relatedness and autonomy as three needs essential to goal-related activity. Their fundamental postulate is that 'humans are active, growth-oriented organisms who are naturally inclined toward integration of their psychic elements into a unified sense of self and integration of themselves into larger social structures' (Deci and Ryan, 2000, p. 229). Some researchers have already begun to apply this theory in studies on institutional care. For example, O'Connor and Vallerand (1994) have focused on the concept of autonomy, which is subtly but significantly different from the concept of control, also an important concept in health psychology. Whereas the literature on locus of control and learned helplessness focuses on the perception of contingency between the person's own behaviours and observable outcomes, autonomy or self determination refers to the experience of freedom in initiating one's behaviour. Control does not ensure autonomy, and autonomy does not ensure control. It is choice which is central to autonomy. Deci and Ryan (2000) describe four types of behaviour that vary along a continuum of autonomy or self-determination. Using these distinctions O'Connor and Vallerand (1994) have developed a measure of elderly motivational style applicable to the domains of life relevant to the lives of older people.

In a study of intermediate-care nursing homes in Montreal, the older people were assessed on the needs for self-determination, and the homes were independently classified on the basis of information they supplied on the degree of self determination provided. As one would expect, residents in high self-determination nursing homes tended to score higher on self-determined motivation. But more interesting was the finding of interaction effects with motivational styles. There was a tendency for low self-determined motivation individuals to report better psychological adjustment in low self-determination nursing homes, and for high self determination motivation individuals to report better psychological adjustment in high self-determination nursing homes.

This is a good example of the so-called 'person–environment congruence' theory of ageing (Lawton, 1980). One cannot expect all elderly nursing home residents to benefit from high levels of autonomy. But O'Connor and Vallerand (1994) suggest the interesting hypothesis that long-term adjustment is better served by an environment that provides opportunities for autonomy that are always slightly greater than one's initial level of self-determined motivation. In a further test of 'person–environment congruence' in institutional settings, O'Connor and Rigby (1996) carried out an intriguing study on 'baby talk' in nursing homes, again independently recording the elderly residents need for succourance and the behaviour shown by staff. Significant interactions were again evident, suggesting the harmful effect of receiving baby talk on self-esteem for those who perceived it negatively. Thus Deci and Ryan's concept of relatedness also has to be seen in the context of a person's history. What can be perceived as 'warmth' by one person may be seen by another as being 'talked down to' by another, thus undermining feelings of competence.

Some of the best examples of work on motivation in institutional settings in Europe are provided by the late Margret Baltes' programme of research in German nursing homes (Baltes and Carstensen, 1996). She has shown how it is necessary to counteract professional carers' 'preference' for older people who give up self-control and thus become more easy to manage. Moreover, a pattern-of-dependency script operates in institutions, whereby dependent behaviour is most likely to result in staff providing social contact and attention. These are usually highly valued by most residents and, in learning theory terms, function as 'rewards'. Baltes et al. (1994) have developed training programmes that have proved effective in reversing these patterns. It is important to note that, in a large representative sample from East and West Germany, older men and women expressed fear of becoming dependent and losing their ability for independent living with advancing old age (Bode, 2003: Dittmann-Kohli, 1995a: Dittmann-Kohli and Westerhof, 2000).

Personality and ageing

The studies just referred to are clear examples of the importance of individual differences in the study of ageing. However, the question whether personality itself changes with age has remained a difficult one to resolve. Answers to this question also depend on how personality is defined. One way of resolving the paradoxes in the literature on this subject is to think of the realm of personality in terms of two types of variable:

- those that remain relatively stable throughout adulthood (typically referred to as personality traits)
- those that develop and change (including attitudes to the self and to the world around, values, beliefs, goals and reference systems).

Unfortunately most research has not taken both aspects of personality into account.

There is now a well established consensus that the 'big five' traits of neuroticism, extraversion, openness to experience, agreeableness and conscientiousness are consistent across age groups, cultures and measurement instruments as dimensions of personality on which individuals differ (John, 1990; Costa and McCrae, 1997). The structural invariance of the measurement techniques means that one can confidently assert the relative stability of these personality traits with age (Staudinger, 2005). Individuals retain the same profile relative to one another. There is consistent evidence for relatively small mean changes with ageing. Neuroticism appears to decrease across adulthood (Mroczek and Spiro, 2003), although it may show some increase in very late life (Small et al., 2003), as also does openness to experience and extraversion (McCrae et al., 2000; Field and Millsap, 1991). Agreeableness and conscientiousness, by contrast, increase (Haan et al., 1986; Helson and Kwan, 2000). Longitudinal evidence of similar changes has led McCrae, Costa and others to speculate whether this developmental pattern may have been selected for by evolution (McCrae et al., 2000).

McAdams (1995) makes a useful distinction between three levels of knowledge of personality. The first level comprises the traits that are independent of context, but are so broad that they give only limited knowledge of the person. McAdams refers to personality traits as the 'psychology of the stranger'. By contrast, when one knows a person better one moves to the second level of understanding their motives, values, attitudes and skills, including ways of coping, all of which McAdams groups under the term 'personal concerns'. But particularly in the modem world even this type of information is insufficient for in-depth awareness of the person. Some additional understanding is needed of the inner story of the self, how people make sense of their lives, how they integrate their past, present and future, and their various characteristics, so as to experience their life as having unity, purpose and meaning. Not everyone succeeds in this integration but this is what McAdams means by 'identity', using the term first coined in this way by Erikson (1963).

Some of the most interesting work on age changes at the second level has been done on ways of coping. Already in the 1980s there was evidence of systematic change with age towards greater control of the emotions and less use of problem solving. Using the methods developed by Lazarus, the pioneer American researcher on stress and coping (Lazarus, 1966; Lazarus and DeLongis, 1983), Folkman et al. (1987) reported that these differences in styles of coping remained even when controlled for the different areas of stress experienced by older and younger people. For example, older people report more stresses having to do with environmental and social issues and less with family, friends and finance. The one exception was the health area where older people appear to be more proactive than younger people (Leventhal et al., 1992), perhaps because of their greater experience of the difficulties caused by neglecting a health problem.

[…]

Recent work on personality and ageing which really does focus on the individual person is scarce. Between the world wars there was an active tradition of case-study analysis carried out by well-known psychologists such as Murray and Allport, but its value was overlooked in the postwar enthusiasm for quantitative methods. Those who have tried to recover this tradition (e.g. Runyan, 1984; Bromley, 1986; McAdams and West, 1997; Fishman, 1999) have emphasised that disciplined study can be carried out and testable generalisations formulated on data collected on individual lives. Coleman has pointed to the particular applicability of case-study research to the study of adaptation in later life (Coleman, 1999, 2002) and has argued for its inclusion alongside qualitative surveys within longitudinal studies of ageing.

[…]

Conclusion

This brief overview of theories and research in the field of psycho-gerontology is necessarily selective and incomplete. We focused on the psychology of the ageing – but still developing – individual facing gains and losses, experiencing cognitive, emotional, motivational and personality changes, but nevertheless, generally, able to maintain a positive self-concept and outlook on life far into advanced old age. […]

References

Bakan, D. (1966) *The Duality of Human Existence: Isolation and Communion in Western Man.* Boston MA: Baecon Press.

Baltes, M.M., Neumann, E.-V. and Zank, S. (1994) Maintenance and rehabilitation of independence in old age: an intervention program for staff. *Psychology and Aging* 9, 179-188.

Baltes, P.B. and Carstensen, L. (1996) The process of successful ageing. *Ageing and Society* 16, 397-422.

Birren, J.E. and Fisher, L.M. (1990) The elements of wisdom: overview and integration. In: Sternberg, R.J. (ed.) *Wisdom: Its Nature, Origins and Development*. Cambridge: Cambridge University Press.

Bode, C. (2003) *Individuality and Relatedness in Middle and Late Adulthood: A Study of Women and Men in the Netherlands, East and West Germany*. Enschede, Netherlands: Print Partners Ipskamp.

Bromley, D.B. (1986) *The Case-study Method in Psychology and Related Disciplines*. Chichester: Wiley.

Carstensen, L.L., Fung, H. and Charles, S.L. (2003) Socioemotional selectivity theory and the regulation of emotions in the second half of life. *Motivation and Emotion* 27, 103-123.

Carstensen, L. L., Isaacowitz, D.M. and Charles, S.L. (1999) Taking time seriously: a theory of socioemotional selectivity. *American Psychologist* 54, 165-181.

Charles, S.L, Reynolds, C. and Gatz, M. (2001) Age-related differences and change in positive and negative affect over twenty-five years. *Journal of Personality and Social Psychology* SO, 136-151.

Coleman, P.G. (1999) Creating a life story: the task of reconciliation. *Gerontologist* 39, 135-154.

Coleman, P.G. (2002) Doing case study research in psychology. In: Jamieson, A. and Victor, C.R. (eds) *Researching Ageing in Later Life,* 135-154. Buckingham: Open University Press.

Costa, P.T. and McCrae, R.R. (1997) Longitudinal stability of adult personality. In: Hogan, R., Johnson, J.A. and Briggs, S.R. (eds) *Handbook of Personality Psychology,* 269-290. New York: Academic Press.

Deci, E.L. and Ryan, R.M. (2000) The 'what' and 'why' of goal pursuits: human needs and self-determination of behaviour. *Psychological Inquiry* 11, 227-268.

Dittmann-Kohli, E. (1995a) *Das personliche Sinnsystem: Ein Vergleich zwischen fruhem und spatem Erwachsenenalter*. Göttingen: Hogrefe.

Dittmann-Kohli, E. (2001) Selbst- und Lebensvorstellungen in der zweiten Lebenshälfte: Ergebnisse aus dem Alterssurvey. In: Dittmann-Kohli, E, Westerhof, G.J. and Bode, C. (eds) *Die zweite Lebenshälfte: Psychologische Perspectiven,* 549-584. Stuttgart: Kohlhammer.

Dittmann-Kohli, F. and Westerhof, G.J. (2000) The personal meaning system in a life span perspective. In: Reker, G.T. and Chamberlain, K. (eds) *Exploring Existential Meaning: Optimizing Human Development across the Life Span,* 107-123. Thousand Oaks, CA: Sage.

Erikson (1963) *Childhood and Society* (2nd edition), New York: W.W Norton.

Erikson, E.H., Erikson, J.M. and Kivnick, H.Q. (1986) *Vital Involvement in Old Age: The Experience of Old Age in Our Time*. New York: Norton.

Field, D. and Millsap, R.E. (1991) Personality in advanced old age: continuity or change? *Journal of Gerontology,* 46, 299-308.

Fishman, D.B. (1999) *The case of pragmatic psychology*. NY: NY University Press.

Folkman, S., Lazarus, R.S., Pimley, S. and Novacek, J. (1987) Age differences in stress and coping processes. *Psychology and Aging*, 2, 171-184.

Gutman, D. (1987) *Reclaimed Powers: Towards a New Psychology of Men and Women in Later Life*, (2nd edition), Chichester: Wiley.

Haan, N., Millsap, R. and Hartka, E. (1986) As time goes by: change and stability in personality over fifty years. *Psychology and Aging*, 1, 220-232.

Helson, R. and Kwan, V.S.Y. (2000) Personality change in adulthood: the broad picture and processes in one longitudinal sample. In: Hampson, S.E. (ed.) *Advances in Personality and Psychology*, vol. 1, 77-166. Philadelphia: Psychology Press/Taylor & Francis.

Holliday, S.G. and Chandler, M.J. (1986) *Wisdom: Explorations in Adult Competence*. Basel: Karger.

John, O.P. (1990) The 'big five' factor taxonomy: dimensions of personality in the natural language and in questionnaires. In: Pervin, L.A. (ed.) *Handbook of Personality: Theory and Research*, 66-100. New York: Guilford Press.

Kramer (1990) Conceptualizing wisdom: the primacy of affect-cognition relations. In: Sternberg, R.J. (ed) *Wisdom: Its Nature, Origins and Development*, 279-313. Cambridge: Cambridge University Press.

Kramer, D.A. (2000) Wisdom as a classical source of human strength: conceptualization and empirical inquiry. *Journal of Social and Clinical Psychology*, 19, 83-101.

Labouvie-Vief, G. (2005) The psychology of emotions and ageing. In: Johnson, M., Bengtson, V.L., Coleman, P.G. and Kirkwood, T. (eds) *The Cambridge Handbook of Age and Ageing*. Cambridge: Cambridge University Press.

Labouvie-Vief, G. and Marquez Gonzales, M. (2004) Dynamic integration: affect optimization and differentiation in development. In: Dai, D.Y. and Sternberg, R.J. (eds) *Motivation, Emotion, and Cognition: Integrative Perspectives on Intellectual Functioning and Development*. Mahwah, NJ: Erlbaum.

Labouvie-Vief, G. and Medler, M. (2002) Affect optimization and affect complexity: modes and styles of regulation in adulthood. *Psychology and Ageing*, 17, 571-588.

Lawton, M.P. (1980) *Environment and Aging*. Belmont, CA: Brooks-Cole.

Lazarus, R.S. (1966) *Psychological Stress and the Coping Process*. New York: McGraw-Hill.

Lazarus, R.S. and DeLongis, A. (1983) Psychological stress and coping in aging. *American Psychologist* 38, 245-254.

Leventhal, H., Leventhal, E.A. and Schaefer, P.M. (1992) Vigilant coping and health behavior. In Ory, M.G., Abeles, R.P. and Lipman, P.D. (eds) *Aging, Health, and Behavior*, 109-140. Newbury Park, CA: Sage.

McAdams, D.P. (1995) What do we know when we know a person? *Journal of Personality* 63, 365-396.

McAdams, D.P. and West, S.G. (1997) Personality psychology and the case study: introduction. *Journal of Personality* 65, 757-783.

McCrae, R.R., Costa, P.T., Ostendorf, E., Angleitner, A., Hrebickova, M. et al. (2000) Nature and nurture: temperament, personality and life span development. *Journal of Personality and Social Psychology* 78, 173-186.

Mroczek, D. and Spiro, A. (2003) Modelling intraindividual change in personality traits: findings from the Normative Aging Study. *Journal of Gerontology*, 58B, P153-165.

O'Connor, B.P. and Vallerand, R. J. (1994) Motivation, self-determination, and person–environment fit as predictors of psychological adjustment among nursing home residents. *Psychology and Aging* 9, 189-194.

Oatley, K. and Jenkins, J.M. (1996) *Understanding Emotions*. Oxford: Blackwell.

Rahhal, T.A., May, C.P. and Hasher, L. (2002) Aging, source memory and source significance. *Psychological Science* 13, 101-105.

Runyan, W.M. (1984) *Life Histories and Psychobiography: Explorations in Theory and Method*. New York: Oxford University Press.

Small, B.J., Hertzog, C., Hultsch, D.F. and Dixon, R.A. (2003) Stability and change in adult personality over 6 years: findings from the Victorian Longitudinal Study. *Journal of Gerontology* 58B, P166-176.

Staudinger, U.M. (2005) Personality and Ageing. In: Johnson, M., Bengtson, V.L., Coleman, P.G. and Kirkwood, T. (eds) *The Cambridge Handbook of Age and Ageing*. Cambridge: Cambridge University Press.

Staudinger, U.M., Lopez, D.F. and Baltes, P.B. (1997) The psychometric location of wisdom-related performance: intelligence, personality and more? *Personality and Social Psychology Bulletin* 23, 2100-2114

Sternberg, R.J. (ed.) (1990) *Wisdom: Its Nature, Origins and Development*. Cambridge: Cambridge University Press.

Taranto, M.A. (1989) Facets of wisdom: a theoretical synthesis. *Journal of Aging and Human Development* 29, 1-21.

Westerhof, G. J. and Bode, C. (2006) The personal meaning of individuality and relatedness: gender differences in middle and late adulthood. In: Daatland, S. and Biggs, S. (eds) *Ageing and Diversity: Multiple Pathways and Cultural Migrations*, 29-44. Bristol: Policy Press.

Westerhof, G.J., Dittmann-Kohli, F. and Bode, C. (2003a) The aging paradox: towards personal meaning in gerontological theory. In: Biggs, S., Lowenstein, A. and Hendricks, J. (eds) *The Need for Theory: Social Gerontology for the 21st Century*, 127-143. Amityville, NY: Baywood.

Westerhof, G.J., Barrett, A.E. and Steverink, N. (2003b) Forever young: a comparison of age identities in the United States and Germany. *Research on Aging* 25, 366-383.

Wink, P. and Helson, R. (1997) Practical and transcendent wisdom: their nature and some longitudinal findings. *Journal of Adult Development* 4, 1-15.

9

Dementia reconsidered: the person comes first

Tom Kitwood

In my own work on dementia I have tried to develop a view of personhood that meets at least four main criteria. It must reveal our moral obligations; it must be valid in terms of a psychology that focuses on experience, action and spirituality; it must illuminate care practice; and it must be fully compatible with the well–corroborated findings or neuroscience. ...

   [...]

The psychodynamics of exclusion

Many cultures have shown a tendency to depersonalize those who have some form of serious disability, whether of a physical or a psychological kind. A consensus is created, established in tradition and embedded in social practices, that those affected are not real persons. The rationalizations follow on. If people show bizarre behaviour 'they are possessed by devils'; 'they are being punished for the sins of a former life'; 'the head is rotten'; 'there is a mental disorder whose symptoms are exactly described in the new diagnostic manual'.

   Several factors come together to cause this dehumanization. In part, no doubt, it corresponds to characteristics of the culture as a whole; where personhood is widely disregarded, those who are powerless are liable to be particularly devalued. Many societies, including our own, are permeated by an ageism which categorizes older people as incompetent, ugly and burdensome, and which discriminates against them at both a personal and a structural level (Bytheway 1995). Those who have dementia are often subjected to ageism in its most extreme form; and, paradoxically, even people who are affected at a relatively young age are often treated as if they were 'senile'. In financial terms, far too few resources have been allocated to the provision of the necessary services.

There is also the fact that very little attention has been given to developing the attitudes and skills that are necessary for good psychological care. In the case of dementia, until very recently this was not even recognized as an issue, with the consequence that many people working in this field have had no proper preparation for their work.

Behind these more obvious reasons, there may be another dynamic which excludes those who have dementia from the world of persons. There seems to be something special about the dementing conditions – almost as if they attract to themselves a particular kind of inhumanity: a sodal psychology that is malignant in its effects, even when it proceeds from people who are kind and well-intentioned (Kitwood 1990a). This might be seen as a defensive reaction, a response to anxieties held in part at an unconscious level.

The anxieties seem to be of two main kinds. First, and naturally enough, every human being is afraid of becoming frail and highly dependent; these fears are liable to be particularly strong in any society where the sense of community is weak or non-existent. Added to that, there is the fear of a long drawn-out process of dying, and of death itself. Contact with those who are elderly, weak and vulnerable is liable to activate these fears, and threaten our basic sense of security (Stevenson 1989). Second, we carry fears about mental instability. The thought of being insane, deranged, lost forever in confusion, is terrifying. Many people have come close to this at some point, perhaps in times of great stress, or grief, or personal catastrophe, or while suffering from a disease that has affected mental functioning. At the most dreadful end of these experiences lies the realm of 'unbeing', where even the sense of self is undermined.

Dementia in another person has the power to activate fears of both kinds: those concerned with dependence and frailty, and those concerned with going insane. Moreover, there is no real consolation in saying 'It won't happen to me', which can be done with many other anxiety-provoking conditions. Dementia is present in almost every street, and discussed repeatedly in the media. We know also that people from all kinds of background are affected, and that among those over 80 the proportion may be as high as one in five. So in being close to a person with dementia we may be seeing some terrifying anticipation of how we might become.

It is not surprising, then, if sensitivity has caused many people to shrink from such a prospect. Some way has to be found for making the anxieties bearable. The highly defensive tactic is to turn those who have dementia into a different species, not persons in the full sense. The principal problem, then, is not that of changing people with dementia, or of 'managing' their behaviour; it is that of moving beyond our own anxieties and defences, so that true meeting can occur, and life-giving relationships can grow.

How personhood is undermined

[T]he standard paradigm feeds into an extremely negative and deterministic view, which can be summed up in the popular image of 'the death that leaves the body behind', and in the headline of an article that appeared a few years ago in a popular magazine, 'Alzheimer's: No cure, no help, no hope'.

If we stay close to mundane reality, and explore how people with dementia live out their lives from day to day, in their own homes and in the settings where formal care is provided, we get a very different picture (Kitwood 1990b). It is clear that many social. or societal. factors are involved: culture, locality, social class, education, financial resources, the availability or absence of support and services. Also, at the interpersonal or social–psychological level, much depends on how far a person with dementia is enabled to retain intact relationships, to use his or her abilities, to experience variety and enjoyment. From the vantage-point of the standard paradigm, these things are externalities, separate from the advancing process of disease. According to the paradigm that I am suggesting, they are also part of the whole process – actually incorporated into the dementing condition, for good or ill (Kitwood 1994a).

A story of our time

Here, in outline, is an account of the process of dementia in an older woman, covering a period of eight or so years in all. I have used it in the form presented here on training courses, as a way of raising awareness of the broader context of the dementing conditions.

> Margaret B. died in March 1995, at the age of 89, in Bank Top Nursing Home. The first episode that really convinced her husband Brian that something was seriously wrong occurred in the summer of 1987, while they were on holiday in Spain, staying in a large hotel. One morning when she was collecting her breakfast in the dining room she got completely lost; she could not find Brian, or their table. When he found her she was very upset and frightened, and apparently had no idea where she was. She seemed to lose confidence from this point forward, becoming increasingly anxious and confused. Margaret had shown some signs of forgetfulness before this time; for example, she had difficulty remembering the names of their six grandchildren. She had also made a few odd mistakes, such as coming home from the supermarket with cat food, despite the fact that their last cat had died several years before.

Brian had simply passed off these things as part of growing older; after all, he and his wife were both approaching 80.

Margaret had always been a very conscientious person, loyal to her husband and family. She had worked part-time for a while, but mainly her life had centred on the home. Brian was a strong and upright man, highly efficient and organized. He was respected in the community, although few people knew him well. He had been a very strict father to their three children, and he had always had a rather formal manner with his wife. As a couple, Margaret and Brian 'kept themselves to themselves'. They had no close friends. Their daughter Susan had emigrated, and both of their two sons had settled in distant places.

After the episode in Spain, life for Brian and Margaret became more and more difficult, although neither of them understood what was happening. Brian found himself resenting Margaret's unreliability, and to his shame he became openly critical of her mistakes. When she showed signs of anxiety or sadness, he often told her to 'pull herself together'. Sometimes she came close to him, pleading with him to hold her and help her to feel safe; usually he pushed her away, or suggested that she go and sit down while he got on with his various jobs. On a few occasions he became really angry with her, which was very unlike how he had usually been. One afternoon she wandered away from home, and when Brian returned she was nowhere to be found. The police picked her up in a distant part of town. He was furious about this, telling her it was a disgrace to the family and all they stood for. From this point forward he felt it was necessary to lock her in the house whenever he went out.

Although Brian knew a little about Alzheimer's disease from television, and things he had read, he did not consciously connect this knowledge with Margaret's behaviour. It was only in 1990, when Susan came on a visit from Australia, that the realization dawned. Susan was a nurse. She immediately recognized the signs of dementia, and insisted that her mother was taken to the doctor. Margaret was given a provisional diagnosis of Alzheimer's disease, and the doctor suggested that Brian should do the best he could to look after Margaret at home.

Brian's response was dramatic. He quickly absorbed all the information about Alzheimer's disease he could lay his hands on, and set about looking after Margaret in the most efficient way. He took over all the housework and cooking. If she hovered around him while he was doing his tasks, he made her return to the sitting room. When he went shopping, he went alone. As soon as Margaret began to have problems with continence, he obtained help from the advisory service, and did all that was necessary to avoid unpleasant accidents. When she developed problems with sleeping, he took her to the doctor, who prescribed some night sedation. Although the task of looking after Margaret was extremely tiring, Brian was determined to play his part well.

By late 1991 Brian knew that it was all getting too much for him. He was becoming increasingly tired and irritable; Margaret was more and more bewildered and tearful. Brian called in the social services. After Margaret's assessment it was decided that she should go to a day centre. This gave Brian some relief. although Margaret was often very upset before going, and sometimes seemed extremely confused on her return. He never went with her to the centre, but kept in touch with the manager by telephone.

A new crisis developed in mid-1992. Brian's health was deteriorating; he had developed angina. Margaret was extremely confused and agitated; her medication was increased. The day centre manager stated that Margaret was no longer an appropriate client because her dementia was too severe. The district nurses who came in to help get Margaret to bed were usually in a hurry, and they talked to each other continually while they gave her a bath and put her to bed. This seemed to make Margaret very upset. One evening she bit one of the nurses on the arm, which caused great distress. For Brian, this was the last straw. After talking things through with the social worker, he came to the conclusion that Margaret would have to go into full-time residential care. He felt extremely guilty and uneasy at the prospect.

Brian had heard that The Gables was a good home. He rang the manager, who immediately offered a place for Margaret. One day in November Brian told Margaret that they were going out for a ride in the car, although he did not say where they were going. This was how she entered residential care. As Margaret was very anxious and tearful, the manager suggested that Brian should not visit for several days, to give time for her to get used to her new home.

Unfortunately, Margaret did not settle in The Gables. Her distress and agitation caused great annoyance to other residents; she would not stay in bed at night. Brian usually visited her three times each week, but soon she appeared not to recognize him and often ignored him. One evening one of the residents shouted very abusively at Margaret, and Margaret hit her in the face, causing severe bruises. The family of this resident immediately lodged a complaint, and insisted on an inquiry.

Two days later Margaret was taken to a psychiatric assessment ward, where she spent six weeks. She was given heavy tranquillizing medication. After this she was placed in Bank Top Nursing Home, which had a wing entirely for people with dementia.

At Bank Top, Margaret remained under sedation. Her life consisted of being got up in the morning, having her breakfast, and then being put in a chair. Here she sat for hours on end, half awake, half asleep, and occasionally wandering around. Around 8.00 p.m. each day she was put to bed. Within four months she had lost the use of her legs. She was becoming very thin, and often left her food. Only one member of staff realized that Margaret was often eager to eat, but needed prompting about actually doing it. Brian's visits became less and less frequent; he saw little point in coming. The two sons did not come at all. For the very last part of her life Margaret spent longer and longer periods lying on her bed. She was fed, mainly with liquid food. One morning it was found that she had died.

Although this narrative taken as a whole is a fiction, each element of it is based on events that have actually happened. Also, while The Gables and Bank Top Nursing Home have no existence in reality, they both epitomize the poorer quality kind of place where people are taken in for residential care. The story of Margaret and Brian is typical of how dementia has been lived out in recent years in Britain, and it has close parallels in other industrialized countries. Several people have said to me, after I have used it in training work, that it almost exactly describes a case they know, or even what has happened in their own family.

If we follow the development of any person's dementing condition closely, again and again we will come to see how social and interpersonal factors come into play, either adding to the difficulties directly arising from neurological impairment, or helping to lessen their effects. In the light of this it is extremely difficult to hold to the view suggested by the standard paradigm: that the mental and emotional symptoms are a direct result of a catastrophic series of changes in the brain that lead to the death of brain cells – and nothing more than that. This narrow conception of the ill-being that dementia often entails can easily divert attention away from the inadequacy of our social arrangements, and it has led to a gross imbalance in research. Insofar as it has done this, it might be regarded as a 'neuropathic ideology' – a body of opinion that systematically distorts the truth.

In moral terms, it is clear even from the brief account given here that there were many points at which Margaret was not treated fully as a person. She needed comfort in her anxiety, but Brian was unable to give it. She pleaded for encouragement and reassurance when her self-confidence was failing, but she met criticism or anger. She wanted a 'way of life', a continuity with her past, but her role as the homemaker was totally stripped away. The day centre was unable to provide her with occupation within her range of capability, and it failed to offer her the kind of company with which she could feel at ease. Neither The Gables nor Bank Top had developed the skills among staff that would enable them to provide effective psychological care for residents with dementia. Margaret's 'behaviour problems' were never explored in a sympathetic way, or traced back to their roots; eventually they were controlled by medication, but at the cost of suppressing much of what enabled her still to be a person, and possibly of adding further damage to her nervous system.

In a case such as this one might be tempted to blame the main carer, but it would be both psychologically inept and morally blind to do so. Those who have this role take on, almost single-handed, a colossal task. The weight of evidence from anthropology is that no individual was ever 'designed' for such an onerous commitment; human beings emerged through evolution as a highly social species, where burdens are carried by a group. Even in those rare instances in industrial societies where the care is genuinely shared by several members of the family, the situation is far less fraught and strained.

Brian, in the story, was left to live out the consequence of the tendency of our kind of society to force into isolation people who are under pressure. Furthermore, he had received no preparation, practical or psychological, for his new role. He was the product of his own upbringing, with its many limitations, and of his own attempts to measure up to the common standards of how to be a man. At many points his own needs were not met, and when the situation became really difficult he received no support. Where 'community care' was available, it consisted mainly of *ad hoc* interventions, and when the situation became really difficult it proved completely inadequate. Some of the things Brian did to Margaret fell far short of true respect for her personhood, but what about his personhood too? Locking his wife in the house when he went out might be considered deeply immoral, but perhaps it was the 'least bad' thing that he could do in the circumstances. As Margaret's dementia grew worse, no one helped Brian with his feelings of anger, inadequacy and guilt; no one enabled him to come to terms with his own tragic predicament.

So this story of one person's dementia is much more than that of an advancing neurological illness. It is absurdly reductionistic to suggest, as some have done, that 'everything in the end comes down to what is going on in individual brain cells'. In very many cases, we find that the process of dementia is also the story of a tragic inadequacy in our culture, our economy, our traditional views about gender, our medical system and our general way of life. In engaging with people who are in Brian's position we should take great care not to be judgemental; it is probable that they already carry a very heavy burden of guilt feelings. The fault lies in the context, and at a systemic level; it is the culmination of a long historical process. That whole context needs radical improvement – through a change in the culture of care. But that is a task that has, until very recently, been almost totally neglected.

[…]

Evidence for a positive view: A case study

A series in the *Journal of Dementia Care* presents accounts of good effects associated with (and almost certainly resulting from) person–centred care (Kitwood 1995c). Each one shows how a deteriorating situation was turned around, or how well-being was maintained, in the face of cognitive disability ….The following story describes the last part of the life of a woman with dementia, after she had moved into sheltered housing.

When Bessy moved into Flower Court, from a village a few miles away, she was already showing early signs of memory problems that were obvious to her close family. Her daughter lived near the scheme and had applied for a flat for her mother so that she could give her extra help.

Two years later, when I first met Bessy, her dementia had increased considerably. However, she appeared to have a very high level of wellbeing. During my visit to her flat she made no real conversation but constantly laughed and made happy fragmented comments. This impression was confirmed by the warden. According to her reports Bessy always showed a considerable amount of humour, frequently initiated social contact with others and was usually relaxed.

When Bessy first moved into the scheme the situation was not as happy as I found it. During her first few months in Flower Court she had often been aggressive, and indeed physically violent, towards people who came into conflict with her. For example, she always refused to be undressed for bed, and if encouraged she would hit out. Her neighbours were afraid of the aggressive outbursts. As a consequence they tended to avoid Bessy, which severely restricted her social life.

In addition a problem of a different kind was occurring. At a similar time every day Bessy would attempt to leave the scheme and search for a bus back to the village where she had previously lived. In sheltered housing, tenants tend to be active enough to come and go as they please, and there are no care staff to look out for them. Therefore as Bessy's dementia developed it was a growing concern that she would be lost and/or injured if this continued.

Luckily for Bessy, she and Janet the warden had 'clicked' on their first meeting and over time became strongly bonded to one another. A number of behaviours on Bessy's part confirmed her attachment. For example, she had learned Janet's name straight away and always used it - 'to my surprise' said Janet. If Bessy hurt herself she would search out Janet to help her. On one such occasion she fell and badly hurt her knee and yet still managed to walk to Janet's office, saying to her, 'Save me'.

Janet was committed to exploring possibilities to lessen Bessy's afternoon disappearances, her aggression and consequent stigmatization by other tenants. So she arranged to discuss the situation with Bessy's daughter. What emerged from their conversation was a rich picture of Bessy's previous life. Before her husband had died, the couple had spent their life as publicans. Apparently Bessy had been extremely extrovert and outgoing – she loved company, jokes, dressing up for work and having a firm routine to her life. Obviously due to such a lifestyle Bessy had also needed to be able to protect herself when threatened, even if this was by just appearing aggressive.

Janet had used this personal information to form a few ideas of ways in which she might lessen Bessy's problems; for example, Bessy refused to undress for bed, becoming aggressive if pushed. Some creative thinking around Bessy's previous love of dressing-up eased the problem. The warden allowed Bessy to sleep in the clothes she had worn during the day. The next morning when the home help would visit Bessy, she would get out lots of outfits and comment, 'It's like C&A in here, let's try on some clothes'. Bessy would then happily try on different things until she was in a new, clean outfit each day.

Turning her attention to Bessy's increasingly dangerous wandering and searching, Janet thought of the boredom she must now be experiencing after such a busy and routine filled life. As a start Janet began to take Bessy with her when she took and picked up her children from school. This gave a very regular format to her day. At exactly the same time each morning and afternoon Bessy would go on what she called 'an outing', meeting other people as she went, which encouraged her sociable nature. With a little encouragement tenants accepted that Bessy would come to some social events in the communal lounge, and a few would pick her up from her flat. Bessy 'had a wonderful time', according to Janet, at these social events. She loved to sing and when tenants walked her back to her flat they would have to sing with her all the way.

Thus the scheme had arrived at the situation I found. Bessy was happy and relaxed, strongly attached to Janet. Her initial aggression had lessened considerably without ever using medication. Other tenants had grown to like Bessy and actively helped her to join in events.

Before my most recent visit to Flower Court, Bessy had a serious fall and was subsequently admitted to a geriatric ward. Three weeks later she died while still in hospital. Until the end of her time in Flower Court she had remained closely bonded to Janet and well liked by other tenants. On the day of her funeral half of the tenants of the scheme attended and paid their respects – an indication of how well thought of she had been.

(Petre 1996)

This story shows, incontrovertibly, some of the effects of person–centred care. The ground of Bessy's well-being, in her widowhood, was the close attachment she had formed with Janet, the warden. Janet also provided a structure for Bessy's day, and helped her to recover enough confidence to recreate her former outgoing pattern of life. As other tenants became involved, a 'virtuous circle' was set in motion. Tracy Petre, who carried out the research, was able to give Bessy an informal Mini-Mental State Examination about a year before she died. Her score was 1 (out of a maximum of 30); this, as well as informal observation, suggests very severe cognitive impairment.

Single examples, of course, cannot be used to prove a general case. They can merely illustrate particular points, and highlight areas where evidence needs to be gathered systematically.

[…]

References

Bytheway, B. (1995) *Ageism*, Buckingham: Open University Press.

Kitwood, T. (1990a) The dialectics of dementia: with particular reference to Alzeimer's disease. *Ageing and Society*, 10: 177-96.

Kitwood, T. (1990b) Understanding senile dementia: a psychobiographical approach. *Free Associations*, 19: 60-75.

Kitwood, T. (1994) Discover the person, not the disease. *Journal of Dementia Care*, 1 (1): 16–17.

Kitwood, T. (1995) Studies in person centred care: building up the mosaic of good practice. *Journal of Dementia Care*, 3 (5): 12–13.

Petre, T. (1996) Back into the swing of her sociable life. *Journal of Dementia Care*, 4 (1): 24–5.

10

The 'Senses Framework': a relationship-centred approach to care

Mike Nolan and Serena Allan

Setting the scene

Concerns about the quality of care provided for frail older people in the UK have been apparent for some 50 years (Townsend, 1962). However, despite considerable efforts to improve the situation, a recent review (Gallagher et al, 2008) concluded that the dignity of older people receiving help and support from health and social services is more compromised now than it was following Barbara Robb's (1967) damning critique in *Sans everything*. Given the number of initiatives that have taken place, particularly over the last 10 years, this is both disappointing and perplexing.

The first decade of the 21st century witnessed the introduction of the National Service Framework (NSF) (DH, 2001) for older people, intended to ensure uniformly high standards of care wherever it was provided. Despite some progress its relative failure to address what appear to be systemic and intractable problems resulted in the launch of the 'Dignity Campaign' (DH, 2006), closely followed by the 'Confidence in Care' initiative (DH, 2008). Such developments have not been confined to central government, with major think tanks such as The King's Fund deeming it necessary to institute their 'Point of Care' programme (Goodrich and Cornwell, 2008), the goal of which is to ensure that older people receive 'compassionate care' at the point of delivery. Professional bodies such as the Royal College of Nursing (RCN) and the Nursing and Midwifery Council (NMC) have also contributed to the debate, highlighting the need to establish a culture of care that recognises the vulnerability of older people and engages both older people and their family carers as 'partners' in care (RCN, 2008; NMC, 2009). The challenges this poses in what has become a 'quick fix, targeted driven culture' (RCN, 2008, p 6) have to be acknowledged. However, it has been argued that currently too much emphasis is given to 'slogans' and not enough on how to turn ideals such as 'dignity' and 'compassionate care' into 'meaningful practice' (Help the Aged, 2008, p 4).

Concepts such as 'dignity' are 'never simple, but always important' (Cass et al, 2009, p 47), and if such commonly used but complex ideas are to be turned into 'meaningful practice' (Help the Aged, 2008, p 4), it is essential that they are expressed in a way that is 'ordinary, accessible, jargon free, and commonly understood' (Goodrich and Cornwell, 2008, p 28). It is here that the 'Senses Framework' (Nolan et al, 2006) and relationship-centred care (Tresolini and the Pew–Fetzer Task Force, 1994) have a potentially important part to play.

Origins of the Senses Framework

The Senses Framework was first suggested by Nolan (1997) who was concerned about the low status of work in long-term care environments and the lack of a therapeutic direction for staff who worked with the most frail and vulnerable older people. Therefore, while staff in acute settings provide 'cure' or 'rehabilitation', work in longer-term settings was seen as 'aimless residual care' (Evers, 1981, p 205) or at best, 'good geriatric care' (Reed and Bond, 1991, p 55), where the aim was to attend to older people's 'basic' needs. Believing that this description failed to recognise the complex and skilled nature of work in long-term care, Nolan (1997) argued that staff should aim to create an environment in which older people experience six 'senses'; these were a sense of:

- security
- belonging
- continuity
- purpose
- achievement
- significance

This, he argued, would create an environment that enhanced older people's quality of life while at the same time raising the status and value of previously denigrated 'care' work. However, it was also suggested that if staff were to create such an environment for older people, then they must experience the 'senses' themselves. Consequently, staff should feel secure in their work, not just physically, but emotionally and psychologically as well. For example, they should feel safe to raise concerns about poor standards of care without being worried about censure or losing their job. They should also feel part of a team and that their contribution is valued, and so on. Fundamentally, however, work in long-term care has to be seen as being significant, and accorded status. Since it was initially suggested, the Senses

Framework has been developed further and underpins the *My* Home Life initiative launched by Help the Aged (now Age UK) with the goal of promoting care homes as important places to live, work and visit (see www.myhomelife.org.uk).

Although the Senses Framework was originally focused on long-term care settings, shortly after it was suggested that a major national study funded by Help the Aged use the framework to identify acute care environments that provided dignified care for older people (Davies et al, 1999). This found that the same 'senses' were equally relevant in acute hospitals, but that what created the 'senses' was different than in long-term environments. For example, creating a sense of belonging in a long-term environment is in large part about making the older person feel part of a community, where they have an ongoing contribution to make (see Davies, 2001). This would be undesirable in an acute setting where discharge is the goal, but while the length of stay may be far shorter, older people in acute settings nevertheless want to feel that they 'belong' (for some examples, see Davies et al, 1999). Furthermore the 'Dignity' project extended the framework by applying it to family carers. Table 10.1 below is based on a number of projects conducted over several years and indicates what the 'senses' mean to older people, family carers and staff.

Later work applied the principles underpinning the Senses Framework to the experiences of students (see Nolan et al, 2006; Brown et al, 2008a, 2008b). Work with older people has always been one of the least preferred career choices for practitioners from all health and social care disciplines, frequently being seen a boring, low 'tech', low status and 'dead end' (for a review, see Nolan et al, 2006). However, a major longitudinal study of student nurses' perceptions of their training (Nolan et al, 2001) found that most of the students' negative attitudes towards work with older people were formed not as a result of a dislike for older people, but because of a poor experience on clinical placement. If students had a positive placement and felt that they had learned something of value, then they were much more likely to choose to work with older people when they qualified. Such a positive experience could also be captured by the Senses Framework, and it was as a result of the 'Dignity' project (Davies et al, 1999) and the work with students (Nolan et al, 2006; Brown et al, 2008a, 2008b) that the idea of an enriched environment emerged.

An enriched environment and relationship-centred care

It was at the time that the Senses Framework were being developed that Tom Kitwood (1997) published his now seminal work on person-centred care that has done so much to raise the status, profile and quality of care

Table 10.1: The 'senses' as they relate to older people, staff and family carers

A sense of security	
For older people	Attention to essential physiological and psychological needs, to feel safe and free from threat, harm, pain and discomfort; to receive competent and sensitive care
For staff	To feel free from physical threat, rebuke or censure; to have secure conditions of employment; to have the emotional demands of work recognised and to work within a supportive but challenging culture
For family carers	To feel confident in their knowledge and ability to provide good care without detriment to personal well-being; to have adequate support networks and timely help when required; to be able to give up caring when appropriate
A sense of belonging	
For older people	Opportunities to maintain and/or form meaningful and reciprocal relationships, to feel part of a community or group as desired
For staff	To feel part of a team with a recognised and valued contribution to make, to belong to a peer group, a community of 'gerontological' practitioners
For family carers	To be able to maintain/improve valued relationships, to be able to confide in people you trust and to feel that 'you're not in this alone'
A sense of continuity	
For older people	Recognition and value of personal biography; skilful use of knowledge of the past to help understand the present and future; seamless, consist ent care delivered within an established relationship by known people
For staff	Positive experience of work with older people from an early stage of their career, exposure to good role models and environments of care; expectations and standards of care communicated clearly and consistently
For family carers	To maintain shared pleasures/pursuits with the older person; to be confident that the older person receives high standards of care, whether delivered by self or others; to ensure that personal standards of care are maintained by others; to maintain involvement in care across care environments as desired/appropriate
A sense of purpose	
For older people	Opportunities to engage in interesting and enjoyable activities; to be able to identify and pursue personally valued goals and challenges; to exercise choice
For staff	To have a sense of therapeutic direction, a clear set of goals to aspire to
For family carers	To maintain the dignity and integrity, well-being and 'personhood' of the older person without ignoring other valued goals
A sense of achievement	
For older people	Opportunities to meet meaningful and valued goals; to feel satisfied with your efforts; to make a recognised and valued contribution; to make progress towards therapeutic goals as appropriate
For staff	To be able to provide good care; to feel satisfied with your efforts; to contribute towards valued therapeutic goals; to use your skills and abilities to the full
For family carers	To feel that you have provided the best possible care, to know 'you've done your best'; to meet challenges successfully; to develop new skills and abilities
A sense of significance	
For older people	To feel recognised and valued as a person of worth, that your actions and existence are of importance, that you 'matter'
For staff	To feel that gerontological practice is valued and important, that your work and efforts 'matter'
For family carers	To feel that your caring efforts are valued and appreciated, to experience an enhanced sense of self

Source: Adapted from Nolan (1997); Davies et al (1999); Nolan et al (2006)

provided for people with dementia. Since then, the idea of person–centred care has extended well beyond dementia and has been used to underpin initiatives such as the NSF for older people (DH, 2001) and, in the guise of patient–centred care, the 'Point of Care' programme (Goodrich and Cornwell, 2008). Indeed person–centred and related concepts such as autonomy and independence lie at the heart of recent government policy for older people. However, person–centred care is based on a consideration of the older person and their needs (DH, 2001), and while these are clearly important, Nolan and colleagues (2004) argue that this promoted a rather narrow view, believing that notions of autonomy and independence failed to acknowledge the reciprocity and 'give and take' that characterise the best relationships. They suggest that the idea of relationship–centred care is more appropriate.

The term 'relationship–centred care' was first suggested by a major task force in the US (Tresolini and the Pew–Fetzer Task Force, 1994) that was charged with considering how future healthcare needs could best be met. It concluded that the current healthcare system in the US focused almost exclusively on acute care, but that the major health challenges for the future would be posed by long–term conditions. These usually require ongoing contact with health and social care systems, and the Task Force advocated that the focus of healthcare should shift from acute, short–term contact to one that emphasised the nature and quality of relationships between those in need of care and support and those providing it. However, at the time they offered no model for achieving this. It is suggested that the Senses Framework captures many of the essential elements of such relationships and better reflects the reciprocity that underpins them. It was from this belief that the idea of an 'enriched environment' emerged, with this being an environment in which all groups experience the 'senses'. This is reflected in the matrix below (see Figure 10.1).

Figure 10.1: Capturing the elements of an 'enriched' environment

	Older person	Staff	Family carers	Students
Security				
Belonging				
Continuity				
Purpose				
Achievement				
Significance				

The 'senses' have been developed with, by and for older people, family carers, staff and students who have been closely involved in defining what they mean and how they can be achieved. Because of this they seem to speak to all these groups in a language that they can understand and relate to. The Senses Framework is also consistent with recent ideas of 'relational practice' (Parker, 2008) that are increasingly influential in debates about providing quality care. Below we present a case study which briefly describes how the 'senses' were introduced into a care home for visually impaired older people and the impact that it has had.

Using the Senses Framework to create an enriched environment: reflections from practice

As charge nurse, I knew that things on my unit were not quite right:

- Although staff were kind and caring, they tended to see residents as 'the work', a series of tasks to be completed.
- They rarely engaged with residents and knew little about their lives and achievements, what made them who they were. Their goal was to provide a good standard of basic care.
- Families were not involved with residents' care even if they had been the main carer at home. Complaints from families were a recurring feature of my working life.
- Relationships between staff were hampered by poor communication and there were frequent minor conflicts.

Learning about the Senses Framework helped me to look at the situation in a different way and inspired me to introduce a series of changes, including:

- Regular staff meetings to improve communication and give everyone an opportunity to be heard.
- Encouraging staff to talk to residents and to treat them as individuals, with a unique life and needs, promoting choice and rights.
- Delegating greater responsibility to care staff such as organising staff rotas and assessing residents' needs for specialist products. This had the added advantage of freeing my time to focus more on resident care.
- A keyworker system was introduced with each staff member having special responsibility for two residents. Each keyworker's photograph was displayed so families would know who they were.
- Regular care reviews were started and residents' families were invited to come and discuss their relative's care with staff.
- Care plans were based around the 'Senses' with an explicit outcome linked to each 'sense'.

These changes have had a significant impact on staff, residents and families. All staff are now genuine partners in care and their senses of purpose and achievement are evident. There is a feeling of belonging to a well functioning team, that is mutually supportive. There is greater clarity about the goals of care, improving continuity. Crucially, staff feel that their input matters and that they are appreciated for their efforts. They are significant.

Residents' lives have improved. Staff are more aware of individual needs and have dropped their 'one size fits all' approach. Care is now based on a better understanding of residents' past lives and their hopes for the future. Because residents are more involved in their own care planning they have greater choice and control.

Relationships between staff and relatives have improved considerably; they now talk openly with staff about their feelings during the regular care reviews and feel that they are an important part of the 'team'. Relatives' meetings are well attended, giving them an opportunity to meet other families in similar situations.

Overall, while the environment of care was never truly impoverished, it is certainly now far more enriched for everyone concerned.

Implementing the Senses Framework: valuing relational practice

As a major literature synthesis recently concluded (Patterson et al, 2011), dignity in care is intimately linked with feelings of well-being, personal worth and self-respect, and that dignity is either enhanced or diminished during the interactions that people have with each other. Dignity and similar concepts are therefore essentially *relational* and are created in the 'small' encounters that characterise the giving and receiving of help.

Like dignity, compassion lies at the heart of good caring relationships, but as Youngson (2007, 2008) contends, existing models of health and social care, especially in acute settings, are too linear and fail to reflect complexity, focusing instead on the 'technical fix'. This overlooks the fact that the health and social care systems comprise the people who inhabit them, and therefore the most important interactions are those between their thoughts, beliefs, circumstances and behaviours.

As The King's Fund notes (Goodrich and Cornwell, 2008), compassion is made manifest by the relational dynamics that occur between people, and that compassionate care can alleviate pain in others. However, if those providing such care are not supported by the system of which they are part, it can also be a cause of pain to them. This is entirely consistent with the ideas underpinning the Senses Framework. Real compassion requires empathy, respect and recognition of each individual and a willingness to enter into relationships that acknowledge every one's limitations, strengths and emotions. This means that practitioners need to engage in a 'real' dialogue with others and focus on the 'little things' that are essential to compassionate care. However, if they are to do so, such 'little things' have to matter and it must be recognised that in giving of themselves to others, practitioners expose themselves emotionally and may require support to deal with their own reactions. Unfortunately, the current emphasis on meeting targets and the devaluing of direct care by delegating it to the least qualified overlooks the importance of such relational work, as does the prioritising of technical competence over interpersonal care in professional training. This is in danger of producing a generation of practitioners who fail to see the value of, and lack the necessary skills for, the delivery of high quality interpersonal care (Goodrich and Cornwell, 2008).

There has recently been a call for a change in culture towards one that values relationships and promotes them as integral to good care (Patterson et al, 2011). This will require a greater recognition of 'relational practice' (Parker, 2008), which Parker sees as those activities 'necessary to develop and sustain interpersonal relationships'. However, the requirement to meet 'targets' results in staff being placed under intense pressure to reduce the type of interactions necessary for relational practice to flourish (Parker, 2008). If the situation is to improve, then relational practices and the conditions that support them must be actively promoted. As Parker (2008, p 206) notes:

> Relational work in caregiving organisations thus depends, not only on the skills of individual practitioners and care workers, but also on the extent to which the workgroup and the organisation are structured and operated in ways that are supportive of relational work behaviours.

The importance of creating an enriched environment in which such relational practices can flourish is well recognised, as is the importance of any such relationships being based on an equal partnership between older people, families and staff (NMC, 2009). Recently Youngson (2007, 2008) has argued for a move away from services that focus on 'fixing' things to one where the goal is to create a 'healing' environment. We would suggest that the term 'enriched' reflects the same aspirations, and that the Senses Framework and relationship–centred care offer a means of creating an environment in which the needs of all groups are valued and addressed.

References

Brown, J., Nolan, M., Davies, S., Nolan, J. and Keady, J. (2008a) 'Transforming students' views of gerontological nursing: realising the potential of "enriched" environments of learning and care: a multi-method longitudinal study', *International Journal of Nursing Studies*, vol 45, pp 1214-32.

Brown, J., Nolan, M.R. and Davies, S. (2008b) 'Bringing caring and competence into focus in gerontological nursing: a longitudinal, multi-method study', *International Journal of Nursing Studies*, vol 45, pp 654-67.

Cass, E., Robbins, D. and Richardson, A. (2009) *Dignity in care*, Adults' Services SCIE Guide 15, London: Social Care Institute for Excellence (www.scie. org.uk/publications/guides/guide15/files/guide15.pdf).

Davies, S., Nolan, M.R., Brown, J. and Wilson, F. (1999) *Dignity on the ward: Promoting excellence in the acute hospital care of older people*, London: Report for Help the Aged/Order of St John's Trust.

Davies, S. (2001) 'The care needs of older people and family caregivers in continuing care settings'. In Nolan, M., Davies, S. and Grant, G. (eds) *Working with older people and their families: Key issues in policy and practice*, Buckingham, Open University Press, pp 75-98.

DH (Department of Health) (2001) *National Service Framework for older people*, London: DH.

DH (2006) *The Dignity Challenge*, London: DH.

DH (2008) *Confidence in Care*, London: DH.

Evers, H.K. (1981) 'Multidisciplinary teams in geriatric wards: myth or reality?', *Journal of Advanced Nursing*, vol 6, pp 205-14.

Gallagher, A., Li, S., Wainwright, P., Rees Jones, I. and Lee, D. (2008) 'Dignity in the care of older people: a review of the theoretical and empirical literature', *BMC Nursing*, vol 7, no 11, pp 1-12.

Goodrich, J. and Cornwell, J. (2008) *Seeing the person in the patient: The Point of Care review*, London: The King's Fund.

Help the Aged (2008) *On our own terms: The challenge of assessing dignity in care*, London: Help the Aged (http://policy.helptheaged.org.uk).

Kitwood, T. (1997) *Dementia reconsidered: The person comes first*, Buckingham: Open University Press.

NMC (Nursing and Midwifery Council) (2009) *Guidance for the care of older people*, London: NMC.

Nolan, M.R. (1997) 'Health and social care: what the future holds for nursing', Keynote presentation at 3rd RCN Older Persons European Conference and Exhibition, The Old Swan, Harrogate, 5 November.

Nolan, M.R., Davies, S., Brown, J., Keady, J. and Nolan, J. (2002) *Longitudinal study of the effectiveness of educational preparation to meet the needs of older people and carers: The AGEIN (Advancing Gerontological Education in Nursing) Project*, London: The English National Board for Nursing Midwifery and Health Visiting,

Nolan, M.R., Brown, J., Davies, S., Nolan, J. and Keady, J. (2006) *The Senses Framework: Improving care for older people through a relationship-centred approach*, Getting Research into Practice (GRIP) Series, No 2, Sheffield: University of Sheffield.

Nolan, M.R., Davies, S., Brown, J., Keady, J. and Nolan, J. (2004) 'Beyond person centred care: a new vision for gerontological nursing', *International Journal of Older People Nursing*, vol 13, no 3a, pp 45–53.

Parker, V.A. (2008) 'Connecting relational work and workgroup context in caregiving organizations', *The Journal of Applied Behavioural Science*, vol 38, no 3, pp 276-97.

Patterson, M., Nolan, M., Rick, J., Brown, J., Adams, R. and Musson, G. (2011) *From metrics to meaning: Culture change and quality of acute hospital care for older people*, Final report to NCCSDO, London: HMSO (www.sdo.nihr.ac.uk/files/project/93-final-report.pdf).

RCN (Royal College of Nursing) (2008) *Defending dignity – Challenges and opportunities for nursing*, London: RCN.

Reed, J. and Bond, S. (1991) 'Nurses' assessment of elderly patients in hospital', *International Journal of Nursing Studies*, vol 28, no 1, pp 55-64.

Robb, B. (1967) *Sans everything: A case to answer*, London: Thomas Nelson and Sons.

Townsend, P. (1962) *The last refuge: A survey of residential institutions and homes for the aged in England and Wales*, London: Routledge & Kegan Paul.

Tresolini, C.P. and the Pew–Fetzer Task Force (1994) *Health professions' education and relationship-centred care: A report of the Pew-Fetzer Task Force on advancing psychosocial education*, San Francisco, CA: Pew Health Professions Commission.

Youngson, R. (2007) 'People-centred health care', International Symposium on People-centred Health Care: 'Reorientating health systems in the 21st century', The Tokyo International Forum, 25 November.

Youngson, R. (2008) 'Compassion in healthcare: the missing dimension of healthcare reform?', NHS Confederation (www.debatepapers.org.uk).

11

Disability and adulthood

Mark Priestley

Extract from *Disability: A life course approach* (2003) Cambridge: Polity Press.

This chapter highlights ... how idealized and gendered notions of adulthood underpin the position of disabled people in contemporary societies. In particular, the discussion draws attention to the concepts of adult 'independence', 'competence' and 'autonomy'. Thinking about disability helps to problematize our understanding of what it means to be an adult in society and reveals more about the way that that both disability and adulthood have been socially produced. In this sense, there is some similarity in the way that the 'non-adult' social categories of disability, childhood, youth and old age have been produced. At the same time, it is important to note how changes in technology, gender roles, work, the family and the nation state have blurred the traditional boundaries of adult citizenship. The discussion draws on the challenges of disability theory and activism to critically examine the concepts of individualism, autonomy and (inter)dependency in a changing world. ...

Thinking about adulthood

... [T]he concept of adulthood ... has attracted much less specific theoretical attention than the study childhood, youth or old age. As a consequence, adulthood remains relatively under-theorized as an analytical or critical concept. ... However, when we look at writing and research about disability adult issues are core concerns. Although issues like adult independent living and employment are prominent in academic and policy agendas (at the expense of disabled children and older people), there has been little overt recognition of their generational significance. Thinking explicitly about the way that adulthood is constructed and produced helps to address this anomaly. The following sections deal with some of the key concepts. In particular, the discussion illustrates how constructions of adulthood (based on ideas about autonomy, competence and individualism) frame our understanding of citizenship and rights.

Adulthood, disability and the generational system

The first point to consider is that the generational category of adulthood can be both positively and negatively defined. On the one hand, adult social status arises from criteria of inclusion (such as the attainment of a certain chronological age or the achievement of adult roles, in relation to employment or parenting for example). On the other hand, adulthood can be a seen as a kind of residual category occupying the territory that is left over when other categories of people are excluded (in particular, those exempt from participation in adult labour markets). Thus, while both older people and disabled people of working age may be included in an age-based definition of adulthood, they may also be excluded from the rights and responsibilities normally associated with adult social status.

More generally, adulthood can be viewed as the pivotal organising concept in a generational system based on the construction and production of dependency. In this sense, other categories (such as children and young people, older people and disabled people) are defined by their perceived dependency on non-disabled adults, as the recipients of adult care or financial resources. By contrast, adults are constructed as independent contributors to the social relations of production and reproduction (for example, through participation in family work or paid employment). So, there is a sense in which disabled 'adults' excluded from productive and reproductive roles exist as a dependent social category outside the traditional realm of 'adulthood' (in the same way that younger and older people do). This suggests that there is an important generational dimension to the social exclusion of disabled people.

The perceived marginality of children, older people *and* disabled people in Western societies is premised upon a particular view of adulthood, based on ascriptions of adult independence, competence and autonomy. In addition, the enforced dependency of these other groups on adult labour (in both the public and private domain) places a generational responsibility on non-disabled adults to engage in productive and reproductive work. These adult responsibilities bring with them the social compensation of adult rights – rights to political participation and citizenship and rights to exercise control over non-adults in caring relationships. There is then a close link between the generational responsibilities of independent adulthood and the legitimation of adult rights and power relationships.

Exploring some of these issues, Hockey and James (1993) argue that concepts of personhood and citizenship in Western societies are heavily symbolized in terms of adult autonomy, self-determination and choice. Comparing young childhood and advanced old age, they show how institutional practices of 'caring control or controlling care' deny very young and very old people a proper recognition of their agency and personhood. Hockey and James argue that such practices are culturally specific to Western industrialized societies, where dependency and impairment are regarded as 'childlike' states. Adopting a symbolic approach, they examine how exclusion maintains the dependency of children and older people and reproduces their generational marginality from adulthood. Making a similar point, Irwin (2001: 18) argues that:

> Childhood and later life are positioned, in cultural representations and in social and institutional constructions, as dependent statuses and as social locations that deny children and those in later life full social participation or a proper measure of dignity. In contrast, independent adulthood is positively valued, carrying social status and prestige…There is a clear parallel, in these constructions, with the positioning of disabled experiences in modern society.

This suggests some important parallels in the construction of disability, childhood and old age, as parallel categories marginal to the domain of independent adulthood. In this sense, the generational system that defines childhood and old age has much in common with the system that produces and regulates disability in modern societies (Priestley, 1997; Priestley, 2000). These issues are discussed in more detail later; suffice to say that just as disabled people have been excluded from participation in adult labour so they have been excluded from full adult rights and citizenship.

To summarize, although the concept of adulthood remains relatively under-theorized within social science (by comparison with other generational categories) it occupies a pivotal place in the construction and institutional regulation of the life course. This paradox may be explained by thinking of adulthood as a kind of residual category, defined by the exemption of other social groups from adult responsibilities (particularly from adult work). The apparent dependency of these other groups on adult labour then contributes to their maintenance as non-adult social categories. In this sense, our understanding of independent adulthood may be defined less by intrinsic adult qualities than by the shifting boundaries of neighbouring categories like childhood, youth, old age and disability.

What kind of independence?

As suggested earlier, independence is a key factor in constructions of adulthood but it can be viewed in a number of ways. For example, independence may be associated with the physical and cognitive functioning of the adult body, with an autonomous sense of adult self-identity, with cultural constructions of adult individualism, or with the successful transcendence of structural dependency upon others. Since each of these themes is relevant to the construction of disabled people as dependent (and in that sense as 'non-adults') it is important to look critically at adult independence and to examine some of the challenges to its definition arising from generational and disability politics.

For Hockey and James (1993: 142) the construction of adulthood as 'a uniquely work-able condition' is contingent upon an individualist model of adult autonomy in Western societies. Thus, Walker and Leisering (1998) argue that Western individualism has been progressively institutionalized during the era of modernity, and that the regulation of the self and the life course has been increasingly detached from relationships to others or community. Similarly, Giddens (1991) points to the dislocation of lives from their embeddedness within contexts of community, placing more emphasis on individual mobility and reflexivity. Indeed, it is this culture of individualism that frames our current understanding of what it means to be an 'independent' adult. In this sense, adult independence is gauged by the degree to which we are seen to function, both physically and socially, as autonomous actors.

Thinking about adult competence and autonomy within the context of individuation helps to explain the apparent emphasis on narrow individualist concepts of independence – in particular, the ability to do things for oneself (see, Stainton, 1994). Clearly, there are parallels here with individual models of disability, which define disabled people's social exclusion as a consequence of their bodily function or 'inability to work'. In particular, medical and therapeutic models of disability have relied heavily on assessments of physical and cognitive function as a measure of actual or potential independence. From this perspective, the presumed dependency of disabled people, like children and older people, is defined by the extent to which these groups demand assistance with social and physical tasks.

There have been considerable challenges to the idea that adult independence can be equated with an absence of any need for assistance from within the disability movement. As Oliver (1989: 83–4) notes:

> In common sense usage, dependency implies the inability to do things for oneself and consequently the reliance upon others to carry out some or all of the tasks of everyday life. Conversely independence suggests that the individual needs no assistance whatever from anyone else and this fits nicely with the current political rhetoric which stresses competitive individualism.

In reality, of course, no one in a modern industrial society
is completely independent: we live in a state of mutual
interdependence. The dependence of disabled people therefore,
is not a feature which marks them out as different in kind from
the rest of the population but different in degree.

Redefining adult independence is thus a key goal for the disabled people's
movement. Within this political context, disabled people have been more
likely to construct adult independence in terms of choice and control than
autonomous physical functioning (e.g. Morris, 1993; Rock, 1988). Two
responses are particularly significant. First, much emphasis has been placed
on the role of assistive technologies in increasing independent functioning
(e.g. Roulstone, 1998). Second, the movement for independent living has
shown how greater choice and control can be achieved through the self-
management of personal assistance (e.g. Priestley, 1999). However, some
have questioned whether preferences for technological assistance or human
assistance reflect different positions in the debate about personal autonomy.
For example, Agree (1999) distinguishes between these two forms of
support, suggesting that people who use assistive technology report lower
levels of 'functional limitation' than those using personal assistance:

> The use of assistive technology differs from personal care on a
> fundamental level. It does not require the ongoing cooperation
> or coordination of other people and therefore increases the
> sense of independence with which a disabled individual can
> meet their long-term care needs. (Agree, 1999: 427)

Similarly, Verbrugge, Rennert and Madans (1997) claim that assistive
technology offers a more 'efficacious strategy for reducing and resolving
limitations' than personal assistance, concluding that the perceived gains to
disabled people were greater where they could complete daily living tasks
'by themselves' (see also, Hoenig, Taylor, and Sloan, 2001). Drawing on such
findings, and on their own research with older people using mobility aids,
Allen, Foster and Berg (2001) note that younger adults in North America
are more likely to use equipment and less likely to draw on personal
assistance than older people. This, they suggest, may be due to generational
norms and expectations about autonomy and independence.

> Older age consistently predicts both having any care and the
> amount of care received. This finding may reflect greater frailty
> among older than younger people with disability, as well as
> greater availability of helping resources. However, it may also

> reflect the desire for greater autonomy among younger people,
> as well as perceptions by family members and people with
> disability themselves that dependency is appropriate for people
> at older but not younger stages of the life course. (Allen et al.,
> 2001: S381)

This kind of reasoning assumes autonomous physical functioning to
be the benchmark of adult independence. Within this approach, the
achievement of adult independence is directly associated with a lack of
reliance on assistance from another *person*. At the same time, increased
function or competence achieved by using *non-human* forms of assistance is
more highly valued. Such examples highlight the idealized individualism of
contemporary adulthood (discussed earlier) and suggest that constructions
of dependence and non-adult status tend to devalue the interdependence
of supportive personal relationships. Adopting a disability rights perspective,
Morris (1997) takes issue with the way that people using personal
support in their daily lives are constructed as 'dependents' upon their
'carers'. Rather, she emphasizes the importance of choice and control,
while recognising the gender inequalities for disabled women who seek
independence though relationships of assistance (Morris, 1995). Similarly,
Goodley (2000) explores the independence achieved by people with a label
of learning difficulties through relationships that promote self-advocacy.

Also from a disability perspective French (1993) examines the narrow
view of independence as autonomous functioning and asks the more
fundamental question, 'What's so good about independence?'. As Reindal
(1999) notes, the idea of 'being able to do things for oneself, to be self-
supporting and self-reliant' is central to thinking about independence in
the context of Western industrial societies, grounded in a modernist view
of the autonomous subject and arising from European Enlightenment
philosophy. This, she argues, limits the discussion of personal autonomy
to discussions of an either/or relationship between independence and
dependence. By contrast, Reindal argues that a more postmodern
understanding of the subject as relational, as 'both embedded and
embodied' allows us to deal more openly with the fact that the human
condition is ultimately one of interdependence between people. Thus:

> When the human condition is viewed as one of
> interdependency and vulnerability, this leads to an
> understanding of independence as 'partnership'.
> Departing from a relational view of the subject,
> independence becomes a two-way responsibility and
> not solely an individual ability. (Reindal, 1999: 364)

Jenkins (1998) makes some similar arguments about competence and incompetence, suggesting that these should be viewed as relational and socially embedded concepts. Reviewing a number of contributions, concerned with the situation of people with learning difficulties in different cultural contexts, Jenkins concludes that (in)competence:

> ... is as much an emergent property of social networks and interactional context as it is an endogenous quality of individuals. Perhaps the most basic competence is the capacity for this *sociality*, rooted in the reciprocations of mutually intelligible, complex communication, that characterises human beings and human social life. (Jenkins, 1998: 227, *original emphasis*)

For this reason, he argues that we should broaden our understanding of competence from a narrow mechanistic property of the embodied individual to one that takes account of its relational character and situated construction. This is quite a complex idea but in essence refers to the fact that competence, in the reality of everyday lives, often reflects things that are achieved by people working *together* rather than in isolation. In this sense, measuring the 'skills' of individuals does not necessarily reveal their competence to perform roles or functions *in collaboration with others*. Thus, Booth and Booth (1998b) suggest that it may make more sense to think about competence as something that is 'distributed' within families and social networks than something located within the individual.

The relational basis of interdependence has been widely employed in feminist debates about disability and health, as a way to reclaim the significance of caring relationships (e.g. Brown and Gillespie, 1992). Drawing on similar themes, Gabriel and Gardner (1999) adopt a gendered approach, asking whether there are in fact 'his and hers' versions of interdependence. Reviewing a number of studies, they argue that women are more likely to emphasize the relational aspects of interdependence while men are more likely to focus on the collective aspects. Similarly, interdependence has been viewed as a key concept in citizenship. As Porter (2001) argues, interdependence, arising from experiences of nurturing in our intimate lives, is at the core of responsible citizenship because it underscores and creates the conditions for connectedness amongst citizens at a political level too.

Key points ...

Idealized notions of adulthood occupy the centre or apex of the constructed life course, as it is produced and regulated through policies and institutions. These dominant discourses of adulthood reflect a view of independence and the autonomous self, grounded in individualistic notions of competence and physical functioning. Within the generational system, assistance with daily living becomes synonymous with non-adult forms of dependency. Thus, life course studies have tended to view independence as something that increases during childhood, reaches a peak during adulthood, and declines again during old age. However, this simplistic linear analysis becomes problematic when we consider the situation of disabled adults. Within an individualist paradigm, where adulthood is defined as functional independence and disability is defined as functional dependence, it is easy to see why disabled people have so frequently been denied adult social status.

Understanding how disability interacts with the generational system, as a social category, is an important step in understanding why disabled adults have been institutionally regulated in such similar ways to children and older people. Expectations about doing things for yourself, doing things on your own, and being independent have been important in defining adult status and citizenship. However, challenges from the disability movement and from feminist critiques suggest that we should reformulate our ideas to take account of the relational nature of human interdependence, both within and between generations. Although many disabled adults (like children and older people) remain structurally dependent on the productive or caring labour of non-disabled adults, it is misleading to suggest that this precludes their ability to exercise adult rights and responsibilities. Indeed, developments within the movements for self-advocacy and independent living suggest that new notions of adult independence can be claimed on the basis of self-determination and relational interdependency.

[...]

References

Agree, E. (1999). The influence of personal care and assistive devices on the measurement of disability. *Social Science & Medicine, 48*(4), 427–443.

Allen, S. M., Foster, A., & Berg, K. (2001). Receiving Help at Home: The Interplay of Human and Technological Assistance. *The Journals of Gerontology Series B: Psychological Sciences and Social Sciences, 56*, S374–S382.

Booth, T., & Booth, W. (1999b). Parents Together: action research and advocacy support for parents with learning difficulties. *Health and Social Care in the Community*, 7(6), 464-474.

Brown, K., & Gillespie, D. (1992). Recovering Relationships – a Feminist Analysis of Recovery Models. *American Journal of Occupational Therapy*, 46(11), 1001-1005.

French, S. (1993). What's so great about independence? In J. Swain & V. Finkelstein & S. French & M. Oliver (Eds.), *Disabling Barriers: Enabling Environments*. London: Open University Press/Sage.

Gabriel, S., & Gardner, W. (1999). Are there 'his' and 'hers' types of interdependence? The implications of gender differences in collective versus relational interdependence for affect, behavior, and cognition. *Journal of Personality and Social Psychology*, 77(3), 642-655.

Giddens, A. (1991). *Modernity and Self Identity: Self and Society in the Late Modern Age*. Cambridge: Polity Press.

Goodley, D. (2000). *Self-advocacy in the Lives of People with Learning Difficulties: the politics of resilience*. Buckingham: Open University Press.

Hockey, J., & James, A. (1993). *Growing Up and Growing Older: Ageing and Dependency in the Life Course*. London: Sage.

Hoenig, H., Taylor, D., & Sloan, F. (2001). Assistive technology is associated with reduced use of personal assistance among disabled older persons. *Journal of the American Geriatrics Society*, 49(4), A40.

Irwin, S. (2001). Repositioning disability and the life course: a social claiming perspective. In M. Priestley (Ed.), *Disability and the Life Course: Global Perspectives*. Cambridge: Cambridge University Press.

Jenkins, R. (Ed.) (1998). *Questions of Competence: Culture, Classification and Intellectual Disabilities*. Cambridge: Cambridge University Press.

Morris, J. (1993). *Independent Lives? Community Care and Disabled People*. Basingstoke: Macmillan.

Morris, J. (1995). Creating a Space for Absent Voices – Disabled Women's Experience of Receiving Assistance with Daily Living Activities. *Feminist Review*(51), 68-93.

Morris, J. (1997). Care or empowerment? A disability rights perspective. *Social Policy & Administration*, 31(1), 54-60.

Oliver, M. (1989). Disability and dependency: a creation of industrialised societies. In L. Barton (Ed.), *Disability and Dependency*. London: The Falmer Press.

Porter, E. (2001). Interdependence, parenting and responsible citizenship. *Journal of Gender Studies*, 10(1), 5-15.

Priestley, M. (1997). The origins of a legislative disability category in England: a speculative history. *Disability Studies Quarterly*, 17(2), 87-94.

Priestley, M. (1999). *Disability Politics and Community Care*. London: Jessica Kingsley.

Priestley, M. (2000). Adults only: Disability, social policy and the life course. *Journal of Social Policy, 29*, 421-439.

Reindal, S. (1999) Independence, dependence, interdependence: some reflections on the subject and personal autonomy. *Disability & Society, 14*(3), 353-67.

Rock, P. (1988). Independence: what it means to six disabled people living in the community. *Disability, Handicap & Society, 3*, 27-35.

Roulstone, A. (1998). *Enabling Technology: Disabled People, Work and Technology*. Milton Keynes: Open University Press.

Stainton, T. (1994). *Autonomy and Social Policy*. Aldershot: Avebury/Ashgate.

Verbrugge, L., Rennert, C., & Madans, J. H. (1997). The great efficacy of personal and equipment assistance in reducing disability. *American Journal of Public Health, 87*(3), 384-392.

Walker, R., & Leisering, L. (Eds.) (1998). *The Dynamics of Modern Society: Poverty, Policy and Welfare*. Bristol: The Policy Press.

12

A sense of belonging: informal support from family, friends and acquaintances

Christine Bigby

Extract from C. Bigby (2004) *Ageing with a Lifelong Disability: A guide to practice, program and policy issues for human services professionals,* London and Philadelphia: Jessica Kingsley Publishers. Reproduced with kind permission of Jessica Kingsley Publishers.

[…]

This chapter begins by examining conceptualizations of informal support, its significance to well-being and factors that influence its provision. The characteristics of informal support networks of older adults with intellectual disability are considered, and finally strategies examined that may reduce the vulnerability of networks as people age, build new or maintain existing relationships.

The significance of informal support

Informal support is a multidimensional concept often imprecisely defined. Terms such as social support, support networks, informal care, or social relationships are used interchangeably. Its defining characteristic however is support provided in the context of an unpaid relationship based on the personal tie between individuals. The depth and quality of informal relationships varies considerably, as does the basis of the tie. Personal ties stem from common membership of a kinship system – family, personal affinity and common interests – friendships, geographic propinquity or use of common spaces – neighbours and acquaintances (Bulmer 1987).

Informal support covers a multitude of different types of exchanges that have been conceptualized in different ways. One of the most common is the dichotomy between instrumental and affective support. Instrumental support is direct and indirect: hands–on assistance with tasks such as personal care, domestic tasks, or household maintenance tasks; and intangible tasks such as advocacy, negotiation, facilitation, coordination of formal services and information collection. Affective support is *less* practical generally involving spending time together, shared activities or celebrations, companionship, listening or reassuring. An alternative conceptualization suggested by Dalley (1988) is that of 'caring for' and 'caring about'. Caring for tasks are associated with direct hands-on support, whilst caring about is expression of affection, or concern and concrete actions such as monitoring service quality to ensure a person's overall well-being.

Value of informal support

Having a social network and receipt of informal support from family and friends is related to 'higher morale, less loneliness and worry, feelings of usefulness, a sense of individual respect within the community and a zest for life' (Hooyman 1983, p 139). Availability of informal support appears to be have protective aspects and is associated with lower mortality, better survival and recovery rates from acute conditions and reduced institutionalization (Mendes de Leon et al. 1999). The mechanisms at play are not clear, although it is suggested that it is the quality and not quantity that is important and that the perceived availability of support may be a crucial factor (Krause 2001). Informal support does not simply equate with presence of relationships, rather it is the salience and nature of the relationships that are important. For example, an older person may have an extensive family network but only be in contact regularly with one member.

Bayley (1997) discusses the cognitive and emotional needs met by informal relationships that he suggests include:

- attachment and intimacy where relationships allow the expression of feelings freely and without which loneliness as distinct from social isolation may be experienced
- social integration where common concerns and interests are shared often by means of joint activities
- opportunities for nurturance, whereby relationships provide an opportunity to give back and achieve a sense of being needed
- reassurance of worth where relationships affirm competence in a social role either at work or in the family
- reliable assistance where network members provide direct assistance
- obtaining guidance from respected others to assist in life decisions
- the exercise of choice, which is fundamental to a sense of autonomy, human worth and dignity.

Bayley suggests that a single relationship is unlikely to meet this range of needs and further that inappropriate behaviour and strain on relationships may occur if too much is expected of anyone. He suggests therefore that various relationships of different styles and intensities are required to fulfil an individual's range of needs.

[...]

The emphasis on valued social roles, community inclusion and social relationships with members of the community who are not disabled has detracted from the value of friendships between people with intellectual disabilities (Chappell 1994). As Knox and Hickson (2001) suggest it is more often the view of outsiders that decide whether and in what way relationships are meaningful and scant attention has been paid to the meanings that people with intellectual disabilities themselves give to relationships. Research suggests that friendships between people with intellectual disability can have depth, richness and longevity. The types of friendships classed as 'good mates' play a pervasive and pivotal role in people's lives (Knox and Hickson 2001). Relationships between people with intellectual disabilities also provide the basis for furthering collective interests through means such as self-advocacy organizations (Chappell 1994). What is important however is to distinguish friendships between people with intellectual disability based on common interests and choice from mere groupings of people whereby individuals although proximate to each other have no common bonds.

Some of the functions played by informal support, particularly direct hands-on assistance, are replicated by formal support services. In some instances paid relationships between workers and people with intellectual disability can replace the informal without loss of quality. However, formal organizations and relationships cannot replicate all the tasks and find it particularly difficult to fulfil those that require long-term commitment, are non-routine and idiosyncratic. These are the 'caring about' tasks that provide affective support, manage and mediate relations with formal services and undertake advocacy. These latter functions are crucial to the quality of life of older people who live in shared, supported accommodation and rely on formal support to meet their day-to-day needs. In situations such as this sources external to formal organizations fully committed to the individual and without divided loyalties are required to monitor and negotiate quality of care, advocate and oversee the well-being of the older adult and their affairs. Formal structures such as standards monitoring, case management, statutory guardianship and advocacy services are in place but undertake only fragments of these tasks for short periods and often work reactively rather than proactively. Formal services cannot provide the same continuing comprehensive commitment to an individual and oversight of their well-being that informal sources can (Bigby 2000). The inability of formal services to substitute for some of the key roles fulfilled by informal network members emphasizes the vulnerability of those people whom as they age lack strong informal networks of support.

Factors affecting networks of support

Litwak's (1985) theory of task specificity argues that family, friends and neighbours each have particular characteristics that differentiate the type of support they are best able to provide. For example, neighbours are characterized by close proximity but loose or non-affective ties, and thus are well suited to support that requires low commitment but either speedy response or proximity such as emergency assistance, monitoring an empty house or feeding the cat. In contrast relationships with spouses or other close family members are characterized by proximity, face-to-face contact on a daily basis and high degree of commitment. They are often the only ones in a network in a position to provide support with primary care tasks, which require these characteristics. Other family members may not be geographically close but still have a strong commitment and be suited to tasks that don't require frequent day-to-day contact such as administration of financial affairs, advocacy or negotiation with formal organizations. Friendships are characterized by affective ties but often not proximity or long-term commitment and may be better suited to tasks such as emotional support, companionship or shared activities that require intermittent contact with a low level of commitment.

Clearly, this delineation of characteristics and functions is based on ideal types. Both relationships and the tasks fulfilled by informal network members are mediated by factors such as gender, social context, individual resources, personal histories, life course stage and negotiated commitments. Nevertheless, Litwak's ideas can provide indications of which functions may not be well performed by a person's network. However, the idea of task specificity together with the absence of close family, traditionally regarded as spouse and children, from the network of older adults with intellectual disability potentially leaves a substantial vacuum. With fewer expectations as to the roles of remaining family members in the support networks of older people, substantial room is left for creative negotiation of role based on affinity rather than obligations or kinship. This opens up the possibility of non-normative roles being played by more distant family or friends.

The notion of a 'convoy of social support' suggests that the history of supportive relationships is central to understanding present relationships, and that people move through life surrounded by a convoy of others with whom they exchange social support (Antonucci and Akiyama 1987). Convoys are lifelong but dynamic, varying across time and situations.

The model is a useful framework to organize factors that determine the structure and functions of an individual's support network over the life course. The properties of the individual, their demographic characteristics, personality and abilities are one set of factors. The properties of the situation, external aspects of the environment, roles occupied, place of residence, organizational membership and life events are another set. Both sets affect the structure of the convoy, its size, connectedness, stability, complexity and homogeneity. The convoy structure in turn affects its functions; the actual support given, received or exchanges by members of the convoy. By stressing the dynamic nature of convoys this model emphasizes changes that occur to social networks over the life course. This highlights the vulnerability of networks as individuals and their convoy members age, and as a result of environmental or situational age-related changes.

Understanding networks

The concept of networks is a framework for analysing informal relationships. A network approach examines relationships between the individual and others in their network, in terms of the origin, duration and strength of ties and the frequency, nature and location of exchanges. It provides a means of understanding the whole as well as the individual components. For example, the structural properties of a network can be described in terms of size, the age, gender and relational balance of members and density, the extent to which members are known to each other. Research has shown that the structural characteristics of informal networks are often predictive of the nature of support provided informally (Wenger 1994). Thus, an understanding of a network per se is useful for considering how it may be vulnerable on the one hand to disruptions by formal supports, or on the other strengthened or complemented by formal services.

Informal networks in later life

In regard to informal networks of support, as for health, adults with intellectual disability embark on the ageing process from a position of weakness rather than strength. A proportion of the current and several future cohorts of older people will have spent much of their lives in institutions dislocated from family and community before relocation to small-scale, supported living in mid or later life. Strategies to build informal relationships for this group with community members are still evolving, but to date have had little success. Research suggests that among adults with intellectual disability moving to the community from institutions 'friendships are frequently non existent' (Rapley and Beyer 1996) and 'most are still not really part of their communities. The majority of these people have few if any friends' (Amado 1993, p.279).

However, adults who live in supported accommodation or in more independent options in the community tend to have larger networks that include more friends and are less dominated by family members than adults who have remained at home with parents. This latter group has smaller informal networks, characterized as family dominated and community insulated (Grant 1993). Friends are likely to be shared with parents and, as a result, their networks are likely to be dense and comprise people from their own or an older generation. Ramcharan, McGrath and Grant (1997) suggest that despite a high proportion of adults that live with family identifying a wish to have more friendships and community activities, opportunities for this are constrained by the attitudes of parents and ensuing difficulties of negotiation encountered by care managers or support workers. Clearly, for some adults with intellectual disability who remain at home with family a form of trade-off exists between opportunities for friendships and the exploration of independence and things such as security, continuity of care and unconditional commitment by family.

[...]

Dynamics of networks when parents die

The informal support network of adults who have remained at home changes dramatically with the death of their parents. At minimum they will lose their source of primary care but often also a dominant force in their lives that was the major source of advocacy and negotiation with formal service systems. ... [A]fter the loss of their parents some adults remain at home, with various sources of in-home support and some move to live with other family members, but over time as people age the majority move to supported accommodation. Thus in later life a characteristic of their informal support networks is the separation of caring for and caring about tasks, both of which were previously performed by parents. Formal services are much more likely to be involved in caring for tasks, whilst other family members and long-term family friends often alter or intensity their roles to absorb some of the caring about tasks. In particular siblings may assume greater responsibility for more concrete caring about tasks, as well as continuing to be an important source of social contact and companionship for older adults with intellectual disability. A defining characteristic of older people's informal networks is the existence of a 'key person' who takes responsibility for oversight of their well-being. Key people have a close long-term relationship with the older person, demonstrate considerable commitment to their well-being and play a plethora of caring about roles, combining them in some instances with primary care. ...

The networks of older adults have many similarities to those of middle-aged adults at home. Networks are small, with between 0 and 20 members and an average of 6 members who have contact at least twice a year. They continue to be dominated by family members comprising the entire network for a third of older people. Very few people have no family, whilst a third have no friends. The most common form of support is affective in the form of visiting and outings. However, three-quarters also get some form of instrumental support from network members, although this is usually from one member only. Types of support included:

1 Caring for:
   ■ provision of hands-on, day-to-day care
   ■ development of skills.

2 Caring about:

   ■ decision making
   ■ financial management
   ■ adoption of formal or legal roles
   ■ mediating, negotiating and advocating with service systems
   ■ monitoring service quality
   ■ supervision of medical needs
   ■ coordinating support from other network members
   ■ provision of back-up or short-term replacement of other members
   ■ emotional support
   ■ listening
   ■ advising
   ■ visiting and companionship.

... Incidental contact with family often decreased when they left the parental home but involvement with family at times of celebration like birthdays and Christmas was an important aspect of informal support.

Indeed for many older people the loss of their parents signified a shift to an adult rather than child role and the opportunity for new – in some instances for the first time – intimate friendships. Key people from a different generation to parents with different attitudes often actively sought out and encouraged new horizons and opportunities for the older adult, having previously felt powerless to counter protective attitudes of parents; yet at the same time understanding and respecting parental stances, acknowledging the different historic and value context in which they gave birth and raised a child with a disability. In addition restrictions and responsibilities placed on an adult with intellectual disability from living with a frail parent who required care or monitoring were also lifted. New opportunities for activities and meeting people were sometimes also offered by the supported accommodation service to which some people moved.

[...]

Summary

The foundations of the relationships that older people with intellectual disability have with family and friends, like so many other aspects of ageing, are built during the life course and reflect their earlier lifestyle and opportunities. Although many older people continue to have at least one strong and committed relationship with a family member, the chances of such a relationship decrease with age. The absence of the younger generation from the networks of older people with intellectual disability make them particularly vulnerable to social isolation and undue control and decision making by formal service providers. Supporting, nurturing and building a breadth of informal relationships, each of which will contribute in different ways to their quality of care, social well-being and quality of life, is a vital role for formal services.

[...]

References
Amado, A. (1993) 'Working with friendships.' In A. Amando (ed) *Friendships and Community Connections Between People with and without Developmental Disability*. Baltimore: Brookes.

Antonucci, T. and Akiyama, H. (1987) 'Social networks in adult life and a preliminary examination of the convoy model.' *Journal of Gerontology 42*, 519-527.

Bayley, M. (1997) 'Empowering and relationships.' In P. Ramcharan, G. Roberts, G. Grant and J. Borland (eds) *Empowerment in Everyday Life*. London: Jessica Kingsley Publishers.

Bigby, C. (2000) *Moving On without Parents: Planning, Transitions and Sources of Support for Older Adults with Intellectual Disabilities*. Sydney, Maclennan and Petty.

Bulmer, M. (1987) *The Social Basis of Community Care*. London: Allen and Unwin.

Chappell, A. (1994) 'A question of friendship: Community care and relationships of people with learning difficulties.' *Disability and Society 9*, 4, 419-433.

Dalley, G. (1988) *Ideologies of Caring: Rethinking Community and Collectivism.* Basingstoke: Macmillan.

Grant, G. (1993) 'Support networks and transitions over two years among adults with mental handicap.' *Mental Handicap Research 6,* 36-55.

Hooyman, N. (1983) 'Social support networks in services to the elderly.' In J. Whittaker and J. Garbarino (eds) *Social Support Networks: Informal Helping in Human Services.* New York: Aldine.

Knox, M. and Hickson, F. (2001) 'The meaning of close friendships: The view of four people with intellectual disabilities.' *Journal of Applied Research in Intellectual Disabilities 14,* 3, 276-291.

Krause, N. (2001) 'Social Support.' In R, Binstock and L. George (eds) *Handbook of Aging and Social Sciences,* 5th edn. New York: Academic Press.

Litwak, E. (1985) *Helping the Elderly.* New York: Guildford Press.

Mendes de Leon, C., Glass, T., Beckett, L., Seeman, T., Evans, E. and Berkman, L. (1999) 'Social networks and transitions across eight intervals of yearly data in the New Haven ESPESE.' *Journal of Gerontology 54,* 3, 162-172.

Ramcharan, P. and Grant, G. (1997) 'Voices and choices: Mapping entitlements to friendships and community contacts.' In P. Ramcharan, G. Roberts, G. Grant and J. Borland (eds) *Empowerment in Everyday Life.* London: Jessica Kingsley Publishers.

Rapley, M and Beyer, S. (1996) 'Daily activity, community participation and quality of life in and ordinary housing network: A two-year follow-up.' *Journal of Applied Research in Intellectual Disabilities 11,* 34-43.

SECTION THREE

The environment: from accommodation to community

13

Environment and ageing

Sheila Peace, Hans-Werner Wahl, Heidrun Mollenkopf and Frank Oswald

[…]

Theoretical perspectives

Historical influences

From its inception, environmental gerontology has emphasised the theoretical understanding of person-environment relations as people age. For recent overviews see Oswald et al. (2006), Scheidt and Windley (1998, 2006), Wahl (2001) and Wahl and Weisman (2003). This is important because there is a tendency in scholarly work to 'de-contexualise' human ageing from the environment, the day-to-day surroundings in which a person's growing older really takes place. Environmental gerontology has focused particularly on the physical/material and spatial component of the context of ageing, while acknowledging that there are close links between physical, social, psychological and cultural environments. The 'Gestalt switch' from ageing persons to ageing person-environment systems has not occurred accidentally; it has taken a number of theoretical avenues and there is still a need to continue to develop and refine existing conceptualisations. That said, we begin by considering the historical roots of environmental gerontology, including a discussion and critique of currently well-accepted theoretical approaches, returning to suggestions for future theoretical development later in the chapter.

The 'birth' of environmental gerontology has been linked to the eminently readable contribution by Kleemeier (1959). However, this work was influenced by a range of earlier authors from sociological and ecological traditions, including the Chicago School of Urban Sociology in the 1920s and 1930s (Park et al., 1925). Built environments such as run-down urban districts were regarded for the first time on an explicit level as having a negative impact on health and welfare. The theoretical writings of German psychologist Lewin in the 1930s and 1940s (see Lewin, 1951, for an overview) – which promoted the view that behaviour should be regarded as a function of the person *and* the environment influenced contextual thinking in the behavioural and social sciences. At about the same time, Murray (1938), an American researcher of personality, introduced the term 'press' as an indication of how personal growth may be affected both objectively and subjectively by the context in which a person is situated. In addition, prominent learning theories in psychology and education during the 1950s and 1960s attributed much to the influence of environment in all stages of human development, and this proved an important stimulus for environmental perspectives in gerontology (see Baltes, 1996, for a review). In its most radical version, the message of learning theories applied to ageing is that it is not chronological age per se but constraining environments that can be non-reinforcing or helplessness-provoking that lead to age-related loss in physical and mental functioning (Seligman, 1975).

The second half of the twentieth century saw these earlier developments overshadowed by the impact of the social sciences within gerontology. Alongside the traditionally strong consideration of biology and medical conditions, social influences such as the role of economic circumstances, family and social surroundings, as well as housing and neighbourhood quality, became acknowledged as factors able to shape ageing. Finally, the emergence of environmental psychology in the 1960s and 1970s provided another set of roots for environmental gerontology. Old age became an attractive area for early work in this field (Pastalan and Carson, 1970) due to the assumed vulnerability of the ageing organism to environmental demands as well as the existence of specially designed environments for ageing people such as long-term care institutions. Such research influenced the development of ecological theories of ageing later in the twentieth century.

Ecological perspectives

The press-competence (PC) model

In Figure 13.1, the central box provides a synopsis of the major person-environment theoretical developments in environmental gerontology, a field that has been dominated by North American researchers. In the press-competence model suggested by Lawton and Nahemow (1973) with direct referral to Murray (1938) and Lewin (1951), there is a major assumption that the lowered competence of the older person in conjunction with strong 'environmental press' negatively impacts on behaviour and well-being (Figure 13. 2). In earlier conceptual and empirical work, the term 'environmental docility hypothesis' was coined to address this basic mechanism in person-environment relations (Lawton and Simon, 1968). Lawton and Simon revealed how the patterns of social interaction of older people in institutional settings depended on physical distances, with greater distances more strongly undermining social relations – thus pointing to the 'environmental docility' of the older organism.

Figure 13.1: Historical influences on theory development in environmental gerontology

Major historical influences on theories of person–environment relations in old age

- Chicago School of Urban Sociology/Human Ecology
- Lewin's field theory
- Murray's environmental press model
- Learning theories
- Evolution of social gerontology within gerontology
- Evolution of environmental psychology

Major person–environment theoretical approaches in current environmental gerontology

- Press–competence model/Environmental docility and proactivity hypothesis
- Person–Environment fit model
- Social ecology concepts/Dependence–support script
- Person–environment stress model
- Place attachment concepts/Place insideness
- Place theory – dementia concepts
- Relocation concepts/Relocation trauma hypothesis

Critique and future challenges

- Better integration of environmental docility and proactivity
- Better integration of the micro and macro level of analysis
- Better integration of temporality
- Better integration of physical and social environment
- Better integration of ongoing cohort dynamics

The press-competence model has been criticised for promoting a one-sided image of older people as 'pawns' of their environmental circumstances, In the 1980s, Lawton introduced the concepts of *proactivity* and *environmental richness* (Lawton, 1985, 1998) in order to address this criticism.

The press-competence model takes quite a general approach in defining both 'competence' and 'environmental press'. For example, 'competence' could relate to sensory loss, loss in physical mobility, or cognitive decline;

and 'environmental press' could relate to low housing standard, bad neighbourhood conditions, or underdeveloped public transport. Also, 'behaviour' can mean basic activities of everyday living (such as dressing or washing) or leisure involvement; while 'well-being' covers positive and negative affect as well as cognitive evaluations such as satisfaction with life. The most central theoretical consequence of the PC model is that there exists for each ageing person an optimal combination of available competence and given environmental circumstances leading to the highest possible behavioural and emotional functioning for this person conceptualised by the adaptation level (Figure 13.2). Much empirical work in environmental gerontology, as well as practical work in terms of housing adaptation and designing institutions for the aged, directly or indirectly adheres to the PC model (Peace and Holland, 2001a; Scheidt and Windley, 2003; Wahl et al., 2003).

However, while acknowledging the importance of environment, it should be noted that the model recognises the complexity of interaction beyond environmental determinism. There is also recognition that in different circumstances levels of environmental press can be seen as positive, as well as negative, being stimulating and promoting engagement (Weisman, 2003).

Figure 13.2: Ecological/Press-competence model

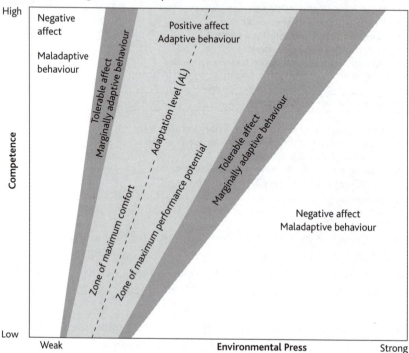

Source: Lawton and Nahemow (1973) © American Psychological Association

134

The person-environment fit (PEF) model

Complexity is also noted in the person-environment fit model, a parallel development that has strongly underlined the role of motivation and personal needs rather than competence within person-environment processes. The basic assumption is that there is a mismatch between personal needs and environmental options, leading to lowered behavioural functioning and well-being. Empirical support for this assumption has emerged from studies conducted in institutional settings (Kahana, 1982).

Carp and Carp (1984) suggested further differentiation for the PEF model in distinguishing between older people's basic and higher-order needs in relation to the potential and limits of a given environment. Here 'basic needs' are conceptualised in a similar way to 'competence' outlined above (for instance, facilitating sensory and walking ability), whereas 'higher-order needs' may relate to issues such as privacy and affiliation which facilitate greater self-actualisation – reflecting Maslow's (1964) model of human needs. According to the Carp and Carp extension of the PEF model, different outcomes of misfit in both of these domains are to be expected. While person-environment misfit in the basic needs domain will predominantly result in reduced behavioural autonomy, misfit in the higher-order realm will predominantly undermine emotional well-being and mental health.

Social ecology (SE) concepts and the person-environment stress (PS) model

The third theoretical perspective outlined here can be defined as *social ecology* (SE) concepts which assume close links between physical surroundings and the social behaviours of persons acting within these settings (Moos and Lernke, 1985). The study of institutional settings has also formed an ideal arena for applying the learning theory perspective to ageing within social ecology thinking, the assumption being that staff will have different reactions to residents' antecedent behaviours, leading to different outcomes.

The empirical application of this model has produced profound insights into the role of the social environment for dependent behaviour in old age by repeatedly identifying robust interaction patterns characterised as a 'dependence-support' script (Willcocks et al., 1987; Baltes, 1996). According to this interaction script, staff tend to overly support dependent behaviours of residents, while independent behaviours are mostly overlooked. There are direct links here to Goffman's work on institutionalisation and the development of 'batch-living' (Goffman, 1961).

The interrelationship of all of these theoretical developments is apparent, nurtured by research that has been dominated by studies within age-segregated institutional settings. The person–environment stress (PS) model argues that environmental conditions, such as a lack of privacy or control due to the built or organisational environment specifically in institutions for the aged, should be regarded as stress.., evoking (Schooler, 1982). How people cope with stress-inducing environments will vary. For instance, some ageing individuals may feel psychological threat, apathy or indifference when faced with similar 'environmental press', rather than the satisfaction of facing such a challenge. Where older people have experienced negative psychological reactions, supportive interventions such as the systematic enhancement of control in institutional settings may enable them to achieve an optimal level of behavioural and emotional functioning (Langer and Rodin, 1976; Rodin and Langer, 1977). However, as already mentioned, institutional control may devalue personal autonomy. Environmental gerontologists work with these issues both theoretically and practically. For example, in Britain, a national study of residential care homes in the early 1980s (Willcocks et al., 1987) suggested the development of 'residential flatlets' that had potential for enhanced levels of privacy and autonomy for older people. This design and organisational innovation foreshadowed developments in both care homes and extra care housing (Netten, 2005; Parker et al., 2004).

Place attachment

In contrast to the foregoing approaches that focus mainly on the role of the objective environment, research concerned with the concept of place attachment addresses the gamut of processes operating when ageing individuals form affective, cognitive and behavioural ties to their physical surroundings (Gurney and Means, 1993; Peace et al., 2006; Oswald and Wahl, 2005; Rubinstein and Parmelee, 1992). Attachment to place may be reflected in the strength of such bonding, as well as in different meanings associated with places such as the home environment or specific landscapes. One approach suggested by Rowles (1978, 1983) has focused on what he calls the many faces of *insideness of place* in old age. Whereas *social insideness* arises from everyday social exchange over long periods, *physical insideness* is characterised by familiarities and routines within given settings such as the home environment, such that the individual is able 'to wear the setting like a glove' (Rowles, 1983, p. 114). He labels the third element of place attachment as *autobiographical insideness* in that 'place becomes a landscape of memories, providing a sense of identity' (p. 114). Rubinstein (1989) focused on the more immediate environment of the home, developing a complimentary model of psycho–social processes linking person to place. According to his terminology, *social-centred processes* include social norms and relationships to other people, *person-centred processes* concern the expressions of one's life-course in features of the environment, and *bodycentred processes* include the 'ongoing relationship of the body to the environmental features that surround it' (Rubinstein, 1989, p. 47).

Place theory and dementia concepts

The body of knowledge is always evolving and within environmental gerontology researchers are conscious of the changing characteristics and circumstances of older people within an ageing world. Gerontologists, particularly those living within developed nations, are concerned for those living with cognitive impairment, and the prevalence of dementing illnesses has increased from the late twentieth century. Consequently, 'place theory and dementia concepts' refers to the theoretical and practical challenge of providing good environments for older people with dementia, which optimise the person-environment interchange processes characteristic of this very specific human condition (Lawton, 2001). This work is driven not least by the hope that environmental design and re-design can make a difference for older people, even when major personal resources such as cognitive capacity are exhausted. Weisman's (1997, 2003) 'model of place' has received due recognition in this regard, and a cornerstone of this concept is its reference to environmental attributes important to secure the life quality of older people with dementia living in institutional settings. Numerous such environmental attributes have been suggested, covering the whole range from basic safety to stimulation, privacy and personal control (Marshall, 2001; Regnier and Pynoos, 1992; Weisman et al., 1996).

Relocation of older people

Finally, there has been a long standing debate within environmental gerontology concerning residential decisions across the life-course. Early research in the 1960s and 1970s was mainly driven by the 'relocation trauma hypothesis' in which negative health effects of relocation from home to an institutionalised setting were stressed (Coffmann, 1981). The empirical evidence was controversial, however, and was plagued by methodological problems such as selectivity of study samples towards the more frail, and missing control groups. Focusing on later life, Litwak and Longino's (1987) distinction between first, second and third moves relied on the assumption of a substantial association between chronological age and the type of move and the motivation for it. Whereas first moves often take place early in the ageing process (close to retirement), and are usually prompted by the amenities associated with the desired place of residence, second moves (roughly appearing in the person's seventies or early eighties) are predominantly characterised by moving back to the place of origin, reflecting a higher need for support and proximity to kinship. Third moves often are to institutions in very old age (Oswald and Rowles, 2006).

Other ways of looking at relocation processes and their differential outcomes concern available coping resources (Golant, 1998) and the distinction between basic and higher-order needs (Carp and Carp, 1984) as motivations for moving (Oswald et al., 2002); while detailed housing histories (Holland, 2001; Peace et al., 2006) have also extended knowledge of the complexity of moving and 'staying put', showing stability and change across the life-course and identifying older people in the UK as migrants, movers and locals. To these debates there is a need to add more recent discussion of cross-national migration, both permanent and seasonal, and to reconsider 'relocation trauma' in the light of the position faced by the diversity of older migrants, whom as Wames et al. (2004) have indicated [...] range from those who are deprived and socially excluded to those with wide personal resources but where all are currently disadvantaged through ageing as migrants.

Final remarks

In sum, pluralism seems to be essential to theorising within environmental gerontology (Wahl and Weisman, 2003). However, this should not be seen as a disadvantage or as an indication of weakness in the field. Instead, the complexity of person-environment relations in later life probably demands a diversity of perspectives and a level of methodological complexity which all contribute to a greater understanding of how environments impact on the course and outcomes of normal and frail ageing – contextualising ageing.

[...]

References

Baltes, M. M. (1996) *The Many Faces of Dependency in Old Age.* Cambridge: Cambridge University Press.

Carp, F. M. and Carp, A. (1984) A complementary/congruence model of well-being or mental health for the community elderly. In: Altman, I. and Lawton, M. P. (eds) *Human Behavior and Environment. Vol. 7 - Elderly People and the Environment,* 279-336. New York: Plenum Press.

Coffmann, T. L. (1981) Relocation and survival of institutionalized aged: a re-examination of the evidence. *Gerontologist* 21, 483-500.

Goffman, E. (1961) *Asylums: Essays on the Social Situation of Mental Patients and Other Inmates.* New York: Anchor Books.

Holland, C. A. (2001) *Housing Histories: The Experience of Older Women Across the Life Course* [PhD thesis]. Milton Keynes: Open University.

Kahana, E. (1982) A congruence model of person-environment interaction. In: Lawton, M. P., Windley, P. G. and Byerts, T. O. (eds) *Aging and the Environment: Theoretical Approaches,* 97-121. New York: Springer.

Kleemeier, R. W. (1959) Behavior and the organization of the bodily and external environment. In: Birren, J. E. (ed.) *Handbook of Aging and the Individual,* 400-451. Chicago: University of Chicago Press.

Langer, E. J. and Rodin, J. (1976) The effects of choice and enhanced personal responsibility for the aged: a field experiment in an institutional setting. *Journal of Personality and Social Psychology* 34(2), 191-198.

Lawton, M. P. (1985) The elderly in context: perspectives from environmental psychology and gerontology. *Environment and Behavior* 17(4), 501-519.

Lawton, M. P. (2001) The physical environment of the person with Alzheimer's disease. *Aging and Mental Health* 5(1), 556-64.

Lawton, M. P. and Nahemow, L. (1973) Ecology and the aging process. In: Eisdorfer, C and Lawton, M. P. (eds) *The Psychology of Adult Development and Aging,* 619-674. Washington, DC: American Psychological Association.

Lawton, M. P. and Simon, B. B. (1968) The ecology of social relationships in housing for the elderly. *Gerontologist* 8, 108-115.

Lewin, K. (1951) *Field Theory in Social Science.* New York: Harper.

Litwak, E. and Longino, C. E, Jr (1987) Migration patterns among the elderly: a developmental perspective. *Gerontologist* 27(3), 266-272.

Marshall, M. (2001) Dementia and technology. In: Peace, S. and Holland, C. (eds) *Inclusive Housing in an Ageing Society,* 125-243. Bristol: Policy Press.

Maslow, A. H. (1964) *Motivation and Personality.* New York: Harper & Row.

Moos, R. H. and Lemke, S. (1984) *Multiphasic Environmental Assessment Procedure: A User's Guide.* Palo Alto, CA: Center for Health Care Evaluations, Dept of Veterans Affairs and Stanford University Medical Center.

Murray, H. A. (1938) *Explorations in Personality. A Clinical and Experimental Study of Fifty Men of College Age.* Oxford: Oxford University Press.

Oswald, F and Rowles, G. D. (2006) Beyond the relocation trauma in old age: new trends in today's elders' residential decisions. In: Wahl, H.-W., Tesch-Romer, C. and Hoff, A. (eds) *New Dynamics in Old Age: Environmental and Societal Perspectives,* 127-152. Amityville, New York: Baywood Publishing.

Oswald, F and Wahl, H.-W (2005) Dimensions of the meaning of home. In: Rowles, G. D. and Chaudhury, H. (eds) *Coming Home: International Perspectives on Place, Time and Identity in Old Age.* New York: Springer. 21-46.

Oswald, F, Wahl, H.-W., Naumann, D., Mollenkopf, H. and Hieber, A. (2006) The role of the home environment in middle and late adulthood. In: Wahl, H.-W, Brenner, H., Mollenkopf, H., Rothenbacher, D. and Rott, C. (eds) *The Many Faces of Health, Competence and Well-being in Old Age: Integrating Epidemiological, Psychological and Social Perspectives,* 7–24. Heidelberg: Springer.

Park, R. E., Burgess, E. W. and McKenzie, R. D. (1925) *The City.* Chicago: Chicago University Press.

Parker, C., Barnes, S., McKee, K., Morgan, K., Torrington, J. et al. (2004) Quality of life and building design in residential and nursing homes. *Ageing and Society* 24, 941–962.

Pastalan, L. A. and Carson, D. H. (eds) (1970) *Spatial Behavior of Older People.* University of Michigan Institute of Gerontology.

Peace, S. M. and Holland, C. (eds) (2001a) *Inclusive Housing in an Ageing Society.* Bristol: Policy Press.

Peace, S., Holland, C. and Kellaher, L. (2006) *Environment and Identity in Later Life.* Maidenhead: Open University Press.

Regnier, V. and Pynoos, J. (1992) Environmental intervention for cognitively impaired older person. In: Birren, J. E., Sloane, R. B. and Cohen, G. D. (eds) *Handbook of Mental Health and Aging,* 2nd edn, 763–792. San Diego, CA: Academic Press.

Rodin, J. and Langer, E. J. (1977) Long-term effects of a control-relevant intervention with the institutionalized aged. *Journal of Personality and Social Psychology* 35, 897–902.

Rowles, G. D. (1978) *Prisoners of Space.* Colorado: Westview Press.

Rowles, G. D. (1983) Geographical dimensions of social support in rural Appalachia. In: Rowles, G. D. and Ohta, R. J. (eds) *Aging and Milieu: Environmental Perspectives on Growing Old,* 111–130. New York: Academic Press.

Rubinstein, R.L. and Parmelee, P. W. (1992) Attachment to place and representation of life course by the elderly. In: Altman, I. and Low, S. M. (eds) *Human Behavior and Environment. Vol. 12 – Place Attachment,* 139–163. New York: Plenum Press.

Scheidt, R.J. and Windley, P.G (eds) (1998) *Environment and Aging Theory: A focus on housing.* Westport, CT: Greenwood Press.

Scheidt, R. J. and Windley, P. G. (2006). Environmmental gerontology: Progress in the post-Lawton era. In J. E. Birren and K. W. Schaie (eds), *Handbook of the Psychology of Aging,* 6th edn, 105–125. Amsterdam: Elsevier.

Schooler, K.K. (1982) Response of the elderly to environment: a stress–theoretical perspective. In: Lawton, M.P., Windley, P.G. and Byerts, T.O. (eds) *Aging and the Environment: Theoretical Approaches,* 80–96. New York: Springer.

Seligman, M. E. P. (1975) *Helplessness: On Depression, Development, and Death.* San Francisco: Freemann.

Wahl, H.-W. (2001) Environmental influences on aging and behaviour. In: Birren, J. E. and Schaie, K. W (eds) *Handbook of the Psychology of Aging,* 5th edn, 215-237. San Diego, CA: Academic Press.

Wahl, H.-W. and Mollenkopf, H. (2003) Impact of everyday technology in the home environment on older adults' quality of life. In: Charness, N. and Schaie, K. W. (eds) *Impact of Technology on Successful Aging,* 215-241. New York: Springer.

Wahl, H.-W. and Weisman, G. D. (2003) Environmental gerontology at the beginning of the new millenium: reflections on its historical, empirical, and theoretical development. *Gerontologist* 43(5), 616-627.

Warnes, A. M., Friedrich, K., Kellaher, L. and Torres, S. (2004) The diversity and welfare of older migrants in Europe. *Ageing and Society* 24(3), 307-326.

Weisman, G. D. (2003) Creating places for people with dementia: an action research perspective. In: Schaie, K. W., Wahl, H.-W., Mollenkopf, H. and Oswald, F. (eds) *Aging Independently: Living Arrangements and Mobility,* 162-173. New York: Springer.

Weisman, J., Lawton, M. P., Sloane, P. S., Calkins, M. and Norris-Baker, L. (1996) *The Professional ..., Environmental Assessment Protocol.* Milwaukee, WI: School of Architecture, University of Wisconsin.

Willcocks, D., Peace, S. and Kellaher, L. (1987) *Private Lives in Public Places.* London: Tavistock.

14

Life course

Caroline Holland and Sheila Peace

Extract from *International Encyclopaedia of Housing and Homes* (2010) Oxford: Elsevier.

Introduction

[...]

Personal circumstances – within wider influences – produce opportunities and constraints that affect choices about moving or staying put. Life course has been described as the patterned progression of individual experience through generational time, anchored in bodily growth, psychosexuality, behavioural conditioning, and cognitive development (Gubrium and Holstein, 1995): an intimate relationship with the deep-seated personal experiences of the passage of time.

[...]

From a sociological perspective, social status may be more important than chronological age in reflecting individuals' experiences of life-course transitions. Therefore, factors such as gender and class must be taken into account. In contrast, environmental gerontologists have considered individual competence to be a key factor in the person-environment fit. It has been argued that this competency, in all its complexity, should be considered across a person's life course.

The timing of specific events – such as marriage, divorce, or unemployment – has been shown to have an effect on housing outcomes; although some evidence suggests that their impact may weaken over time. The relationship between earlier experience and later outcomes is not fixed and is subject to other influences. For example, people who receive higher education may not live in high-quality housing for some years as an immediate effect of continuing in education, but may subsequently have the resources to move up the housing ladder rapidly.

The chronological timing of life-course events is also significant. For example, owing to the worldwide financial recession in 2009, young adults in the United Kingdom and elsewhere looking for their first independent adult homes found themselves in a quandary. Their position was quite different from those of cohorts of a few years previously, with regard to the availability of mortgages, credit, and sufficiently well-paying jobs to give them financial independence.

Housing and stages in the life course

Life course has been a powerful organising concept for understanding in general terms how, when, and why people move between and experience houses and homes. This further extends to understanding the home range of neighbourhoods and locales beyond the dwelling place itself. In very general terms, the life course of a person from birth to death tracks a pattern of widening personal reach into the environment. This interaction with the environment begins from the cradle at birth; proceeds through gradually increasing access that varies with age, gender, personality, and status to the personal maximum range in adulthood; and then begins to shrink once again in old age towards the eventual grave. Individuals can and do differ in the choices as well as in the timings of their entry into particular 'life stages' – such as parenthood or retirement – and in the shape of their reach across the life course into the wider environment. However, these generalised concepts are reflected in standard recognised patterns across populations.

Early years

The homes that people inhabit at birth and in early childhood are necessarily provided by others. They are based on others' ability to provide shelter and on changing ideas about what is appropriate: for example, the separation of male and female children at certain ages or levels of privacy and comfort. Traditionally, the child exercises little influence over this 'parental' environment; yet, in later life, these are often among the most vividly remembered and emotionally resonant of homes. … Some studies have suggested that social deprivation in early life can have lasting effects on certain health conditions in later life. Social deprivation is related to poor housing conditions, such as dampness or lack of safety, which can affect health. Children from families that have been homeless for long periods, or which have been long-term residents of temporary or overcrowded accommodation, are at a disadvantage in terms of education and, in particular, health. This may affect their opportunities, as they become adults.

The first transitional stage in housing career, broadly coinciding in many cultures with the lifecourse event of transition to young adulthood, occurs when young people leave the parental home. This is seen as a critical stage in terms of psychosocial development; although … timing … and

… circumstances … vary considerably. Influences may include elements of class and gender. … Cultural and religious attitudes may be significant here, as are the availability and affordability of housing for people at the beginning of their working lives. In the early twenty-first century, leaving the parental home is not necessarily a once-and-for-all event. It may instead be a process of gradually developing autonomy – with episodes of returning home – before the young persons can establish their own separate households. This 'boomerang-kids' phenomenon potentially puts pressures on family resources and creates conflicts between the lifestyles of coresident generations.

Middle years

Much of the literature on life course and housing is concerned with mobility during the extended 'middle' period of working life and family formation. … Marriage and parenthood can precipitate a transition from renting to homeownership, whereas divorce may result in one or both previous partners moving back into renting, at least temporarily. Patterns of household formation thus affect - and are affected by - housing, as partnerships form, split, and rejoin. Consequently, the social aspects of setting goals and negotiating family needs must be considered along with market influences. Likewise, residential relocation in response to the needs of one family member – for example, for reasons of work or education – may have a detrimental effect on the others.

Employment, especially of … men …, is considered to have a major impact on household decisions about relocation and the type and tenure of housing, as these households move up, down, and through the housing markets. Traditionally, the employment of the women … has been less influential because they get lower pay and their employment opportunities are fragmented. The effects of periods of unemployment can be of greater or lesser significance, depending on the frequency, persistence, and the timings of these periods: for example, the long-term unemployed members are more unlikely to become owner-occupiers. Long-term ill health and disability in the middle years, including caring for a disabled child, are also associated with lower income and poorer housing, unless mitigated by social and financial support.

Later years

… As individuals and couples move into middle age and later life, two life-course events have been marked as being particularly significant: the 'empty nest', when all children of the family have permanently left home; and retirement, when people take stock of their future options.

Adaptation

For many people these events bring about a change in their relationships with home, which can be exacerbated if there are also persisting health problems. Adapting to the phenomena of personal ageing and a changing person-environment fit may take the form of 'downsizing' to accommodation that is more manageable and affordable. This may also be associated with relocation in pursuit of better climate, amenities, social or cultural arrangements, or proximity to family. For the majority of older people ..., 'staying put' in the mainstream domestic housing seems to be the preference throughout later life. This may make it necessary to carry out adaptations to the dwelling to compensate for disability, ill health, or increasing frailty. In many countries, there is also an increasing move towards the use of assistive technologies. ...

Relocation

Older people seeking a combination of manageable housing and social inclusion – but wishing to maintain independence as householders – may relocate to age-related 'retirement housing', some of which provides accommodation-with-care. A minority of older people, with higher proportions in great old age, move out of independent housing altogether and into a care home. Age-related housing takes many different forms (see Table 14.1), which may include some or all of the following characteristics:

- compact size of unit (typically one or two bedrooms or a studio flat);
- multiplicity of units, often with communal facilities and resources;
- availability of security measures, such as personal alarm systems and personnel;
- design that is age-friendly, ranging from basic adaptations to ergonomically designed 'lifetime homes';
- ethos of maintaining independence; and
- availability of formal care and service.

Research shows the pivotal role of the physical, psychological, and social environment in the lives of older people. However, it is argued that in later life, as at other stages of the life course, the ontological importance of 'home' can outweigh the need for physical change affecting the way individuals manage the person-environment 'fit' in later life.

Table 14.1: Housing situations and types across the life course

Age-related?	Age-integrated?
Child foster care	Homelessness
Adult foster care	Living alone
Children's homes	Home sharing
Hostels	Flat (apartment) sharing
Halls of residence (students)	Terraced housing
Sheltered housing	Flats – high rise
Cohousing (adults)	Flats – conversions or adaptations
Extra-care housing	Semidetached houses
Assisted living	Bunglaows
Care homes (adults: residential or nursing)	Caravans or mobile homes
Care housing for people with dementil	Detached houses
Long-stay hospitals	Hospital
Hospices	Hospices

Source: Adapted from Figure 1. Peace S and Holland C (2001, p. 3)

[...]

Housing histories and the life course

Table 14.2 provides abbreviated data from the three case studies within a study in England. The study used biographical methods to produce data on housing and home across the life course. The three profiles drawn from detailed biographical narratives show how the study of actual life-course experiences gives insights into the relationships between people and their environments. These profiles are situated in a combination of individual, familial, and collective histories where generation, social class, gender, culture, intergenerational transfers, and location have all had an impact. Table 14.3 represents a timeline of how the life-course events and housing histories of the three persons overlap. The life-course events in the individual lives are positioned differently in relation to the common historic events and circumstances. The three narratives are drawn from the study of environment and identity by Peace et al (2006). This study looked at the physical or material, social, and psychological aspects of the person–environment fit in both mainstream and age-segregated housing. To reflect the diversity in housing types and neighbourhoods, the study focused on geographically contrasting areas: metropolitan or urban (the London borough of Haringey); small town, urban, or suburban (Bedford); and small town, village, or semi-rural (Northamptonshire).

Housing histories and relocation

Housing histories may involve relocation or migration within or between the boundaries of nation states. They can take many different patterns and present with different effects on housing opportunities and experiences of home. In some cases, there are multiple voluntary relocations; in others, migrations forced by political, economic, or environmental circumstances. Clark and Dieleman (1996) related the emotional impact of any move as being either positive or negative. They further drew a distinction between moves that allowed the retention of webs of contacts and those that caused a partial or total disruption of those ties. The life-course approach to housing enables the effects of relocation to be considered alongside the cause.

Table 14.2: Housing histories of three residents in the 'Environment and Identity' study

Henry, aged 85 Haringey	Nerys, aged 73 Northamptonshire	Ben, aged 61 Bedford
1917: born in Barking, Essex – lived with parents and brother in private rented accommodation 1939: enlisted in the army (Second World war) – lived in barracks accommodation. Met future wife who lived with her family in Hornsey, North London 1940s: postwar, moved to Hornsey and married – lived at first in sister-in-law's home 1950s: moved to own rented flat in Weston Park, commuting to work near Woolwich. Birth of child 1960s: moved to flat in Tottenham, nearer to new work Mid-1990s: became a widower 2001: entered care home for rehabilitation after being attacked in the High Street. Hoping to move on to 'sheltered housing' when allowed to go home, because no longer able to cope with stairs within the flat	1929: born in small village in Wales – lived with parents and two older sisters in three-storey terraced house 1930s: moved because of father's job to a larger town with a secondary school and college 1948: moved to Leeds to work – lived with sister 1952: moved to Northamptonshire, close to other sisiter. Met husband (widower with a 7-year-old daughter) who had been posted during the war to the village of Rushden 1954: married and moved to Rushden to a three-bedroomed council house with large garden. Two more daughters 1980s: bought the house 1999: widowed – living alone	1940: born in Peterborough – lived in grandmother's house 1946: family moved to Potter's Bar 1961: family moved to London and bought a council house 1987: moved to Bedford for work in law firm— settled with wife and daughter in his own home; enjoyed the river and greenery 1992: marriage broke up and he had a stroke, leading to his early retirement. Walked with difficulty 1993: moved to a two-bedroomed council flat in a block where most people were over 40 years of age. Area was peaceful, secure and green 2000: moved to another flat within the same block with easier access for persons with disabilities 2003: deceased
Note: Impact of neighbourhood change on safety and security	*Note: Ageing in place: attachment to place*	*Note: Changing person–environment fit in relation to health and well-being*

Table 14.3: Housing careers of three people of different cohorts in the 'Environment and Identity' study

Date	1890	1900	1910	1920	1930	1940	1950	1960	1970	1980	1990	2000
Context	Private renting WW1					WW2 NHS	Social housing boom		Social housing decline/mass ownership			
Henry			b			m	p					w ↑
Nerys					b		mp	p p				w ↑
Ben						b		m	p		d	

b = born; m = married; p = parent; w = widowed; d = divorced

148

References

Clark WAV and Dieleman FM (1996) *Households and Housing: Choice and Outcomes in the Housing Market.* New Brunswick, NJ: Center for Urban Policy Research.

Elder G and O'Rand A (1994) Adult lives in a changing society. In: Cook K. Fine G. and House J (eds.) *Sociological Perspectives on Social Psychology.* Boston, MA: Allyn & Bacon.

Gubrium J and Holstein J (1995) Life course malleability: Biological work and deprivatization. *Sociological Inquiry* 65 (2):207-223.

Glossary

Age-related housing The terms age-related and age-segregated are usually applied to accommodation designated and (generally) designed for older people. This is distinct from the types of communal accommodation that are provided for relatively narrow age ranges, such as student residences and military barracks. Forms of age-related housing vary from country to country with respect to amenities, tenure, the provision of care and social services, and the minimum age of residents.

Ageing in place Most people age in place, that is, they remain resident in non-age-segregated housing into great old age, This is generally regarded as the preferred option of most of the older people. Initiatives to enable ageing in place include the provision or facilitation of home improvements, adaptations, and domiciliary care.

Housing career This is the movement of individuals or households through a series of different dwellings. It has been frequently linked to other aspects of personal biographies including life-course events such as child bearing, employment, careers, and power within markets (availability and affordability of housing).

Housing history This is a development of a history of the housing career, used particularly when considering individual experiences rather than predicting outcomes.

Life course This concept was developed to encapsulate both individual chronological ageing and the cultural expectations of age-related social roles and statuses, mediated by socialisation and rites of passage. It includes elements of the chronological approach to normative stages in human development found in life-cycle and life-stage studies.

Further reading

Allen, G. and Crow, G. (eds.) (1998) *Home and Family: Creating the Domestic Sphere.* Basingstoke: Macmillan.

Heywood, F,. Oldman, C., and Means, R. (2002) *Housing and Home in Later Life,* Buckingham: Open University Press.

Laslett, P. (1989) *A Fresh Map of Life.* London: Weidenfeld and Nicholson.

Lawton, M.P. (1989) *Environment and Aging.* Monterey, CA: Brooks/Cole Publishing Company, pp 159-78.

Mulder, C.H. and Hooimeijer, P. (1999) Residential relocations in the life course. In: van Wissen, L.J.G. and Dykstra, P.A. (eds.) *Population Issues. An Interdisciplinary Focus.* New York: Springer.

Oswald, F. and Wahl, H.-W. (2003) Place attachment across the life span. In: Miller, J.R., Lemer, R.M., Schiamberg, L.B. and Anderson, P.M. (eds.) *Human Ecology: An Encyclopedia of Children, Families, Communities, and Environments.* Santa Barbara, CA: ABC-Clio.

Peace, S., Holland, C. and Kellaher, L. (2006) *Environment and Identity in Later Life.* Maidenhead: Open University Press.

Thomson, H., Petticrew, M., and Morrison, D. (2001) Health effects of housing improvements: Systematic review of intervention studies. *British Medical Journal* 323 (7306): 187-190.

15

The role of technologies in the everyday lives of older people

Caroline Holland

Technology is all about applying scientific and experiential knowledge to using tools, techniques or systems in order to solve problems or make things easier to do. In general terms, humans have a long history of using technology, and in modern societies it is inescapable – even people who declare themselves to be technophobes use many and various technologies every day.

Technologies have sometimes been described as 'high', 'medium' or 'low', reflecting the extent to which highly advanced or specialised systems are involved. 'Intermediate' or 'appropriate' are terms generally applied to technologies adapted or designed for use in less developed countries where access to resources is limited. However, in the UK, current discussions about technological inclusion and exclusion, and the appointment in 2009 of a Digital Inclusion Champion, focus more specifically on 'high tech' information and communication technologies (ICT), where older people are repeatedly identified among technologically excluded groups

This chapter aims to investigate the nature of older people's interactions with ICT, within the context of older people's uses of technologies more generally and particularly within the environments where they live, and the potential for ICT products and services to enhance the everyday lives of older people.

Electronic computing as we understand it today emerged gradually from pre-20th century mechanical computing machines via incremental advances until it really started to take off after the Second World War, with innovations in electromechanics/electronics and programmability. The rate of development gathered pace through the latter part of the 20th century to the point where personal computers became a mass consumer product. ICT in one form or another is now ubiquitous with integrated circuits (computer chips) in a wide range of everyday products: from ATM (cash) machines to television remote controls, from barcode readers in shops to central heating systems in the home. In the seemingly relentless tide of innovation of recent years many people, including many older people, have at times felt swamped by new technologies. Yet it is unhelpful to position older people *per se* as particularly resistant to changes in technology. I am writing this chapter a few miles from Bletchley Park, where the development of the Colossus electronic computing device played a significant role in the outcome of the Second World War. The women and men who developed, worked with and kept very quiet about that cutting-edge technology are now in their nineties. During their lifetime they and their contemporaries have developed and embraced the mass use of telephones, home electrical equipment such as washing machines, and a myriad of other kinds of domestic appliances, wireless radio and television. In addition older people have often fashioned impromptu devices for themselves to help with practical tasks, for example, to reach or to carry, and many devices that initially older people used rarely over time have gained more general acceptance.

Openness to new ways of doing things is not a simple matter of being youthful or aged, or indeed of belonging to a particular generation – a person's attitude to new technologies relates to their present circumstances, their general inclinations and attitudes to innovation, their previous experiences, work, education and knowledge and their past and current exposure to different technologies. To understand exactly why some older people are wary about new technologies, reluctant to use them or refuse to take on board what others see as useful technologies, requires a 'person-centred approach'. Research has shown that most older people are happy to try technologies that they think will be really useful to them and that are affordable and not difficult to service or maintain. On the other hand, faced with an apparently unending stream of new devices, some of which are costly, unproven and liable to be superseded in a short time, many older people are justifiably wary of committing time and resources to getting involved where they feel that the effort to learn the technology outweighs the probable benefit of using it; and they may well feel that they have more urgent things to spend their money on. Nor does everyone agree that technological advances are necessarily social advances. Some argue that using technologies can be deskilling for individuals, and older people may be particularly aware of skills such as mental arithmetic or map reading which, having learned as children, they do not want to lose through reliance on devices. It is vitally important that technologies are used to support and enhance rather than to replace or undermine existing skills. Furthermore, some people argue that technologies can all too easily be used to replace human contacts, whether socially or with carers, face to face.

As potential users of ICT, older people and people with disabilities have been particularly targeted in the development of teleheath/telecare systems and assistive technologies, some devised specifically for people with sensory, mobility or cognitive impairments. But older people and their requirements have in general been less well considered in the development of the internet and in social media technologies, and with a few exceptions the marketing of these products has tended to ignore older consumers.

Telehealth, telecare and assistive technologies

Telemedicine is an advanced form of *in absentia* medical care, where information is transferred between locations for the purposes of consulting, diagnosis or procedures: it has primarily been used by clinicians and other medical professionals. *Telehealth* is a more general extension of this idea, combining devices and services to enable people to self-monitor or be monitored by others, including health professionals. It allows continuous monitoring of specific physical measures such as blood pressure or blood glucose levels. Telehealth systems tend to be commissioned by providers of healthcare services from commercial companies that specialise in developing 'ecosystems' of different kinds of devices, with information management and data storage, in integrated systems. An older service user will typically be able to decide whether or not to use particular devices, but only from among those on offer from the organisation providing their care service package. *Telecare* takes this one step further to enable the monitoring of activities that might have an effect on the older person's health or safety; examples include emergency alarms, motion sensors and fall detection devices. Telecare can include 'the continuous, automatic and remote monitoring of real-time emergencies and lifestyle changes over time in order to manage the risks associated with independent living. Sensors around the home are linked via a telephone line to a call centre. The system monitors a person's activities and, if a problem occurs, triggers an alarm to a relative, keyholder or call centre' (Alzheimer's Society, 2008). Generally speaking most of these technologies are designed to be used by older people, either actively or passively, as providers of information that will be recorded, assessed and acted on by others.

Assistive technologies have been defined as: 'any device or system that allows an individual to perform a task that they would otherwise be unable to do, or increases the ease and safety with which the task can be performed' (Royal Commission on Long-term Care, 1999). Assistive technologies can include telecare and telehealth, but also extend to a range of more familiar medium and low technology devices such as slip-resistant mats, cutlery and kitchenware designed for people with arthritis, or compartmented pill boxes to help people to take the right medicines at the right time. These technologies have often been designed with the focus on specific needs with the intention of supporting or extending independent living as far as possible. *Smart Homes* are domestic houses where there are a number of such technologies, usually combined with accessibility features, to enhance independent living. The term 'assistive technology' can also include technologies designed for the more general population. Examples are the internet and the mobile global positioning system (GPS) used to support independence and well-being (Beech and Roberts, 2008); many common household technologies such as microwave ovens and washing machines can be regarded as assistive in helping people to maintain independence in everyday activities. One categorisation of assistive technology (Doughty, 2004) has described it as including:

- supportive technologies for helping individuals to perform tasks that they might otherwise find difficult;
- detection and reaction technologies to help individuals to manage risks and raise an alarm if necessary;
- prediction and intervention (preventative) technologies to help prevent dangerous situations from arising and raise an alarm if they do.

Technologies for specific health conditions and disabilities

Some technologies have been identified as being particularly useful for people with specific health conditions, while others have been purposely developed or adapted with their needs in mind. Mobility, sensory and cognitive impairments are among the conditions where technological solutions have been proposed to help people to cope with everyday challenges; the examples discussed here are just a sample of those available with others continually being developed.

Mobility technologies

Physical mobility aids tend to be either for indoor or outdoor use, with relatively few spanning both. Some of these technologies are long-standing and familiar, for example, stairlifts and walkers ('zimmer frames') that enable independent movement within the home. Others such as powered stairclimbers, which can be used where there is no fixed stair lift or elevator, are at an earlier stage of availability and use. Outdoors, mobility scooters and powered wheelchairs for use on and off roadways are a common sight in the UK, where there are regulations regarding their specifications and permitted use (Use of Invalid Carriages on the Highways Regulations, 1988). Alongside these aids to physical mobility, there is a growing market in devices and systems that aid navigation and wayfinding. These can range from the familiar signs and signals used to assist people with visual impairments (tactile surfaces, colour contrast equipment, audio signals), to satellite-based signalling systems such as GPS used in car navigation and smart phones. In addition, older people are being encouraged in some places, including in care homes and community centres, to use products designed for leisure activities (at present, for example, Wii and Kinect consoles with sports/activity software) to maintain a degree of physical flexibility and stamina in a sociable context.

Sensory augmentation

There is a long history of inventions and adaptations to mitigate the effects of sensory impairments. As with mobility aids, they have often been relatively familiar and understood – for example, magnifiers or hearing aids – but at the same time also often felt as labelling or even stigmatising. Consequently modern developments have tended to focus not only on increasing the efficacy of devices but also on improving their look, feel, usability and discretion. For example, over the years there have been progressively smaller, more discrete and more effective hearing aids, and lighter, thinner lenses for spectacles. The growth in ICT has brought with it new aids, including computer screen readers and voice recognition software for people with visual impairments or following stroke. More recently, developments in haptic technologies, using the sense of touch, offer new ways of enabling people with disabilities to navigate and manipulate their worlds (see, for example, Lévesque, 2005).

Cognitive support

Various cognitive training software products have been developed and marketed to older people with the claim that regular use can help to prevent age-related cognitive decline. These often take the form of games to exercise memory, reasoning, focus, problem solving etc, either on hand-held devices or using television or computer monitors. To date there is no convincing evidence that such products are more effective than similar activities in more traditional forms (such as playing dominoes or doing crossword puzzles). A large-scale study by Owen et al (2010) reported in *Nature* found that the improvements that participants aged 18-60 gained in the context of 'brain training' tasks did not transfer to other tasks. Acceptance of these products does, however, point to the concerns that many people have about cognitive decline in later life and their willingness to take steps to protect themselves against it.

However, other technologies demonstrably benefit people who already have a degree of cognitive impairment, and the use of supportive technologies have been particularly welcomed in aspects of dementia care because of their potential for enabling people to live longer in their own homes in the community. The Alzheimer's Society (2008) describes assistive technology as being potentially helpful for people with dementia and their carers by:

- increasing independence and choice, both for the person with dementia and those around them;
- reducing the risk of accidents in and around the home;
- reducing avoidable entry into residential and hospital care;
- reducing the stress on carers, improving their quality of life, and that of the person with dementia.

The Alzheimer's Society gives some examples of fairly simple devices that can provide low-key support for day-to-day independence. These include audio reminder messages to prompt the person to remember their door keys, be careful about who they let in or remember that day's appointments; clocks that also show visually whether it is evening or morning to help prevent disorientation; locator devices using a radio transmitter which can be attached to objects such as keys or glasses cases; and software to evoke memories and stimulate conversation, using familiar music, photographs, videos etc.

   Clearly while some of the devices and systems described so far have been developed with the specific needs of older and disabled people in mind (whether or not they actually fit the bill for any given individual), many more are designed for general use by a much wider population. In the latter case some devices may need further development to meet specific needs – for example, bigger buttons, more accessible text – while others can be used straight 'out of the box'. This is important because the modern everyday environment is not primarily a world of purpose-designed assistive devices, but one dominated by ICT used for communication in many forms, and it is essential that older people are not excluded from this pervasive aspect of modern life. Thus it is vital to think about how older as well as younger people might use communication technologies.

The internet

The development in the early 1990s of the World Wide Web signalled the start of a revolution in communication which, by 2010, has linked well over a billion people, and rising, across the planet. Needless to say, the quantity and speed of uptake has varied widely between and within populations. According to Ofcom, the UK's independent communication industries regulator, in 2009 the growth in internet take-up that year in the UK appeared for the first time to have been driven by those aged over 55, for whom the use of email was particularly important (Ofcom, 2010). However, this concealed a more complex pattern of access by older users, and in 2010 it was still the case that 64 per cent of those individuals who had never accessed the internet were aged over 65 (ONS, 2010), indicating differences between those approaching retirement age or fairly recently retired, and much older cohorts. Older people who do not use the internet do not necessarily regard this as a problem and it varies as to whether they wish to get involved. The use of the internet in general is closely associated not just with age but also with other socioeconomic and demographic indicators, with people on lower incomes and with less education much less likely to have access. Governments internationally have identified this 'digital exclusion' as a problem and a form of social exclusion, because as use of the internet has become more and more ubiquitous, lack of access to it means that people may be cut off from ready sources of current information, access to lower tariffs for goods and services and convenient ways of maintaining social contacts as well as administrative tasks such as banking. As a result there have been many initiatives aimed at the digitally excluded. Just a few examples are an EU-wide 'Get Online' campaign, offering free courses sponsored by consortia of companies and organisations (www.getonlineweek.com); projects to introduce older people and their families and carers to video conversations via webcam (www.connectmk.com); and the establishment of an annual Silver Surfers' Day of activities and promotions.

Social media

The internet has many uses, such as commercial purposes (business, buying and selling), education purposes (for example, the Open University provides open access courses through iTunes U), and many other purposes including research, leisure and gaming. Among these uses the rise of social media has been particularly striking, moving from the very first handful of emails between computer programmers in the early 1970s to mass use. In the spring of 2011, for example, Facebook, Twitter and other forms of blogging made a recognised contribution to fast communications during political upheaval in the Middle East and disaster relief in Japan. These kinds of media enable people to express themselves both personally and publicly, combining technologies with social interaction in ways that are quick, inexpensive and easy to learn compared to conventional media such as television and newspapers. But generally speaking these technologies, as they have developed, have been seen as the domain of the young, and typically not regarded as useful or relevant to older people. Notable exceptions have been fêted in online communities as bucking this trend.

For example, María Amelia López blogged regularly from when she was 95 until her death at 97 in 2009, and the centenarian Ivy Bean (@ IvyBean104), until her death in 2010, regularly posted on Twitter from her care home, and said that she would be miserable without it. Both women had a mass following of people of all ages who communicated with them until the end of their lives.

Singh (2010) has suggested that the social web could help to reduce the social exclusion of older people by:

- enabling decision making;
- increasing self-reliance;
- helping people adjust to new circumstances;
- improving the quality of life in terms of social contact, entertainment and physical movement; and
- providing a means by which older people may be introduced to and eventually appropriate technological devices for their own interests.

Reflections

A combination of ideas has prompted increasing interest in understanding older people's relationships with technology and in securing their input to design. These ideas include concerns about social/digital exclusion; propositions about the contributions that technologies can make to supporting independence while reducing demands on carers and potentially saving money; and an awareness of a largely under-served (or under-exploited) market of older consumers. Some older people have also encountered problems when their tried and trusted technologies have become obsolete, for example, non-digital cameras and audio and video equipment. Furthermore, where advertising, marketing and indeed campaigning have, so far, addressed older consumers, the tone and age-related labelling (such as 'silver surfer') has been regarded by some as patronising while not necessarily taking seriously older consumers' preferences.

This all rather begs the question of the relevance of age. Some disabling conditions that can affect the person–technology relationship, such as sight loss, hearing loss and mobility problems, become generally more prevalent in older populations, although some individual older people may not experience significant impairment until very late in life, if at all. Others may have had lifelong sensory impairments, with which they age. Here the question is whether ageing *per se* is relevant, over and above the condition. In addition to possible effects of the individual ageing process, the shared experience of successive cohorts is relevant because of differing exposure to technologies, especially in the workplace.

Designers and developers sometimes aim to produce products and services of a universal good design that are accessible to all; one benefit is that the aesthetic look of a product for the general market is important, and labelling for age or disability is minimised. On the other hand, people sometimes need bespoke, individualised or exact-fit products to meet a precise need, and it is one of the features of advancing technology that the making of one-off products may become increasingly more cost-effective through computer-aided design (CAD) and manufacture. Will it become possible, through good design, to emphasise the kudos of 'exclusivity' above the stigma of 'special needs'?

Simulation exercises have been used for some time in helping medical and care staff, designers and others to get a 'feel' as well as an intellectual understanding of the effects of specific age-related impairments, aiming to produce empathy as well as understanding. At a very simple level this may involve, for example, wearing clothing that restricts movement or spending some time moving around in a wheelchair. Technological advances have enabled the development of more sophisticated simulations, and there is now a whole range of aids, from goggles that represent specific visual impairments to body suits that emulate arthritis or stroke-related disabilities. With the turn to user consultation as part of the design process, and a growing acknowledgement of the significance of individual biographical experiences, there is reason to be hopeful that older people's concerns will be taken more into account in designing products.

Yet information remains key to accessing both products and the means to acquire them, and as more and more products and indeed whole new technological approaches become available, many older people are turning to family, friends and carers for support in finding out about and getting to grips with technologies that might improve the quality of their lives. It is important that these intermediaries listen to the older person's aspirations rather than imposing their own prejudices about technology and what is or isn't suitable on account of age.

References

Alzheimer's Society (2008) 'Assistive technology' (http://alzheimers.org.uk/site/scripts/documents_info.php?documentID=109).

Beech, R. and Roberts, D. (2008) *Assistive technology and older people*, SCIE Research Briefing 28, August, London: Social Care Institute for Excellence.

Doughty, K. (2004) 'Supporting independence: the emerging role of technology', *Housing, Care and Support*, vol 7, no 1, pp 11-17.

Lévesque, V. (2005) *Blindness, technology and haptics*, TR–CIM–05.08, Haptics Laboratory Centre for Intelligent Machines, Montréal, Canada: McGill University.

Ofcom (2010) *Ofcom Communications Market Report* 2010 available at http://stakeholders.ofcom.org.uk/market-data-research/market-data/communications-market-reports

ONS (Office for National Statistics) (2010) *Internet access 2010, Households and individuals*, Statistical Bulletin, 27 August, London: ONS.

Owen, A.M., Hampshire, A., Grahn, J.A., Stenton, R., Dajani, S., Burns, A.S., Howard, R.J. and Ballard, C.G. (2010) 'Putting brain training to the test', *Nature*, vol 465, pp 775-8.

Royal Commission on Long-term Care (1999) *With respect to old age: Long-term care rights and responsibilities*, London: The Stationery Office.

Singh, R. (2010) *In what ways might the social web reduce older people's experiences of social exclusion?*, London: UCL (www.ucl.ac.uk/network-for-student-activism).

16

Accommodating older and disabled prisoners in England and Wales

Barbara M. Glover

Introduction

There are currently in the region of 142 different types of penal establishments in England and Wales, with a useable operational capacity of just under 88,500 people, and a population of around 85,000 male and female adult, young and juvenile offenders. Around 108 prisons are used to accommodate male and female adult offenders over the age of 21, with only one in Wales. During the past decade it has been recognised that there is a steadily increasing number of older prisoners.[1] The increase is not the result of a surge in crime among older citizens but because of stricter sentencing policies: courts are not only imprisoning far more people over the age of 60, but are also giving them longer sentences (HMIP, 2004), thus creating further health and overcrowding implications for the Prison Service. These implications are discussed in more detail in the following sections.

Older and disabled prisoners

The chances of living with an impairment increase with old age. However, it should not be assumed that all prisoners over the age of 60 consider themselves to be old, or that they will all begin or end their sentences with (or having had) an impairment or illness, just as it should not be assumed that every prisoner between the ages of 21 and 59 is physically agile and healthy. A high percentage of chronically ill and disabled inmates *are*, however, much older than the rest of the prisoner population. The growing number of older prisoners inevitably increases the number of the disabled and, over the years, the terms 'disabled' and 'elderly'[2] have tended to become synonymous within the prison context. This means that in many establishments disabled individuals – of all ages – are housed with older prisoners who may or may not have chronic illnesses and impairments, as it is assumed that not only are many of their *personal* needs and interests the same, but that they would *benefit* from living together.

In 2007, guidance for the care of older offenders was published by the Department of Health, but the Home Office had no plans to develop a national strategy for them, even though they were described as living in 'institutions designed for the young and in circumstances that merely hasten their deaths' (*The Guardian*, 1 February 2005). In the space of one year alone (2003), there were 21 deaths from natural causes among prisoners aged 65 and over, prompting the director of the Howard League for Penal Reform to point out that it was 'not a rational use of resources to use prison as a high security nursing home', and that 'continuing to imprison older people at this rate raise[d] the spectre of the Prison Service having to take over whole cemeteries' (ibid). As recently as August 2008 Her Majesty's Chief Inspector of Prisons expressed concern that not only was there still no national strategy for elderly prisoners but that prisons were still not being fitted with equipment suitable for their needs. Furthermore, she criticised the fact that too many prisons did not have a designated disability lead, and that many officers had no idea which of their prisoners would require personal assistance in an emergency, or which non-disabled prisoners could be relied on to help them with the old and infirm in these situations.

Older and disabled prisoners are expected to cope with the physical and attitudinal barriers to full participation in prison life, and their feelings of powerlessness and invisibility could be described as the 'hidden injuries' of imprisonment (Sennett and Cobb, 1973). They must also cope with the debilitating and humiliating effects of other long-term or permanent illnesses and conditions that may add to their feelings of isolation. Many of them worry about being cut off from the outside world (Howse, 2003), and others suffer from 'relocation stress' (Sieber et al, 1993), while men who have been married for a long time may find the separation from their wives unbearable (Crawley, 2005). Some of them worry that they might become seriously ill and die in prison (Gross, 1991), or that their wives will die before they can be together again, and so, in an attempt to reduce potential distress, they sever all ties with family and friends long before this happens (Crawley, 2005).

Other 'hidden injuries' of imprisonment are caused by 'institutional thoughtlessness' (Crawley, 2005, p 356). Older prisoners are frequently sent to prisons that are overcrowded and unsuitable for their particular needs, and this raises concerns about general healthcare and the opportunities for exercise. Many have little to occupy them and are left to spend their days in enforced idleness in their cells. Prisoners of any age who have impairments or who are chronically sick are expected to fit in with the schedule of activities arranged for young healthy inmates, and are not always given any special dispensation (Owen, 1998; Crawley, 2005). While the majority of prisoners may enjoy the daily hour of exercise in the yard, the lack of toilet facilities causes others acute physical discomfort and distress, and prison clothing is often of too poor a quality to offer adequate protection against colder weather (Crawley, 2005). Extra bedding and warmer clothing are supplied to older and disabled prisoners in South West England (Clarke, 2007), but apparently not elsewhere. This not only suggests that prison managers have some discretion in the matter but that many are unaware of (or choose to ignore) the needs of some of their most vulnerable (but least vocal) residents.

Living with a disability in prison: design faults and facilities

The architects of prisons from Victorian times onwards apparently assumed that prisoners would be young and able-bodied, and no thought seems to have been given to those who, although apparently healthy on arrival, may become ill or disabled during their incarceration. This is reflected in the designs of the buildings, many of which have small cells, no purpose-built accommodation for older and disabled people, narrow doorways and corridors, and several storeys reached by steep, open staircases. Design faults and omissions inevitably affect the quality of life and the morale of these prisoners, and add to their feelings of vulnerability and isolation. Many who are frail or have impaired mobility find that they cannot cope with the constant noise, or are unable to access some parts of the jails 'constructed in blithe unconsciousness of the needs and sensibilities of the old' (Crawley and Sparks, 2005, p 350).

As a service provider, the Prison Service was expected to comply with the Disability Discrimination Act (DDA) 1995 (DfEE, 1996; Heager et al, 1999), yet it was still dragging its feet years after most reasonable adjustments had been made in the wider community. It was not expected to undertake large-scale building or alteration work, or to make all of its establishments accessible to disabled and older prisoners, but it was expected to try to accommodate their needs in its policies and planning, and to ensure that each prison was in possession of, and able to offer, auxiliary aids, portable induction loops for the hearing-impaired, handrails and ramps (HMIP, 2004). Prisons were also expected to offer all prisoners access to other facilities such as the library. The Prison Service disability strategy and *Prison Service Order (PSO) 2855: Prisoners with disabilities* (Her Majesty's Prison Service, 2008) made it clear that one of the mandatory actions of each prison governor was to nominate a disability liaison officer (DLO) from the staff who, as well as carrying out his or her normal duties, would be allowed sufficient time to familiarise him/herself – and subsequently the prisoners and staff – with any new information on policy and good practice.

In July 2005 the Offender Policy and Rights Unit of the National Offender Management Service distributed a disability accommodation survey to the 142 prisons and/or Young Offender Institutes across England and Wales in order to collate information for a central database on the types of accommodation and facilities (such as wheelchair accessibility, adapted toilets and any other modifications that had been made) which were available for disabled prisoners. The results of the survey showed that there were 619 adapted cells/bed spaces in 142 establishments, but they were not evenly spread across the estate and, in some, the only suitable disability accommodation was in the healthcare centre. A number of prisons could offer cells with wider doorways but no other special facilities, and 73 prisons were reported as having no disability-designated accommodation or facilities whatsoever.

Research base

The research (Glover, 2009) on which this chapter is based focused on a range of issues including: changes to the professional identity of the discipline officers who were not trained as carers; the impact of disability on the relationships between the staff and the older and disabled prisoners; and the external and internal structural barriers which compromised the equality of, and access by, prisoners with physical and sensory impairments. The research was based on the social model of disability that believes that it is society, and not impairments, which disables people from fully and equally participating in everyday life (Oliver, 1996; Thomas, 1999). The research investigated whether the Prison Service was making every attempt to provide a safe, secure and equal environment for these prisoners in accordance with the requirements of the DDA 1995.

Disability Acts

The DDA 1995 was introduced to protect the civil rights of disabled people, and it required service providers to make 'reasonable adjustments' to their policies, practices and procedures in order to ensure that disabled people were given equal access to goods, facilities and services. From December 1996 it was considered unlawful to treat anyone 'less favourably' because of their impairments, and by October 1999 service providers were to have modified their services and made extra assistance available to whoever needed it. The modification or removal of structural barriers or the provision of an alternative method of access were to be in place by October 2004.

The DDA 2005 amended the earlier Act quite substantially, and extended the rights of disabled people in public transport, education, employment, advertisements, large private clubs, local and public authorities and the buying or renting of property and land. It also gave a wider definition of disability, and introduced a duty on public bodies to promote awareness of, and equality of opportunity for, all disabled people.[3] The Disability Equality Duty came into force on 5 December 2006.

Both Disability Discrimination Acts, but not the Disability Equality Duty, were replaced by the Equality Act 2010, which became law in October 2010. This continues to protect the civil rights of disabled people, and also includes the rights of people wrongly perceived to be disabled and people who are associated with anyone who is disabled.

Research fieldwork

The fieldwork took place in six adult prisons in the north of England during 2004/05. Five of these were from the male estate: Garth (category B),[4] Kirkham (category D, or open)[5] and Lancaster Castle, Risley and Wymott (all category C). The sixth prison, Low Newton, was from the female estate. Methods included semi-structured interviews with a total of 25 disabled/older prisoners and 20 members of staff/management. The interviews – most of which were recorded (with the participant's permission) – lasted for an average of one hour and, where possible, records were made of the physical environment. In this chapter attention is given to material concerning the person and their environment.

Physical/material environment

The standard regulation measurements for disabled facilities are given in Table 16.1, while Tables 16.2 and 16.3 give similar data for the facilities available for disabled/older prisoners in these six prisons. Such random and frequently inadequate facilities suggest that there was no coordination or planning at policy level, and that there had been no input from consultants with professional and/or personal knowledge of gerontology and disability. None of the prisons was properly equipped to cater for the many and diverse needs of its older and disabled prisoners, thus compromising their health and safety, as well as their equality with the other prisoners.

Table 16.1: Regulation measurements of disabled facilites in accordance with Part III of the DDA 1995

	HEIGHT (from floor)
Available space	A minimum area of 5' x 5" to allow for easy manoeurve of wheelchairs
Doorway (inner measurement)	(2" 7" W)
Window control	5' 8" (max) (obstructed access) 6' 4" (max) (unobstructed access)
Light switches	2' 6" to 3' 4"
Coat hooks	3' 6" to 4' 8"
Bed (to top of mattress)	1' 7"
Shower head	4' 0" to 7' 4" (adjustable)
Water control	2' 5" to 3" 4"
Tip-up-seat	1' 8"
Bath (to top of rim)	1' 8" (5' 4" to 5' 8" L; 2' 4" W)
Wash basin (to top of rim)	2' 6"
Toilet (to top of seat)	1' 7"

Source: ODPM (2004)

In-cell facilities

There was little consistency in the size and shape of the cells – including those described as being particularly suitable for older and disabled prisoners – as the positioning of their fixtures and fittings was often ill-conceived, and handrails and emergency cords were the exception rather than the norm. The width of the doorways varied considerably and, while some wheelchair users could gain access to the cells, others found it difficult without the help of other prisoners or members of staff. Typically, the emergency call button was located next to the door and could be about 5 feet up from the floor, thus rendering it useless if the occupant was unable to reach it; the privacy board[6] merely served as another obstruction in an already-crowded living space. The specifications of the toilets and washbasins varied widely between the different wings within each prison and across the estate, and not one cell – including those said to be disability-designated – had been fitted with a vibrating clock or a flashing light to waken the prisoner or to alert him/her to the next change in activity.

Table 16.2: Specifications of in-cell facilities for the disabled in, and between, the prisons

	Garth	Kirkham	L/Castle	Low Newton	Risley	Wymot
Cell	Health Care Centre (not all measurements available	Intermitten Custody Unit L 13ft. W 10ft 1in.	n/a	E Wing (facilities not in use) I Wing L 9ft. 10 in. W 9 ft. 10in.	G Wing L 11ft. 6in. W 9ft. 11in.	G/H Wing L 11ft. W 14ft. 2in.
Shower room	–	L 10ft. 4 in. W 6ft. 4 in.	n/a	n/a	–	–
Bathroom	–	–	n/a	n/a	n/a	–
Doorways	2ft. 8 in. (cell) 2ft. 7in. (s/room) 2ft. 5 in. (b/room)	2ft. 8 in. (cell) 2ft. 10in. (s/room)	n/a	– 2ft. 7in.	3ft. 3in. (cell) 2ft. 4 in. (to shower, on landing)	3ft. 3in. (cell) 2ft. 6in. (s/ block)
Bed (floor to top of mattress)	–	1ft. 7in.	n/a	– 1ft. 6 in.	2ft.	2ft.
Toilet (floor to top of seat)	–	1ft 5in.	n/a	–	1ft. 4in.	1ft. 6in.
Washbasin (floor to rim)	–	2ft. 4in.	n/a	–	2ft. 8in.	–

Out-of-cell facilities

The out-of-cell environment could also be disabling. Although several of the prisons had more than one induction loop for the hearing-impaired, and one establishment had a specially-adapted telephone, there was no other evidence across the six prisons of any attempt to assist vision-impaired prisoners by providing them with colour-coded routes[7] or texture boards. There was some evidence of doorframes having been painted in a contrasting colour to the doors themselves, but the contrast was not always sufficiently clear. Some library books and information for prisoners had been transcribed into Braille, but there was no signage in Braille on the walls of the buildings, inside or out, and no clear marking to the edges of steps or any sharp corners.

Communal services could also be problematic. Many of the shower and bathing facilities were of the wrong height according to health and safety guidelines. For example, while some care had been taken to position showerheads and water control buttons where someone in a wheelchair could easily reach them, others had been placed too low down for other disabled prisoners, and some were far too high for anyone to use.

Table 16.3: Specifications of washing facilities (height from floor) for the disabled in, and between, the prisons

	Garth	Kirkham	L/Castle	Low Newton	Risley	Wymot
Showerhead	6ft.	3ft. 10in. to 5ft. 10in. (adjustable)	n/a	5ft. 3in. n/a	6ft. 7in.	6ft.
Water control	4ft.	3ft. 4in.	n/a	3ft. 3in. n/a	3ft. 2in.	3ft. 9in.
Shower seat	–	1ft. 7in. (fold down)	n/a	n/a n/a	1ft. 10in. (bench)	n/a
Bath	2ft. [4ft. 9in L 1ft. 10 in W]	n/a	n/a	n/a n/a	n/a	n/a

Conclusion

Not one of the six prisons could provide a full range of specialist equipment and facilities to people with physical and sensory impairments, and the failure to do so automatically highlighted the 'difference' of these people from the rest of the prison population, placing them at a disadvantage. They were expected to cope with what was, in effect, double punishment: the loss of personal freedom and of dignity and equality. The non-slip flooring became slippery when wet/soapy; handrails, hoists, chairlifts, special shower chairs, toilet raiser seats and ramps were generally conspicuous by their absence; and only one prison had a specialist bath (although it had apparently never been used). Narrow doorways, insufficient floor space, steps and retaining walls often obstructed wheelchair access. Such design faults and omissions of even small changes in the environment were the result of a lack of funding or thoughtlessness, and they inevitably affected the quality of life of these vulnerable prisoners.

It was known across the prison estate that the structures of Garth and Lancaster Castle[8] were unsuitable for disabled prisoners, but there were occasions when the working procedure between them and the feeder prison at Preston failed or could not be adhered to because of overcrowding. Therefore each prison should have attempted to provide at least the basic facilities for such eventualities, but both failed to do so. The cells in the healthcare centre at Garth could accommodate wheelchair users (as long as they were able to self-transfer onto the bed), but there were very few disability aids, and these rooms were really for the treatment of in-patients. As a listed building, Lancaster Castle was more at a disadvantage, but the addition of handrails and an alarm system in the washing areas could have provided some support when necessary. The facilities in the intermittent custody unit at Kirkham were considered the most favourable, but even they had faults; those at Low Newton were, in the main, more than adequate, but unused, because they were located in the part of the prison now occupied by girls in the young offender institution which formed part of the prison building. Although Risley housed its older and disabled men together on one wing, this could not be described as a community, and the structure of the prison meant that the more spacious cells on another wing were unused by those who needed them most. The woefully inadequate facilities at Wymott were by far the most disappointing, given the prison's unofficial status as the disability prison for the north of England, and many of the disabled prisoners sent there to receive what they believed would be care more suited to their needs felt disappointed and betrayed. It was only the determination of the officers to help the men, the friendships which developed between the men as a result of acting as carers for each other, and the relatively quiet atmosphere which prevailed on the unit that kept morale from sinking too low.

During the research the prisons were each assessed according to the resources, facilities and equipment provided, and then ranked accordingly from high (1) to low (6) (see Table 16.4). The results were not inspiring. While it was to be expected that Lancaster Castle and Garth would not rank highly because of their inherent structural difficulties, Wymott – with its unit for older and disabled prisoners – *should* have come in first place.

Table 16.4: Ranking of the prisons according to their facilities for the disabled

Prison	Ranking
Garth	5
Kirkham	1
Lancaster Castle	6
Low Newton	2
Risley	4
Wymott	3

It is fair to say that the response of the Prison Service to the DDA 1995 has been random, inconsistent and painfully slow. Despite the rising profile of disability across the prison estate Disability Liaison Officers were neither trained to do this extra work nor given the time within their normal shift in which to do it. Frontline officers were ashamed of the conditions in which older and disabled prisoners were expected to live, and tried their best to think up new coping strategies in order to help them overcome the difficulties they faced on a daily basis. They acknowledged that although they were first and foremost discipline officers, they needed to extend their skills to include the care of the rising numbers of older and disabled prisoners, and had repeatedly asked management to provide them with appropriate training courses on the correct way to lift prisoners, and how to care for the bereaved or the dying; so far nothing had come of these requests.

Changes for the better

During visits to Wymott and Risley[9] early in 2011 I found that, while there is still a long way to go, many positive attempts have been made to facilitate the needs of the prisoners and to give them a better quality of life. Handrails have finally been fitted on the landings in the Elderly and Disabled Community at Wymott, and a special, lightweight plastic chair is now provided in the showers. A multipurpose day centre (The Annexe) has 10 slightly larger cells (which are currently closed due to budgeting constraints), a communal space with a small kitchen, and a classroom that is used for a range of courses and where resources for advice on health and welfare issues are available. The men meet in The Annexe to talk or play cards and dominoes, keep fit on the exercise bikes or listen to talks by external speakers. At Risley some re-organisation to meet the needs of wheelchair users, and other disabled and older prisoners has occurred, while health and well-being through regular exercise is explained and discussed at meetings organised by the physical education officers. Individual care plans have also been introduced at both prisons, and copies of information for disabled prisoners (PRT, 2004) are now available.

The role of the DLO is increasingly becoming recognised across the estate as an important part of prison life. There are now regular meetings with regional colleagues to discuss best policy and practice, and some extra training is available for this particular role.

Security and control must always take priority across the prison estate, but the personal needs of the prisoners should also be considered. There will always be many justifiable and necessary claims on funding, but it is essential that a proportion of this money is invested in accelerating the provision of facilities and accommodation for all older and disabled prisoners in order to provide them with fair and humane containment.

Notes

[1] Opinions differ regarding the base age of the older people in prisons, but it is usually taken as being somewhere between 50 and 65. Her Majesty's Inspectorate of Prisons, and the Prisons Reform Trust (PRT), have both used 60 in the past, but the PRT has now lowered this to 50.

[2] In this chapter the terms 'elderly' and 'elderly prisoners' are used where it reflects the use as language in policy and practice.

[3] For further information see www.inclusion.me.uk; http://webarchive. nationalarchives.gov.uk; www.direct.gov.uk

[4] Category A is the highest security category.

[5] Prisoners in an open prison are allowed out to work in the community during the day, but they must return to the prison immediately afterwards. Other prisons are referred to as closed establishments.

[6] This is a small hardboard partition meant to afford some privacy to a prisoner using the toilet, but which only shields the prisoner's lower half from view, and does not prevent sounds and smells from escaping into the room.

[7] This is where internal walls are painted a different colour for each main area of the building.

[8] HMP Lancaster Castle was closed in March 2011.

[9] In 2005 these were the two establishments, within the closed estate, where at least some facilities for older and disabled prisoners were available.

References

Aday, R.H. (1999) 'Responding to the Graying of the American Prisons: a 10-year Follow-Up'. Unpublished report. Murfreesboro, TN: Middle Tennessee State University.

Clarke, S. (2007) *Older and Disabled Prisoners in the South West: Report on the Findings of a Survey carried out in Ten Prisons in the South West region in October 2006*. Bridgwater: Care Services Improvement Partnership.

Crawley, E. (2005) 'Institutional thoughtlessness in prisons and its impacts on the day-to-day lives of elderly men', *Journal of Contemporary Justice*, vol. 21, no. 4, p. 350-63.

Crawley, E. and Sparks, R. (2005) 'Older Men in Prison: Survival, Coping, and Identity', in A. Liebling and S, Maruna (eds) *The Effects of Imprisonment*. Cullompton: Willan Publishing.

DfEE (Department for Education and Employment) (1996) *Disability Discrimination Act 1995: Guidance on Matters to be Taken into Account in Determining Questions Relating to the Definition of Disability*. Norwich: HMSO.

Fox, L.W. (1952) *The English Prison and Borstal Systems.* London: Routledge & Kegan Paul.

Glover, B.M. (2009) 'Prison Staff and Disabled Prisoners: Potential Conflict in Role and Identity'. Unpublished thesis. Lancaster University.

Gross, D.A. (1991) *Dying in Prison: Counseling the Terminal Inmate.* Eugene, OR: The Hemlock Society.

Her Majesty's Prison Service (2008) *Prison Service Order (PSO) 2855: Prisoners with Disabilities* (revised edition issued 3 April).

HMIP (Her Majesty's Inspectorate of Prisons) (2004) *'No Problems – Old and Quiet': Older Prisoners in England and Wales. Thematic review.* London: The Stationery Office.

HMIP (2008) *Older Prisoners in England and Wales: A Follow-Up to the 2004 Thematic Review.* London: HMIP.

Howse, K. (2003) *Growing Old in Prison: A Scoping Study of Older Prisoners.* London: Prison Reform Trust.

Meager, N., Doyle, B, and Tachey, N. (1999) *Monitoring the Disability Discrimination Act (DDA).* London: Department for Education and Employment.

ODPM (Office of the Deputy Prime Minister) (2004) *Building Regulations 2000. Access to and Use of Buildings: Approved Document M.* Norwich: The Stationery Office.

Oliver, M. (1996) *Understanding Disability: From Theory to Practice.* Houndmills: Macmillan Press.

Owen, B. (1998) *'In the Mix': Struggle and Survival in a Women's Prison.* Albany, NY: State University of New York Press.

PRT (Prison Reform Trust) (2004) *Information Book for Disabled Prisoners,* London: PRT.

Sennett, R. and Cobb, J. (1973) *The Hidden Injuries of Class.* New York: Vintage Books.

Sieber, M.J., Gunter-Hunt, G. and Farrell-Holton, J. (1993) *Coping with Loss of Independence.* San Diego, CA: Singular Publishing Group.

The Guardian (2005) 'Warning over rising number of older prisoners'. 1 February.

Thomas, C. (1999) *Female Forms: Experiencing and Understanding Disability,* Buckingham: Open University Press.

17

Community care and support for Black and African Caribbean older people

Josie Tetley

Introduction

As a multicultural society, the UK is ageing across all ethnic groups (Toofany, 2006). However, population data identifies that in terms of ethnicity and ageing, nearly 18 per cent of White British are aged 65 but that other minority ethnic groups have younger populations (Lievesley, 2010). Moreover, current generations of older people from minority ethnic populations are most commonly first generation migrants who primarily came from the Caribbean in the 1950s and 1960s, followed by a slightly later arrival of people from India and Pakistan. It was not until the 1980s that people from Bangladesh and China (Hong Kong) migrated, followed later by refugees and asylum seekers from a wider range of nations. This historical context is important as specific age-related data for minority ethnic populations illustrates that the Black Caribbean population for people aged over 65 is 13.4 per cent (ONS, 2008) and is the closest to White British in this respect (see Figure 17.1), thus demonstrating that migration history shapes the age structure of the ethnic population (Lievesley, 2010).

Figure 17.1: England and Wales, 2007, Ethnicity: Black Caribbean

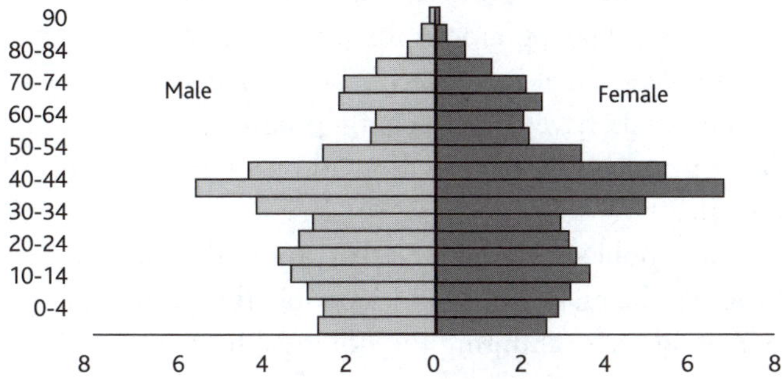

Source: Lievesley (2010). Reproduced from *The Future Ageing of the Ethnic Minority Population of England and Wales*, with permission from the Centre for Policy on Ageing and the Runnymede Trust.

Data on ageing, health and ethnicity also show that non–White British older people may experience similar conditions in ageing, but patterns of health and ill health are different, with Black Caribbean older people more likely to experience health problems related to diabetes and cardiovascular disease (Toofany, 2006; Karlsen and Nazroo, 2010). However, when older people from minority ethnic communities experience problems with their health it is argued that they have limited choice and tend to under-use statutory and voluntary services because care and support are perceived to be insensitive to their needs (Peckham and Meerabeau, 2007). Blakemore (2000), Bowes (2006) and Nazroo (2003) further suggest that choices are limited because services are not adequately developed due to mistaken assumptions about the presence of family support and misunderstandings about specific communities' health needs.

Of course, issues of individual choice and decision making concerning health and social care services are not unique to minority ethnic communities. Since the late 1980s there has been a raft of policies that have aimed to improve access to care and support for older people and their carers by:

- developing care management systems that aimed to put the older person and their carers at the centre of assessment processes;
- introducing a 'quasi-market' where services once provided by the local authority were contracted out to commercial and voluntary organisations and purchased to meet the client's individual needs;
- enabling more older people to remain in their own homes, thus reducing the proportions of older people in institutional care.

The intention has not only been to reduce the costs associated with providing community care but to encourage service users to see themselves as 'customers' instead of passive recipients. It was hoped that this would make services more accountable, responsive and flexible (Gilleard and Higgs, 1998; Cowen, 1999). The aspirations for service users to be at the centre of assessment processes, making choices about what services they purchase to meet their needs, have more recently progressed through the introduction of direct payments, personalisation and personal budgets (DH, 2007, Manthorpe et al, 2010).

Commenting on these policies, Slasberg (2010) argues that despite the aspirations of these policies, in reality older people find it difficult to engage in these new processes limiting the potential for real change. The challenges of engagement with the new processes are potentially compounded for older people from minority ethnic communities who are more likely to experience poor health, exclusion from mainstream processes and lower economic status (Karlsen and Nazroo, 2010). Against this backdrop, a study that included Black African Caribbean older people was undertaken in a city in the north[1] of England to explore how developments in community care policies and services have had a practical impact on the choices and decision-making experiences of those seeking help (Tetley, 2007).

Setting up the research

As people have lived experiences that are multiple and complex, this research was guided by a constructivist and participatory methodology where a partnership between participants and researcher is argued to lead to greater mutual understandings (Guba and Lincoln, 1989; Lincoln and Guba, 1985; Lincoln, 2001). A mixed method approach was adopted using participant observation and interviews, and ethics approval was gained from an NHS ethics committee.

The study setting was a day centre/community support service for Black African Caribbean older people. The centre and the community outreach services were established by the Black African Caribbean community. Approximately 40 people normally attended the day service and a further 20 people received outreach support; of these, 25 agreed to the author taking notes of activities and conversations. From this initial phase of the study eight people were purposefully sampled for interview as their stories and experiences highlighted particular issues related to contemplating, using, refusing or ceasing to use particular services.

Learning about the decision-making processes

Older people from the Black and African Caribbean community identified three issues that had particularly influenced their decision-making processes when using or contemplating using health and social care services:

- aspirations for care
- means testing and assessment processes
- personal resilience and coping mechanisms.

Aspirations for care

Decision and choice-making processes were in part affected by the tensions between what services were able to offer and what the older person wanted. Some clients, such as Mrs North, were still receiving an ironing service arranged many years previously. However, service provision and contract arrangements with local social services had altered, and management found it complex to sustain this arrangement. The field notes recorded that:

> Mrs North was aware that the support team wanted to stop the ironing service but she ... was unable to iron herself because of back problems that were a result of a work-related injury. She explained that she was supported by her granddaughter, but she worked full-time and had her own family so was limited in the support that she could provide. Mrs North also told me that she didn't receive the attendance allowance and didn't see the point of applying for it as she didn't know anyone who she could pay to help her.

Mrs North's story revealed how some people will refuse certain benefits if they have limited social networks and cannot see how they can use the financial resource to purchase the help and support that would meet their own needs. This reflects the concerns of Slasberg (2010), who argues that many older people do not want to be responsible for managing budgets, or finding services and purchasing services, but instead want to have supported access to services that are responsive to their needs.

Mr Maxwell, a primary carer for his wife who appeared to be struggling at home, also attended the day centre. He said:

> 'Whatsoever is to be done, it's me who's got to do it. One of the times when I realise that it was a bit too much for me, I went round seeking help but couldn't get none, so I've got to still struggle with her. And then I went down here and asked, the most thing they want to do is shopping, and there's nothing much we want at shop but they just want to do shopping, they just want to spend the money.
>
> What they want is to get her, wash her, that's all and do shopping, but I can wash her and if anything the little bit that we want of shopping I can just jump in the car and go and buy it from Netto or Morrisons and come back. So a lot of those people what they say, is more they can do, but they cannot hoover and they don't allow to hoover nor do anything more.'

So while home care was available, the service they offered did not match his aspirations for help and he refused the care that was being offered. As a consequence Mr Maxwell felt that this has contributed to him becoming psychologically and physically ill:

> 'I was really broken down, really, really broken down, and then everything just built up on me and then it drove my blood pressure right up and my sugar was gone right up, through the worries and all those things coming back.'

The issue of service inflexibility has been reflected in the findings from the Joseph Rowntree Foundation Older People's Research Programme (JRF, 2004), which concluded that:

> There is a paradox of sorts in that older people may be offered a service they don't want while they cannot get access to a service that they do want. Sometimes the mismatch is in terms of agreeing or not agreeing with the assessment of need. But at other times it seems that resources are still locked up in services that don't do what people want or in service practices that don't meet people's needs. (p 37)

Reports on the traditional provision of community care for older people (JRF, 2004, 2005; new economics foundation, 2004; Wanless, 2006) have also concluded that home care services are an essential part of community care, but continue to struggle to meet people's expressed needs for care and support.

The lack of services to meet daily living needs, such as shopping, cleaning and gardening, that people regard as 'a little bit of help', is also highlighted as an important aspect of community care that needs rethinking (JRF, 2004). While direct payments, personalisation and personal budgets have been identified as a key way forward, there is concern that more community resources will have to be developed, so that the services that people want are available for them to access and purchase (Clarke et al, 2004; JRF, 2004; Slasberg, 2010).

Means testing and assessment processes

The older people in this study encountered several difficulties when they sought support or applied for services. Mr Smith had had a stroke and had limited mobility. He had applied for a stairlift to get to the bathroom upstairs, but found the financial assessment very intrusive. He described the assessment:

> '... [she] wanted to know how much money you have in the
> bank....I had to go to the bank and get bank statements ... to
> show them....Yeah.'

He later confirmed that this experience affected his decision making as
it had made him wary of seeking help in future outside of his immediate
family.

   In other instances people described how and why they had not applied
for benefits to which they were entitled. Mrs James at the day centre
explained how she became aware of attendance allowance but had not
completed the application form:

> 'Well a man, a gentleman came to me and said Nadine can
> claim for help for me, because she baths me. I said me daughter
> helps me and she wash me clothes and she does my cleaning
> and cleans the house for me.'

She went on to explain that, although her daughter provided a lot of care
and support, they did not complete the application form because of the
length and details required:

> 'She say she can't be bothered. She says too much complication
> and worry, she can't be doing it.'

People were also deterred from applying for services and benefits because,
to be eligible, they had to prove how disabled they were. Mrs Purdy had
been thinking of applying for aids and adaptations to help her get in and
out of the bath but was put off by the application form:

> '... the forms that they sent me just said you've got to be very
> disabled, and I'm not very disabled but I'm disabled, and I didn't
> bother with it and it's still at home there.'

The older people's experiences demonstrated how people may prefer to
continue struggling or getting by in preference to completing paperwork
or going through a detailed assessment process. These processes were
viewed as unfair and devalued their previous contributions to society.
While some people were prepared to persist and complete paperwork,
others just refused. If people did go through the process and found it
invasive or were refused support or benefits at the end of the process, this
was reported as a significant factor in deterring people from making future
applications for help and support. Understanding this is important as a

study of means-tested benefits, tax credits and pension reforms found that, despite attempts to improve uptake, many eligible pensioners still do not claim, resulting in 29 per cent of Black or Black British pensioners still living in poverty (House of Commons, 2009).

Personal resilience and coping mechanisms

While the decision-making processes were influenced in part by the nature and quality of assessment processes and service quality, the research also showed that personal resilience and individual coping mechanisms also appeared to influence people's decision-making processes. Resilience has been defined 'as a positive personality characteristic enhancing individual adaptation' (Wagnild, 2003, p 42), and this quality was seen in the interviews. Although participants were accessing some form of care or support service, being able to manage some aspects of their daily lives without help or support was often described as being particularly important. For example, Mrs Harris said:

> '… that's two things I'm glad for. I can cook a bit of dinner for myself and I can wash me clothes and keep myself clean.'

However, she went on to say that although she could manage some things, getting dressed and undressed was more difficult:

> 'Yes I can't I'm stiff. I can't get me tights or me knickers on. If you should be here to see me get my tights off. I just push it and struggle and get me tights off and go into bed.
> '… sometimes I can't I just sit there, sit there almost, I've got to make myself go because I have got no other way of doing it more than going. So it's not very easy for me but I've got to keep going, keep going, keep going, going that's all I've got to do, keep going.'

Mrs Harris also talked about the importance of her inner strength:

> '… one of the best things that you can do, when you are not very well, is to fight back, because if you don't fight back you've had it.'

Fighting was what kept Mrs Harris going:

'Yes! You don't feel like it but you have to do it, maybe if I
didn't fight back I would have turned good for nothing, we call
it Jamaican term – worthless.'

Her Christian faith also influenced her decision making and ability to cope
with ill health and life events. Indeed, her strength of mind and faith in
God gave her the will to keep going:

'But I took faith in the Lord and came out of it....'

Likewise Mrs James spoke about the importance of both her faith and the
devotion group that they held at the day centre. She described how at one
time in her life she had been unable to get out of bed, because she felt so
ill, but she prayed and God had helped her recover. As this comment shows
she engages in religious discussions with some of the other elders:

'... the most important things that we talk about the Lord, you
know we sit down and we talk about the Lord Jesus and tell
them about the holy commandment of the Lord, how the Lord
want us to live, loving with one another, kind with one another,
without, without Jesus we are nothing and I don't care me you
going to do, without God is in it, we aren't going nowhere, so
I always put God first, in this argument what we have in here
you don't put Jesus. You must put God first, that's what we learn
to put God first and then will God will make the way for you
... so that's what I do, you know all the day, you know I try to
love one another and I love you and I love everyone that come
in the centre here and we try to get on very well. And I feel
healthy.'

So although both women were receiving various forms of care and
support, their faith and inner strength also contributed to their ability to
cope and manage at home.

   The value and use of religious belief as something that can be drawn on
to help the older person cope with health-related problems is reinforced
by findings from other studies where older people with high support needs
and carers of partners with advanced HIV reported that where individuals
had a belief in God, this provided them with a positive form of emotion-
based coping (Bower, 1996; Folkman, 1997). However, while the Black
African Caribbean older people in this study identified that a belief in
God was positive and something that helped them maintain some degree
of independence from services, research has suggested that while minority

ethnic status limits health, the impact of religious faith to physical health differs across different religious groups (Karlsen and Nazroo, 2010). Karlsen and Nazroo (2010) therefore caution against the use of broad assumptions that religious faith has a universally positive impact on independence, health and well-being.

Conclusion

This research was conducted during a time of increasing interest in the development and provision of community services to support older people and family carers living in their own homes. The findings identified that mainstream health and social care services often failed to meet the needs of older people and their carers from the African Caribbean community because of a mismatch between individual aspirations for help and the nature of the service and support available. But is this a different experience from the majority White British older population? This question needs ongoing discussion. While older people across all ethnic groups may express concerns about the limited availability of low level support at home, the experiences of Black African Caribbean older people, as illustrated by Mrs North and Mr Maxwell, demonstrate how limited social networks and the increased likelihood of physical ill health compound issues of service mismatch and limit people's use of services.

Reports on the funding of health and social care have also recognised that means testing for services and benefits deters people from applying for services that would otherwise enable them to stay in their own homes for longer (Wittenberg et al, 2004; Wanless, 2006; Burke, 2008; DH, 2010). Personalisation may provide one solution to this issue, but its impact on service use in the Black African Caribbean community could be limited as the people in this study were not only deterred from applying for services by the assessment processes but also because they doubted their eligibility for support and funding.

This study further highlighted how specific decision and choice-making processes can be complex and not just related to issues of service provision. The use of emotional-based coping strategies was an unexpected but important finding, as this illustrated how people gained a sense of personal pride when they were able to manage practical difficulties. In light of these findings, if future services are to effectively meet the needs of Black African Caribbean older people there must be support from workers who recognise and can respond sensitively to cultural issues. However, as the work of Karlsen and Nazroo (2010) highlights, issues relevant to one minority ethnic community cannot simply be transferred to other minority ethnic communities.

There is continued recognition that for service reforms to make a positive impact on the specific communities they are serving there needs to be greater user participation and consultation in the development processes. While this study provides some insights into the factors that affected a recent cohort of Black African Caribbean older people, it should also be recognised that these older people were first generation Black African Caribbean migrants. As a result, the views of the participants in this study may not hold true for future cohorts of older people who identify themselves as Black African Caribbean.

Note

[1] Data from the 2001 Census, accessed through the Office for National Statistics, identified that this is an ethnically diverse city with over 15 per cent of the population identifying themselves as being from black and minority ethnic community backgrounds. These include Pakistani, Black Caribbean, Black African, Chinese Yemeni and Indian backgrounds.

References

Blakemore, K. (2000) 'Health and social care needs in minority communities: an over problematized issue?', *Health and Social Care in the Community*, vol 8, no 1, pp 22-30.

Bower, G. (1996) 'Relational resilience: a new perspective for understanding the elderly person's relationship to the notion of God', *Journal of Geriatric Psychiatry*, vol 29, no 1, pp 83-104.

Bowes, A. (2006) 'Mainstreaming equality: implications of the provision of support at home for majority and minority ethnic older people', *Social Policy & Administration*, vol 40, no 7, pp 739-57.

Burke, S. (2008) 'Who will pay for better care?', *The Political Quarterly*, vol 79, no 4, pp 628-36.

Clarke, H., Gough, H. and Macfarlane, A. (2004) *'It pays dividends': Direct payments and older people*, York: Joseph Rowntree Foundation.

Cowen, H. (1999) *Community care, ideology and social policy*, London: Prentice Hall.

DH (Department of Health) (2007) *Putting People First*, London: DH.

DH (2010) *A vision for adult social care: Capable communities and active citizens*, London: DH.

Folkman, S. (1997) 'Positive psychological states and coping with severe stress', *Social Science and Medicine*, vol 45, pp 1207-21.

Gilleard, C. and Higgs, P. (1998) 'Older people as users and consumers of health care: a third age rhetoric for a fourth age reality', *Ageing & Society*, vol 18, no 2, pp 233-48.

Guba, E.G. and Lincoln, Y.S. (1989) *Fourth generation evaluation*, Newbury Park, CA: Sage Publications.

House of Commons (2009) *Tackling pensioner poverty. Fifth report of Session 2008-09*, London: The Stationery Office.

JRF (Joseph Rowntree Foundation) (2004) *From welfare to well-being: Planning for an ageing society*, York: JRF.

JRF (2005) *The Older People's Inquiry: 'That little bit of help'*, York: JRF.

Karlsen, S. and Nazroo, J.S. (2010) 'Religious and ethnic differences in health: evidence from the Health Surveys for England 1999 and 2004', *Ethnicity & Health*, vol 15, no 6, pp 549-68.

Lievesley, N. (2010) *The future ageing of the ethnic minority population of England and Wales*, London: Runnymede Trust/Centre for Policy on Ageing.

Lincoln, Y.S. (2001) 'Engaging sympathies: relationships between action research and social constructionism', in P. Reason and H. Bradbury (eds) *Handbook of action research*, London: Sage Publications, pp 124-32.

Lincoln, Y.S. and Guba, E.G. (1985) *Naturalistic inquiry*, Beverley Hills, CA: Sage Publications.

Manthorpe, J., Kharicha, K., Goodman, C., Harari, D., Swift, C. and Iliffe, S. (2010) 'Smarter working in social and health care: professional perspectives on a new technology for risk appraisal with older people', *British Journal of Social Work*, vol 40, pp 1829-46.

Nazroo, J. (2003) 'The structuring of ethnic inequalities in health: economic position, racial discrimination, and racism', *American Journal of Public Health*, vol 93, no 2, pp 277-84.

nef (new economics foundation) (2004) *A well-being manifesto for a flourishing society*, London: nef.

ONS (Office for National Statistics) (2008) *Population Trends 134*, Houndmills: Palgrave Macmillan.

Peckham, S. and Meerabeau, E. (2007) *Social policy for nurses and the helping professions* (2nd edn), Maidenhead: Open University Press.

Slasberg, C. (2010) 'Can personalisation be a reality for older people?', *Working with Older People*, vol 14, no 3, pp 15-22.

Tetley, J. (2007) 'Older people's decision-making about the use of health and social care services: a constructivist inquiry', Unpublished PhD thesis, University of Sheffield.

Toofany, S. (2006) 'Cultural competencies', *Nursing Older People*, vol 18, no 7, pp 14-18.

Wagnild, G. (2003) 'Resilience and successful aging: comparison among low and high income older adults', *Journal of Gerontological Nursing*, vol 29, no 12, pp 42-9.

Wanless, D. (2006) *Wanless social care review. Securing good care for older people: Taking a long-term view*, London: The King's Fund.

Wittenberg, R., Comas-Herrera, A. and Pickard, L. (2004) *Future demands for long-term care in the UK: A summary of projections of long-term care finance for older people*, York: Joseph Rowntree Foundation.

18

'Exclusion is necessary': excluding people from society

Daniel Dorling

Extract from *Injustice: Why social inequality persists* (2010) Bristol: The Policy Press.

Just as the post-Second World War surfeit of resources in affluent nations was initially directed at targets such as eliminating ignorance, but came through time to be focused more on education spending in support of elitism, so the old social evil of want, of poverty, of having too little, was initially the direct target of spending in many postwar states. Additional resources for extra personal expenditure, social security benefits, were initially aimed at the elimination of want, but then, when the worst of want was seen to have been eliminated, public monies, redistribution and state attention moved elsewhere in a way that supported growing exclusion. Tax rates were reduced for the rich, benefit levels tagged to inflation (or less) for the poorest. The income of the rich moved away from that of average earners, who in turn saw their incomes increase faster than those on welfare benefits. The initial compressing (reducing the spread) of income distributions that came with the introduction of social security in many affluent nations, and the taxation needed to fund it, was removed most quickly in those countries which began to choose to become most unequal. High social security spending was not essential for high levels of social inclusion, but low levels of income inequality were. Thus relatively few people would describe themselves as poor and needing to take out loans just to get by in countries as diverse as Japan and the Netherlands, whereas in Britain and the US relative rates of poverty have grown greatly in recent decades, simply because inequality has grown.[1]

Poverty that mostly results from inequality comes in the form of a new kind of exclusion: exclusion from the lives, the understanding and the caring of others. This is now not through having to live in abject poverty, but through social norms becoming stretched out along such a wide continuum, as most additional income becomes awarded to the most affluent, more of that left to the next most affluent and so on. The elimination of the worst of early 20th-century poverty, coupled with the tales of elitists who believed that those who were poorer were inferior, reduced the power of argument of groups that had previously succeeded in bringing down inequalities in resources between families and classes within many affluent societies. It is slowly becoming clear that growing financial inequality results in large and slowly growing numbers of people being excluded from the norms of society, and creates an expanding and increasingly differentiated social class suffering a new kind of poverty: the new poor, the indebted, the excluded.

The new poor (by various means of counting) now constitute at least a sixth of households in countries like Britain. However, these are very different kinds of households from those who lived through immediate postwar poverty. What the poor mostly had in common by the end of the 20th century were debts they could not easily handle, debts that they could not avoid acquiring and debts that were almost impossible to escape from. Just a short step above the poor in the status hierarchy, fewer and fewer were living average 'normal' lives. The numbers of those who had a little wealth had also increased. Above the just-wealthy the numbers who were so well off they could afford to exclude themselves from social norms were hardly growing, although their wealth was growing greatly. This wealth was ultimately derived from such practices as indirectly lending money to the poor at rates of interest many of the poor could never afford to fully repay.

Indebted: those most harmed by exclusion, a sixth of all people

There are many ways of defining a person or household as poor in a rich society. All sensible ways relate to social norms and expectations, but because the expectations as to what it is reasonable to possess have diverged under rising inequality, poverty definitions have become increasingly contentious over time. In the most unequal of large affluent nations, the US, it is very hard to define people as poor as so many have been taught to define 'the poor' as those who do not try hard enough not to be poor.[2] Similarly, growing elitism has increased support for arguments that blame the poor for their poverty due to their apparent inadequacies, and there has been growing support for turning the definition of the poor into being 'that group which is unable or unwilling to try hard enough'.

The suggestion that at least a sixth of people live in poverty in some affluent nations results from arguments made in cross-country comparisons which suggest that a robust way of defining people as poor is to say that they are poor if they appear poor on at least two out of three different measures.[3] These three measures are: first, do the people concerned (subjectively) describe themselves as poor? Second, do they lack what is needed (necessities) to be included in society as generally understood by people in their country? Third, are they income-poor as commonly understood (low income)? It is currently solely through low income that poverty is officially defined, in Europe in relative terms and within the US in absolute terms. A household can have a low income but not be otherwise poor, as in the case of pensioners who have accrued savings that they can draw on. Similarly a household can have an income over the poverty threshold but be unable to afford to pay for the things seen as essential by most people, such as a holiday for themselves and their children once a year, or Christmas presents or a birthday party, the kind of presents and party that will not show them up. A family that cannot afford such things is likely to be expenditure- (or necessities-)poor and very likely to feel subjectively poor even if just above the official income poverty line.

[...]

Necessities, worries and strife

In Britain, by the start of the 21st century almost as many households were poor because they lacked the necessities required to be socially included and because their constituent members knew they were poor (5.5%), as were poor because they fell into all three poverty categories (5.6%). When the population was surveyed as to what items were necessities and what were luxuries, the two key essential expenditures that the current poverty line pivoted on were, first, an ability to make small savings each month (£10 in the case of Britain); and, second, to be able have an annual holiday away from home and the wider family. These were the two items that a majority of people in Britain thought others should, as a minimum, be able to afford and which the largest numbers could not afford.[4]

The injustice of social exclusion had, by the 21st century, debt at its heart in place of the joblessness, destitution and old age that were the key drivers of 'want' when today's pensioners were born. It is now debt that prevents most poor people from being able to afford necessities – you cannot save each month if you have debts to pay off and holidays are affordable to almost anyone except those with too much unsecured debt. As debt grew in importance over time, the link between low income and low expenditure on necessities weakened slightly, with the smallest overlap in Figure 18.1 being between those two poverty measures. This is because low income does not initially prevent the purchase of necessities if there is access to debt.

In countries where inequality is higher, debts are accrued to pay for holidays, and to allow the newly income-poor, those who lose their jobs, divorce or see their spouse die, to be (for a little while at least) less expenditure-poor. The effect in Britain of the increased necessity of falling back on debt and of keeping up appearances, in what has become one of the most unequal countries in Western Europe, was that half of the mountain of all credit card debt in all of Western Europe was held solely by British citizens by 2006.[5] A not insignificant proportion of that debt had been amassed to finance going on holiday. People were taking holidays more than ever before, because in Britain being able to take a holiday had become the marker of social acceptability, just as being able to wear a suit to church had been in a previous era, and just as being able to afford to run a car if you had children became a social norm not long after that. In the US another significant purchase, a second car for a family of four or more, serves the same purpose of establishing yourself as someone currently coping rather than not. It is not the object itself, but what it signifies and makes possible that matters. The US built suburbs without pavements. The UK built up the idea that those who worked hard would be rewarded with holidays. [...]

Figure 18.1: Proportion of households poor by different measures (%), Britain, 1999

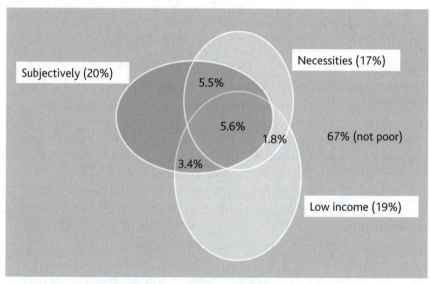

Note: The sixth who are poor on at least two criteria are shown in the areas with percentages labelled in them (5.5%+3.4%+1.8%+5.6%=16.3%, and 67%=100%−16%−6%−4%−7%).

Source: Drawn from figures given in table 6 of the original study: Bradshaw, J. and Finch, N. (2003) 'Overlaps in dimensions of poverty', *Journal of Social Policy*, vol 32, no 4, pp 513-25.

Holidays matter now in most rich countries because they have become such a clear marker separating those who are just getting by from those who are doing all right from those who are doing well or very well. 'Where did you go on holiday?' is now an extremely intimate question to ask of another adult; the answers divide parents picking up children from school into groups; they divide work colleagues into camps; they divide pensioners by their employment history as it is that history that determines their pensions and hence their holidays.

[...]

In an age where holidays are common people mostly take holidays because other people take holidays. It has become an expectation, and as a result holiday making in affluent countries is remarkably similar within each country as compared to between countries. Most people in Japan take only a few days' holiday a year, but household working weeks and working lives are not excessively long. In contrast, the two-week 'summer holiday' and one-week 'winter break' have become standard in parts of Europe. In contrast again, only minimal holidays are common in the US where holiday pay is still rare. Everyone needs a rest, but whether that rest comes in the form of an annual holiday depends on when and where you are. Holidays became the marker of social inclusion in affluent European societies by the start of the current century because they were the marginal item in virtual shopping baskets, that commodity which could be afforded if there was money to spare, but which had to be forgone in hard times.

Safeguarding social standing

In any society with even the slightest surplus there is always a marginal commodity. It has been through observing behaviour historically in relation to those marginal commodities that the unwritten rules of societies were initially unravelled. The necessity of having furniture, televisions, cars and holidays came long after it was observed that workers needed good quality shirts and shoes (recognised in 1759), that in order to have self-respect they should not to have to live in a 'hovel' (observed by 1847), and that it was not unreasonable to ask to be able to afford a postage stamp (at least by 1901).[8] Mill-loom woven shirts, brick-built terraced houses, postage stamps, all became necessities less than a lifetime after the mass production of looms and large-scale brick making and the introduction of the Penny Post in Britain and equivalents in many similar countries. Within just one more lifetime, the mechanisation of looms, automation of brick making and (partly) of letter sorting had made shirts, brick-built homes and postage stamps parts of life that all could enjoy, no longer marginal items that the poor had to go without. Slowly a pattern was emerging.

Towards the end of the Second World War it was becoming clear to those studying (male-dominated) society that the '... outstanding discovery of recent historical and anthropological research is that man's economy, as a rule, is submerged in his social relationships. He does not act so as to safeguard his individual interest in the possession of material goods; he acts so as to safeguard his social standing, his social claims, his social assets'.[9]

However, what was far from clear in 1944 was in what ways, as men's (and then women's) individual interests in material goods, their basic needs, were better met, would people need to act differently to maintain their social standing. Pecking orders and rank do not simply disappear in an abundance of goods. For men, social standing had largely been secured through earning enough to safeguard their family, enough to be able to afford to put a good shirt on their own back, enough to feel they were not living in a hovel. Occasionally a man might have spent the excess on trinkets such as a postage stamp for a letter to a lover, and much more often beer, the poorest of men and women drinking themselves to death on gin. However, from the 1960s onwards those times began to fade in memory, as mass consumption followed mass production.

Mass consumption often consists of what appear to be trinkets and trivia, of more clothes than people possibly need, no longer one good linen shirt, or of more shoes than can easily be stored, no longer just one good pair, of houses with more rooms than can easily be kept clean, and in place of that postage stamp, junk mail. However, trinkets, trivia and fecklessness only appear as such to those not over-purchasing or over-consuming. From the trading of shells in ancient Polynesian societies, to curvier cars in 1950s America, we have long purchased with our social status foremost in mind.

Trinkets have always held great social importance and mechanisation did not decrease this. Mass-produced trinkets, such as jewellery in place of shells, and production-line cars, and their purchasing, wearing and driving, soon came to no longer signify high standing; that requires scarcity. Mass-produced goods soon become necessities, and after that are simply taken for granted. In Europe in 1950 to be without a car was normal; 50 years later it is a marker of poverty. In Europe in 1950 most people did not take a holiday; 50 years later not taking a holiday has become a marker of poverty (and holidays can now easily cost more than second-hand cars).

Most of the increase in debt that has occurred since the 1950s has been accrued by people in work. Of those debts not secured on property (mortgages), most have been accrued by people in low-paid work. Work alone no longer confers enough status and respect, not if it is poorly paid. People working on poverty wages (in Europe three fifths of national median wages) tend to be most commonly employed in the private sector, then in the voluntary sector, and most rarely in the state sector.[10] The private sector pays higher (on arithmetical but not median average) because those in charge of themselves with little accountability to others tend to pay themselves very well, and by doing so reinforce the idea that the more valuable a person you are the more money you should have. The state sector pays its managers less because there is a little more self-control levied when accountability is greater. In the absence of accountability people in the state sector are just as capable of transgressing, as state-employed members of the UK Parliament illustrated when many of their actions were revealed in the expenses scandal of 2008/09. What they bought with those expenses illustrated what they had come to see as acceptable purchases in an age of high and rising inequality. The voluntary sector is a mix of these two extremes. God or the charity commissioners might be omnipresent in theory, but in practice he/she/they are not spending government money. In all sectors if you find yourself at the bottom of each pyramid, and the pyramids are being elongated upwards (to slowly look more like upside-down parsnips than ancient tombs), to then value your intrinsic self when others are so materialistic requires either great and unusual tenacity, or borrowing just a little extra money to supplement your pay. You borrow it to buy things which others like you have because 'you're worth it', and you want to believe you are like them, not inferior to them.

[...]

Notes

[1] Wilkinson, R.G. and Pickett, K. (2009) *The spirit level: Why more equal societies almost always do better*, London: Allen Lane, p 143.

[2] Alesina, A., Tella, R.D. and MacCulloch, R. (2004) 'Inequality and happiness: are Europeans and Americans different?', *Journal of Public Economics*, vol 88, pp 2009-42.

[3] Wolff, J. and de-Shalit, A. (2007) *Disadvantage*, Oxford: Oxford University Press, p 110, using arguments from Bradshaw, J. and Finch, N. (2003) 'Overlaps in dimensions of poverty', *Journal of Social Policy*, vol 32, no 4, pp 513-25.

[4] Dorling, D., Rigby, J., Wheeler, B., Ballas, D., Thomas, B., Fahmy, E., Gordon, D. and Lupton, R (2007) *Poverty, wealth and place in Britain, 1968 to 2005*, Bristol: The Policy Press.

[5] Irvin, G. (2008) *Super rich: The rise of inequality in Britain and the United States*, Cambridge: Polity Press, p 189. A fifth of the entire population had outstanding debt on credit cards by 2007; they were no longer a middle-class-only niche: ONS (Office for National Statistics) (2008) *Wealth and Assets Survey: Initial report*, London: ONS.

[8] In 1759 Adam Smith wrote about the linen shirt and shoes and has been endlessly quoted thereafter. In 1847 Karl Marx wrote on how homes would appear as hovels if a castle was built nearby. In 1901 Seebohm Rowntree wrote on the necessity of being able to afford a stamp to write a letter to a loved one.

[9] Karl Polanyi's writing of 1944 quoted in Magdoff, H. and Magdoff, F. (2005) 'Approaching socialism', *Monthly Review*, vol 57, no 3.

[10] Almond, S. and Kendall, J. (2001) 'Low pay in the UK: the case for a three sector comparative approach', *Annals of Public and Cooperative Economics*, vol 72, no 1, pp 45–76, at p 45.

Have I done enough?

Ros Coward

Extract from *The Guardian*, 18 October 2008. Copyright Guardian News & Media Ltd 2008.

... It's Mum's birthday and I'm not spending it with her. I'm away. In Amsterdam, in fact. This is the first time for many years that I haven't been with her on her birthday. I ring before leaving to say sorry that I won't be with her to celebrate her 84th birthday. "Is it my birthday?" She says. "Oh well. I'm not bothered about that stuff. I'm all discombobulated."

Although it feels strange not to be with her, I am also relieved. It's a time to get away and take stock: of Mum's care, of my exhaustion and my decision to finish the column, which I've been writing since January 2007.

My exhaustion is not physical, because others are now taking on more of Mum's care – my brother and sister, and her grandchildren. My exhaustion is mental, the result of the parallel existence that has to be lived trying to keep someone with dementia relatively independent – the organising and paying of carers, the endless appointments, the worrying about Mum's shopping and supplies, dealing with emergencies and, of course, wondering when the next one will strike.

... Over the past two years I've become increasingly aware how little the medical profession and social services recognise the reality of looking after people with dementia. I've been with doctors who insist on talking only to Mum, giving her complicated instructions that she'll never follow. I've witnessed hospitals treating Mum as if she is just a collection of different ailments all requiring endless follow-up appointments, which it is assumed she will travel to herself. I've seen the way that there is no coordination or continuity of her care. Most strikingly, I've witnessed what sometimes feels like a convenient blindness as to just how much goes into keeping a dementia sufferer afloat in her own home, what they call "coping reasonably well independently".

So I need a break. But once away in Amsterdam, I'm assailed by sadness. It's Mum's enthusiasms that keep waylaying me. We're walking in the Hortus Botanicus and all I can think of is how, with her enthusiasm for plants and gardens, she would have loved to be here. Hers has never been the sort of enthusiasm of the doughty ladies who appear on Gardeners' World strolling round beautifully tended grounds identifying plants by their Latin names. Mum has lived most of her adult life in a council flat with a small balcony. But she was always passionate about plants and greenery and nature, and had a strong eye for design...

Later in Amsterdam, we go to the Van Gogh museum. He was never one of her favourites but again it's Mum who immediately comes to mind, with the passions she had at one time for drawing and, latterly, art. Like many things she did, her drawing was untutored, but she was naturally able – "teachable", as my artist friend would say. She used to sketch branches, trees and flowers so it's Van Gogh's rather Japanese blossom paintings that remind me of her.

I buy her a print to take back, but what I really want is for her to be here, for her to be able to enjoy it. Why did I never make the time to bring her? Sadly, Mum never had any confidence – in her intuition, her abilities, her tastes or herself. When we were young, she was always ashamed of our small flat and discouraged us from bringing our "posh friends" home. We stayed crammed into this flat even through adolescence with tensions between my parents and us children seething and erupting mainly because my father – prescient man – thought that mortgages were "immoral". But Mum hated it and hated domesticity and railed against her fate. "You can't bring them back to this pigsty," she would say, usually in my father's hearing, as a dig at what she felt were his failures.

I've long ceased to dwell on those difficulties and have come to appreciate her extraordinary spirit. What she lacked as a mother she more than made up for as a grandmother. Not through gifts, but by "being there", offering to take them out, riding the front of buses, taking them to galleries, never judging through adolescent excesses. In return, they all adore her. For all its terrible problems, what this period of dementia ... has given me is a chance to process ambivalent feeling and old resentments, something denied to people who lose their parents suddenly. It's like a long, slow goodbye.

In spite of beautiful weather in Amsterdam, it's the sadness that clings. Everything reminds me of her. I buy bulbs thinking that I'll plant some for her balcony and then wonder, where will she be next spring? I want so much to take her to places like this and now I'll never have that chance.

... the person I want to remember is that one, with her enthusiasms and energy, raising her glass to life, greeting most things with "Oh sooper."

Already it's becoming difficult. It's as if someone has taken a rubber and smudged the edges off her. So much is about health and illness now, about tussles with the NHS, the horrors in which Mum and her sharp humour find ever fewer opportunities to shine. I feel I've been able to pay Mum tribute not as someone pathetically dependent and old but still with her sharpness intact, and her free spirit, still somehow outfoxing the patronage of the medical institutions and, even in the havoc her condition brings, causing laughter. But if I am to remain truthful, the coming hardships may strip her of this. I want to leave it where, as one reader kindly said, there is still joy among the sadness.

If I continued [writing a regular column], it would be increasingly with the indignities and decline. Mum herself does not really seem to mind. "No, no," she said the other night, "write what you like. I'd like to find out about myself." But not everyone in my family has seen it that way and I've met some opposition for "invading her privacy". I know there are greater difficulties ahead, decisions we will have to take about how she is looked after, how we deal with decline, and sadly there will probably be more family conflict. While I genuinely believe it has been, and would continue to be, a good thing to explore this publicly – because these issues affect so many people now – simultaneously I know that to continue would not leave open the possibility of healing family division.

Writing this column, I've realised that there is a taboo about being explicit about the process of ageing. This is not so much about death, but about the disintegration, decay and indignities of ageing and the shifts in dependency that come with it. Ageing may be a perfectly natural process, but somehow detailing these changes, and the care needed, is seen as "shaming" the person involved, robbing them of their personhood. It can rub off on the writer. I think some people are so horrified by the process that they would rather not have to think about it.

In the mid 1980s, when my children were born, I remember the late Angela Carter advising me in typically flamboyant terms never to let newspaper editors hear the children in the background. If they knew I was distracted by caring for children they wouldn't take me seriously. Well, feminism, including Angela herself, changed those attitudes, but not attitudes towards that other caring that goes on unseen, the care for elderly parents. I've sat through several work meetings recently where men have left early. "I have to pick up the children on Tuesdays," they say, striding out with an aura of being "good dads". I wait to the end. How would it go down if I said, "I need to get over to my old mother's to check she's had her tea"?

It will take another revolution like feminism to make society accept that this is something that can't be hidden away, needing as much respect and support as childcare. I know from the large amount of correspondence that vast numbers are affected by this, people who are struggling with the lack of coordinated support for them as carers and the lack of recognition of the needs of the elderly, especially the increasing numbers of those with Alzheimer's and dementia.

I've also learned from readers' emails that the seeds of change are there. I've been told about support networks such as the Alzheimer's Association, about new research into caring for dementia. But there's a long way to go before this awareness becomes so powerful that it changes social attitudes and provision. As one reader wrote to me about fighting for improvements to her mother's treatment, "I'm doing this not for my mother but because this is the fate that awaits all of us."

... The birthday present I've left her turns out to be strangely apposite. Earlier in the year at the Chelsea Flower Show I had bought various things bearing this year's insignia – tulips. Not so long ago, before her dementia, Mum had come to Chelsea with me, my partner, John, and my friend Lee. At one point, in true Chelsea style, it poured with rain and we found ourselves sitting watching a brass band playing with rain dripping into our Pimm's, dressed in giveaway macs. We laughed so much at the daftness of it all that we were hysterical, and no one more than Mum.

When I ring her from Amsterdam I ask her whether she likes the present from Chelsea and whether it brings back memories of that day. But she doesn't seem to have registered the presents at all. "Well, there's such a big heap here it might have got lost."

"Really?" I say and I'm wondering if I'm jealous.

"No," she says. "I'm being sarcastic."

So although we spend her birthday apart, she's on my mind. I feel sad, free, torn. I'm sad I didn't do those things with her I always thought I would one day. I wonder if I have done enough. Happy birthday, Mum.

Going the distance: a family journey after acute stroke

Julia

Two years ago on an ordinary Tuesday morning, my husband James tumbled down the last few steps of our stairs and slumped unconscious on the hall floor. I knew it was serious (but not *how*). Part of me had feared a heart-attack or a stroke as a man like James with high blood-pressure, high cholesterol and a high-five attitude to alcohol is hardly in rude health.

My 999 call was calm and almost immediate, a paramedic arrived by car within minutes – followed by two more in an ambulance minutes later and, within an hour, a helicopter was waiting in the local football field. The general clatter had woken our two boys – and, to keep them occupied, I sent them off to get dressed in their school uniforms. Meanwhile I was told by the tallest if not the most senior paramedic that it seemed to be "something cerebral" (a stroke I thought .. hopefully not too bad ..they can do so much...) But the bigger shock was the advice not to send the children to school – to bring them with me to the specialist hospital (50 miles away) ... and that the boys should say goodbye to their Daddy before the ambulance whisked him off to the helicopter.

The "goodbye" advice was a bit too much – it dawned on me that James might die. I locked myself in the bathroom to cry – only for a moment and very quietly – then pulled myself together. Composed Mum made sure the boys kissed Daddy and we all waved him off on his helicopter flight. I even managed to 'phone work (James' and mine) – and the boys' schools before setting off in the car.

By the time we arrived at the hospital (long after the helicopter) James was still unconscious, hooked up to an array of machines and tubes looking grey – but still with us. The Head of Emergency care offered the option of giving me news alone or with the children. We decided together – we all sat down to hear what was what. (I am so glad we did this *together* – we were a team.) The Doctor was extremely clear and kindly so – Dad had had a stroke a blood clot – probably doing its worst over some days. Was that why Dad had a dreadful headache on Sunday? – Yes possibly – but NO, they couldn't do anything about the clot – too late (no fabulous thrombolytic drugs then … my heart sank a bit). We heard the word infarct for the first time; we were able to ask questions; we saw the scans which indicated a very extensive area of the left brain essentially dead. The left side, we were told, governed right side movement – and also speech, language and expression; communication looked like being the biggest challenge.. but it was too early to say. The next 48 hours would be critical; Dad would be monitored in Medical Assessment – and hopefully moved to the acute stroke ward for treatment. And, privately.. in the corridor, the kindly Doctor said to me alone, "It's about as bad as it can be"….

I sat with James in Medical Assessment – talking, reassuring, praying. Each time new nurses, doctors approached I went through a litany of – this is my husband, James, he's 48 years old; I love him , our children love him and they need their Dad. I thought if I let them know how he was loved they would fight all the harder for him.

James made it through those critical few days – into acute stroke care (four months) and residential rehab (just two months). In acute care he was a star – one of the youngest patients, one with a beautiful smile and one with regular visitors, cards and greetings. He hated the rehab "home" – physio was first class, but he wasn't getting anything like the speech therapy he needed (one of the SALT[1] team on maternity leave – no cover) – he wasn't socialising (how could he – he was hardly able to talk – but no-one seemed to make an effort) – he hated the food – and he wanted a beer! After two months, he was discharged home to family life – but not as we knew it.

You'd think home-coming would be such a celebration. We'd had many a mini party with family and friends each weekend James came home from hospital or rehab … But home for ever? And at such short notice? I have never seen my older son so angry. Dad can't come home – 'he's not well – he can't talk – he doesn't understand us – he's not better yet. My younger one, who had been unfailingly positive and cheerful thus far was clearly shaken (and remains so). They both saw the stroke as an illness from which their Dad would recover – they knew it could be a long haul – but he *would*

---

[1]   SALT Speech and Language Therapy

be well again. For them the home-coming was a bewildering defeat. It was frightening and overwhelming for me too – what are we going to do now?

Despite the number of different professionals working with James – doctors, nurses, physiotherapists, occupational therapists, speech and language therapists and even psychologists and social workers – our family felt ill-prepared for adjusting to life with a needy, disabled, frustrated man in place of my husband – in place of a loving Dad.

My fear for the future was sky-high – could James be left alone? Would I be able to carry on work? How are we going to manage physically, financially and in every other way? But along side my fear, I knew that we, as a family, had to take over – it was our job now to love, support and encourage – this was a long, journey for all of us.

Two years on – it's less bewildering, some of us are less angry (I am). My younger son is still finding it tough – his whole outlook on life is coloured by his Dad's stroke – ("*I want my Dad back*"). It's affected his school life and his friendships (one of his friends described James as "creepy" ... I despair).

More positively, James can walk (hurrah!) – but not long distances. He hasn't recovered full use of his right arm ("learned non-use") – we keep trying to encourage him. The biggest challenge of all is communication – a normal conversation is impossible. We try to take pleasure in every new word James says; we talk with words, pictures, writing and gestures – we even sing songs together. (James can sing more words in a song than he could ever say.) Occasionally James' frustration and rage boils over (and that is frightening) – we're all adjusting.

Most of the time I feel exhausted – I've gone from being a wife and mother of two to single mother/carer for *three* boys – one of which is James, being particularly challenging – the other two being more needy than ever. My biggest fear now isn't James' staying power – it's will I be able to go the distance?

PART II

Transforming adulthood

Introduction

In this part of the reader, the principle of human rights is the foreground for examining the potential to transform adulthood. It focuses on some of the challenges and realities of practising and using health and social care services and how these can have an impact on policy making in a national and international context.

'What is the nature of the problem?' **Peter Townsend** suggested that a body of thought, which could be characterised as 'acquiescent functionalism', attributed the causes of the problems of old age to the natural consequences of physical decrescence and mental inflexibility. In answer to his question, this is institutional ageism and has contributed to 'structured dependency'. This dependency of older people on the state and other institutions is created in market, residential and hospital care, private and public social care policies. Townsend argued that a new analytical framework – based on the European Convention on Human Rights – has rapidly evolved, offering hope of breaking down blanket discrimination and of using resources more appropriately in a society where things are still going depressingly wrong.

Drawing on the tragic death of Mayan Coomeraswamy, **Tim Spencer-Lane** argues that the starting point for practitioners in determining an appropriate balance between individual autonomy and protection is the European Convention on Human Rights. He discusses how a range of law exists to help and protect people who neglect themselves but demonstrates the complexity of the need to intervene by ending with a quote from Lord Justice Mundby, 'What good is it making someone safer if it merely makes them miserable?'. **Gordon Grant** suggests that adopting a life course approach to safeguarding requires an understanding of the contexts in which abuse and neglect arise. He argues that it is important to recognise the shift from seeking to 'explain' abuse as a by-product of pathologies to an approach rooted in human rights in relation to life course perspectives.

Moving the debate forward to consider aspects of practice in relation to health and social care, Section 5 begins with **Janet Bardsley** debating the question 'Why collaborate?'. She suggests that the feedback and views of people who may be in need of support, and which is fundamental to the principle of the notion of person–centred health and social care, is the primary reason for joint working between and within organisations. Continuing with the holistic theme of seeing people as a whole, **Geraldine Crewes** examines the realities of working within teams, raising questions about what this means in practice and how the complex interplay between internal and external dynamics shapes how teams function.

Two quite different perspectives highlight the complexity and challenges of being in practice in health and social care. First, **Gillian Woolhead and colleagues'** cross-European study explores older Europeans' experiences of dignity in relation to receiving health and social care and contrasts these findings with the views of health and social care professionals. Their study highlights how, despite being aware of good communication practices – for example, use of appropriate forms of address, listening, giving people choice, respecting their autonomy, rights for privacy and politeness and enabling them to feel valued – professionals often fail to apply these. Second, **Ian Buchanan** uses the case of Maria and her family to highlight how assessment of adults – their eligibility and suitability – for the purposes of receiving health and social care is illustrative of a complex and contested process despite the aim of creating a single process.

Beyond the specifics of practice, Section 6 broadens the arena to include not only an international dimension but also how this has an impact on social policy. **Sandy Sieminski** argues that one positive aspect of globalisation is that it has created opportunities for sharing ideas about policy and practice issues which can lead to better understanding of people's needs in relation to health and social care. Equally one of the challenges of globalisation is meeting these needs adequately, and **Geraldine Lee-Treweek** raises some of the issues in relation to adult vulnerability by examining the 'real world' examples of migrants. She sends a clear signal to policy makers, practitioners and the public of the necessity to understand adult vulnerability in the context of a person's home country and culture, demonstrating how a person's needs in this respect are not always visible. The assumption that all adults have rights and, crucially, can deploy these rights, reveals one example of where the hope of 'breaking down blanket discrimination and of using resources more appropriately in a society' falls through the cracks.

The next two chapters identify issues central to understanding governance and inequality. **Charlotte Williams and Gerry Mooney** use *devolution* to open up the debate for 'theorising' within the discipline of social policy. They argue that a new discursive terrain is emerging through recognising the ways in which devolution is intertwined with the creation of a new social topography that reflects, for example, territorial politics, inequalities and entitlements and issues of social justice and citizenship on a UK-wide basis. In his analysis of the intellectual origins of *social capital*, **Andrew Gibson** notes that in most developed countries health inequalities have not decreased despite rising national wealth (as measured by increasing gross national product [GNP] per capita). He suggests that this has provoked discussion of how social factors other than material deprivation may affect health outcomes.

Finally, this section returns to the impact that political ideology, philosophical differences and actions may have for people as they age and for people with mental health needs. First, health and social provision for older people in Cuba is a consequence of the Cuban policy commitment to healthcare being free and a human right and the responsibility of the state, with volunteerism playing a central role. **Elizabeth Bertera** suggests that Cuba continues to be unique in how its model of healthcare involves moral rather than material exchanges and reciprocities. Respect for older people is taught through intergenerational programmes in schools and as such, being old is not seen as anything to be ashamed of. In contrast, **Minichiello and colleagues** writing in Australia suggest that although various forms of stereotyping and discrimination may have an impact on the lives of older people, the language used in the gerontological literature to talk about how older people are treated and perceived is not necessarily understood and used by all older people. They suggest that some groups of older people are challenging stereotypical notions of older people by focusing on ageism, advocating more positive images of ageing, and in this sense they are making their own contribution to transforming the image of older people and creating a politically correct agenda. 'I know I look older, but I don't feel old. I haven't arrived at the feeling of feeling old' (Mrs Smith, quoted in Minichiello et al, 2011 in this volume, p335).

Finally, **David Pilgrim** examines the complexities of mental health in a global context, suggesting that most of the contention about mental health issues stem from philosophical differences and empirical claims. Crucially, he argues, the point is not to prove or disprove any particular viewpoint but in a postmodern context, and in transforming adulthood, we might want to proceed with caution when thinking about the desirability of 'mental health interventions'.

SECTION FOUR

Human rights and the life course

19

Using human rights to defeat ageism

Peter Townsend

Extract from *The Peter Townsend Reader* (2010) Bristol: The Policy Press.

[...] This chapter, initially prepared to celebrate many years' work of British social gerontologists, provides an excellent opportunity to stand back and assess the 'big picture' and to review not only previously influential ideas, but also ideas that may not yet have found a place in the sun.

Rise of social development policy

What is the nature of the problem? The volume of research studies, pamphlets and media programmes about the maltreatment of older people grew steadily after the war of 1939-45. A number of social and economic historians (see, for example, Macnicol and Blaikie, 1989) have traced the commissioning of surveys explicitly on old age, the emergence of geriatric medicine after the inauguration of the NHS, the looming prospects of population ageing and so-called 'dependency ratios', and the way in which state pensions were given new priority in the political interest generated after the 1939 war. Because of the respective histories of sociology and social policy, as newly arrived major disciplines, the shock-horror of the most extreme conditions, rather than cause, attracted greatest attention. Theories or explanation of poor conditions and maltreatment were over-weighted towards the demographic, or supposedly naturalistic, on the one hand, or fragmented into the convenient sub-divisions of policy subject-matter – housing, mental or physical health, education, institutional or family care, and social insurance and social assistance, on the other.

Where theory had a part, and that part summary or undeveloped, it occupied a middle level designed to be immediately practical to the locations and individuals immediately at issue. Larger statements about the record of governments and of policies as instruments of cause were not much attempted. The connections between themes or subjects, and their possibly common antecedents, were not seriously addressed. The achievements of the welfare state in the early years of the 20th century and then again in the immediate post-war situation of 1945, were not hammered home, and the theory of success sustained by continuing political education. The door of public service accessible to all was not slammed shut on interlopers and thieves. In Harold Macmillan's famous comment on one of Margaret Thatcher's privatisations, assaults on public ownership and public service could be likened to 'selling the family silver'.

The gains of 'welfare' could be expressed in many ways. Certainly collective, or universal, interests, public service, interdependence and redistributive rights and responsibilities would figure largely. The recent language of 'reform' from the critics has in some measure found the advocates of welfare embarrassed or defenceless. I would want to suggest that the critics have gained ascendancy mainly because defence has been neither multidimensional nor multinational. [...]

Several European Union countries have put up a steady defence of welfare. Many have maintained substantial levels of social transfers on behalf of social services, measured by percentage of Gross Domestic Product (GDP). Redistribution of income to pensioners remains considerable in all member countries. However, discussion of the European social model has become heated, and some individual governments have sought to curtail expenditure on pensions. In the UK, in particular, schemes with final salary pensions are declining rapidly, plans are being put in place to raise retirement and pension ages and comprehensive state second pensions are being phased out. The battle both to preserve, and to raise to a reasonable level, basic state pensions continues.

Formulation of theory: 'acquiescent functionalism'

[...] I was one of those trying to make sense of the poor conditions being experienced by many older people. By good fortune I had worked on different national and cross-national projects before that time in residential homes [...], hospitals and nursing homes, and in private households [...]. It became inevitable that I should reflect on the wider as well as immediate causes of the problems that were recognisably severe in particular locations as well as scattered more widely across the general population (see Townsend, 1981, 1986). Connections had to be made.

What could then be called the 'liberal–pluralist' tradition, now referred to as the 'neoliberal' or even Washington Consensus, was dominant. There existed a 'family' of theories – like neoclassical economics, democratic pluralism, sociological functionalism and certain theories in social psychology – that not only reflected but tended implicitly to approve the staged development of the capitalist democracies into and through the processes of industrialisation. By accepting as givens the changing structural inequalities of a competitive market, this 'family' reinforced individualistic and not social values and gained spurious authority. The continuities of economic individualism within classical economic theory, neoclassical theory, monetarism and neoliberal economics, and on the way even Keynesianism, had to be traced to reveal better what came to be built into social policies.

This 'family' of theories came to be applied to the emerging conditions of rapidly increasing numbers of older people. This can be followed in the wake of many of the social gerontologists of the earliest generation, including Donahue and Tibbitts (1957), Parsons (1942, 1964) and Cumming (1963) (see Townsend, 1986, pp 16-19). Their work, I considered, could be characterised as 'acquiescent functionalism'. This was a body of thought about ageing that attributed the causes of the problems of old age to the natural consequences of physical decrescence and mental inflexibility, or to the failures of individual adjustment to ageing and retirement, instead of the continuing as well as new exertions of state economic and social policy partly to serve and partly to moderate the play of market forces. Social inequality was thereby 'reconfigured' in the language that is now being applied to universal social services.

[...]

And still today there are features of that institutionalised ageism that have to attract our primary attention if, along with other forms of discrimination by gender, 'race', class and disability, it is to be radically reduced and dispersed so that our whole attention may be turned to the more practical fine-tuning of policy.

Alternative theory: structured dependency

In demonstrating the value of new policies in the 1970s the consequences of conventional theory had first to be exposed. I came to understand the debt I owed to social anthropologists like Radcliffe-Brown and economic sociologists like Marx and Weber (especially Weber's *Theory of economic and social organisation*, 1947) for putting concepts of social structure, class and economic and social change at the heart of scientific analysis of society and therefore of ageing and the conditions experienced by the third, and fourth, generations. Retirement, poverty, institutionalisation and restriction of domestic and community roles are the experiences that help to explain how the dependency of older people came to be artificially structured or deepened. Each of these required extensive investigation and assessment.

A great deal of evidence relevant to these forms of dependency emerged in the 1960s and 1970s. There were the examples of: a fixed age for pensions; the minimal subsistence afforded on the state pension; the substitution of retirement status for unemployment; the near-compulsory admission to residential care of many thousands of people whose faculties were still relatively intact; the enforced dependence of many residents in homes and of patients in hospitals and nursing homes; and the conversion of domiciliary services into commodity services. By the 1980s "an artificial dependency [was] being manufactured for a growing proportion of the population at the same time as measures [were] being taken to alleviate the worst effects of that dependency" (Townsend, 1986, p 43). A critical view has to be taken therefore of welfare – weeding out elements that had at the time infiltrated the concept, like parsimony and coercion. But a critical view cannot be allowed to become dismissive or override the massive evidence for extensive national, and now international, 'welfare' action.

Historically, planning as a determinant of social structure and therefore of 'welfare' had seeped into the consciousness of generations in the mid–20th century. This was the end–result of the work of theorists like Marx but also of policy advocates, like Sydney and Beatrice Webb, in European countries. I became acutely conscious of the events leading up to the establishment of the British welfare state after 1945 and understood policy as cause. I was influenced too by early 'planning conscious' social gerontologists like Yonina Talmon, who wrote revealingly about the experimental collective settlements, the *Kibbutzim*, and their value to older people, then being set up in Israel (Talmon, 1961). She understood the importance of maintaining extended family relationships in a new society struggling to introduce egalitarian values, and was especially sensitive about the values of reciprocation and location, as well as organised support for severely disabled people (Talmon, 1961, pp 288, 290, 294).

[...]

Human rights and welfare

First, some general arguments. The language of human rights has particular virtues of *moral obligation*. Each of the rights is 'universal'. Non–fulfilment is a 'violation'. Rights are 'human' and not only civil or political. Rights are multiple and interdependent. Corrective anti–discriminatory measures have to be directed not at the separate existence of racial, religious, gender, disability or ageist discrimination but in a comprehensive, connected and proportionate manner against all forms of discrimination.

Second, the *methodology* of human rights is in its infancy. The operational definition of rights and therefore violations demands imaginative and sustained quantitative, but also qualitative, methods of investigation. The violations are not those only that end life, or involve extreme abuse, the scale of which have to be assembled in statistical handbooks, but those that represent affronts to human dignity and identity. For older people, the Quality of Life research studies carried out in the UK under the auspices of the Economic and Social Research Council's (ESRC) Growing Older Programme offer rich contributions to this objective (see, for example, Walker and Hennessy, 2004; Walker, 2005). In operationalising a definition of rights for people of all ages perhaps there has been too much readiness to adapt familiar indicators of human development or health, or economic growth, as single indicators of sometimes complex conditions or entitlements rather than build requirements for survey data about extreme conditions from scratch.

The 'indivisibility' of human rights seems to have deterred some social scientists – I include lawyers – from developing *multiple* indices of certain general conditions or priorities. And the seeming inflexibility in defining a threshold or line between satisfaction and non-satisfaction of each right listed in the Articles of rights – either the individual has a right or she or he has not – creeps into the use of a single indicator testing whether that right has or has not been fulfilled (because selecting multiple indicators raises a lot of questions about multiple criteria in agreeing a threshold when different individuals are in reality on a point in the scale from extreme non-fulfilment to generous fulfilment).

Only in recent years have serious efforts been made to organise operational definitions in a form that allows multiple non-realisation of rights to be measured reliably and relatively unambiguously. [...]

Third, the *politics of rights*. This is crucial in the choice of methodology, investigative priorities and persuasive assessment of needs and policies. As many as 191 nations have ratified the Convention on the Rights of the Child (CRC) and numbers of signatories are almost as high for the original Universal Declaration of Human Rights and still impressively high for other human rights instruments. Access to rights plays a crucial role in public discussion about economic and social developments – for example in responses to conflict, anti-terrorism measures and different types of discrimination. Acknowledgment of the influential role of human rights has spread rapidly among campaigning organisations, departments of state and international organisations of every kind. To base both research and action on human rights instruments is to apply the leverage of accepted authority and democracy.

To traditional positive national arguments for welfare can therefore now be added the perceptions as well as revelations of cross-national agreed rules of a quasi-legal kind – a growing number of which have been and are being incorporated into domestic laws. Knowledge of that process can now enthuse those concerned with domestic disputes of a familiar kind that affect older people [...]

Human rights from a UK and European perspective

I am arguing that a new analytical framework has evolved very rapidly, with which social scientists must necessarily engage. [...] Based on the European Convention on Human Rights (ECHR), the Human Rights Act of the UK dates from 1998. The rights are not guaranteed against repeal or amendment by Parliament, and the courts cannot strike down incompatible primary legislation. Nonetheless, following precedents elsewhere, the expressed rights are beginning to have a substantial impact on the law, and also on the activities and thinking of administrators, lawyers and politicians.
[...]
The UK Act incorporates the ECHR, but the emphasis is on civil and political rights and not also on economic, social and cultural rights. The rights to life, to not being subjected to torture, or inhuman or degrading treatment, or forced labour, to an effective remedy and to non-discrimination raise questions of social protection and reconstruction, and therefore stray into a range of possible social and economic rights, but this cannot be pressed strongly in law. However, the counterpart of the ECHR is the European Social Charter (ESC) (Council of Europe, 2002; Samuel, 2002). As many as 30 of the member states of the Council of Europe had signed and ratified the Charter by 2001. After the Amsterdam Treaty of 1997 came into force the revised Charter has become an integral part of the structure of the European Community. The newly elected Labour government signed the Charter in 1997. Many of the Articles reflect European agreement on the 'European Social Model' and several are relevant to conditions for older people. In particular, Article 4 of the additional protocol of 1988 spells out the right of older people to social protection....

Violations of the rights of older people in the 21st century

Both the ESC (Council of Europe, 2002; Samuel, 2002) and the ECHR can be widely used in the analysis of conditions experienced by older people and necessary alternative policies. For example, Age Concern and Help the Aged have given worrying contemporary evidence on lack of rights. Help the Aged explained that "older people whose human rights are violated are often not in a position – or do not choose – to take action themselves" (JCHR, 2003, II, Evidence 310). Few staff, and few members of the public were yet informed about the 1998 Act. Older people subjected to abuse rarely complained.

Failure to accept Sutherland

[...] In Britain, perhaps the most authoritative review so far in this century is the Sutherland Commission on Long-term Care (Sutherland Report, 1999). The Commission argued that the long-term costs of care should be split between living costs, housing costs and personal care. Personal care should be available after assessment, according to need and paid for from general taxation; the rest should be subject to co-payment according to means. A National Care Commission had to be created. Private insurance would not deliver what is required at an acceptable cost, nor would the industry want to provide that degree of coverage. The recently evolving private infrastructure of residential and nursing home care had grown rapidly in cost and "the 'market' was shaped in a particular way, driven by what could be paid for rather than what people needed". [...]

Partly prompted by a querulous note of dissent from two of the Commissioners, the government set aside the recommendations of the Royal Commission. With hindsight it is perhaps unfortunate that the Royal Commission did not strengthen its powerful case by formal reference to human rights generally and the new UK Human Rights Act in particular, and to the rapid developments in the treatment of both the ECHR and the ESC, together with the momentum in Europe and elsewhere in the world in favour of linking current concerns about particular problems of the day that gain wide publicity with human rights. [...]

Practicality of human rights

... [M]ultiple material and social deprivation must be acknowledged and investigation based on identifying and then counting different types of deprivation, or abuse. One type of horror, and the identification of horror in one location, must be placed into a context that is national, multigenerational, applicable to public and private sectors, and international. I have taken the view for many years that specialised research can only carry force if there is generalised research as well, and vice versa. The best national work is that which is also international or cross-national. Of course it is never easy to ride two horses and improvisations and shortcomings will exist. But that is the first necessity. The effort remains crucial and will allow what is truly international and objectively scientific to emerge. [...]

Let me give [...] examples of the methodology. One is old-style multiplication of material and social deprivation. [...] After setting aside certain overlapping indices there remain 31 items representing commonly agreed necessities of life. As many as 37 per cent of people of pensionable age were deprived of at least one necessity, but as many as nine per cent deprived of five or more, including a third of these deprived of ten or more necessities. These nine per cent represent more than one million older people. That figure does not include half a million older people who are in hospitals, nursing homes and residential care. Severe multiple deprivation is therefore a common experience, and one that raises acute questions about human rights.

[...]

[...] The next stage has been to apply Articles of human rights to the measurement of multiple deprivation among adults. For older people we can move in successive stages from the ECHR, through the ESC to the International Covenant on Economic, Social and Cultural Rights. I cannot yet offer the statistical results. What I can do is outline the stages of research.

The first is to show ways in which the ECHR can be illustrated [see Table 19.1]. Additional use could be made, of course, with other Articles, like the right to marry (Article 12) and some of the Protocols, such as Articles 1 and 5 of Protocol 7, respectively on safeguards in the expulsion of aliens, and on equality between spouses.

The next step is to do the same for the ESC, which opens the door to a more sophisticated set of measurements. [see Table 19.1]. A third step in anticipating the growing acknowledgement of economic and social rights, and partly through the slow influence of the ESC on the UK government, is to examine the International Covenant on Economic, Social and Cultural Rights.

One method developed lately of accelerating progress in developing countries with the measurement of multiple violation of human rights, has been to focus on violations representing different features of material and social deprivation so that priorities in policy may be identified (Gordon et al, 2003). Another method would be to focus on the twin rights to social security and an adequate standard of living – Articles 22 and 25 of the Universal Declaration of Human Rights, Articles 26 and 27 of the CRC and Articles 9 and 11 of the International Covenant on Economic, Social and Cultural Rights (Table 19.2). The advantages to be derived from building afresh on these two rights are especially promising.

Globalisation and the human rights of older people

In deciding the future direction of the work of social gerontologists, the growing inequality within countries as well as between poor and rich countries must provide the structural context (Townsend and Gordon, 2002). The globalisation of market, technology and communications

Table 19.1: Types of violations of human rights and possible indicators

Source document and human right	Indicator
A. European Convention on Human Rights	
Right to life (Article 2)	Premature death, by location, age and gender
Prohibition of torture or 'inhuman or degrading treatment or punishment' (Article 3)	Degrading care practices in residential and home care
Right to respect for private and family life (Article 8)	Wish in disability to stay in own home; access to surrounding possessions of a familiar kind
Prohibition of discrimination 'on any ground such as sex, race, colour, language, religion, political or other opinion, national or social origin, association with a national minority, property, birth or other status' (Article 14)	Acceptance for care services, standardised for disability, by minority or gender status
B. European Social Charter	
Resources adequate for full and active life	Annual subjective/objective survey assessment of amount required to escape poverty/multiple deprivation
Facilities and information to lead an active, participating life	Access to range of public and private services, and facilities providing information
Opportunity to lead a life in a home of their choosing	Type of accommodation by degree of disability and preference
Access to appropriate health care	Frequency and speed of utilisation in relation to degree of disability, degree of material and social deprivation and whether and when need for health care identified
Freedom of action and quality of living conditions in residential institutions	Subjective expression of opportunities to act freely; objective assessment of living conditions in relation to measured degree of disability

(see, for example, Walker and Deacon, 2003) affects the organisation of all societies, including the conditions and prospects of older people. Recent failures of privatisation schemes, and even of major transnational corporations such as Enron and WorldCom and parts of the financial services industry, have led to calls for radical new policies. Fresh reports of instances of corporate corruption have paved the way for new calls for collective approaches through law and regulation that go a lot further than the minimal and highly variable expressions so far of 'corporate social responsibility'.

On globalisation, support for a change has come from unexpected sources. For example, the former chief economist at the World Bank, Joseph Stiglitz, has written revealingly about corporate greed (Stiglitz, 2002a, 2002b). Again, in the wake of the $4 billion (£2.1 billion) WorldCom scandal in 2002 Digby Jones, the then Director-General of the Confederation of British Industry, called for new forms of business

Table 19.2: International Covenant on Economic, Social and Cultural Rights and 1995 World Summit Action Programme

International Covenant on Economic, Social and Cultural Rights (1966-76)	Article 9: The States Parties to the present Covenant recognise the right of everyone to social security, including social insurance	Article 11 (1): The States Parties to the present Covenant recognise the right of everyone to an adequate standard of living for himself and his family, including adequate food, clothing and housing, and to the continuous improvement of living conditions
Copenhagen World Summit for Social Development (1995) relevant decisions by 117 countries	Action Programme 38: Social protection systems should be based on legislation and ... strengthened and expanded ... to protect from poverty people who cannot work ...	Action Programme 8: Equitable and non-discriminatory distribution of benefits of growth among social groups and countries and expanded access to productive resources for people living in poverty

leadership and for stronger statements about corporate responsibilities in accountancy and administration (Jones, 2002).

Public faith in agreements reached at World Summits to deal with the world's needs has begun to dwindle. Public expectations raised by the announcement of the Millennium Development Goals in 2000 and the closing statements of successive World Summits since then – including those of Monterrey on financial developments and New York on the needs of children – have been disappointed. Some of the earlier international agreements – such as that at the 1995 Copenhagen World Summit for Social Development – had a more lasting impact. The Copenhagen Declaration and Programme of Action followed a coherently organised summit and the recommendations were more specific than in other similar events (UN, 1995). The programme of action has begun to have constructive results and has considerable potentiality for the future, if governments and interest groups, including international bodies, are held regularly responsible – and accountable – for widely agreed objectives in establishing human rights and reducing inequalities and poverty. Compared with diminishing confidence in World Summits, public trust in the charters and conventions expressing human rights has continued to grow. Public support for the values upholding human rights and legally backed action remains strong.

Universal rights

The world has seen only mixed success for the declared objective in the past 50 years of reducing the violations of human rights, including those that address different forms of severe deprivation that were selected earlier in this chapter for special attention. Our findings prompt re-examination of the links between 'universalism' or human 'rights', and both comprehensive public social service and social security. 'Targeting' as a strategy in developing countries to reduce poverty has become highly controversial and the forms of targeting that have been adopted are increasingly criticised. Reports of persisting poverty and deepening inequality in many countries outweigh the modest results that at best reflect the structural adjustment programmes and their successors, including the social funds that were introduced. In developing countries, the Programme of Action to Mitigate the Social Cost of Adjustment was set up in the late 1980s to correct the excesses of structural adjustment programmes, but was criticised for being underfunded and lacking direction (Donkor, 2002). Success for programmes intended both to restrict public expenditure and yet relieve extreme poverty by targeting resources has turned out to be elusive. Action on behalf of children is a priority, but huge numbers of older people will also continue to suffer unless comprehensive, and principled, action is taken on behalf of society as a whole.

Conclusion

The idea of 'structured dependency' helps to explain the box before death within which many older people are placed. Unintentionally, as well as for deliberate reasons of economy and profit or convenience on the part of the state and of other institutions, their dependency is created in market, residential and hospital care and private and public social care policies. There are exceptions from which lessons can be learned about countervailing policies. [...]

The various problems of 'structured' dependency persist. And those problems seem set to grow in many parts of the world. Human rights offer a framework of rigorous analysis and anti-discriminatory work. Success depends on good operational measurement – for purposes of producing reliable evidence of violations and monitoring progress – and the incorporation internationally as well as nationally of institutions and policies that reflect those rights. Human rights instruments offer hope of breaking down blanket discrimination and of using resources more appropriately, and more generously, according to severity of need. But investment in human rights is not only a moral and quasi-legal salvation from things that are still going depressingly wrong. Used best, human rights offer a framework of thought and planning early in the 21st century that enables society to take a fresh, and more hopeful, direction.

[...]

References

Council of Europe (2002) *European Social Charter: Collected texts* (3rd edn), Strasbourg: Council of Europe.

Cumming, E. (1963) 'Further thoughts on the theory of disengagement', *International Social Science Journal*, vol 15, no 3, pp 377-93.

Donahue, W. and Tibbitts, C. (1957) *The new frontiers of aging*, Ann Arbor, MI: University of Michigan Press.

Donkor, K. (2002) 'Structural adjustment and mass poverty in Ghana', in P. Townsend and D. Gordon (eds) *World poverty: New policies to defeat an old enemy*, Bristol: The Policy Press, pp 226-8.

Gordon, D., Nandy, S., Pantazis, C., Pemberton, S. and Townsend, P. (2003) *Child poverty in the developing world*, Bristol: The Policy Press.

JCHR (Joint Committee on Human Rights) (2003) *The case for a Human Rights Commission*, Sixth Report of Session 2002-3, vol I and II, HC 489-I and II, London: The Stationery Office.

Jones, D. (2002) Business and media supplement, *Observer*, 30 June.

Macnicol, J. and Blaikie, A. (1989) 'The politics of retirement, 1908-1948', in M. Jefferys (ed) *Growing old in the twentieth century*, London: Routledge, pp 21-42.

Parsons, T. (1942) 'Age and sex in the social structure of the United States', *American Sociological Review*, vol 7, no 5, pp 604-16.

Parsons, T. (1964) *Essays in sociological theory* (paperback edn), New York, NY: The Free Press.

Samuel, L. (2002) *Fundamental social rights: Case law of the European Social Charter* (2nd edn), Strasbourg: Council of Europe Publishing.

Stiglitz, J. (2002a) 'Corporate corruption', *The Guardian*, London, 4 July.

Stiglitz, J. (2002b) *Globalisation and its discontents*, London: Allen Lane.

Sutherland Report (1999) *With respect to old age: Long term care – rights and responsibilities. A report by the Royal Commission on Long-term Care*, Cm 4192-1, London: The Stationery Office.

Talmon, Y. (1961) 'Ageing in Israel: a planned society', *American Journal of Sociology*, vol 67, no 3, pp 284-95.

Townsend, P. (1981) 'The structured dependency of the elderly: a creation of social policy in the twentieth century', *Ageing and Society*, vol 1, no 1, pp 5-28.

Townsend, P. (1986) 'Ageism and social policy', in C. Phillipson and A. Walker (eds) *Ageing and social policy: A critical assessment*, Aldershot: Gower, pp 15-44.

Townsend, P. and Gordon, D. (eds) (2002) *World poverty: New policies to defeat an old enemy*, Bristol: The Policy Press.

Walker, A. (ed) (2005) *Understanding quality of life in old age*, Milton Keynes: Open University Press.

Walker, A. and Deacon, B. (2003) 'Economic globalisation and policies on ageing', *Journal of Societal and Social Policy*, vol 2, no 2, pp 1-18.

Walker, A. and Hennessy, C.H. (eds) (2004) *Growing older: Quality of life in old age*, Milton Keynes: Open University Press.

Weber, M. (1947) *Theory of economic and social organisation* (revised and edited edn), London: Palgrave.

20

To empower or to protect: does the law assist in cases of self-neglect?

Tim Spencer-Lane

Mayan Coomeraswamy who suffered from Schizophrenia died in January 2009, aged 59, from natural causes, aggravated by neglect. According to the inquest into his death, his flat was in a state of grave disrepair and barely fit for human habitation. While a remedy for the cleaning, decorating and reliable heating was available and urged on him by his family and others, he would not accept these. At the time of his death, Mayan Coomeraswamy was compliant with depot medication from his community psychiatric nurse, and according to the media reports had been assessed as having decision-making capacity (Harding, 2010). The coroner in this case, Paul Knapman, blamed "a piecemeal legal framework" which he claimed was riddled with contradictions and inadequacies, and individual mistakes by the workers concerned. (Letter to Phil Hope MP, 18 March 2010)

Introduction

The tragic death of Mayan Coomeraswamy highlights the challenging and sometimes intractable dilemmas that can arise in cases of self-neglect. Professionals often need to find the appropriate balance between promoting individual autonomy and ensuring adequate protection for those who need it. This chapter considers whether the law assists professionals in cases of self-neglect, or whether it is riddled with contradictions.

What is self-neglect?

Many people when they speak about abuse and neglect refer only to acts or omissions by third parties. However, self-neglect is one of the most commonly reported forms of mistreatment (Dyer et al, 2007). It can be described as an inability to meet one's own basic needs. Manifestations include failure to take medication or seek support from services, even for life-threatening conditions; impaired ability to perform daily living tasks such as bathing, dressing, cleaning and paying bills; the accumulation and hoarding of certain objects; and ownership of several pets but an inability to care for them. Consequently, many people who neglect themselves have poor hygiene, live without utilities and some live in complete squalor.

The explanations of self-neglect are varied, ranging from medical and psychiatric explanations, which link it to certain illnesses or syndromes, such as depression and Diogenes syndrome, to socio-cultural models where different lifestyle habits such as self-care are viewed as distinct parts of certain cultures (Braye et al, 2010). Self-neglect is seen as occurring predominately in older people, although it is also associated with people with mental health problems (Braye et al, 2010).

Self-neglect and autonomy

Self-neglect will vary from the relatively minor to extreme cases, where professionals will need to intervene proactively. However, identifying a threshold at which self-neglect may require a proactive response is fraught with difficulties and will vary according to the particular circumstances of the individual case. Professionals often battle with issues of risk levels when dealing with self-neglect. How much risk can be accepted before professionals begin to question the person's mental capacity?

For practitioners, there is a difficult balance to be struck between maximising autonomy and ensuring adequate protection for those who need it. Public intervention in the lives of children is often based on the assumption that they lack competence, but with adults a contrary assumption applies. Where an adult lacks capacity and is self-neglecting, the need for intervention may be heightened. Where a person has capacity and is self-neglecting, the position is less clear. There may be a need to investigate whether or not the person's refusal of help is a competent decision and free of coercion and undue duress.

In determining an appropriate balance between individual autonomy and protection, the practitioner may also need to take into account the views of family, friends and carers, and the wider interests of the public. For, example, if a person is hoarding rubbish and living in a rodent-infested home, a conflict is created between the desire to stay at home and the neighbours' desire to live in a clean environment and the desire of family members to keep the individual safe.

How can the law assist?

Even the most clearly drafted law or guidance will not provide clear solutions for every scenario. However, the law can provide a framework to assist the practitioner to decide on the most appropriate response, and provides a range of possible interventions to implement that decision.

Human rights

The starting point for practitioners should be the European Convention on Human Rights, which is a binding international agreement that the UK helped draft. It sets out 16 fundamental human rights and freedoms. Some of these rights are *absolute*, which means they cannot be interfered with under any circumstances, but the majority are *limited* or *qualified* rights, which means that interference can be justified in certain circumstances. In cases of self-neglect, Article 8 of the Convention is most relevant. This provides that everyone has the right to respect for their private and family life, and this right can be restricted only in specified circumstances, such as to protect health and the rights and freedoms of others. Any interference must also be in accordance with the law, legitimate and necessary. Although practitioners often interpret Article 8 as restricting intervention, in legal terms this is not necessarily correct. It requires a balance between the rights of the individual and the need to, for example, protect the wider needs of the community.

What legal interventions are available in cases of self-neglect?

The range of interventions available to practitioners may range from the most intrusive and restrictive, to the least coercive, representing minimal or limited threats to self-determination.

Service provision

Section 47 of the NHS and Community Care Act 1990 governs the assessment for and provision of community care services by local authorities in England and Wales. If a person *appears to be in need* of such services (for example, as a result of self-neglect), the local authority is required to do an assessment and decide if services should be provided. The law therefore establishes a low qualifying threshold for an assessment – the duty arises irrespective of whether or not the person consents, refuses to participate, or will qualify for services.

A person who is self-neglecting may be eligible for home help or
cleaning services under the Chronically Sick and Disabled Persons Act
1970 or services for older people under the Health Services and Public
Health Act 1968. To assist local authorities to decide if the person is
eligible for services, the government in England and in Wales has issued
statutory guidance (Welsh Assembly Government, 2002; DH, 2010). This has
a higher legal status which means it must be followed unless there is good
reason not to.[1] Although the detail of the guidance in England and Wales
differs, they are materially the same, setting out an eligibility framework
that is graded into four bands: *critical, substantial, moderate* and *low*. Each
band includes a number of descriptors or risk factors that describe the
seriousness of the risks to independence or other consequences if needs
are not addressed. Local authorities have discretion to decide which bands
it will provide services to meet (the *eligibility criteria*). In deciding which
bands to include, the local authority can take account of its resources,
local expectations and local costs. However, if a person is assessed as
falling within one of the bands that the local authority has included in its
eligibility criteria, there is a duty to provide services to meet those needs.
So, for example, if a person is neglecting themselves to such an extent
that they have been assessed as having *substantial needs*, then if the local
authority has set its eligibility criteria to meet *substantial and critical needs*
only, it must provide services for the person.

Of course, this is often not the end of the story. The person may refuse
services or any services provided may be subject to a charge (depending
on the financial circumstances of the person) that may make the person
reluctant to agree to the service provision.

Local authorities are not the only agency that can provide support to
people who self-neglect. Health service provision may be necessary, such
as registered nursing care or NHS continuing healthcare. These services are
provided free of charge under the NHS Act 2006 and the NHS Act (Wales)
2006. In cases where the person refuses help, then non-consensual forms of
intervention may be needed.

Safeguarding

Although safeguarding is often referred to as a separate and specialist area
of practice, in England and Wales it has no specific statutory basis and
therefore in legal terms is best understood as linked to local authorities'
existing statutory functions under community care legislation. In Scotland,
however, the position is different and this is discussed later in this chapter.

In England, the relevant government guidance on safeguarding adults
is *No secrets*, which has been issued as *statutory guidance* (DH and Home

Office, 2000). However, this guidance fails to mention self-neglect. It does mention *neglect* as a form of abuse but links this to issues of omission by third parties. It is expected that *No secrets* will be replaced in future and hopefully this serious omission will be rectified. The official guidance in Northern Ireland also fails to mention self-neglect (Volunteer Now, 2010). In contrast, the Welsh statutory guidance, *In safe hands*, not only defines self-neglect (*a failure to provide for self, through inattention or dissipation*) but also lists various examples and indicators, such as inability to manage personal finances and activities of daily living, suicidal acts, refusal of medication, lack of utilities, malnourishment and dehydration (National Assembly for Wales, 2000).

Both *No secrets* and *In safe hands* refer to the concept of a 'vulnerable adult' in order to help practitioners identify who may need to be safeguarded against abuse or neglect. A vulnerable adult is defined as any adult who:

> ... is or may be in need of community care services by reason of mental or other disability, age or illness; and who is or may be unable to take care of him or herself, or unable to protect him or herself against significant harm or exploitation. (DH, 2000, para 2.3)

However, this definition is not without its difficulties. The guidance fails to define terms such as 'significant' that can make it subjective and open to varying interpretations. The use of significant harm can be seen as a way of limiting the numbers of cases to manageable levels that local authorities would be required to investigate. On the other hand, *significant harm* may set the bar too high, thus undermining preventative measures, and suggests that some forms of abuse and neglect are acceptable and not worthy of being investigated.

Mental incapacity

If a person lacks capacity to choose their living situation then the Mental Capacity Act 2005 may provide a solution in cases of self-neglect. Section 1 of the Act requires that any decision made or action taken on behalf of a person who lacks capacity must be in their 'best interests'. The decision maker must consider the past and present wishes and feelings of the person, the views of anyone else with an interest in their welfare and any other relevant consideration when taking the decision or action. Subject to the outcome of a best interests decision, the person could be, for example, required to move temporarily to allow their accommodation to be cleaned or works to be carried out. In implementing this decision, a proportionate degree of force can be used. However, if the person is living at home and needs to be detained in their best interests then an application to the Court of Protection for authorisation may be necessary.

In practice, however, it can be difficult to assess the capacity of people who are self-neglecting if they are reluctant to engage with services. Similarly, making a best interests decision can be difficult if there is limited knowledge of previously expressed attitudes, opinions, values and preferences.

Mental disorder

In cases of mentally disordered people who self-neglect, the Mental Health Act 1983 may be of assistance. This Act can be used to detain a person in hospital in the interests of their own health and safety. Many people who are detained under the Act will lack capacity, but unlike the Mental Capacity Act 2005, there is no requirement that the person lacks capacity. In practice, the prevalence of mental incapacity among detained patients is high but not invariable (Owen et al, 2008).

In relation to cases of self-neglect, the 1983 Act does not provide any express powers to enforce environmental improvements but can be used to treat any underlying disorder that has contributed to the state of disrepair, and since the property is vacated temporarily while the person is in hospital, services may be able to carry out cleaning or repairs. However, these powers only apply if the person satisfies the criteria for detention under the 1983 Act. Many disordered people who are neglecting themselves will not need to be detained in hospital for assessment or treatment of a mental disorder, and therefore will not come within the remit of the 1983 Act.

Some powers of the 1983 Act do not require the person to be detained in hospital. For example, Section 135(1) enables a person who is believed to be suffering from a mental disorder and is being neglected or unable to look after themselves to be detained at a place of safety for up to 72 hours for the purposes of making alternative arrangements for care and treatment. The relatively short time limit of this power, however, may limit its effectiveness in dealing, for example, with cases of extreme self-neglect. Alternatively, the use of guardianship under the 1983 Act may assist by putting in place a formal community-based support structure under which care and treatment can be provided more coercively than in ordinary situations. It allows a nominated person or body (often the council) to assume responsibility for the supervision of a person's care in the community. However, guardianship provides few powers to override a refusal by the relevant individual, for example, refusal to comply with medicine, have their accommodation cleaned or move out of their home.

Compulsory removal

Section 47 of the National Assistance Act 1948 allows local authorities to apply to a magistrates' court for an order to remove a person from their home if they are suffering from grave chronic illness or living in insanitary conditions, and not receiving proper care and attention. The person can be detained for up to three months. However, this power contains serious flaws. Section 47 is one of the few principles of the old Poor Law that has remained in place and its wording is based on local legislation drafted in Bradford in 1925 designed to assist in slum clearance (Muir, 1990). In many cases the use of Section 47 breaches the European Convention on Human Rights due to the broad range of people who can potentially be detained and limited rights of appeal. The limited evidence available indicates that Section 47 is used rarely but may not be entirely obsolete.

Public and environmental health powers

Public bodies have compulsory powers to enter and cleanse premises where there are risks to public health. The Public Health (Control of Disease) Act 1984 allows a magistrate to order the removal of a person from a house where an infectious disease has occurred, and to place or detain a person in hospital if they are suffering from a notifiable disease. There is further power for a magistrate to order the removal of people who are or may be infected or contaminated in such a way that presents a significant risk of harm to human health. Under the Public Health Act 1936 there are powers to temporarily remove people from their homes where fumigation of the premises is required. The state of the dwelling must be such that it represents a risk to health. There is further power to remove individuals from their homes, detaining them for the purpose of cleaning them or their clothing where either are 'verminous'. Under the Environmental Health Act 1990 a local authority has powers of entry in order to determine if a statutory nuisance exists or to take action or execute work. This includes premises that are in a state prejudicial to health or nuisance or any accumulation or deposit prejudicial to health or a nuisance.

However, the thresholds for intervention under this legislation are high, and accordingly, the powers are only used as a last resort. In any event, these powers are aimed at protecting *public* health, rather than being focused on the harm that may be caused to the person responsible for the insanitary conditions.

Inherent jurisdiction of the High Court

Where statute law fails to provide a solution, then the High Court may make decisions on behalf of vulnerable adults under its 'inherent jurisdiction'. Traditionally this has been used in relation to those who lack capacity but in some cases it has also extended to those who have capacity.[2] However, the inherent jurisdiction cannot be used to compel a capacitated but *vulnerable* person to do (or not do) something which they have, after due consideration, decided to do (or not to do); the jurisdiction acts to 'facilitate the process of unencumbered decision-making' by those who have capacity 'free of external pressure or physical restraint in making those decisions'.[3] Also, High Court proceedings can be costly and time consuming and are therefore an inappropriate way of dealing with emergency safeguarding cases.

Adults at risk of harm

Finally, in Scotland the Adult Support and Protection (Scotland) Act 2007 includes all the main powers and duties of councils to protect adults who are unable to safeguard their own interests. The Act includes express reference to self-neglect in the definitions of an 'adult at risk' and 'harm' for the purposes of the legislation. It includes a number of compulsory powers, such as the power for a council officer to visit premises to determine whether or not further action is needed to protect an adult at risk of harm, using warrants of entry if necessary; the power for a sheriff to issue an assessment order or an order to remove the adult at risk to a specified place; and the power to ban abusers from a specified place for up to six months.

Conclusion

A range of law exists to help and protect people who neglect themselves. These powers range from the provision of care and support with the consent of the individual concerned to more coercive forms of intervention. In deciding how to intervene (if at all), practitioners need to achieve an appropriate balance between maximising autonomy and ensuring adequate protection for those who need it. The need for such balance was summed up by Lord Justice Munby, when he was a High Court Judge, in the following words:

> The fact is that all life involves risk, and the young, the elderly and the vulnerable, are exposed to additional risks and to risks they are less well equipped than others to cope with. But just

as wise parents resist the temptation to keep their children metaphorically wrapped up in cotton wool, so too we must avoid the temptation always to put the physical health and safety of the elderly and the vulnerable before everything else. Often it will be appropriate to do so, but not always. Physical health and safety can sometimes be bought at too high a price in happiness and emotional welfare. The emphasis must be on sensible risk appraisal, not striving to avoid all risk, whatever the price, but instead seeking a proper balance and being willing to tolerate manageable or acceptable risks as the price appropriately to be paid in order to achieve some other good – in particular to achieve the vital good of the elderly or vulnerable person's happiness. What good is it making someone safer if it merely makes them miserable?[4]

Notes

[1] *R v Islington London Borough Council ex p Rixon* (1997-98) 1 CCLR 119.

[2] *Re SA* [2005] EWHC 2942 (Fam).

[3] *LBL v RYJ* [2010] EWHC 2665 (COP) at [62].

[4] *MM (An Adult)* [2007] EWHC 2003 (Fam), [2009] 1 FLR 443, at [120].

References

Braye, S., Orr, D. and Preston-Shoot, M. (2011) *Self-neglect and adult safeguarding. Findings from research*, London: Social Care Institute for Excellence

DH (Department of Health) (2010) *Prioritising need in the context of Putting People First*, London: The Stationery Office.

DH and Home Office (2000) *No secrets: Guidance on developing and implementing multi-agency policies and procedures to protect vulnerable adults from abuse*, London: The Stationery Office.

Dyer, C.B., Pavlik, V.N. and Kelly, P.A. (2007) 'The making of a self-neglect severity scale', *Journal of Elder Abuse and Neglect*, vol 18, no 4, pp 13-23.

Harding, E. (2010) 'Intervening behind closed doors', *The Guardian*, 31 March (www.guardian.co.uk/society/2010/mar/31/mental-health-law-vulnerable-people-intervention).

Muir, J.A. (1990) 'Section 47: Bradford 1925 – United Kingdom 1988', *Journal of Public Health Medicine*, vol 12, no 28, pp 29-30.

National Assembly for Wales (2000) *In safe hands: Implementing adult protection procedures in Wales*, July, Cardiff: Welsh Government.

Owen, G., Richardson, G., David, A.S., Szmukler, G., Hayward, P. and Hotopf, M. (2008) 'Mental capacity to make decisions on treatment in people admitted to psychiatric hospitals: cross sectional study', *British Medical Journal*, vol 337, a.448.

Volunteer Now (2010) *Safeguarding vulnerable adults: A shared responsibility*, Belfast: Volunteer Now.

Welsh Assembly Government (2002) *Health and social care for adults: Creating a unified and fair system for assessing and managing care*, Cardiff: Welsh Assembly Government.

21

Safeguarding vulnerable adults over the life course

Gordon Grant

Introduction

As we grow older we want to continue to make contributions to society, to feel valued, to be part of a family and community, and to feel safe. Ageing can provide fresh opportunities for personal development and socialisation, and for the chance to acquire even more resilient qualities. But just as this is not inevitable, ageing can also bring threats and demands that have devastating and life-threatening consequences. This chapter considers why life course trajectories should figure more prominently in a robust approach to safeguarding, informed by an understanding of the contexts in which forms of abuse and neglect arise.

Vulnerable adults, the life course and safeguarding

However vulnerable adults are defined, they have typically been characterised by long-term conditions: chronic illness or disability in later life, dementia, mental illness, learning disability, or perhaps drug and alcohol dependence. But is this really helpful? Most of the literature on the safeguarding of vulnerable adults either assumes sufficient homogeneity between these categories or else deals only with singular categories, such as people with dementia. With one or two notable exceptions (Bowes and Daniel, 2010; Johnson et al, 2010), it is surprising that few efforts have been made to consider how life course considerations might shed light on the contexts in which abuse and neglect arise and perhaps lead to a questioning of constructions of abuse that might be experienced, the categorisations of vulnerability that ensue and the safeguarding practices that might follow.

A life course perspective assumes that individuals become more or less autonomous under conditions of changing cultural, social and historical settings, entailing both continuities and discontinuities (Clausen, 1998). The paths taken involve twists and turns as a result of interactions between a 'minded self' (human agency) and different environments. Life course experiences of vulnerable people are therefore culturally embedded and socially contingent (Priestley, 2000), and do not necessarily follow the more predictable stages of the life span.

So, what are the implications of this thinking for a better understanding of contexts of abuse and ensuing safeguarding practice?

Most obviously, a life course perspective incorporates the key dimension of *temporality* into practitioner thinking. A reflective practitioner will therefore be seeking to minimise biographical disruption in the lives of vulnerable adults and as far as possible help to sustain their continuity, well-being and safety over time as far as this is possible. This implies a capacity for *anticipatory thinking and intervention*, perhaps the most necessary device in the practitioner's toolkit dedicated to safeguarding vulnerable people.

Second, abuse can have insidious and long-term effects in people with reduced mental capacity and there is as yet little reporting of this, which means that the lives of many people continue to be blighted through their unacknowledged and silent suffering. Symptoms of abuse they display can still too easily be confabulated (O'Callaghan et al, 2003) or assumed to be associated with behavioural phenotypes. There is also evidence of what some commentators describe as 're-victimisation', where experience of abuse or harm earlier in the life course can indicate risk of future victimisation.

Third, a life course perspective would require an aligning of 'disability trajectories' with other trajectories linked to people's lives and welfare. These would include: family life cycle changes, institutional calendars and service transitions, and wider social and cultural changes taking place within historic time. These trajectories run in parallel, and may be helpful in highlighting when things are becoming asynchronous and potentially dangerous, for example, when the death of a key family carer coincides with a sudden deterioration in the cognitive functioning of an older person with dementia.

Fourth, as suggested at the beginning of this chapter, the risk literature can too easily lead to a pathologising of responses. Life course literature, whether addressed to vulnerable children, adults or families (Hawley and DeHaan, 1996; Rutter, 1996), tends to emphasise how individuals can become resilient following trauma and abuse at earlier periods in their lives, leading to a better understanding of the role of protective factors in histories of 'personal overcoming'.

Finally, as Bowes and Daniel (2010) suggest, it is important to explore the problem of harm and abuse from the point of view of victims and perpetrators. We might add victims and families since the latter can provide crucial information about symptoms of abuse when family victims do not necessarily have the capacity to talk about third party perpetrators. This would also be important in work with people of different ethnicities where constructions of harm and typical responses to them might well be informed by norms and values rooted in culturally embedded beliefs and practices.

Understanding abuse

Adopting a life course approach to safeguarding requires an understanding of the contexts in which abuse and neglect arise. In what is arguably the single most important national policy document to emerge in England on the subject of adult protection, *No secrets* (DH and Home Office 2000), in its foreword, declared that:

> Abuse is a violation of an individual's human and civil rights by any other person or persons ... [it] may consist of a single act or repeated acts. It may be physical, verbal or psychological, it may be an act of neglect or an omission to act or it may occur when a vulnerable person is persuaded to enter into a financial or sexual transaction to which he or she has not consented, or cannot consent ... can occur in any relationship and may result in significant harm to, or exploitation of, the person subjected to it.... (paras 1.1, 1.2, 2.5-2.7)

Abuse may therefore be the result of actions that are *intentional*, like sexual abuse, or *unintentional*, like failure to follow a correct medical procedure.

No secrets was addressed to the circumstances of those adults thought to be most at risk of abuse and neglect, that is, vulnerable adults. It defined as a vulnerable adult any person aged 18 years or over, 'who is or may be in need of community care services by reason of mental or other disability, age or illness; and who is or may be unable to take care of him or herself, or unable to protect him or herself against significant harm or exploitation' (DH, 2000).

It is important to recognise the shift from seeking to 'explain' abuse as a by-product of pathologies associated with ageing, for example, in terms of personal factors such as changing behavioural patterns, the onset of dementia or even chronological age itself, something subsequently recognised by the Commission for Social Care Inspection (CSCI), Association of Directors of Social Services (ADSS) and Association of Chief Probation Officers (ACPO) (2007), to more nuanced approaches that have their roots in human rights, production of welfare and life course perspectives (see, for example, Whitelock, 2009; Bowes and Daniel, 2010; Johnson et al, 2010). The developments marked by the latter references are important since they represent a shift in perspective from the older person as the source of the problem to one more concerned with the social construction of the relationships adults and older people have with others and with the environments in which they live. In other words, they stress the importance of understanding the *context* of abuse and neglect, the *life stage* of the abused person and *societal/cultural responses.*

Careful reviews (Cooper et al, 2008) show that abuse of older people is not uncommon, and can take physical and psychological forms. However, abuse and neglect continue to be under-reported for a variety of linked reasons:

- *disempowerment or fear:* the offender is likely to be in a position of power over the victim, and may be threatening to withdraw support or services;
- *isolation:* the offender may be an intimate either as a support worker, paid or family carer and could be threatening to withdraw their help or friendship;
- *poor access to mediation, counselling or advocacy:* the most vulnerable victims lack access to good and reliable information about services and to advocacy or support systems that hold those with a duty to care to account;
- *credibility:* categories of disabled people are too easily stigmatised or are disadvantaged by being considered as unreliable witnesses – one of the reasons why so few cases of reported abuse ever get to court or lead to convictions;
- *limited articulacy:* people with intellectual, cognitive or neurological impairments may have difficulties in making themselves understood and are likely to be frustrated, upset and traumatised by not being able to communicate directly what has happened to them. People in such circumstances who have survived abuse can experience effects such as difficulties sleeping, self-harm, aggression, reliving the event and "startle" responses, not unlike criteria for post-traumatic stress disorder.

(See Wilson 1994; O'Callaghan et al, 2003, p 175; Fitzpatrick and Hamill 2010 among others.)

Those most at risk of abuse are also likely to be the most vulnerable – individuals least able to speak for themselves, with psychological or mental health problems, learning disabilities, dementia or other life-limiting conditions associated with ageing, and anyone deemed to be without capacity (Mental Capacity Act 2005; Berzins and Petch, 2003; Cooper et al, 2009; Beadle-Brown et al, 2010).

New and insidious forms of abuse seem to develop as newer technologies permit – cybercrimes are but one manifestation where people's identities and bank accounts can be intercepted through the internet in the pursuit of fraudulent activity; 'cold calling' and persuasive salesmanship over the telephone, an almost daily experience nowadays, can lead especially vulnerable older people into very suspect and exploitative 'deals'. Cultural factors also confound what constitutes abuse – honour crimes are perhaps an extreme example.

Abuse or harm largely occurs in contexts where there is not only a premium on privacy and trust, but also expectations for best care. This means that those responsible for inflicting abuse or harm are typically well known to their victims.

Flynn and Brown (2010, pp 220-1) have helpfully reflected on the types of abuses of adults that have been reported as well as possible responses to them:

- hate crime, which takes place in public places, requires: bullying (including sexual bullying and cyber bullying) policies, public engagement, youth education, policing, and safe havens in the community;
- sexual abuse and predatory financial abuse which requires workforce regulation, very careful policing based on long-term intelligence, alert neighbours, healthcare, social care and housing professionals;
- parasitic abuse in which abuser(s) move in on a vulnerable person, (perhaps presenting themselves as "befrienders"). This type of abuse requires concerted intervention from housing providers, social care staff, emergency services, post offices, banks, local communities and shops;
- abuse in institutions and residential care settings that require sound commissioning, good policies especially around control and restraint, challenging behaviour, recruitment and supervision, and appropriate specialist knowledge on behalf of their staff;
- not all family homes are sanctuaries so abuse in family settings needs to be prevented by safe care planning and appropriate levels of support, regular review, alert health care input, public education and good links with domestic violence services;
- ethically challenging situations, for example whether to put a PEG tube in for someone with Down's Syndrome with early signs of dementia, or whether and how to treat cancer in someone with dementia and learning disabilities: these require consistent application of, and probably an extension of, the Independent Mental Capacity Advocacy.

Given the scope of actions suggested above, tackling abuse, but more preferably preventing abuse, requires a strategically well planned, coordinated, multi-agency approach, backed by strong legislation.

The policy response

The national policy response in England began in earnest with the publication of *No secrets* (DH and Home Office, 2000). This required the work of national bodies to be realigned and refocused. The Criminal Records Bureau (CRB), the Care Quality Commission (CQC) (formerly the CSCI), the Independent Safeguarding Authority (ISA) and the General Social Care Council (GSCC) were pressed to tighten inspection processes and minimise the risks of recruiting people not fit for work with vulnerable people through the introduction of barring schemes, and rights of entry to places where people are at risk of harm. There was to be devolved leadership and coordination of adult protection systems, with local authority social services departments tasked to take the lead.

These arrangements, unlike those in child protection, did not carry the force of law, so much was left to the discretion of local agencies about how policies and procedures were to be established. However, implementation has been rather uneven around the country (Reid et al, 2009).

Although not mandated in *No secrets*, serious case reviews (SCRs) have become an important part of the safeguarding landscape as attempts to learn lessons when things have gone badly wrong either in individual cases or within and between agency systems. They therefore mostly concern investigations following deaths, life-threatening injuries or major system failures. However, there is no agreed basis about when SCRs should be undertaken, the terms of reference they should have or the local and national reporting arrangements. Because individual circumstances and contexts can be so diverse in SCRs (Sinclair and Bullock, 2002), it can be difficult to draw general lessons from retrospective case reviews.

Meanwhile the Coalition government has made *protection* one of the seven central planks of its new strategy for social care (DH, 2010a). Reflecting the lexicon of the 'Big Society' it wants local communities to be the eyes and ears of safeguarding, speaking up for people who may not be able to protect themselves through Neighbourhood Watch schemes or initiatives by local HealthWatch (DH, 2010a, para 6.2). The government also intends to work with the Law Commission to strengthen the law in respect of safeguarding (DH 2010a, para 6.7).

In announcing its proposed reforms for the NHS (DH, 2010b), the Coalition government has again recognised the growing concerns about safeguarding by:

- requiring better information about levels of healthcare-associated infections, adverse events and avoidable deaths, broken down by providers and clinical teams;
- making the safety of the care and treatment of patients one of the three key quality domains of the NHS Outcomes Framework;
- establishing HealthWatch England, a new independent consumer champion within the CQC.

Nevertheless, the combined proposals for safeguarding contained in these two new Coalition government initiatives look rather piecemeal when set against systemic changes needed to underpin a full blown preventive strategy.

Putting safeguarding into practice

Structural reforms aside, health and social care practitioners will continue to bear the brunt of responsibility for the safety, health and well-being of vulnerable adults.

Strengthened barring schemes and rigorous application of CRB checks are helping to keep predatory individuals from getting near to vulnerable people, but the system is still not 100 per cent foolproof, and probably never will be. This means that peer support and whistleblowing must have key roles in maintaining close checks of both professional standards and also of the rights and dignity of vulnerable adults.

Continuing professional development (CPD) is crucial when predatory individuals are constantly looking for new avenues to exploit or harm those least able to look after themselves. Frontline workers should therefore be armed with best evidence and guidance about tackling or preventing abuse. It has also been recognised that professional qualifying training needs to be ratcheted up in relation to safeguarding, including ways to minimise unintended harm to patients (House of Commons Health Committee, 2009).

With most abusers being well known to victims, it seems self-evident that assessment should incorporate family or social systems frameworks (see, for example, Landau, 2010; Trivette et al, 2010). This would at least bring a focus to potentially all those who have a close relationship – as kith, kin or professionals – to vulnerable adults, allowing questions to be asked about the nature of their roles, affinities and dependability. Confidentiality smokescreens cannot be used as an excuse not to ascertain the probity and integrity of the individuals involved.

The recent report, *Enabling risk, ensuring safety*, from the Social Care Institute for Excellence (SCIE) (Carr, 2010) appears to reinforce family systems thinking by suggesting that there is evidence that social work skills and relationship-based working with the person using the service is required, both to promote risk enablement as part of self-directed support and to detect and prevent abuse as part of safeguarding. The report further concludes that practitioners need support from local authorities to incorporate safeguarding and risk enablement into relationship-based, person-centred working, and that good quality, consistent and trusted relationships and good communication are particularly important for self-directed support and personal budget schemes.

The final report of the evaluation of the individual budgets pilot programme (Glendinning et al, 2008) acknowledged that there were safeguarding issues still to be addressed. There were concerns about potential exploitation of vulnerable adults by family or neighbours taking responsibility for budgets, and by the nature of contracts set between clients and a largely unregulated workforce – personal assistants – exacerbated by an inattention to monitoring of these relationships.

Where abuses have been alleged, in this case in residential care services, it is reported that multi-agency collaboration, transparency of practice, training, reflective practice and effective supervision of frontline staff, appear to assist managers and care workers in negotiating the positive and negative experiences of the implementation of adult protection systems (Rees and Manthorpe, 2010).

Conclusion

Evidence about good safeguarding is expanding quickly. The full extent of abuse and harm of vulnerable adults is still not known, but valuable insights are coming to light from continued analysis of the contexts in which abuse and harm can occur, and not least from the vigilance of well trained practitioners supported by joined-up inter-agency safeguarding protocols. The incorporation of life course perspectives into frontline practice is likely to assist preventive work with vulnerable adults, and to ensure that safety and well-being are maintained as a top priority.

References

Beadle-Brown, J., Mansell, J., Cambridge, P., Milne, A. and Whelton, B. (2010) 'Adult protection of people with intellectual disabilities: incidence, nature and responses', *Journal of Applied Research in Intellectual Disabilities*, vol 23, pp 573-84.

Berzins, K.M., Petch, A. and Atkinson, J.M. (2003) 'Prevalence and experience of harassment of people with mental health problems living in the community', *The British Journal of Psychiatry*, vol 183, pp 526-33.

Bowes, A. and Daniel, B. (2010) 'Introduction: Interrogating harm and abuse: a lifespan approach', *Social Policy and Society*, vol 9, no 2, pp 221-9.

Carr, S. (2010) *Enabling risk, ensuring safety: Self-directed support and personal budgets*, Adults' Services SCIE Report 36, London: Social Care Institute for Excellence.

Clausen, J.A. (1998) 'Life reviews and life stories', in J.Z. Giele and G.H. Elder (eds) *Methods of life course research: Quantitative and qualitative approaches*, Thousand Oaks: Sage Publications, pp 189-212.

Cooper, C., Selwood, A. and Livingston, G. (2008) 'The prevalence of elder abuse and neglect: a systematic review', *Age and Ageing*, vol 37, no 2, pp 151-60.

Cooper, C., Blanchard, M., Selwood, A., Walker, Z., Blizard, R. and Livingston, G. (2009) 'Abuse of people with dementia by family carers: representative cross sectional survey', *British Medical Journal*, vol 338, p 155.

CSCI (Commission for Social Care Inspection), ADSS (Association of Directors of Social Services) and ACPO (Association of Chief Probation Officers) (2007) *Safeguarding adults protocol and guidance*, London: CSCI.

DH (Department of Health) (2010a) *A vision for adult social care: Capable communities and active citizens*, London: The Stationery Office.

DH (2010b) *Equity and excellence: Liberating the NHS*, Cm 7881, London: The Stationery Office.

DH and Home Office (2000) *No secrets: Guidance on developing and implementing multi-agency policies and procedures to protect vulnerable adults from abuse*, London: The Stationery Office.

Fitzpatrick, M. and Hamill, S.B. (2010) 'Elder abuse: factors related to perceptions of severity and likelihood of reporting', *Journal of Elder Abuse and Neglect*, vol 23, no 1, pp 1-16.

Flynn, M. and Brown, H. (2010) 'Safeguarding adults with learning disabilities against abuse', in G. Grant, P. Ramcharan, M. Flynn and M. Richardson (eds) *Learning disability: A life cycle approach* (2nd edn), Maidenhead: Open University Press and McGraw Hill Education, pp 217-31.

Glendinning, C., Challis, D., Fernandez, J.L., Jacobs, S., Jones, K., Knapp, M., Manthorpe, J., Moran, N., Netten, A., Stevens, M. and Wilberforce, M. (2008) *Evaluation of the Individual Budgets Pilot Programme: Final Report*, London: Department of Health.

Hawley, D. and DeHaan, L. (1996) 'Toward a definition of family resilience: integrating lifespan and family perspectives', *Family Process*, vol 35, pp 283-98.

House of Commons Health Committee (2009) *Sixth report: Patient safety*, London: The Stationery Office.

Johnson, F., Hogg, J. and Daniel, B. (2010) 'Abuse and protection issues across the lifespan: reviewing the literature', *Social Policy and Society*, vol 9, no 2, pp 291-304.

Landau, J. (2010) 'Communities that care for families: the LINC model for enhancing individual, family and community resilience', *American Journal of Orthopsychiatry*, vol 80, no 4, pp 516–24.

O'Callaghan, A.C., Murphy, G. and Clare, I.C.H. (2003) 'The impact of abuse on men and women with severe learning disabilities and their families', *British Journal of Learning Disabilities*, vol 31, no 4, pp 175–80.

Priestley, M. (2000) 'Adults only: disability, social policy and the life course', *Journal of Social Policy*, vol 29, no 3, pp 421–39.

Rees, P. and Manthorpe, J. (2010) 'Managers' and staff experiences of adult protection allegations in mental health and learning disability residential services: a qualitative study', *British Journal of Social Work*, vol 40, no 2, pp 513–29.

Reid, D., Penhale, B., Manthorpe, J., Perkins, N., Pinkney, L. and Hussein, S. (2009) 'Form and function: views from members of adult protection committees in England and Wales', *The Journal of Adult Protection*, vol 11, no 4, pp 20–9.

Rutter, M. (1996) 'Transitions and turning points in developmental psychopathology as applied to the age span between childhood and mid-adulthood', *International Journal of Behavioural Development*, vol 19, no 3, pp 603–26.

Sinclair, R. and Bullock, R. (2002) *Learning from past experience: A review of serious case reviews*, London: Department of Health.

Trivette, C.M., Dunst, C.J. and Hamby, D.W. (2010) 'Influences of family systems interventions on parent–child interactions and child development', *Topics in Early Childhood Special Education*, vol 30, no 1, pp 3–19.

Whitelock, A. (2009) 'Safeguarding in mental health: towards a rights-based approach', *Journal of Adult Protection*, vol 11, no 4, pp 30–42.

Wilson, G. (1994) 'Abuse of elderly men and women among clients of a community psychogeriatric service', *British Journal of Social Work*, vol 24, no 6, pp 681–700.

SECTION FIVE

Practice: ways of doing – or not?

22

Why collaborate?

Janet Bardsley

> It is important that organisations work well together and that
> departments tackle the barriers to joint working so that long
> lasting improvements are made to the quality of services that
> the public receive. (Sir John Bourn, Head of the National Audit
> Office, quoted in NAO, 2001)

This statement offered to Parliament in 2001 might be considered a
truism. Working well together means better quality services. However, the
evidence is that partnership is not a straightforward goal (Cameron and
Lart, 2003; Atkinson et al, 2007). Its achievement may create emotional,
financial and practical bounty (Ham and Smith, 2010), but it is also a road
littered with good intentions and a spirit of acrimony and retrenchment
to professional and organisational bunkers (Hudson, 2002; Brown et al,
2003). It is therefore important to understand why it is necessary to rise
to the challenge personally, professionally and organisationally, to embark
on shared ways of working … when, let's face it, getting on and doing for
yourself, or directing others to produce, to the standard you expect, can
seem a lot easier.

Any consideration of joint working has to acknowledge the diversity of
forms it can take. Atkinson et al (2007) collated 14 definitions of multi-
agency activity, and as time passes there is a tendency to proliferate rather
than consolidate the vocabulary, for example, the recent increased use of
the term 'co-production'. This is understandable, given the complexity
of the aspiration, and the multiple ways in which organisations, teams,
individual workers or members of the public can overlap in both their
intentions and actions. The language reflects the nuances of the nature and
quality of collaborative activity. Carnwell and Buchanen (2005) illustrate
this in their suggested continuum of terms that represent the growing trust
and reciprocity that can emerge in shared arrangements with service users:

Involvement → *Collaboration* → *Participation* → *Partnership*

Joint working could be perceived as an issue primarily between
health and social care organisations, or between different parts of the
NHS (predominantly the acute and community services). However,

in considering the health and well-being of adults using a life course perspective, these narrow organisational boundaries do not reflect the only areas where more collaboration could be perceived to be beneficial. All parts of the welfare state, and the social environment, are part of the make-up of the support that enables us to live healthy lives of quality. For the purposes of this chapter the broadest possible view of collaboration is taken, both in terms of the level of change and commitment to the principle, and to the range of partners who might engage.

'Because service users say so'

The first and perhaps primary reason to collaborate is because of the feedback and views of those people who might need support in their lives. A growing feature of the delivery of public services has been the appreciation of the importance of listening to service users and patients about their experience of the services that are delivered to them. This perspective is obviously fundamental to the whole principle of 'person-centred' health and social care. It is anomalous to suggest that such care can happen if nobody involved in delivering services has listened to, and acknowledged, what the 'person' thought was important about their situation. However, there are also other more generalised forms of comment and perspective from the types of 'customer care' and quality systems such as, for example, complaints procedures.

There have also been concerted moves to include service users in policy making and larger scale planning and design of services. This is not an uncontested process and raises concerns about power and control, tokenism and representation (Schehrer and Sexton, 2010). However, one of the clear messages from these sources is about the need for greater collaboration. The consultation about person-centred services, *Our voice in our future*, noted the process:

> ... highlighted service users' holistic approach to their lives and the services that they need, and that social care needs to become part of a "whole systems" approach taking in health care, benefits, transport and support with training and employment.... (Turner et al, 2003, p 25)

There is abundant evidence of the frustration felt about the lack of communication and coordination between services. Events organised to canvass views consistently raise issues of wanting less bureaucratic, more easily understood and accessible services (Beresford and Hasler, 2009; CQC, 2010).

The centrality of people's experience is also reflected in the concern for their inclusion in measures of 'outcomes' as the bases for integration. The Darzi review of the NHS (DH, 2008, p 70) emphasised this as the focus of joint work, stating the importance of putting '… the needs of patients and communities before organisational boundaries…'. In a similar way, guidance to local authorities, as part of *Putting People First*, highlighted the impact on service user lives as the basis for assessing the coordination of the services delivered (Bennett et al, 2009).

'Because the government says so'

> It is difficult to find a contemporary policy document or set of good practice guidelines that does not have collaboration as the central strategy for the delivery of welfare. (Dowling et al, 2004, p 309)

Although not new at that time, the principle of 'seamless' and 'joined-up' government is closely associated with the Labour administration from 1997. However, the centrally driven requirement to collaborate is unlikely to disappear with future administrations. Even in the early months of the new Coalition government, they were able to make statements on social care that stated a commitment to 'break down barriers between health and social care funding to incentivise preventative action' (DH, 2010). And Eric Pickles, the Secretary of State for Communities and Local Government, radically and, somewhat provocatively at the time, suggested the sharing of chief executive and other senior roles as a cost-saving strategy (Pickles, 2010).

There are various ways in which governments approach driving a central agenda for more joint working. Besides exhortations in public policy statements, there have been a number of examples where collaborative ways of working have been piloted and used as exemplars to replicate as national models. For example, integrated care organisations tested out 15 pilots of joint working between a range of health and social care departments (Rosen and Ham, 2008; DH, 2009). Central governments can also use less 'facilitative' approaches to achieving collaborative ways of working and adopt more authoritarian tactics. Parton describes a 'statutory voluntarism' where joint working no longer becomes an option reflecting good practice, but a local requirement (Parton, 2004, cited in Dowling et al, 2004). The Delayed Discharges Act 2003, where local authorities are practically fined for apparently 'blocking' acute hospital beds, might seem to be among the most punitive example of such a strategy.

The imperative to restructure and work differently is the inheritance every recent government has acquired from the organisation of the welfare state set up in the period of postwar crisis, a framework that could be considered not entirely fit for purpose for the early part of the 21st century. Miller (2004) suggests that the immediate postwar construction of the welfare state sat well with the experience of wartime centralised planning and coordination. Beveridge also achieved political consensus in his articulation of the role of the state to abolish the five giants of social evil of 'Want', 'Idleness', 'Ignorance', 'Squalor' and 'Disease'. In such a climate the 'organisational architecture of the welfare state' was one where centrally driven bureaucratic forms administered by privileged professionals became the only way to ensure basic services were available to all at the point of need (Newman and Clarke, 1994 citied in Miller, 2004, p 15). The divisions between the centrally funded NHS and local authority services of housing and social care were made, and the contracts that divided GPs, and therefore primary services, from secondary healthcare in hospital were set. However, the monolithic state bureaucracies acceptable at this time are not appropriate to postmodern conditions of increased demographic pressures, an emphasis on continual change and innovation, individualised and specialised interventions. It is from these conditions that the inevitable pressures to make connections across organisational and professional boundaries and reconstruct delivery through collaboration and partnership emerge.

The other tenet that has been central to all administrations over the past 30 years has been the role of 'markets', in some form, as a mechanism for the delivery of public services. The underlying principle of competition could be seen as the antithesis of collaboration and partnership. In the absence of a free market system, the role of 'quasi-markets' have centred largely on the provision of a range of provider services including those from the third sector, that is, hospitals, and residential care. Ham (2008) suggests that for the NHS such a competitive scenario has been an effective means of coordination in areas of predictable provision (for example, in planned admissions and reduction of waiting times), but that it is a structure that 'sucks resources into hospitals'. The concern is about whether such a mechanism is likely to be effective in responding to other new priorities such as those of disease prevention and chronic disease.

'Because we want to do better'

Further imperatives for collaboration come from the aspirations about the lifestyles that are expected to be supported. Basic principles of service, which are now seen as standard, are relatively new. For example, Enoch

Powell, speaking as Minister for Health, in his famous 'Water Tower' speech, summed up the nature of the task as he foresaw it in closing the large mental hospitals:

> "This is a colossal undertaking, not so much in the new physical provision which it involves, as in the sheer inertia of mind and matter which it requires to be overcome. There they stand, isolated, majestic, imperious, brooded over by the gigantic water-tower and chimney combined, rising unmistakable and daunting out of the countryside – the asylums which our forefathers built with such immense solidity to express the notions of their day." (Powell, 1961; emphasis added)

In considering residential and other services to people with mental health problems 50 years later, the 'inertia of mind' has been overcome and ideas have changed. There is now no call for a single hospital-based asylum accommodating hundreds of people that Powell describes having to dismantle. Modern patterns of service require collaborative engagement across multiple providers and service users themselves

Grint (2010), in his evaluation of 'Total Place', suggested the challenges facing public bodies required different responses and leadership styles 'Total Place' was another pilot in collaborative services, initiated centrally to explore mechanisms for joint working and devolving power more locally. Grint developed a typology of the problems faced by the organisations in this project:

- A *critical* problem is presented as self-evident in nature, as leaving very little time for action, and is associated with authoritarianism. Examples could be responding to a major train crash or a heart attack;
- A *tame* problem is associated with only a limited degree of uncertainty and is thought to be amenable to management intervention such as timetabling the railways or planned heart surgery;
- A *wicked* problem is more complex, rather than just more complicated; it shows no clear relationship between cause and effect and it cannot be extracted from its environment, solved and returned without affecting the environment. (Grint, 2010, cited in Hudson, 2010, p 21)

The expectations about services could be increasingly categorised as 'wicked problems', requiring levels of collaboration and leadership that distinguish them from previous agendas in health and social care. An example of this transformation is illustrated by the 1971 White Paper '*Better services for the mentally handicapped*' (DHSS, 1971). This dealt with the need for day time activities at a number of places in adult training centres. This could be categorised as a 'tame' problem, addressed by a numerical target to be met by the single agency responsible, that ie. the local authority. The next statement, 30 years later, in the White Paper '*Valuing People: A strategy for learning disability for the 21st century*' (DH, 2001), covered the issue by two objectives:

- *to lead full and purposeful lives* in their communities and to develop a range of friendships, activities and relationships.
- to participate in all forms of employment, wherever possible in paid work and *to make a valued contribution to the world of work*.
  (DH, 2001 p 33; emphasis added)

No single agency could address these aspirations. Like other modern principles of services, such as support to independence and autonomy, disease prevention and behaviour change, challenges to stigma and changing attitudes, requires a blossoming of service arrangements and approaches. They fall within Grint's typology of 'wicked problem' where the objectives of the service become inextricably linked to changes within wider political priorities and social contexts.

New understandings of effective ways to support people also impel joint working. Increased knowledge produces more specialism's, specialist teams and ranges of providers that need to work together to be effective for the individual at the centre of the service. If these specialist responses can be viewed sequentially as a 'pathway', or what Hudson (2010) refers to as vertical integration, then the issue for collaboration is about clarity of the process and information sharing between the different relevant stages. However, even this basic and obvious requirement to work together can be problematic when roles and functions are separated. The Care Quality Commission (CQC) reported that 17 per cent of residential homes did not receive basic information about exposure to infections from admission from acute hospital, and 3% per cent of Ps did not receive information about medical procedures or treatments their patients had received while in acute hospital care (CQC, 2010). More challenging are the situations Hudson (2010) suggests require horizontal integration. These are where the understanding of the issue and what needs to be done to support a person require simultaneous and co-ordinated delivery of specialist service.

'Because it could be a matter of life and death'

In this final section the argument for collaboration comes to matters of life and death, or at least, the fact that there are some very distressing and difficult situations that have to be responded to. Significant learning about joint working emerges from the various enquiries and reviews that occur when it appears something has gone wrong, and that an untimely death has occurred. The evidence from these situations in relation to children, for example, Victoria Climbié and Baby Peter, have been well documented, publicised and instrumental in bringing about legislative and organisational change (Driscoll, 2009) Sadly the messages from parallel forms of investigation in relation to adults also frequently note the key role of miscommunication or misunderstanding between organisations as being a key feature of a pattern of service breakdown that leads to tragic consequences (Manthorpe and Martineau, 2011).

Unfortunately any sort of review is just that, looking back when something has gone wrong. They are symptomatic of the complex and uncertain situations individual workers and organisations have to respond to routinely to manage risk (Clarke et al, 2011). While there has been some effort to work together to provide a single assessment of a person's situation using the Single Assessment Process (Miller and Cameron, 2011), there is also a need to ensure shared responsibility for the decisions surrounding risk in the ongoing delivery and review of the support a person might need.

The predominance of risk as a concern may be seen to be a feature of our age (Beck, 1992). However, it also presents particular complexities when balanced by the increasing acknowledgement of the legal rights and adult status of those who are described as 'vulnerable'. There is a balance for services between respecting a person's choice to live eccentric and unusual lifestyles, or to make decisions others perceive as perilous, while still addressing professional standards and a duty of care (McDermott, 2010). The processes to achieve this balance necessarily require collaboration to give the fullest picture of a person's choices, health and capacity to understand the risks they are taking. This holistic view is also required to develop positive strategies to manage the risks individuals wish to take in living their lives, rather than to only have to adopt a narrow consideration of oppressive strategies of risk avoidance (CSCI, 2006).

Conclusion

In the need to work together to manage risk, the focus is again towards the individual service user. Modern standards, aspirations and values of respect to all, whatever their situation, appear to necessitate an open appreciation and acknowledgement of all players involved in seeking to support adults in living the lives they want. Whatever the difficulties in achieving this goal, it is this positive and constructive prize that makes working across organisational boundaries a necessity in the 21st century.

Reference

Atkinson, M., Jones M. and Lamont, E. (2007) *Multi agency working and its implication for practice: A review of the literature*, Slough: NFER

Beck, U. (1992) *Risk society: Towards a new modernity*, London: Sage Publications.

Bennett, T., Cattermole, M. and Sanderson, H. (2009) *Putting people first: Outcomes-focused reviews, A practical guide*, London: Department of Health.

Beresford, P. and Hasler, F. (2009 *Transforming social care: Changing the future together*, Uxbridge: Brunel University Press (www.shapingourlives.org.uk/documents/132459TransformingSocialCareFinal150dpi.p1)

Brown, L., Tucker, T. and Domokos, T. (2003) 'Evaluating the impact of integrated health and social care teams on older people living in the community', *Health and Social Care in the Community*, vol 11, no 2, pp 8–94.

Cameron, A. and Lart, R. (2003) 'Factors promoting and obstacles hindering joint working: a systematic review of the research evidence', *Journal of Integrated Care*, vol 11, no 2, pp 9–17.

Carnwell, R. and Buchanan, J. (eds) (2005) *Effective partnership in health and social care: A partnership approach*, Maidenhead: Open University Press.

Clarke, C., Wilcockson, J., Gibb, C., Keady, J., Wilkinson, H. and Luce, A. (2011) 'Reframing risk management in dementia care through collaborative learning', *Health and Social Care in the Community*, vol 19, no 1, pp 23–32.

CSCI (Commission for Social Care Inspection) (2006) *Making choices: Taking risks*, London: CSCI.

CQC (Care Quality Commission) (2010) *The state of health care and adult social care in England: Key themes and quality of services in 2009*, Newcastle upon Tyne: CQC.

DH (Department of Health) (2001) *Valuing people: A strategy for learning disability for the 21st century*, White Paper, London: The Stationery Office.

DH (2008) *High quality care for all: NHS next stage review. Final report* (Darzi review), Cm 7432, London: The Stationery Office.

DH (2009) *Integrated care pilots: An introductory guide*, London: The Stationery Office.

DH (2010) *A vision of adult social care: Capable communities, active citizens*, London: The Stationery Office.

DHSS (Department of Health and Social Security) (1971) *Better services for the mentally handicapped*, White Paper, London: HMSO.

Dowling, B., Powell, M. and Glendinning, C. (2004) 'Conceptualising successful partnerships', *Health and Social Care in the Community*, vol 12, no 4, pp 309–17.

Driscoll, J. (2009) 'Prevalence, people and processes: a consideration of the implications of Lord Laming's progress report on the protection of children in England', *Child Abuse Review*, vol 18, pp 333–45.

Grint, K. (2010) *Purpose, power, knowledge: Time and space. Total Place final research report*, Coventry: Warwickshire Business School.

Ham, C. (2008) 'Competition and integration in the English National Health Service', *British Medical Journal*, vol 336, pp 805–7.

Ham, C. and Smith, J. (2010) *Removing the policy barriers to integrated care in England*, Briefing Paper, London: The Nuffield Trust.

Hudson, B. (2002) 'Interprofessionality in health and social care: the Achilles' heel of partnership?', *Journal of Interprofessional Care*, vol 16, no 1, pp 8-17.

Hudson, B. (2010) 'The three Ps in the NHS White Paper: partnership, privatisation and predation: which way will it go and does it matter?', *Journal of Integrated Care*, vol 18, no 5, pp 15–24.

McDermott, S. (2010) 'Professional judgements of risk and capacity in situations of self neglect among older people', *Ageing & Society*, vol 30, pp 1055–72.

Manthorpe, J. and Martineau, S. (2010) 'Serious case reviews in adult safeguarding in England: an analysis of a sample of reports', *British Journal of Social Work*, vol 41, no 2, pp 224–41 (18).

Miller, C. (2004) *Producing welfare: A modern agenda*, Basingstoke: Palgrave.

Miller, E. and Cameron, K. (2011) 'Challenges and benefits in implementing shared inter-agency assessment across the UK: a literature review', *Journal of Interprofessional Care*, vol 25, no 1, pp 3–45.

NAO (National Audit Office) (2001) 'Joining up to improve public services', Press release (www.nao.org.uk/publications/press_notice_home/0102/0102383).

Pickles, E. (2010) 'Townhall waste and duplication', Speech by the Secretary of State for Communities and Local Government, Hammersmith & Fulham Town Hall, London, 13 October (www.communities.gov.uk/speeches/corporate/townhallwaste).

Powell, E. (1961) Address to the National Association of Mental Health Annual Conference, 9 March (www.nhshistory.net/watertower.html).

Rosen, R. and Ham, C. (2008) *Integrated care: Lessons from evidence and experience, Report of the 2008 Sir Roger Bannister Annual Health Seminar*, Nuffield Trust Summary Report, London: The Nuffield Trust.

Schehrer, S. and Sexton, S. (2010 *Involving users in commissioning local service*, York: Joseph Rowntree Foundation.

Turner, M., Brough, P. and Williams-Findlay, R.B. (2003) *Our voice in our future: Service users debate the future of the welfare state*, York: Joseph Rowntree Foundation.

23

Working in teams: relationships in balance?

Geraldine Crewes

Introduction

Any involvement in the health and care arena gives some insight to a complex set of organisational and decision-making systems. Such systems can become characterised by functional approaches in which individuals may regard themselves as a small cog in a very large apparatus. Where do patients, service users and carers find themselves in this busy, intangible mechanism?

Within this context lies the reality of day-to-day teamwork, the process that supports the delivery of critical services. In this chapter, the focus is on what this might mean in practice, alongside questions about the nature of teams, roles and dynamics, and how this has an impact on working effectively across teams of different types. How are individual strengths and skills appreciated, valued and nurtured within teams? How does a team move forward when agendas remain contested? Are service users and carers recognised as colleagues in the team?

At the heart of these questions is a consideration of relationships. It may be a truism to suggest that meaningful practice relies on meaningful relationships. The possibility is explored that by using the principles of relationship-based practice, and the skills of assertiveness, it is feasible to create working practices that provide foundations for credible and enlightening teamwork.

More than just a sum of its parts?

It would be easy to assume that any team in the health and care professions is imbued with an unspoken shared motivation to work in collaboration with others, to meet the needs of patients, carers and service users. Experience indicates such assumptions are flawed and perhaps underestimate the emotional skills and adaptations involved in developing and sustaining a productive team of diverse practitioners. As social animals the preference is to work together, but this may conflict with a fondness for 'getting things done' in a way that works best for the individual. Indeed, it is noted by Laing that the natural inclination towards 'relatedness to others'

252

is matched only by an equal inclination towards 'separateness' (Laing, 1959, p 26). As such, how can these apparently opposing forces be balanced when placed within the confines of a team? Furthermore, how can there be the development of an effective system of collaboration that achieves its goals (Douglas, 1976) and remains relevant to the world in which it sits?

If teams are considered as a specific sort of created (rather than naturally occurring) group, brought together and defined by the nature of its management and task (Heron, 2008), then much can be learnt about teams by considering the dynamic connectivity of individuals, groups and tasks (Adair, 1986). In doing so, we can recognise the organismic nature of a team which (contrasting to a mechanistic model) is able to grow and emerge into a transformed system and thus 'more than just the simple sum of its parts' (Shulman, 1999, p 535). Hence, developing effectively as a team requires attention, not just to outcomes, but also to process; not just to objectives, but also to relationships. Too much emphasis on one aspect at the expense of another will alter the dynamic of a team and thus present different models and outcomes. Teams may thus seek to balance their apparently contradictory introvert and extrovert drives, at once focusing on reviewing skills and refreshing expertise from within the team, while simultaneously reaching out to engage in inter-personal and inter-agency networks (Payne, 2000). In holding this delicate balance, a team can be seen to be capable of growth, and in its more effective, self-aware and reflexive state, a team displaying many of the characteristics of collective emotional intelligence (Howe, 2008).

Coordination and collaboration: boundaries and expectations

Much has been written about the roles, structures and systems of multi or inter-agency teams. The contrasting examples of a 'coordinated professional team' as opposed to a 'collective responsible team' (Øvretveit, 1997) may be helpful here as a means of distinguishing between two patterns of teamwork. As such, a coordinated model provides pathways of service provision, running alongside each other, offering separate but complementary resources, such as nurses, doctors and physiotherapists on a hospital ward. Meanwhile, a collaborative model merges such provision into a shared structure of accountability, such as community psychiatric nurses, social workers and psychologists within a community mental health team. The complexity of such models is intensified when the boundaries of practice become sufficiently blurred as to create confusions of accountability and culture (Payne, 2000).

It is often in the context of team dynamics that issues of power, role contention, role confusion, conflicting expectations and individual choice can come to the fore. The particular qualities of team members, clarity of task and group relationships will be greatly influenced by, and in turn have an impact on, the psychological well-being of a team as it seeks to make sense of this inter-related structure (Douglas, 1976).

The tenet offered by Thompson is that constructive collaboration is built on the principles of clarity, both in boundaries and expectations (Thompson, 2009). At the heart of these principles lie the key skills of communication and most particularly, the ability to share an understanding of role and purpose alongside the ability to recognise and value the perspectives of others. Belbin, in his widely cited research, highlights distinct and complementary group roles to indicate the concept of skills balance to affect task development, delegation and completion (Belbin, 2010). In the meantime, Bion draws attention to the idea of 'good group spirit' (Bion, 1961) which can be used to enhance resilience and continuity in the evolving life of teams.

Live and learn

Such sophisticated skills of assertive negotiation, implicit in the communication necessary to establish clarity and role and expectation, rely on a level of motivation and drive, powered by values central to the health and care professions. Care, in this context, is bound up in the ideology of compassion, compassion for those you work with and alongside. Hence being clear about the shared values and purpose within the team helps establish the motivation to work effectively together to meet the needs of others. There is much resonance here with those models of cultural competence which advocate a process of living and learning with others to gain insight into their perspectives and experiences. This also requires a sustained commitment to fostering, respecting and revising relationships with others, in the light of what is learnt (Carballeira, 1997; Laird, 2008).

So if that is agreed, why is it so much easier to offer these aspirational words than it is to practise in their spirit? What are the restraining forces at play that throw down obstacles to the good intentions and invitations to loosen fixed principles?

What can go wrong? Working with involuntary colleagues

The literature in relation to 'involuntary clients' can offer some intriguing insight to relationships with colleagues from different professional groups (Rooney, 1992; Calder, 2009). There are parallels here when some staff may be expected to develop constructive working relationships with colleagues, across disciplines and departments, without seeing either the relevance of such relationships, or what there might be to gain from this enforced 'team spirit'. As such, motivation may not be shared evenly, and any recognition of aim, purpose and the use of authority may remain unresolved (Trotter, 2008). While pressure (in this instance, to conform) can provide a stimulus for energy and performance, it may also provide a source of unwanted tension that is potentially debilitating and unproductive (Thompson, 2007).

A team facing dissonance in motivation and purpose, already fragmented in its foundations, may be further hindered by conflicts in styles of communication. While it may be too easy (and unhelpful) to categorise differences solely within such powerful discourses as gender and culture, it may be equally unrealistic to underestimate their impact here. Assessing the interaction between discourse, individual character and context will offer some insight to the interchange between team members.

Other pressures

It is useful to consider what approaches team members favour – a collaborative style in which members seek to explore and encourage a collective viewpoint, and thus garner a shared meaning, or alternatively a more dominating style vying to obtain and retain an audience in order to present their comparative ideas and articulate their own meaning. Some research has attributed collaborative styles more commonly with women and comparative approaches more commonly with men (Case, 1994), while other psycho-social factors may be considered influential in terms of cultural 'norms' regarding levels of autonomy, risk-taking and deference (Hofstede, 1991).

Some team members may feel disenfranchised if they are not included in the problem-solving process, while others may be impatient with a perceived lack of leadership. Either group may have developed strategies that have previously served them well in getting the response they desire and resort to game-playing to preserve their position (Berne, 1968).

'All tragedy is the failure of communication' (Wilson, 1956, p 9)

So far, the picture is painted in such bold themes as power and trust woven into the practice of teams, with communication acting as both cause and effect. Thus the relationship is often acted out between language and wider social systems – language at once both reflecting and reinforcing discrimination in society (Thompson, 2009). It is possible to consider such systemic dynamics within the culture of teams and reinforce those habitual practices which create discourses more resistant to critical examination (Brown et al, 2006). As such, not only might teams find themselves restricted by dominant styles of communication, but also underpinned by dominant assumptions about goal achievement, status and professional hierarchies. A race to reach a solution may offer a false sense of efficiency in which answers may be offered before all the questions have been asked. By missing an opportunity to balance organisational learning with 'unlearning' it is likely that an opening for individual and team growth is also closed down (MacDonald, 2002, cited in Gould and Baldwin, 2004).

What unlocked potential is trapped within a team when such communication blocks prevail? How might questions of power and trust exert themselves when inter-professional constraints of eligibility, priority, inflexible operational systems and cultures are interlinked? After all, safe working practice is a fragile commodity, in need of careful attention, wherein 'professional judgement and decision-making is inherently uncertain' (Parton, 2001).

With so many obstacles in the way, it is all too easy to lose sight of the very people that we are seeking to help, as they become hidden behind the impenetrable camouflage of bureaucratic barriers. It is within this context that people are lost. As with any Shakespearean tragedy, information is mis-interpreted, mis-represented or hidden at the expense of the literary victim.

Overcoming the obstacles to effective multi-professional teamwork

Perhaps, not unlike some of those qualities identified as promoting resilience in children facing difficulties, a team member may benefit from developing a capacity to harness their strengths in the face of adversity and stress. As such, developing good relationships with peers alongside autonomous coping strategies and supports (including an appropriate use of humour) translate to useful teambuilding skills. Applying to this a sense of self-efficacy and reflection offers a practitioner a sense that they are valued and able to make a positive contribution – in short, the skills of reflexive practice as the person interacts with the lived experience, reflecting, reinterpreting and responding to the complexities of professional relationships (Adams et al, 2009).

In the context of 'involuntary colleagues' it is possible to make links with the field of pro-social modelling. Clarity of role and shared principles alongside collaborative problem solving are seen as being enhanced when legitimate 'pro-social' skills are encouraged. From a behaviourist stance, this may be in keeping with offering attention and praise to constructive team behaviour and presenting an accurate and considered model of good practice (Trotter, 2008).

Such approaches to teamwork are not without the concept of challenge. In fact, it is argued that constructive challenge is a key skill used by practitioners to advocate and represent the needs of others (Lishman, 2009). Such skills should be transferable into teamworking skills. To get this right, the timing, manner and motivation for challenge needs to be assessed. Presenting constructive challenges will involve skills of assertiveness and negotiation alongside those of reframing and flexibility (Petch, 2002, cited in Coulshed and Orme, 2006). In this context, it is worth keeping a close eye on those interwoven responses of aggression and passivity. Individuals may delight in angry confrontation or keep a veiled 'score of wrongs', both being habitual practices that are at risk of causing harm (McBride, 1998). It could be argued here that challenge that lacks elegance (Thompson, 2003) and compassion may serve only to distract from the original area of concern, leading to a loss of trust and respect.

Good-enough teamwork or a higher aspiration?

A range of research has identified the value that is placed on clear, tangible, material help within the context of good inter-personal skills (Mayer and Timms, 1970; Rees and Wallace, 1982; Harding and Beresford, 1995). A focus on assertive practice in which honest expression, used with integrity, forms the backbone of practice that aids others to change their behaviour (Jakubowski, 1977, cited in Thompson, 2009). For many, a concept of 'good-enough' teamwork may restrict the opportunities for the self-aware and responsive practices required for growth and thus not mirror the reflexive expertise required in wider practice.

Herein may lay the potential for emotional incongruence, as team members experience a lack of fit between the values expressed within their profession and the practices governing their own development. Such incongruence may stimulate well-established defence mechanisms (Munro, 2010), which in turn take their emotional toll as a worker who senses a lack of influence in this scenario is likely to feel powerless and vulnerable to stress. Contributing to an environment in which staff feel encouraged and understood (by peers as well as managers) offers a sense of hope in which change can happen and suggests a humanitarian cultural 'norm'. The importance of reflective supervision is paramount to this process.

So, returning to the fundamental principles of communication in collaborative work, the key skills here are those of feedback, assertiveness and relationship-based engagement. An empathic and transparent clarity of role, purpose and authority can build professional relationships based on trust, accountability and recognised strengths. The guidance for such work is inherent in many of the central skills of care practice. With a mutuality of enterprise and solidarity, such skills create territory for a constructive 'community of practice' (Wenger, 1998).

References

Adair, J. (1986) *Effective teambuilding*, London: Pan.

Adams, R., Dominelli, L. and Payne, M. (2009) *Social work: Themes, issues and critical debates* (3rd edn), Basingstoke: Palgrave Macmillan.

Belbin, R.M. (2010) *Management teams: Why they succeed or fail* (3rd edn) Oxford: Butterworth Heinemann.

Berne, E. (1968) *The games people play*, Harmondsworth: Penguin.

Bion, W.R. (1961) *Experiences in groups and other papers*, London: Tavistock.

Brown, K., Rutter, L. and Keen, S. (2006) *Partnerships, continuing professional development (CPD) and the accreditation of prior learning (APL): Supporting workforce development across the social care sector*, Birmingham: Learn To Care.

Calder, M. (2009) *The carrot or the stick? Towards effective practice with involuntary clients in safeguarding children work*, Lyme Regis: Russell House Publishing Ltd.

Carballeira, N. (1997) 'The LIVE and LEARN model for cultural competent family services', *Continuum*, January-February, pp 7-12.

Case, S.S. (1994) 'Gender differences in communication and behaviour in organisations', in M.J. Davidson and R.J. Burke (eds) *Women in management: Current research issues*, London: Paul Chapman, pp 144-67 [cited in M. Payne (2000) *Teamwork in multiprofessional care*, Basingstoke: Macmillan].

Coulshed, V. and Orme, J. (2006) *Social work practice* (4th edn), Basingstoke: Palgrave Macmillan.

Douglas, T. (1976) *Groupwork practice*, London: Tavistock.

Gould, N. and Baldwin, M. (2004) *Social work, critical reflection and the learning organisation*, Aldershot: Ashgate.

Harding, T. and Beresford, P. (1995) *What service users and carers value and expect from social services staff: A report to the Department of Health*, London: Department of Health.

Heron, J. (2008) *The complete facilitator's handbook*, London: Kogan Page.

Hofstede, G. (1991) *Cultures and organisations*, London: HarperCollins.

Howe, D. (2008) *The emotionally intelligent social worker*, Basingstoke: Palgrave Macmillan.

Laing, R.D. (1959) *The divided self: An existential study in sanity and madness*, Harmondsworth: Pelican Books.

Laird, S.E. (2008) *Anti-oppressive social work: A guide for developing cultural competence*, London: Sage Publications.

Lishman, J. (2009) *Communication in social work* (2nd edn), Basingstoke: Palgrave Macmillan.

Mayer, J.E. and Timms, N. (1970) *The client speak: Working class impressions of casework*, London: Routledge & Kegan Paul.

McBride, P. (1998) *The assertive social worker*, Aldershot: Ashgate.

Munro, E. (2010) *The Munro Review of child protection: A systems analysis*, London: Department for Education.

Øvretveit, J. (1997) 'How to describe interprofessional working', in J. Øvretveit, P. Mathias and T. Thompson (eds) *Interprofessional working for health and social care*, London: Macmillan, pp 9-33.

Parton, N. (2001) '*Risk and professional judgment*', in L.-A. Cull and J. Roche (eds) *The law and social work*, Basingstoke: Palgrave, pp 137–47.

Payne, M. (2000) *Teamwork in multiprofessional care*, Basingstoke: Macmillan.

Rees, S. and Wallace, A. (1982) *Verdicts on social work*, London: Edward Arnold.

Rooney, R. (1992) *Strategies for work with involuntary clients*, New York: Columbia University Press.

Shulman, L. (1999) *The skills of helping individuals, families, groups, and communities* (4th edn), Itasca, IL: F.E. Peacock.

Thompson, N. (2003) *Promoting equality: Challenging discrimination and oppression* (2nd edn), London: Palgrave Macmillan.

Thompson, N. (2007) *Anti-discriminatory practice* (4th edn), Basingstoke: Palgrave Macmillan.

Thompson, N. (2009) *People skills* (3rd edn), Basingstoke: Palgrave Macmillan.

Trotter, C. (2008) 'Involuntary clients: a review of the literature', in M. Calder (ed) *The carrot or the stick? Towards effective practice with involuntary clients in safeguarding children work*, Lyme Regis: Russell House Publishing Ltd, pp 3–11.

Wenger, E. (1998) *Communities of practice: Learning, meaning and identity*, Cambridge: Cambridge University Press.

Wilson, J. (1956) *Language and the pursuit of truth*, Cambridge: Cambridge University Press [cited in H. Prins (2005) *Offenders, deviants or patients* (3rd edn), London: Routledge].

24

'Tu' or 'vous?': A European qualitative study of dignity and communication with older people in health and social care settings

Gillian Woolhead, Win Tadd, Josep Antoni Boix-Ferrer, Stefan Krajcik, Barbara Schmid-Pfahler, Barbro Spjuth, David Stratton, Paul Dieppe on behalf of the Dignity and Older Europeans (DOE) project

Extract from *Patient Education and Counseling*, (2006) no. 61, pp. 363–71.

Introduction

Maintaining the dignity of patients, and communicating well with them, are listed as high priorities in health and social care strategy documents in most European countries, particularly in the context of older people [1–6]. [...] However, what is meant by dignity in the context of health and social care for older people, are not well defined [...] The distinction between health care and social care may not be clear in some countries. In this paper, health care refers to all care relating to a physical or mental illness or condition, whether it is provided in a hospital, residential setting or the person's own home. Social care on the other hand is care related to personal aspects such as washing, dressing, feeding, shopping, and such like. Such care may take place in the person's own home, in sheltered housing or in a residential facility such as a nursing home. Social care is not distinguished from health care in the hospital setting.
   [...]

The importance of communication

It has been well documented that good doctor–patient communication is an integral element of high quality health care: good communication has been shown to influence patients' ability to recall doctors' recommendations [8], achieve satisfaction [8–11], adhere to treatment regimens [8–10], achieve favourable biomedical health outcomes [12], and prevents misunderstandings and unnecessary expenses. Poor communication between doctors and patients interferes with patients' ability to understand their options, cope with anxiety caused by illness, and make informed choices about the next diagnostic and therapeutic steps to take [9,12,13]. Unfortunately, patients frequently highlight poor communication skills of professionals when commenting on their care [14]. Doctors also experience frustration with patients who have difficulty discussing their symptoms, expressing their concerns and understanding recommendations [15].

One of the possible reasons for these criticisms may be that some doctors underestimate the importance of taking time to talk with and listen to patients, and perhaps see it as a diversion from their goals [16]. Furthermore, language that uses "nursery school" vocabulary may accentuate the differences in power between doctor and patient. Phrases such as "slip out of your clothes," and "be a good chap", or being addressed as "love" or "sweetheart" may seem condescending to the patient [17]. 'Talking at' a patient is very different to 'talking with', although it is acknowledged that sometimes factors other than the professional's communication skills influence this and these are discussed below.

The 'Dignity and Older Europeans' (DOE) project, of which the study reported here is a part, was funded by the European Commission to explore the meaning and importance of dignity in the context of health and social care for older people [18]. In this paper we report our findings on the impact of professionals' communication practices on the patients' perception of dignified care.

Methods

We performed a qualitative focus group study in six countries, as part of a large international project. Ethical approval was granted from the appropriate committees within each country. Full details of the methodology can be found on the project website http://www.cf.ac.uk/dignity.

Participants

The participating countries were France, Ireland, Slovakia, Spain, Sweden and the United Kingdom. In each of these countries focus groups and interviews were carried out with groups of older people, as well as with groups of health and social care professionals. Older participants were chosen to represent a mix of socio-economic status, ethnicity, gender, age (65 plus) and levels of fitness and functional ability which was assessed using WONCA. Where participants fitness or functional ability prevented them from participating in a focus group then individual interviews were performed in either the person's home or residential setting.

Ninety-one focus groups with older people were held, involving a total of 391 participants. Participants were, with a few exceptions, aged over 65 years, and represented both the 'young-old' (65–79) and the 'old-old' (80 plus) age groups. They were from a range of educational, social and economic backgrounds and displayed considerable variation in functional ability. Males were under represented, despite most centres making considerable efforts to specifically involve more men. Table 24.1 details the age range and gender of the focus groups with older people in each participating country.

Table 24.1: Age range and gender of older people

Centre	Male	Female	Age	
			79<	80+
France[a]	8	53	28	25
Ireland[b]	21	38	29	13
Slovakia	20	57	55	22
Spain[c]	31	50	49	31
Sweden	13	28	28	13
United Kingdom	15	57	52	20
Totals	108	283	241	124

Notes: [a] France missing eight age data; [b] Ireland missing 17 age data; [c] Spain missing one age data.

Selection criteria for health and social care professional's participation included occupational group (medical, nursing, allied health and social work professionals), level of status (assistant, manager, professional), length of service, and setting (residential, community, hospital). We attempted to promote homogeneity of group members in order to avoid potential hierarchical problems.

Eighty-five focus groups were held with health and social care professionals, involving a total of 424 participants. The participants were aged between 18 and 77 years. Of the 424 participants, 55 were male and 369 female. The length of time since qualification ranged from 3 weeks to 46 years, with a mean of 14.47 years. One-hundred and thirty-four (31.60%) of the participants were involved in nursing and 41 (9.6% were involved in medicine. 112 (26.42%) were employed as health care assistants (HCAs) or care workers and 24 (5.66%) were social workers. 25 (5.9%) held senior managerial positions, 22 (5.19%) worked in physiotherapy and

14 (3.3%) were involved in some kind of medical study. The remaining 52 (12.2%) were either psychologists, pharmacists, occupational and speech therapists or dieticians. Table 24.2 outlines the age and gender of the health and social care professionals.

Table 24.2: Age and gender of health and social care professionals

Centre	Male	Female	Age								
			18–29	30–39	40–49	50–59	60–69	70–77	Missing	Age range	Mean age
France	9	74	9	24	31	16	2	0	1	24–60	42
Ireland	8	59	16	18	14	10	1	0	8	21–64	28
Slovakia	13	76	23	27	22	14	3	0	0	18–63	38
Spain	12	49	13	18	20	7	1	1	1	21–77	46
Sweden	5	67	4	12	30	21	5	0	0	22–63	46
United Kingdom	8	44	17	9	16	8	1	0	1	18–60	38
Totals	55	369	82	108	133	76	13	1	11	18–77	41

Data collection

The focus groups with the older people were conducted between April and October 2002, while the focus groups with health and social care professionals were carried out between September 2002 and June 2003. All group and individual interviews were held in private rooms and schedules were developed to ensure that the same issues were covered within each focus group in each country, although leeway was given for informants to raise issues that were meaningful to them [19]. The groups involving older people, lasted approximately two hours, and explored various aspects of dignity and dignified care. A schedule with specific themes was used to direct the group discussions but the emphasis, at least in the initial stages of the discussion, was on spontaneous talk where informants discussed various aspects of their lives. Stimulus materials involving culturally appropriate images representing 'dignity' or 'dignified people' and indignity or undignified people were also used to stimulate spontaneous discussion. Prompted questions were used where necessary and included: 'What does dignity mean to you personally?' 'What would treating you with dignity involve?' 'Can you describe an example of how you or anyone you know has been treated in a (un)dignified way?' Although the literature on focus groups suggests that between 8 and 12 participants are appropriate, it was agreed in the common training held for all researchers involved, that groups involving older participants should contain no more than seven participants and the range across centres was 4–7 older participants.

The focus groups with the health and social care professionals, lasted approximately one hour and focussed on the factors that influenced the provision of dignified care, Probes such as 'Can you describe an example of how an older person has been treated in an (un)dignified way by health or social care professionals?' or 'Which situations or circumstances affect your ability to treat someone with dignity?' were used when necessary. Again the aim was to encourage spontaneous discussion initially and to achieve this, appropriate images were used. The group sizes were larger than those with older people and usually ranged from 8 to 10 participants.

In an attempt to ensure a consistent approach to data collection, all researchers involved in data collection received common training in both focus group methodology and qualitative analysis. Within each focus group, a moderator coordinated the groups and an observer took detailed notes and observations of the verbal and non-verbal communication that occurred. With the consent of the participants all interviews were audio-recorded.

[...]

Findings

In all of the six countries, 'communication', 'addressing', 'listening', or 'interpersonal relationships' emerged from the older peoples and professionals focusgroups as having a direct impact upon the experience of 'dignified' care. Dignity, especially the dignity of personal identity and that of 'menschenwurde', was enhanced or alternatively jeopardised depending on the communication between patients and professionals. Despite the wide range of backgrounds and situations of participants and the wide country variations there was substantial agreement about the effect of communication patterns on the experience of dignity. In relation to impact of communication on dignity, four major categories emerged from the analysis, including (1) forms of address, (2) politeness and privacy, (3) feeling valued, (4) inclusion and choice.

Forms of address

Many of the older participants commented that the form of address chosen when staff spoke to them affected their experience of dignity. The use of first names without prior consent, and the use of pet names were particularly disliked and felt to show a lack of respect. Other poor communication practices included labelling older people as 'tasks', which also failed to demonstrate respect: 'I have got three bed baths left to do' or 'I have got three rheumatoids to see'. In Sweden the 'Du reform',

[Handwritten margin note: Dignity impacted by care.]

which had popularised the familiar word for 'you', even to strangers, was thought to have contributed to the lack of respect for older people. Similar comments were made in France with respect to the use of the word 'tu' rather than the formal 'vous'.

> We didn't 'tu' before
> It is not our generation, here there are some who do
> It is so ordinary to say 'tu'
> It is the question of new life
> It is modernism (Residential care, France)

The majority of older participants disliked being addressed by pet names, such as 'dear' or 'love', or by their Christian name, as they found it humiliating and patronising.

> As people get older especially when they are in sort of hospitals or in residential homes and they're called by their Christian names, I do not think that's right, ...because especially say our age group when we were either Mrs. or Mr. or something like that, I mean it enables with respect. You go into hospital and the first day there they call you by your Christian name (Health shop, UK).

The practice of routinely calling people by their first names emphasised the inequality in professional/client relationships.

> In fact, they're [older people] in a position of decided inferiority with regard to health, vigour and knowledge. That sense of inferiority can be subtly reinforced by first-naming, since to some people it conjures up memories of helplessness in the classroom. Choice hardly exists. I mean whether you're Mrs. Jones or Mary. You are Tom or Mary before you know where you are, and then it's too late. Perhaps you want to be addressed by your first name. Do you then call the doctor Tom or Harry? Because if you do not you're asking to be treated like a child. (Health Council, UK).

Many older participants believed the use of first names signified a close relationship, which they did not have with the majority of health professionals. However, older participants living in residential or care preferred being called by their first names, which seems to reinforce the significance of the nature of relationships.

> Oh yes, it makes it more homely doesn't it, in a home, it's quite
> nice to be called by your first name. Everyone wants to be
> called by their first name (Nursing home, UK).

Explanations as to why the older people participating in the study did not
comment on such inadequate communication centred on their perceived
vulnerability and their desire to be seen as compliant by those caring for
them. The majority of older participants felt it would be a mark of respect
to at least ask how they preferred to be addressed as this offered choice,
rather than assuming that they did not mind how they were referred to.

The professional participants also discussed this issue. They were aware
that older people should be given a choice about how they are addressed.
However, some confessed that they had become blasé and lax in practice.

> Sometimes we might be very casual about calling older people
> by their first names, instead of Mr. or Mrs., the old fashioned
> way. All those things have gone for us, but not necessarily for
> them (Nurses, Ireland).

Others admitted that this lack of choice was a result of professionals failing
to exchange information. When older people gave permission for one staff
member to use their first name, other staff assumed that it was acceptable
for them to do likewise. However, this could cause offence to the older
person.

> We have to ask what they would like to be called. That's possibly
> the thing that slips because the nurses will introduce them as
> 'Annie' so you call them 'Annie'. It's been done by someone else
> (Physiotherapists, UK).

Using first names as a matter of course was acknowledged as a sign of
disrespect and inappropriate in the health care setting. Professionals also
believed that the situation or environment determined whether people
were addressed in a formal or informal manner.

Politeness and privacy

Politeness and privacy were cited as highly important and were often
remembered by individuals and their relatives. Kindness and politeness on
the part of professionals were attitudes cherished by older participants and
were often displayed in communication by professionals. Asking permission
to perform examinations and providing information were further ways

in which dignity was maintained and respect displayed, as older people were involved in decisions. Simple actions, such as knocking on a door before entering, or maintaining eye contact, were aspects of care that older people responded to. Other examples included acknowledging the need for privacy when performing bed baths.

> My husband could not stand it if they washed his private parts. But here in the hospital you see nurses who know how to do it with gentleness, how they cover the parts that are already clean or that they don't have to wash yet, so that the person doesn't feel bad (Nursing home, Spain).

Conversely, block treatments, such as being told when to go to the toilet and rough treatment, were examples of care that robbed the individual of dignity as they denied privacy and involved rudeness of the most basic form.

> One [caregiver] came in with a list to check who had to go to the toilet. People don't have to go to the toilet by list. They have to go when they need to. Someone asked her to take them. She looked at the list and said, 'it's not your turn'. That's not treating someone with dignity. (Nursing home, Spain).

The consensus of the professional participants was to treat the person as an individual. Appropriate touching was seen to convey a sense of worth and value and was an important means of communicating concern and respect. Furthermore, professionals acknowledged that for communication to be effective, they needed to ensure that teeth, spectacles and hearing aids were in place. Although such elements of care could be described as fundamental, many participants admitted that they frequently forgot them. Others knew of the importance of this but also confessed that they did not apply this knowledge in their practice.

> You know exactly what to do, you change the nappy and wash the old person, and it's just a matter of routine. You do it and actually forget that it's a person lying there. (Nurse/ Care Assistants, Sweden)

Feeling valued

Another way in which dignity can be promoted is ensuring that someone feels valued as a human being as this promotes a sense of both self-respect and that others respect you. One of the ways in which older participants felt valued was being listened to, acknowledged as a person, and given time. They considered these aspects of care central to the preservation of their dignity.

> The nursing staff up here work very, very hard. They do. But I always find time to talk to them or they to me and they have always treated me with dignity. It didn't matter whether they were just passing, you were acknowledged and you were treated like the person you are (Older Peoples Meeting Group, Ireland).

Many professional participants agreed that listening and giving older people time was important.

> It's very important when you are talking, to listen to them and give them time to speak to you because very often you finish a sentence off for them, just to give them time to get their words out (Community Unit, Ireland).

However, examples were given where older participants felt they were not listened to.

> We are nothing to our doctor, she has no time or interest in us, she only tries to send us away as soon as possible (Retirement Club, Slovakia).

It was not only professionals' poor communication skills that deterred good communication and therefore denied people dignity. Many participants claimed that organisational barriers, such as their work situation, reduced the opportunities to fulfil the older person's need for social recognition, as there was limited time to sit and listen to them.

> There is no time to sit down and talk to them, for instance. It would be wonderful to do that once, perhaps in the morning when they are having breakfast (Assistant nurses, Sweden).

It was stated that the 'system' valued more obvious, measurable activities and specific tasks, such as finishing a clinic on time, which was seen as more important than providing the humanistic, less quantifiable, elements of care, such as dignified care and treatment. One of the ways in which these measurable targets were achieved was by reducing the amount of communication between patient and professional.

> The care overload often causes you to be short of time. The
> context of conversations, time spent together, sitting down
> together. Today, in a system that's seeks efficiency through the
> cost/time ratio, well in hospitals they're pushing us to reduce
> the average stay as much as we can (Hospital ward, Spain).

Lack of staff, financial resources, awareness and increased bureaucracy
were also cited as barriers that impeded quality communications between
professionals and their clients and therefore reduced the feeling of value
experienced by individual patients. It is important to note that a number of
professional participants stated that they provided dignified care despite the
constraints of social and organisational circumstances.

Inclusion and choice

Communication practices could also enhance dignity by ensuring people
were included, especially in decisions that affected them, and by offering
choice whenever possible.

   Many older participants stated that one of their worst experiences was
of being treated as an 'object'. For instance, it was claimed that some nurses
or doctors totally ignored the person's existence when they performed
interventions.

> I went into this particular specialist and he had an assistant.
> Instead of talking to me, he was writing all the time. I could
> have been an elephant. He said 'Take her in there and tell her
> to strip down', and I just said, 'Am I invisible?' (Social club,
> Ireland).

Feeling included in decision-making processes also emphasised one's
worth as a person. However, in many instances, older participants had the
impression that they were not considered as a person and their opinions or
views were not respected.

> Dignity of older people can be kept if they feel the others listen
> to them. Absolutely, this is dignity. And understood. Yes, to be
> understood, but someone first has to listen to you. Yes this is
> dignity, that someone considers your thoughts and observations
> (Residential care, France)

Professionals' attitudes which emphasised exclusion also affected the older
persons' experience of dignity, especially if they were scolded.

> They do not want you to hear what they are talking about. And
> if you want to know a bit more about something, they'll say
> 'you're being nosey, mind your own business' (Hospital ward,
> Spain).

Inclusion and choice were also seen as important by health and social care professionals. They stated that creating opportunities for older people to exercise autonomy and providing them with real choices were important.

> Affording people choice and making sure that people are
> supported and given as much say in the way that they are
> supported (Social workers, UK).

Conversely, in Slovakia, many doctors and nurses felt uncomfortable including older people in discussions about their treatment as they were of the opinion that older people should comply with treatment and advice without explanation.

Numerous examples were given in relation to promoting autonomy and enhancing opportunities to exercise choice. For example, respecting the older person's right to say 'no' to certain activities or treatment regimens, and choosing between everyday activities, such as whether to have a bath or a shower, or to have a say about the gender of the nurse or care assistant providing their care. Despite this view, choice was not always offered. For example, instances were highlighted where older patients were automatically assigned to treatment regimens without asking their preference. Many of the professional participants believed that older people were too vulnerable to object or make a formal criticism. Some consultants stated that because of the multiple tasks they perform in their day-to-day clinical work, it was easy to forget patients and exclude them from conversations.

> When we do a ward round you are trying to pay attention to
> the patient and any interaction they are having while at the
> same time listening to the doctors who are telling you things
> that are going on, so you are almost in stereo trying to do
> different things and you need to be doing both, but at the same
> time. And the patient is there and it is very easy to actually,
> once you introduce yourself to the patient, to then almost cut
> them out of the loop while you then set about sorting out
> their problem and I have found myself doing that, and will
> consciously try not to, but I am guilty of it (Geriatricians, UK).

It was further acknowledged that it was easy to put one's own values onto older people. Often health professionals were accused of deciding what was best for patients without considering their views.

> It is very easy to put our values onto patients than it is to find out what is really important to individual patients and whether that importance or that particular thing that is important to them is altered by changing their medication, (Rheumatology research team, UK).

Discussion

[...] The analysis of the individual country reports showed far more similarities than differences and frequently highlighted the same issues and concerns facing older people regardless of where they lived or their personal circumstances. Both groups of participants also held similar views on what matters in communications. Forms of address, privacy and politeness, feeling valued and inclusion and choice were identified as key themes, and have been documented as prerequisites for good communication in the general literature [21–23]. However, many examples of poor communication in practice were also highlighted.

[...]

Professional participants provided several explanations to highlight the difficulties in providing good communication, such as the lack of staff, lack of time, awareness and the increased amount of bureaucracy. Many claimed that priorities in health care were based on productivity and cost efficiency with more emphasis being placed on completing tasks than on responding to people as individual human beings.

It is acknowledged that this study has a number of limitations. Despite the use of the participant selection criteria, there was a predominance of women in the groups, and in the health and social care professionals' focus groups some occupational groups were more representative than others. Bearing in mind the majority of people working in health and social care, this reflects the gender and occupational situations in these settings. The reports of practice were also based on subjective views of participants and were not based on observed practice. It is important to note that communication is an interactive process: patients also need the skills and support to take part in decision-making and to raise questions about quality [26]. Thus, ethnographic studies, such as observation methods, may provide further direct information about communication, and reveal information about the interaction between the two groups. As with all research, the participants were self-selected and, therefore, they may have a specific interest in dignity, or research in general. In addition, although several people in residential care were involved, the most disadvantaged, and those most likely to be adversely affected by poor interactions with professionals (such as those with dementia), could not be included. Another possible limitation of this article is the fact that the primary aim of the focus groups was to investigate dignity and not communication. The study also has strengths. A large number of participants were involved, and in spite of their diversity, and the fact that the study took place in six countries, there was a remarkable consistency within the themes and findings, suggesting that the data presented represented a general 'truth'.

Practice implications

These data show communications between older people and the health or social care professionals is of great importance. Within six European countries, the use of appropriate forms of address, listening, giving people choice, including them, respecting their need for privacy and politeness, and making them feel valued emerged as significant ways to maintain older peoples sense of dignity and self-worth. Despite being aware of good communication practices, professionals often failed to apply these to their practice.

These findings have important implications for health and social care professionals when they engage with older people.

[...]

References

[8] Bartlett EE, Grayson M, Barker R, Levine DM, Golden A, Libber S. The effects of physician communications skills on patient satisfaction, recall, and adherence. J Chron Dis 1984;37:755–64.

[9] Kaplan SH, Greenfield S, Gandek B, Rogers WH, Ware JE. Characteristics of physicians with participatory decision-making styles. Ann Intern Med 1996;124:497–504.

[10] Ong LML. DeHaes JCJM. Hoos AM, Lammes FB. Doctor–patient communication: a review of reviews. Soc Sci Med 1995;40:903–18.

[11] Stewart M. What is a successful doctor–patient interview? A study of interactions and outcomes. Soc Sci Med 1984;19:167–75.

[12] Kaplan SH, Greenfield S, Ware JE. Assessing the effects of physician-patient interactions on the outcomes of chronic disease. Med Care 1989;27.

[13] Ruusuvuori J. Looking means listening: coordinating displays of engagement in doctor–patient interaction. Soc Sci Med 2001;52:1093–8.

[14] Buller MK, Buller DB. Physicians' communication style and patient satisfaction. J Health Soc Behav 1987;28:375–88.

[15] Levinson W, Stiles WB, Inui TS, Engle R. Physician frustration in communicating with patients. Med Care 1993;31:285–95.

[16] Adams P. Gesundheit. Rochester, Vermont: Healing Arts Press, 1993.

[17] Curtis AJ. In: Routledge, editor. Health psychology. New York:2000.

[18] Woolhead GM, Calnan M, Dieppe P, Tadd W. Dignity in Old Age: what do older people think? Age Ageing 2004;33:165–70.

[19] Hammersley M, Atkinson P. Ethnography. Principles in practice, 2nd ed., London: Routledge, 1995.

[21] Draper J, Weaver S. Exploring blocks to effective communication in the medical interview. Educat Gen Pract 1999;10:14–20.

[22] Radcliffe S, Campion P. What can general practitioners learn from third party feedback of their consultations? Education for General Practice 1997;8:292–302.

[23] Levine C. The good doctor: the carer's perspective. Clin Med 2004;4:244–5.

[26] Meryn S. Improving doctor–patient communication. Br Med J 1998;316:1922–30.

25

Assessment: mastering a technical process or exercising an art?

Ian Buchanan

Introduction

The assessment of adults for health and social care services has a long history. It has always been central to nursing practice; indeed Florence Nightingale, in her *Notes on nursing* (1969), said that the most important lesson a nurse could learn was how to observe. This chapter focuses on how assessment has developed within different professional and organisational contexts in more recent years. It can be argued that contemporary assessment of adults developed out of the requirement for systematic practice in health and social care introduced in the National Health Service and Community Care (NHSCC) Act 1990. In promoting both technical aspects of assessment processes and the exercise of professional 'wisdom' (Parker, 2008), the NHSCC Act raises the question of whether assessment is mastering a technical process or exercising an art. This question is addressed by exploring initial ideas about assessment in nursing and social work contexts before examining policy developments that have led to the introduction of a common framework – the Single Assessment Process (SAP) (DH, 2004), how it has developed in practice, and has been experienced – the SAP in action.

So how can we define assessment? It is a central activity in all professions that deal with people in society and is guided by the values, ethics and body of knowledge of each profession seeking to determine action when action is needed, and in doing so sometimes acting as a gatekeeper to the use of resources. This is done on the basis of eligibility and suitability. These ethical and knowledge systems are no longer the exclusive province of professional elites but can be contested and defined by the people who use the systems, by service users and by expert patients.

Obviously, nursing and social work practitioners have their own knowledge base and draw on a range of academic disciplines, each with their own rigorous training and registration.[1] The task of health monitoring within nursing care led to an emphasis on the technical or measurable that is still evident today in what we now call assessment (McDonald, 2001; McGann et al, 2009; Serrant-Green, 2010). The origins of social work casework and assessment lie in the 19th century (Mowat, 1961), but social work did not have a recognised national qualification until the 1970s. Its focus on social problems has made the profession much less reliant on technical and measurable aspects of assessment (Parker, 2008), and perhaps it is not surprising that there is no simple definition or understanding of what constitutes assessment in social work (Whittington, 2007; Parker, 2008) or in nursing (McIntosh, 2006; Cowley et al, 2008).

In social work it is generally accepted that there are four or five identifiable stages to the process: assessment, intervention, review and evaluation and a fifth by separating planning out from intervention (Parker, 2008). These stages are not necessarily discrete, linear or cyclical but they are closely linked to making judgements and taking decisions. Staged models such as this are comparable to the systematic approach to nursing emerging during the 1980s where a number of models used a structured approach to nursing patients (Roper et al, 1996). However, systematic staged models tell us little about working within the variety and complexity of individuals' social circumstances. Indeed, while considerable research on structured assessment in nursing has established its reliability in identifying patient need, according to McIntosh (2006), it fails to engage the patient. However, in 2006 she identified two distinct approaches to assessment in community nursing: the formal, structured questionnaire-based approach and the informal conversation-based approach. Formal approaches derive from the profession's practice history of observations and accurate recording while informal approaches are a response to the growing recognition of the importance of relationship building in assessment, drawing not only on nursing concepts and theories but engaging with nursing's worth and purpose (Cowley et al 2008).

Between the professions there are similarities and differences in practice and this discussion begins to address the overarching questions for the chapter. Despite its centrality to social work and nursing, the assessment remains a work in progress. In a Social Care Institute for Excellence (SCIE) learning and teaching guide for social work drawing on Crisp et al's (2005) knowledge review, Whittington identified orientations associated with four assessment types. These are 'ideal types' derived from the distinctive characteristics identified in textbooks in the review and are used later in this chapter to critique processes (see Table 25.1).

The introduction of common assessments

The NHSCC Act 1990 placed assessment at the centre of both community health and social care through the creation of an internal market in health and a quasi-market in social care, separating purchasers and providers of services. It introduced the system of care management based on a systematic assessment of individual need carried out with the service user aiming to lead to flexible packages of care drawn from an expanded range of services and service providers. It also required greater inter-agency working and the intention was that care managers should be drawn from both social work and nursing. Moreover, the advent of the need to address choice for service users and the drive for quality in services brought with them a requirement for measurement on which to base judgements, a trend parallelled by the accelerated use of information and communications technology (ICT). At the same time a holistic understanding of the service user was sought in assessment.

Table 25.1: Orientations of assessment

	Orientation
Process-focused	Professional and organisational judgements
Contingent	Variation by type of service
Contestation-focused	Limited by contested policies, perspectives and priorities
Critical social constuctionist	Process objectivity undermined by constructed meaning

Source: Derived from Whittington (2007, p 19)

Concepts of partnership and collaboration became central to inter-agency working in community care and have endured. Lymbery (2006) has argued that these terms are imprecise and difficult to operationalise, and identifies problems in differences in professional power and in competition between professions operating on the same territory. To this one might add agencies with different governance and different structures (national and local).

Partnership and, particularly information sharing, was reaffirmed in the National Service Framework (NSF) for older people (DH, 2001). To address problems of duplication (of assessment and other activities), fragmentation (of contact and help and support) and the need to share information (between and within health and care sectors) in inter-agency work the NSF for older people information strategy (DH, 2002a) identified a common data set as the basis of a SAP for older people.

The Single Assessment Process: policy and practice

Having developed out of the NSF for older people, the SAP is regarded as a precursor to a Common Assessment Framework (CAF) for adults proposed in the White Paper *Our health, our care, our say* (DH, 2006a; 2006b). At the time of writing CAF for adults had not moved beyond the pilot stage, and the SAP is used here as the basis for critically looking at the first attempt to develop multi-professional assessment with adults. Person-centredness is its principal practice theme (Milner and O'Byrne, 2009, Chapter 11), but there has been recognition that it would build on the Care Programme Approach (CPA) in relation to people with mental health problems and particular person-centred approaches in use in learning disabilities.

The SAP operates at different levels through:

- *Contact Assessments* – which collect personal information, presenting problems and initial assessment details
- *Overview Assessments* – which identify risks and define needs and are carried out in a conversational way
- *Specialist Assessments* – in which the best placed health or social care professional explores specific needs sometimes using a formal assessment tool, and
- *Comprehensive Assessments* – which are multi-agency and multi-disciplinary processes used when the person is very frail and vulnerable with many and complex needs.

It also includes:
- *Carers Assessments* – which consider the needs of informal carers separately. (Milner and O'Byrne, 2009, p 212, Figure 3)

Figure 25.1: The context for developing the Information Strategy for Older People

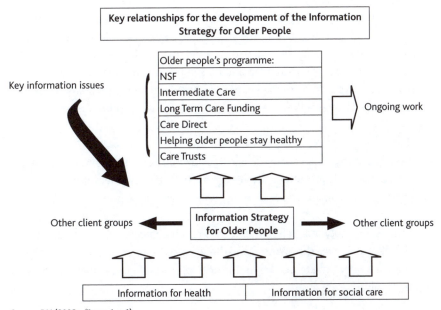

Source: DH (2002a, Figure 1, p 1)

Where complex needs are being considered in a Comprehensive Assessment the work of different professions is integrated under a lead professional. To date research shows that use of the SAP is not widespread except where the outcome may be 'care-home-with-nursing', and even then a systematic multidisciplinary approach has been absent (Challis et al, 2010). However, examining the SAP gives us a useful perspective on assessment in itself and assessment across organisational and professional boundaries. We have already indicated some real differences between agencies and between their professional workers which suggests that joint working may be dependent on more than a common data set.

Disagree with this situation

The case of Maria is now used to examine the SAP in more detail. The case is heavily disguised but it is based on real experiences. It is compiled from notes of a social worker's comments, attendance at a case 'conference' and views and information provided to the social worker. It has been edited. Reading about Maria raises the question of how the SAP and assessment should work in practice. No one person's experience could possibly be used to engage fully with a system as extensive as the SAP. However, Maria's experiences have a bearing on different parts of the SAP and provide the basis for a critical examination of assessment processes in organisational and professional contexts that follow.

Maria: a case study

Maria and her family

Maria is now 87 years old. She was widowed when she was 68 as her husband, Billy, died of a heart attack. She has a son, John, 200 miles away and a daughter, Sarah, nearby. Maria lives in a small town in the north of England.... Maria has five grandchildren, all adults. She has seven great grandchildren. She has always seen all members of her immediate family regularly; weekly in the case of Sarah's family and about every six weeks in John's case.

Maria

Maria has always been energetic and has devoted her adult life to her family. She was mentally and physically very quick; fiery and argumentative. She has never been a woman who rests easily and is very house proud.

Maria is intensely independent. She was much changed after her husband, Billy, died. However, she adapted and threw herself even more into her family. Maria is a very private person and is not comfortable in company outside her family.

Around the time Maria turned 80 she began to be seriously troubled by arthritis. Adaptations to her home gave her a new lease of life but still heavily focused on her family. She was again able to cook meals and enjoy her time with 'the kids'. She is proud and resisted using her zimmer frame for walking.

Maria had a stroke when she was 85. Her children were shocked and wondered if she would survive. She was not able to speak and could not move her left arm and leg. Over two to three months Maria recovered well in hospital but did not fully engage in physiotherapy or occupational therapy sessions.

It soon became obvious that the professional opinion was that Maria would be best cared for in a residential care home. The social worker's main consideration seemed to be residual problems with incontinence. Maria also had significant short-term memory loss and partial and confused recall of past events. She was, however, adamant that she wanted to return home. Her children began supporting her in pursuing her wish to go home. It was not a simple or easy decision. John pressed hard and questioned the absence of information which resulted in a conference involving therapists and a geriatrician (nothing resembling a systematic assessment was ever shown to him). The only thing that was handed out was what appeared to be a partially completed set of tests that had been conducted by a psychologist just prior to the meeting.

The pressures on Sarah who had become ill supporting her mother meant Maria going home wasn't possible. Maria went into a friendly care home which provides a good standard of care. It took her some time to adjust and she asked when she would be going home at her first annual review.

The current reality of the Single Assessment Process

Maria's case can be interpreted on many levels. The information gathered is closest to that in an Overview Assessment. Although she had the stroke that led to her moving into a care home around the beginning of 2008, the SAP was not used. However, what it does tell us about inter-agency working and information flows is significant. A conference was held on the hospital ward without any form of assessment report or other evidence of a systematic approach to decision making. This is consistent with Abendstern et al (2010) finding little evidence of a systematic approach within SAPs. To learn more about the assessment process Maria's case can be compared with the *Single Assessment Summary (Example)* (DH, 2002b), which has six sections:

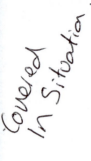
Covered in Situation

- Basic personal information
- Needs and circumstances (including the older person's perspective)
- Evaluation of needs
- Summary of current care plan
- Additional personal information
- Perceptions of family members and principal informal carers

Only the first three sections are considered in relation to Maria's case. Despite her admission to a care home no additional personal information was collected systematically as required in the SAP, there was no current care plan, and family and informal carer perceptions are not known. Apart from excluded personal information the case study provides most of the basic personal information for an Overview Assessment. The narrative only provides part of the data required on needs and circumstances; recording these requires more factual descriptions, some covering specific periods, and entries in tables with boxes. As there was no assessment report concern about the art of eliciting patient-centred information and the technical skills needed to complete a form need to be considered. Maria's case cannot support required judgements of need adequately.

Here Whittington's four assessment types are used to consider the case. This example illustrates a flawed process which falls short of requirements for *process-focused assessment* (Whittington, 2007, see Table 25.1). It is difficult to argue that information collected by SAP's systematic process-focused approach is not relevant to Maria's situation. While reliance on measurement can be criticised in this case, a weak narrative account is less useful than the *Single Assessment Summary (Example)* scores for activities, cognitive functioning, depression or impact on carers (see ref website, DH, 2002b).

There is some evidence for arguing that Maria's case is an example of a *contingent* process-focused approach and of *contestation* where different professions and policies address the issues in different ways (Whittington, 2007). In Maria's case the lead professional in the assessment was the social worker and her children John and, to some extent, Sarah wondered if the process might be contingent on Maria going into care, that is, 'thought to be the only solution and encouraged by professionals'. They also wondered if using their mother's house to pay for residential care was influential in discounting a community care package. Notwithstanding community care goals, John wondered if, in the absence of financial constraints, Maria's failure to engage with the therapy staff had left her without a professional advocate. Yet no one seems to have encouraged Maria to communicate her wishes.

To some degree the SAP is an audit tool that records professionally generated information and judgements. Although its systematic use is a basis for an objective approach, it is open to a *social constructionist critique* (Whittington, 2007). Meaning is made in the interaction between actors (service users, patients, nurses, social workers, medical practitioners, carers and care workers). They each bring their own perspectives and the professional power is of importance according to the context, professional history and culture and the situation. This is evident in the SAP itself which is an official record system with administrative and 'situated routines' (Scott, 1990) that construct knowledge by admitting and rejecting information through their processes and definitions. Objective tests may have the same effect.

There are important limitations in the SAP, which is not universally used in assessment of older people, and there are many reasons for this. McIntosh (2006) has pointed out that most research is concerned with reliability and consistency of parts of the SAP. Yet collaborative working remains hard to achieve (Lymbery, 2006), and there are problems in sharing and managing information because complexities and duplication in the NSF for older people largely remain. Moreover, there is no early evidence that using ICT systems or the SAP have had any direct positive impact on outcomes in integrated care (Glendinning et al, 2007; Loader et al, 2007).

Conclusion

Assessment is a work in progress which continues to struggle with mastering a technical process *and* exercising an art that understands the person. It seems fitting to conclude with a number of contradictory statements and questions that continue to underpin its development:

- Professions bring different histories and knowledge to assessment – how can these be integrated and valued?
- How should this affect inter-professional working?
- Objective tests may be discounted out of hand from an anti-positivist position – what is the benefit of a mixed method approach?
- Self-assessment and supported decision making are inconceivable without a narrative approach. But are narratives selective, especially in relation to what is recorded?
- Record keeping and ICT is important in assessment – but recording is not assessment.

To answer the question posed at the start of this chapter, we need to bring both parts together.

Note

[1] The registration of nurses by Nurse Registration Acts dates from 1919, whereas social workers have only been registered with the General Social Care Council since 2005.

References

Abendstern, M., Hughes, J., Clarkson, P., Sutcliffe, C., Wlson, K. and Challis, D. (2010) '"We need to talk": communication between primary care trusts and other health and social care agencies following the introduction of the Single Assessment Process for Older People in England', *Primary Health Care Research and Development*, vol 11, pp 61-74.

Challis, D., Abendstern, M., Clarkson, P., Hughes, J. and Sutcliffe, C. (2010) 'Comprehensive assessment of older people with complex care needs: the multi-disciplinarity of the Single Assessment Process in England', *Ageing & Society*, vol 30, no 7, pp 1115-34.

Cowley, S., Bergen, A., Young, K. and Kavanagh, A. (2008) 'A taxonomy of needs assessment, elicited from a multiple case study of community nursing education and practice', *Journal of Advanced Nursing*, vol 31, no 1, pp 126-34.

Crisp, B.R., Anderson, M.T., Orme, J. and Lister, P.G. (2005) *Learning and teaching in social work education: Textbooks and frameworks on assessment*, Knowledge Review 18, London: Social Care Institute for Excellence.

DH (Department of Health) (2001) *National Service Framework for older people*, London: DH.

DH (2002a) *Information strategy for older people*, London: DH.

DH (2002b) *Single Assessment Summary (Example)* (www.dh.gov.uk/prod_consum_dh/groups/dh_digitalassets/@dh/@en/documents/digitalasset/dh_4060244.pdf).

DH (2004) *The community care assessment directions*, LAC (2004) 24, London: DH.

DH (2006a) *Our health, our care, our say: A new direction for community services*, Cm 6373, London: DH.

DH (2006b) *A new ambition for old age: Next steps in implementing the National Service Framework for older people*, A resource document from Professor Ian Philp, National Director for Older People, Department of Health: DH.

Glendinning, C., Clarke, S., Hare, P., Maddison, J. and Newbronner, L. (2008) 'Progress and problems in developing outcomes-focused social care services for older people in England', *Health and Social Care in the Community*, vol 16, no 1, pp 54-63.

Loader, B., Hardey, M. and Keeble, L. (2007) 'Health informatics for older people: a review of ICT facilitated integrated care', *International Journal of Social Welfare*, vol 17, no 1, pp 46-53.

Lymbery, M. (2006) 'United we stand? Partnership working in health and social care and the role of social work in services for older people', *British Journal of Social Work*, vol 36, no 7, pp 1119-34.

McDonald, L. (2001) 'Florence Nightingale and the early origins of evidence-based nursing', *Evidence Based Nursing*, vol 4, pp 68-9.

McGann, S., Crowther, A. and Dougall, R. (2009) *A history of the Royal College of Nursing 1916–90. A voice for nurses*, Manchester: University of Manchester Press.

McIntosh, J. (2006) 'The evidence base for individual patient and client assessment by community nurses', *Primary Health Care Research and Development*, vol 7, pp 299-308.

Milner, J. and O'Byrne, P. (2009) *Assessment in social work*, Basingstoke: Palgrave Macmillan.

Mowat, C.L. (1961) *The Charity Organisation Society, 1869–1913*, London: Methuen.

Nightingale, F. (1969) *Notes on nursing: What it is and what it is not*, New York: Dover Publications, Inc.

Parker, J. (2008) 'Assessment, intervention and review', in M. Davies (ed) *The Blackwell companion to social work* (3rd edn), Oxford: Blackwell, pp 94-101.

Roper, N., Logan, W.W. and Tierney, A.J. (1996) *The elements of nursing: A model of nursing based on a model of living*, Edinburgh: Churchill Livingstone.

Scott, J. (1990) *A matter of record: Documentary sources in social research*, Cambridge: Polity Press.

Serrant-Green, L. (2010) 'Community nursing must shed its non-technical image', *Nursing Times*, 1 April.

Whittington, C. (2007) *Assessment in social work: A guide for learning and teaching*, London: Social Care Institute for Excellence.

SECTION SIX

International dimensions

26

Globalisation and health and social welfare: some key issues

Sandy Sieminski

Introduction

In an increasingly interconnected world, the needs of service users and carers accessing health and social welfare services need to be understood within a global context. This chapter considers the relationship between global economic developments and people's health and welfare. It is suggested that globalisation presents challenges and opportunities for practitioners working in health and social care services. One of the challenges that globalisation brings relates to developing effective practices to meet the needs of people who have recently migrated to the UK. One positive aspect of globalisation is that it has increased opportunities for sharing ideas about policy and practice issues which can lead to a greater understanding of service users' and carers' needs.

The increasing interconnection between the global and the local has been attributed to processes of globalisation. Globalisation is a contested concept (Hirst et al, 2009) but there is some consensus within the literature that its key features include: the increasing interconnectedness between countries across the globe through trade with movement of capital and flows of people and information facilitated by advances in communications technologies leading to a compression of time and space. Giddens (1990, 1999) has argued that the processes of globalisation are not solely driven by the integration of global marketplace. He suggests that the communications revolution that started in the late 1960s has transformed the way people are able to relate to one another across the world, which has contributed to the transformation of many of our basic social institutions such as the economy, government, family, gender and sexuality. One example Giddens provides of this is the way in which family relationships have changed for some people, partly through the existence of new communications technologies, which enable people who move to other parts of world to continue to support children and older family members across borders.

Economic crisis: the implications for poverty and health

Since the mid-1990s there has been a trend in the movement of capital from one country to another in the form of outsourcing work which has led to the creation of global production chains. Multinational corporations have used this strategy to drive down labour and operational costs. An example of this kind of practice is the relocation of several call centres for financial groups from the UK to India where labour costs are much lower (Simpson and Lawrence, 2009, p 17). The establishment of global production chains has resulted in an increase in employment opportunities for many workers in some developing countries in the Global South but for workers in the developed countries in the Global North it has been associated with job losses.

Dominelli (2010) expresses concern about the way globalisation has supported industrialised capitalist growth at the expense of the poor. She notes how multinational corporations' search for profit-making opportunities for shareholders has contributed to economic crisis. Unsustainable loans made in the housing market resulted in the financial banking crisis in 2008 and led to economic recession which had an impact on the lives of people living in the US and UK. She explains:

> In 2008, it was estimated that each person in the UK had contributed around £50,000 to bail out the country's financial sector. Saving ailing financial institutions has cost the British taxpayer £1.5 trillion in public funds (Waugh, 2009)....
>
> Taxpayers are paying for the crisis as "bank aid" to keep the financial sector afloat and in reduced public expenditure on items intended to curb the worst excesses of capitalism – education, health, personal social services and income support. Gross inequalities in wealth challenge social workers struggling to find resources, for example, to pay heating bills for children in homes, fund personal care or feed refugees. (Dominelli, 2010, p 605)

Dominelli argues that it is the poor who are most likely to be affected by recession through job losses, low paid work, health hazards and rising food and energy prices. Harrison and Melville (2010) similarly argue that economic recession is accompanied by higher levels of unemployment that leads to higher levels of relative poverty in the countries affected by it.

There is a well-established correlation between poverty and illness (Rose, 2009), and the vast inequalities that exist in life expectancy within countries reflect inequalities in income and wealth. For example, the life expectancy of men living in inner-city Glasgow was found to be 54 years in comparison to 82 years for men living in a neighbouring suburb (CSDH, 2008). Discrepancies in life expectancy in neighbouring geographical locations in the UK are not uncommon. Recent research has uncovered inequalities within Camden: men living in the most deprived areas of the borough have a life expectancy of almost seven years less than those from the least deprived areas (APHO, 2008). In addition to income and wealth, Bywaters et al (2009) note that other factors associated with difference and discrimination, such as gender, disability, sexual orientation or ethnicity, may also be significant in explanations of life expectancy rates. These authors note, for example, that in the US, one of the richest countries in the world, there is a 12-year gap in life expectancy between black males living in Washington DC and men in the US a whole. In Australia there is a gap of life expectancy of 17 years between Australian indigenous peoples and the majority population.

Life course research reveals a social gradient of unequal health chances, related to socioeconomic position, and has shown how social factors influence physical and mental health. Kuh et al (2003) discuss the way the body accumulates socially created advantages and disadvantages from the moment of conception to death: they argue that the social and physical environment leaves imprints on the body system (Kuh and Ben-Shlomo, 2003). Poverty can have an impact on health chances prior to birth. For example, if expectant mothers live in poverty before and during pregnancy they may lack key nutrients which can affect foetal development and put their child at risk of chronic disease in later life (Barker, 1998). Children living in poverty have greater risk of exposure to health-damaging environments during childhood and adulthood. This is reflected in higher death rates, which are twice as high for middle-aged men and women born into poorer families than those growing up in more affluent circumstances (Graham, 2010, p 46).

Poverty and related stressors such as unemployment increase the risk of poor health for those affected by it. Meeting the cost of basic provisions to sustain health such as food, energy and housing inevitably becomes harder for the many people who are reliant on state benefits. Fryer (1995) found that in the western societies people's psychological health may be damaged by the experience of unemployment because it can lead to a loss of social status and sense of loss of purpose in life that can be damaging for a person's self-esteem.

Migration

The ethnic and cultural diversity of the UK population cannot be simply attributed to the processes of globalisation. Migration is not new for the UK. The development and expansion of the British Empire was dependent on an inhumane Transatlantic slave trade and the UK's history of colonial relationships is associated with the arrival of many people from black and minority ethnic groups. Simpson and Lawrence (2009) note that:

> The demand for cheap labour, as well as highly skilled professionals to address skills shortages was often dependent upon colonial relationships, where a common language and special migration arrangements were in place. (Simpson and Lawrence, 2009, p 21)

Factors associated with globalisation, such as global communications systems and affordable means of travel, have made it easier for people to move across borders and take up employment opportunities. In the UK, between 2001 and 2002, 25 per cent of all new social work recruits had trained overseas (Welbourne et al, 2007). A significant number of migrants contribute to work in the care sector. In relation to Ireland, Timonen and Doyle (2009) report that in urban areas in particular, the majority of carers in many occupational categories in institutional, hospital and domiciliary care settings are migrant workers. Adjusting to life in a new country can be challenging, especially if people have to contend with hostility and racism. A 2002 NHS UK survey found that 40 per cent of minority ethnic nurses had experienced discrimination from work colleagues and 65 per cent reported encountering racial harassment from service users and their families (Timonen and Doyle, 2009, p 4). These findings led the authors of the survey, Shields and Wheately Price, to conclude that racism was entrenched within the NHS (Shields and Wheately Price, 2002, cited in Likupe, 2006). Negative stereotypes of foreign workers and communication problems have been identified as contributing to racism and discrimination in the nursing sector (Allan et al, 2004; Allan and Larson, 2003, cited in Timonen and Doyle, 2009). This finding is echoed in research on migrant domiciliary carers and domestic workers, which has found that employers often held racial stereotypes of carers based on their nationality, and that they had a preference for employing nationalities that were assumed to have submissive temperaments (Anderson, 2007, cited in Timonen and Doyle, 2009). The value base for workers in health and social care is clearly linked to anti-discriminatory and anti-oppressive practice, but it seems that there is still a long way to go before this is embraced by all sections of the workforce.

Increasingly in the UK, practitioners working in the fields of health, social care, social and community work come across people whose health and social welfare has been affected by international events which has resulted in their migration to this country. Statistics from the Annual Population Survey published by the Office for National Statistics (2009, cited in Lee-Treweek, 2011, p 1) showed 4.1 million foreign nationals resident in the UK in the year to June 2008, compared with 3.8 million in the year to June 2007. People's reasons for migrating are often complex and varied but may include factors such as economic deprivation and the desire to improve quality of life. Migration may be motivated by ecological disasters in people's country of origin, or by the need to escape war, persecution or oppression. A global perspective considers the reasons for migration, the experiences that these service users and carers have had in their countries of origin, and how these have had an impact on their current experience in the country to which they have chosen to migrate, enhancing the practitioner's understanding of the diverse health and welfare needs that migrants may present.

In relation to refugees and people seeking asylum, Williams et al (2009) note that the experience of war and violence is common, suggesting that:

> [the] ... consequences of these experiences include: people's sense of self being destroyed because of persistent states of fear and vulnerability; the destroying of people's status within their community, for example as a result of rape. People may have lived in areas where family and neighbours are expected to report on each other; which destroys trust and mutual support. Homes and property may have been destroyed; food removed; massacres could have taken place; children may have been kidnapped to become solders; or in the case of girls taken as sexual slaves for the army. Gender abuse, through systematic rape, is often used against civilians of all ages, particularly women, and including children, while others may be made to witness it. (Williams et al, 2009, p 70)

Ramon (2009) notes that political conflict increases the level of stress of those affected by it but that this may not be reflected immediately in a rise in severe rates of mental illnesses, such as psychosis. The impact on people's mental health may only become apparent when the conflict has ended. It is often then that people become aware that they have survived physically, but psychologically many survivors begin to realise that they must confront irreversible losses that have resulted during the conflict. Ramon suggests that for some people, feelings of guilt about surviving and the experience of loss can become overwhelming. This illustrates the way traumatic experiences associated with conflict in one part of the world may have an impact on services users' lives at a later stage, in another location.

Obtaining appropriate support to work with psychological trauma can be especially problematic for some black and ethnic minority people who have travelled to the UK because they may experience a range of discrimination practices in relation to the mental health services they receive. This problem has on occasions been attributed to institutional racism, reflected in inequalities within some mental health services. For example, the Commission for Healthcare Audit and Inspection (2005) report that black African–Caribbean people seeking support from mental health services are 14 per cent more likely than white service users to be turned away when they seek help, and when they do receive services, they are more likely to be placed in seclusion and be subject to control, restraint or be detained for treatment against their will under the provisions of mental health legislation.

Cultural exchange of practice knowledge

Timonen and Doyle's (2009) research considered the extent to which migrant care workers and care recipients interacted harmoniously and understood each other's expectations and ways of communicating. Their study focused on migrant care workers employed in the institutional and domiciliary car sector in Dublin and revealed generally positive carer–care recipient relationships. Domiciliary care workers expressed a great deal of respect and empathy for the older people whom they worked with. Many respondents drew parallels between caring for members of their own families and the people they worked with. These carers were able to form intimate relationships with the people they cared for, which many equated with family type relationships. A commitment to person-centred approaches to working with older people was apparent among both domiciliary care worker and carers working in institutional settings. However, the level of intimacy with service users in institutional settings was not so strong because of the intensity of care workers' workloads which left them with little time for social interaction. Tensions arising from racist attitudes of service users were reported to be rare, but when they had arisen, carers had developed strategies to overcome them.

> To bridge the cultural divide between the carer and care recipients in both the domiciliary and institutional care context,

a gentle understanding approach towards the care recipient was generally adopted. Bringing gifts of traditional cooking was used by an Iranian home carer, while humour was used by many carers to bridge the cultural barrier and to put care recipients at their ease. (Timonen and Doyle, 2009, p 9)

Robertson (1992) acknowledges that globalisation has created opportunities to engage with different cultures and ideas. There is the potential to take ideas and practices from one part of the world to another and apply them to local conditions to produce hybrid cultural practices. Global awareness can be raised and ideas can be shared through media coverage, international conferences and papers published in academic and professional journals, international links between institutions providing training for health and social welfare workers and through the work of a growing number of international organisations such as the International Federation of Social Workers and other international service user and carer movements. Insights gained from a global perspective can inform the development of the practice by enabling health and social care practitioners to identify relevant approaches and skills, acquired during their training, which can be adapted to meet the needs of people affected by the negative effects of globalisation.

There are numerous examples of how practices developed in one country have been adapted to the needs of other populations. For example, Harrison and Melville (2010) note how US models of social work practice have been exported to other parts of the globe and modified and indigenised according to local needs. Family group conferencing, an approach used in work with children and families, originated from the traditions of Maori culture in New Zealand and has been adapted and used in several other countries including the UK. In relation to service user involvement in healthcare, patients' councils in hospitals were initially established in the Netherlands by service users and have since been adopted in the UK. Also within the UK, emphasis is placed on the importance of effective inter-professional work in health and social care to provide a holistic approach to person-centred care for work with service users, accessing both children and families, and adult services. To meet the professional needs of those working in this context in the UK the Centre for the Advancement of Inter-professional Education was established. This organisation disseminates research relating to inter-professional education for professionals working in the statutory, voluntary and independent sectors. Milburn and Walker (2009) report that interest in inter-professional education developed initially in the US in the late 1960s, with the first federal initiative being offered in 1994 by the Institute for Healthcare Improvement. This kind of initiative provides opportunities for practitioners from a range of professional backgrounds to share good practice.

Conclusion

This chapter has highlighted some of the ways in which global events which contribute to increases in poverty and other forms of social disadvantage can have an impact on the health and social welfare needs of service users and carers in the UK. To effectively respond to the complex and varied needs arising from global conditions, it is important that practitioners appreciate how the global affects the local and vice versa. Practitioners can support service users by drawing on knowledge and skills developed through their training, and develop this in the context of greater cultural and global awareness and understanding. There is much to be gained from sharing of ideas and practices globally. In relation to social work, Dominelli (2010) argues that what is called for is the development of new paradigms for practice which place greater emphasis on social and community development and which incorporate an appropriate concern for the environmental circumstances of service users' lives. This perspective has relevance for both health and social welfare practices as it suggests methods and approaches from other parts of the globe cannot simply be applied to other parts of the world without careful consideration of how they can be adapted to meet needs presented in a local context. Therefore, gaining insight into the service users' experiences and perceptions is essential for developing and enhancing practice.

References

Allan, H.T. and Larsen, J.A. (2003) *We need respect! Experiences of internationally recruited nurses in the UK*, London: Royal College of Nursing.

Allan, H.T., Larsen, J.A., Bryan, K. and Smith, P.A. (2004) 'The social reproduction of institutional racism: internationally recruited nurses' experiences of the British health services', *Diversity in Health and Social Care*, vol 1, pp 117-25.

APHO (Association of Public Health Observatories) (2008) *Health profile 2008 Camden*, APHO.

Barker, D. (1998) *Mothers, babies and health in later life*, Edinburgh: Churchill Livingstone.

Bywaters, P., McLeod, E. and Napier, L. (eds) (2009) *Social work and global health inequalities: Practice and policy developments*, Bristol: The Policy Press.

Commission for Healthcare Audit Inspection Services (2005) *Count me in: results of a national census of inpatients in mental health hospitals and facilities in England and Wales*, London: Commission for Healthcare Audit Commission.

CSDH (Commission on the Social Determinants of Health) (2008) *Closing the gap in a generation: Health equity through action on the social determinants of health*, Final report of the CSDH, Geneva: World Health Organization.

Dominelli, L. (2010) 'Globalization, contemporary challenges and social work practice', *International Social Work*, vol 53, no 3, pp 599-612.

Fryer, D. (1995) 'Labour market disadvantage, deprivation and mental health', *The Psychologist*, vol 8, no 6, pp 265-72.

Giddens, A. (1990) *The consequences of modernity*, Cambridge: Polity Press.

Giddens, A. (1999) *Runaway world: How globalisation is reshaping our lives*, London: Profile Books Ltd.

Graham, H. (2010) 'Poverty and health: global and national patterns', in J. Douglas, S. Earle, S. Handsley, L. Jones, C. Lloyd and S. Spurr (eds) *A reader in promoting public health: Challenge and controversy*, Milton Keynes/London: The Open University/Sage Publications, pp 39-51.

Harrison, G. and Melville, R. (2010) *Rethinking social work in a global world*, Basingstoke: Palgrave Macmillan.

Hirst, P., Thompson, G. and Bromley, S. (2009) *Globalisation in question* (3rd edn), Cambridge: Polity Press.

Kuh, D. and Ben-Shlomo, Y. (eds) *A life course approach to chronic disease epidemiology: Tracing the origins of ill health from early adult life* (2nd edn), Oxford: Oxford University Press.

Kuh, D., Ben-Shlomo, Y., Lynch, J., Hallqvist, J. and Power, C. (2003) 'Life course epidemiology', *Journal of Epidemiology and Community Health*, vol 57, pp 778-83.

Lee-Treweek, G. (2011) 'Falling through the net of social policy: impoverished and invisible migrants in the UK today', Working Paper Series, Department of Interdisciplinary Studies, MMU Cheshire.

Likupe, G. (2006) 'Experiences of African nurses in the UK National Health Service: a literature review', *Journal of Clinical Nursing*, vol 15, pp 1213-20.

Milburn, P. and Walker, P. (2009) 'Beyond interprofessional education and towards collaborative person-centred practice', in G. Koubel and H. Bungay (eds) *The challenge of person-centred care: An interprofessional perspective*, Basingstoke: Palgrave Macmillan, pp 11-28.

ONS (Office for National Statistics) (2009) *Annual population survey*, London: ONS.

Ramon, S. (2009) 'The health impact of political conflict: new engagements for social work?', in P. Bywaters, E. McLeod and L. Napier (eds) *Social work and global health inequalities: Practice and policy developments*, Bristol: The Policy Press.

Robertson, R. (1992) *The three waves of globalization: A history of developing global consciousness*, New York: Zed Books.

Rose, S.M. (2009) 'Health, equity and social justice', in P. Bywaters, E. McLeod and L. Napier (eds) *Social work and global health inequalities: Practice and policy developments*, Bristol: The Policy Press.

Simpson, G. and Lawrence, S. (2009) 'Global is local is global', in S. Lawrence, K. Lyons, G. Simpson and N. Huegler (eds) *Introducing international social work*, Exeter: Learning Matters.

Timonen, V. and Doyle, M. (2009) 'Caring and collaborating across cultures? Migrant care workers', *European Journal of Women's Studies*, vol 17, no 1, pp 1–17.

Welbourne, P., Harrison, G. and Ford, D. (2007) 'Social work in the UK and the global labour market: recruitment, practice and ethical considerations', *International Social Work*, vol 50, no 1, pp 27–40.

Williams, J., Foggin, J. and Joubert, M. (2009) 'International perspectives on social work with people with mental health issues', in S. Lawrence, K. Lyons, G. Simpson and N. Huegler (eds) *Introducing international social work*, Exeter: Learning Matters.

27

Falling through the cracks in social welfare: invisible adult migrants in the UK

Geraldine Lee-Treweek

Extract from Working Paper Series, (January 2011) Department of Interdisciplinary Studies, Cheshire: MMU.

Contemporary Western notions of adulthood presuppose that adults are individual, independent people who are able to make choices freely and to direct their own lives (Pilcher, 1995). Such a construction of adults fails to take into account diverse notions of adulthood, which may be framed by a host of factors, including global social change. A major feature of such change has been the increase in transmigration (migration that takes people across national borders) and human trafficking (where people are forced or deceived into moving to undertake exploitative work). Migration can offer opportunities for adults and their families ... However, transmigration is a topic of contention ... whilst in good economic times there are fears about who will fill low status and unwanted jobs, under recessionary conditions the concerns become the 'taking' of jobs, the 'abuse' of welfare and the 'costs' of migration (Huysmans 2006). ... Likewise ... the full extent of the exploitation and vulnerability of trafficked people is also not understood. ... By understanding the dynamics of exploitation and low power that many newcomers to the UK experience, it is possible to perceive the multiple points of vulnerability that some adults suffer. Social welfare provision often fails these groups because of a lack of understanding of these dynamics.

This chapter presents two case studies of recent European Union (EU) migrants to the UK. Both cases illustrate that even migrants who appear protected by UK and EU social policies can face processes that leave them ... invisible to agencies that should protect them. The first case study concerns Halina[1], a Polish migrant, who entered the country legally as a migrant worker but finds that unemployment leaves her and her child vulnerable in the face of benefits errors. Halina's case is a real one and a

---

[1] All names are pseudonyms

group of professionals living and working in the town of Northton, with which I am involved, supported her. Halina gave permission for use of her case but some personal details have been altered. The second case study involves Anda, a Romanian national, who was brought to the UK, through deception by agricultural gangmasters, to harvest crops. Anda's case is derived from the amalgamation of details from non-governmental agencies working with trafficked people, and exemplifies common experiences of trafficked workers. A complicated benefits system, the existence of criminals who exploit people, a lack of understanding by health, and social care professionals … and a paucity of third sector provision for those in difficulties … influence why some people who come to the UK fail to be supported by welfare systems and professionals.

Migration to the UK

Migration to the UK is not new. The UK has always experienced waves of newcomers, as invaders, as settlers and so forth. Some people have been moved to the UK by force and against their will, such as during the slave trade. From the 1950s onwards, others chose to migrate to the UK to fill labour shortages, coming from both Commonwealth countries and from European states (Peach, 1967) … During the 1970s refugees and people seeking asylum also began to be more prominent in the UK media, raising public awareness (Boswell 2003). During these periods, the many newcomers to the UK experienced hostility in settling in new towns and work places, as is the case today. …

Globalisation, a term used to describe the way that geographically dispersed parts of the globe are becoming more interconnected, has altered the numbers and types of migrants entering the UK and their rights when resident. … Processes of globalisation mean that workers can be moved to fill labour shortages quickly, recruited through the internet, transported swiftly between countries and be deployed in various sectors. … Worryingly, those same processes of social change have also encouraged the exploitation of some workers through their forced movement (trafficking and bonded labour). …There are many adults living in the UK today who could be defined as 'new' migrants; arriving over the last ten years. Since 2004, various states have acceded to the EU, the asylum and refugee systems have 'processed' thousands of cases and UK boundaries have been 'challenged' by increasing numbers of illegal and trafficked workers (House of Commons Home Affairs Committee 2009).

This chapter focuses on the case of European migrants coming to the UK. Contrary to popular understanding, not all EU citizens have a right to come and work in the UK. Citizens of A8 states (which joined the EU in 2004, Poland, Czech Republic, Slovakia, Slovenia, Hungary, Latvia, Lithuania, Estonia) have free access to work here. But A2 states, which joined in 2007 (Bulgaria, Romania) have quotas. Quotas mean selection of who gets into the UK; this can lead to exploitation, for instance, by traffickers who claim they will arrange employment and permits. According to the Council of Europe Convention on Action against Trafficking in Human Beings (2005), trafficking means,

> "the recruitment, transportation, transfer, harbouring or receipt of persons, by means of the threat or use of force or other forms of coercion, of abduction, of fraud, of deception, of the abuse of power or of a position of vulnerability or of the giving or receiving of payments or benefits to achieve the consent of a person having control over another person, for the purpose of exploitation."

Trafficked people are effectively invisible and, as they are illegally in the UK, they can not claim social assistance even if their traffickers allowed them to do so. Human trafficking into the UK is illegal but various laws have consistently failed to yield prosecution. Individuals who coerce people into forced labour (slavery or servitude), and who are caught, are guilty of a criminal offence (Coroners and Justice Act 2009). However, this law has only been in place since April 2010 and has yet to be tested.

In recessionary conditions even those migrants who have right of free movement in Europe can become vulnerable; either to traffickers or to others who wish to exploit them. ... Economic migrants from the EU do have some rights in the UK to social assistance but, as noted by the AIRE Centre in London (the leading non-governmental agency supporting the individual rights of European migrants in the UK), the welfare state often fails migrants and their families leaving them vulnerable and open to abuse (AIRE 2010). Moreover, the rules for gaining unemployment benefits are highly complex; so much so that even trained civil servants struggle to understand and apply them. Misapplied rules, delays and awaiting tribunal mean time without money and this can put migrants at risk of other forms of vulnerability and exploitation, due to poverty. It is not unheard of for A8 migrants to become trafficked from within the UK when they have no access to funds to live (AIRE 2010). Others 'choose' to undertake sex work and crime to cope with poverty (Shelley 2007). The two case studies below highlight the vulnerability of migrants and trafficked people.

Case Study 1: Halina

Halina is a 28 year old single mother who lives in Northton, a small town in the North West of England. Halina arrived in Northton in 2005 ... from the Upper Silesia area of Poland, a impoverished region with considerable social problems. Halina' mother died when she was in her early teens, leaving her in the care of her father, who she reported to be a violent alcoholic. ... The EU accession of Poland enabled Halina to gain work in a factory in Northton. Halina settled into monotonous factory work, packing industrial equipment. During this time she met her boyfriend; they moved in together and had a baby, Pawel. When Pawel was a couple of months old Halina found her boyfriend had been stealing and committing fraud; she left with the child and within a few weeks was placed in social housing in Northton. At this point Halina lost the support of her friendship network in the 'Polish community', many of whom considered that Halina should have stayed to make the relationship work.

Halina was employed when she moved into social housing but after two years, she was made redundant ... and went onto Job Seekers Allowance (JSA), a fact that Halina found shameful .... Sometime after Halina was informed she would have to apply for Income Support (IS) instead. Halina asked me to attend her meeting with Job Centre Plus as a note taker. The advice worker reiterated that she would have to come off the contributory benefit and reapply for IS; this would take "approximately 2 weeks". Halina was given a short-term small loan by the social fund. However, when applying Halina reported she was told by the man assessing her that she should ration her sanitary towels; a comment she found humiliating. Nine weeks later Halina contacted us again, she had heard nothing but by now she had no food and no money. With no food bank[2] in Northton ... an emergency food and money collection was arranged privately.

A week after we began providing Halina with food a letter arrived stating that the IS claim was declined because Halina "did not fulfil the criteria for being habitually resident". Again, we attended Job Centre Plus and Halina explained she had no money. The adviser said her hands were tied, "decisions are handled in Wick in Scotland". In the Job Centre, Halina and I wrote a letter requesting a tribunal and tried to address what the problem might be with the claim. We noted the length of Halina's residency (nearly 5 years) and

---

[2] Food banks are provided by the third sector and distribute food aid in some parts of the UK.

that monthly payslips going back to 2005 were available ... Taking the letter to the post office Halina was distressed,

> 'I can't take this ... I have no money for food or heating ... do they think I am bad person? Why they do this to me and my son?'

She felt ashamed that I had to pay postage but Job Centre Plus ... had "run out of freepost envelopes". A week after this, Halina reported she could not stop crying. She attended her GP and was prescribed anti-depressants. At this time, it emerged Halina had received letters about eviction from the social housing provider. ... It transpired that anyone who defaulted, irrelevant of circumstances or payment history, received the same letter. Liaison with the social housing provider stopped the eviction process but this situation illustrated that few health and social welfare services in Northton spoke to each other. Once people were in difficulties it seemed there was no system to identify service users like Halina and her son as vulnerable. ...

After twelve weeks of waiting for an appeal, Halina was on a higher dose of anti-depressants, would not leave the house and ... her mental health was deteriorating ... At points she talked about undertaking sex work to get money, to my knowledge, this never happened, but I was worried that Halina's vulnerability would lead her into such activities. ... Northton's MP wrote supporting Halina's case ... and we were preparing to go to tribunal. Legal support from the AIRE centre in London showed the case was very strong. Five months after her benefits stopped Halina received a letter, it began, "there has been an error in your benefits" and all owed money was returned. Halina's and Pawel's case was reduced to an administrative mistake ... Halina continues to live in social housing and is still under treatment for depression. The experience of the welfare system being against her has damaged Halina's sense of belonging in the UK; it is hard to belong where systems and structures fail to recognise your basic needs.

Case Study 2: Anda

Anda's case is about her experience of being trafficked into agricultural work in the UK from her home in Romania. Anda is one of an invisible army of workers who are brought to the UK illegally and forced to undertake labour in any sector where cheap labour may be required, such as agriculture, factory labour, domestic work, hospitality and food preparation and the sex industry (Geddes 2005). Whilst some people are literally abducted, others are lied to and/or not told about the conditions under which they will work.

For many trafficked people the impetus for moving is extreme poverty, not being able to provide for family (Craig et al, 2007) or (ironically) escaping abuse. People are trafficked as individuals, in family groups, as adult men or women, or as children.

The International Fund for Agricultural Development states that 44% of Romania's population live in rural areas and 38% of this rural population live in poverty (IFAD 2009). Romania is one of the poorest countries in Europe. Anda lived in Maramures, a rural area bordering Ukraine. Living in an area with limited access to education and to employment Anda ... had little opportunity in the local area. When an 'agent' for home helps in the UK visited her village, Anda was selected. The agent ... said he could get her a job in the UK; all she needed to do was ensure she paid back her flight once working. Knowing nothing of employment quotas and the need for a permit, Anda arrived at Heathrow and was met by a Romanian national, once she was in his car he explained that the job as a cleaner had fallen through but he had found her work on a farm. This would cost more as he had to drive her there but she could work this off in time; Anda ... accepted this.

Anda was taken to Lincolnshire to live in a rundown cottage with eight other male and female Romanians. There was no heating and no hot water, food was provided for one meal a day and Anda began to fear the men she worked for, who were aggressive. The group were woken at five each morning and taken by minibus to fields to pick asparagus until the evening. One night the person in charge of the group, the 'gangmaster' took her passport and said this was 'for safekeeping'. After a few weeks Anda began to ask to go home. However, she was told she would have to work off her debt or her family back in Romania would be made to pay. Commonly trafficked workers are kept in 'debt bondage' and they are told they have to pay for their transit with work. However, trafficked people are usually paid well below the minimum wage for their labour, if at all (Craig et al 2007). Some trafficked workers are kept physically captive but usually threats to harm family at home, trafficked children and or intimidation of the trafficked person are used. Moreover, physical and sexual assault of the trafficked adult are also common strategies deployed to make them compliant (Unseen(uk) 2011). As in Anda's case, the taking of documents is also a means of control often used. Fearing for her own and her families safety, Anda had no choice but to do as she was told.

One morning Anda was moved to a caravan on a farm outside Wrexham to harvest potatoes. Anda realised that she no longer worked for the first gangmaster and that she, along with her passport, has been 'sold'. This gangmaster told her that if she was found without documents she would be in serious trouble and UK immigration would put her in prison. By deceiving Anda, the gangmaster exerted control through using her lack of knowledge of UK law. This control strategy was effective and Anda did not attempt to run away. After two years, Anda was 'allowed' to return to Romania, having earned virtually nothing.

Discussion

This paper has provided case studies of two migrants ... which have served to show how global social change can affect social welfare issues in the UK. Under conditions of globalisation, some migrant adults become extremely vulnerable; many will not understand UK systems, they may not have English language skills, they may require advocacy and support to implement their rights and some will experience exploitation and abuse. Due to such factors, it is imperative that consideration is given to the types of ... needs that arise from migration and human trafficking in the UK. This demands that the general public, professionals and policy makers understand some adult welfare needs as framed by global social change. Moreover, the concept of 'adult vulnerability' needs to be separated from an assumption that this is always about care needs or palpable incapacity issues. Sometimes in order to comprehend vulnerability it is necessary to see the situation of the person in the context of their home country, culture, circumstance and the ... dynamics of exploitation that prevent full adult agency.

By examining 'real world' examples of migrant adult experiences, the possession of adult agency and choice can be revealed to be unevenly dispersed in society. Those who have few resources and complex problems are unlikely to have the same level of personal control than those with a reasonable income and choice in how they respond to their problems. The people who 'fall through the cracks' in social welfare ... need to be identified and supported by professionals working in a range of settings. Halina's case exemplifies what can happen when adults who are coping well are failed by inadequate welfare support responses in times of crisis. ... A female migrant like Halina, even with a child, is not a priority. ... With no jobs and no recourse to public funds, sex work and crime are the only activities that could provide money. Another risk was Halina's deteriorating mental health, she already had some risk factors for mental health problems ... and had little social support. The stress of the current situation had led to Halina experiencing depression ... There are no systems that are automatically triggered when a person in Halina's position is left in an unsafe situation. ... From a safeguarding perspective, both adult and child become vulnerable when they are forced into poverty by welfare errors. In Anda's case, her agency and control end when she signs up to be a 'home help' … Anda lost her liberty and physically and psychologically was manipulated by gangmasters. Realisation that one has become a commodity, a 'thing' to be bought and sold to labour for the benefit of others, damages self-esteem, destroys trust in other people and negatively effects belief in your own capacity as an adult. Human traffickers keep those they enslave in an enforced state of vulnerability, designed to strip away a sense of adult entitlements …

Adult independence, identity and autonomy are fragile personal resources. The sense of safety that many experience as adulthood in the UK is based upon assumptions that all adults have rights and status and that people can deploy these to equal degree. The experiences of some migrants provide an insight into the contingent, vulnerable and plural nature of contemporary *adulthoods* in the UK.

References

AIRE Centre (2010) *Guide to the Rights of EEA Nationals who have been Trafficked to the UK,* London: AIRE Centre.

Boswell, C. (2003) 'Burden-Sharing in the European Union: Lessons from the German and UK experience' *Journal of Refugee Studies,* 16 (3), 316–335.

Council of Europe (2005) *Convention on action against trafficking in human beings* (http://conventions.coeint/treaty/en/treaties/html/197.htm, accessed January 2011).

Craig, G. Gaus, A. Wilkinson, M. Skrivankova, K. and McQuade, A. (2007) *Modern Slavery in the UK,* London: Joseph Rowntree Foundation.

Geddes, A. (2005) 'Chronicle of a crisis unforetold: the politics of irregular migration, human trafficking and people smuggling into the UK' *British Journal of Politics and International Relations,* 7 (3), 324–329

House of Commons Home Affairs Committee (2009) *The Trade in Human Beings: Human trafficking in the UK,* London: The Stationery Office Ltd.

Huysmans, J. (2006) *The Politics of Insecurity: Fear, migration and asylum in the EU,* London: Routledge

IFAD (The International Fund for Agricultural Development (2009) *Romania: Country factsheet* (www.ifad.org/events/gc/34/nen/factsheet/romania.pdf, accessed January 2011).

Peach, G.C.K. (1967) 'West Indian migration to Britain' *International Migration Review,* 1 (2) 34–45.

Pilcher, J. (1995) *Age and Generation in Modern Britain,* Oxford: Oxford University Press.

Shelley, T. (2007) *Exploited. Migrant Labour in the New Global Economy.* London: Zed Books.

Unseen (UK) (2011) *Human Trafficking, the Facts.* Available online at, http://www.unseenuk.org/ (accessed 07/01/2011).

Further Online Non-Governmental Resources:

The AIRE Centre

"The AIRE Centre is a specialist law centre whose mission is to promote awareness of European law rights and assist marginalised individuals and those in vulnerable circumstances to assert those rights."
Web address – http://www.airecentre.org/ Accessed 07/01/2011

Anti-Slavery

"Anti-Slavery International works at local, national and international levels to eliminate all forms of slavery around the world."
Web address – http://www.antislavery.org/english/ Accessed 07/01/2011.

Migrant Rights Network

"The Migrants' Rights Network works for a rights-based approach to migration, with migrants as full partners in the development and implementation of policies which affect them. MRN aims to strengthen the voice of migrants in discussions and debates, both with civil society, regional and national authorities. Towards this goal, MRN conducts research and projects to enable migrant community organisations to engage with key legislative and policy issues."
Web address – http://www.migrantsrights.org.uk/ Accessed 07/01/2011

Unchosen

"Unchosen is an anti-trafficking charity promoting human trafficking film campaigns nationwide"
Web address – http://www.unchosen.org.uk/ Accessed 07/01/2011.

Unseen (uk)

"unseen(uk) is a charity established to disrupt and challenge human trafficking at all levels. unseen's specific focus is to combat the trafficking of women for sexual exploitation."
web address – http://www.unseenuk.org/ Accessed 07/01/2011.

28

Decentring social policy? Devolution and the discipline of social policy: A commentary

Charlotte Williams and Gerry Mooney

Extract from C. Williams and G. Mooney, 'Decentring Social Policy? Devolution and the discipline of social policy: A commentary', *Journal of Social Policy* (2008) vol. 37, no. 3, pp. 489–507, reproduced with permission.

[...]

... [T]he potential of devolution for social policy cannot be fully grasped through a focus on those policies which have been devolved alone, but only through an understanding of the ways in which this is intertwined with and contributes to new forms of territorial politics, inequalities and entitlements, and with issues of social citizenship and social justice on a UK–wide (that is, transnational) level. In other words, devolution helps to create what we might term a new social topography, contributing to the emergence of a new discursive terrain. The focus of this chapter is, therefore, not the detail of policy differentiation but the detail of differentiation in the social relations of social policy that prompt a reframing within the discipline.

[...]

Redrawing the terrain: nation and 'nation-building'

The organising concept for a consideration of devolution is nation, and 'nation-building' is a key component of the political projects of the devolved governments. The significance of nation to social policy has been well documented (see Williams, 1989; Lewis, 2000). Clarke's work is instructive here, analysing the nation/state/welfare 'trinity' (2004: 28) and suggesting nations as a 'potent source of attachment', which have both material and symbolic resonance for the citizen. The 'multiple contexts' approach to UK social policymaking (and *remaking*) provides a particular 'spin' on the analysis of nation and social policy. Simply stated, Scotland/ Wales/Northern Ireland become the frame of reference for a consideration of/or construction of 'social problems' in themselves, and act as primary sites for the contestation of social citizenship. This contemporary indigenisation of policy has a strong political referent in terms of 'nation-building' and cannot be seen as simply pragmatic responses to the specificity of the sub-UK contexts. In Scotland, for instance, policies such as on free long-term care for elderly people or student fees are couched notably in terms of their 'Scottishness', the idea of 'Scottish solutions to Scottish problems' (see Mooney and Scott, 2005).

'Nation-building' suggests a picture of homogenisation which is ever far removed from the mix of identities, class and national backgrounds that increasingly characterise Scotland, Wales and Northern Ireland. However, the idea that these countries are somehow distinct in the problems they throw up and that they provide the most appropriate locale for determining responses is in the case of Scotland and Wales further paralleled by a strong 'ethnic' or 'nationalistic' case for self-determination. We call this a process of 're-nationalisation' and, however problematic, its symbiotic relationship with the processes of Europeanisation, globalisation and neo-liberalisation dictates new terrains of analysis.

The construction of national 'publics' in the constituent parts of the UK is well underway with a number of concomitant spin offs. As the policy community is transmogrifying to a much more network-based system of governance (Newman, 2001) so new actors appear in the political arena. This is occurring everywhere, but, it can be argued, subject to a particular construction within the national contexts. In the new constituencies, organisations and groups have been mobilised in response to 're-nationalisation'. For example, in Wales the idea of a 'Welsh civil society' is emerging, as opposed to a civil society in Wales (Hodgson, 2004; Day, 2002), as is the mobilisation of English ethnicity in Wales around access to key resources of welfare such as housing. Lines of association that might previously have been co-national now follow country borders. These new lines of association bring together amalgamations of different stakeholder groups and change the nature of relationships between them and in turn produce novel experiments in the democratisation of welfare.

Alongside this redrawing of the parameters of the terrain there has been significant institutional realignments. Post devolution a number of organisations have rebranded themselves to follow national borders. In Wales, for example, Stonewall Cymru, Citizens Advice Cymru, Barnardos Cymru are organisations that have shifted their focus to Welsh concerns, moved their head offices into Wales, developed infrastructures for national coverage and altered their practices to respond to the new government bodies. There are shifting relationships here between professional bodies, trade unions, the third sector, business organisations and different government departments across the UK. As such, Wales and Scotland are being redrawn and reconstructed institutionally as geo-political entities.

These new configurations suggest something about the construction of social problems and its national referents but also raise questions about conditionalities, solidarities and the reworking of welfare settlements. Clarke aptly points out that the 'coexistence of residual and emergent formations alongside the current dominant tendencies is a reminder that the formations of welfare, state and nation are unsettled and that their reconstruction is *unfinished* '(2004: 29)(emphasis in original). It can be suggested, therefore, that devolution foregrounds this 'unfinished' business of destabilisation and/or reconstructions of nation as a site of contestation.

Visions and utopias: geo-political pluralism

There may be considerable disagreement as to the extent to which devolution represents a significant departure in terms of divergent policymaking. It is a simple enough task to point to policy differences such as free personal care for the sick and elderly or the student fees policy in Scotland, or free prescriptions and the abolition of school league tables in Wales. Some would argue the differences are marginal to the overarching continuities ensured by Labour-dominated administrations (at least prior to the May 2007 elections) across the devolved polities, and the quiet manipulation of the policy strings by civil servants in Whitehall (Hudson and Lowe, 2004). It is clearly important to view devolution within the context of the New Labour 'modernising' project and as a product of its wider socio-economic and neo-liberal agendas. The devolved Scotland, Wales and Northern Ireland are part of this mission. However, it can be argued that the devolved nations open up new sites of struggle and contestation, new processes and practices which challenge the ideological and geo-political boundaries of the British Welfare State, and this encapsulates a significant shift which impacts on the central concerns of the discipline. Interestingly, Clarke, writing within a transnational frame, draws our attention to these very limits of neo-liberalism in practice as it forms an interface with particular geopolitical and cultural entities, when he says this philosophy may encounter 'diverse forms of resistance and refusals to "go with the flow"'(2004: 9).

Mishra (1977) raised a number of issues in relation to the normative basis of social interventionism, not least the identification of its ideological underpinnings. His concern was with the parameters of liberal capitalism and the tension this posed for what he calls 'honest' welfare-orientated values. This tension appears as a theme of devolution with, for example in Wales, an avowed rhetoric to offer some resistance to neo-liberal welfare policy, and more recently claims by the SNP following their election success in May 2007 that they would reject New Labour's approach to public services. It has been forcefully argued (and indeed problematised) that Scotland and Wales are developing welfare discourses that diverge from the strictures of mainstream New Labour-speak (see, for example, Davies, 2003). In Scotland this may have a long history and arguably these can be reinforced through devolution. In Wales the First Minister, Rhodri Morgan, at the opening of the second term of office, committed himself to placing 'clear red water' between Westminster and Cardiff (Morgan, 2002), and constructed his arguments around what he identified as three 'ideological fault lines' in approaches to social welfare: universalism versus means testing, equality versus choice, and equality of opportunity versus 'the fundamentally socialist aim of equality of outcome'. There have been several policy directions that indicate the Welsh direction as built on a philosophy that markedly differs from Westminster, not least the citizen-focused approach to public services (WAG, 2007) and the principle of distribution based on the notion of 'progressive universalism' (Drakeford, 2007). It can be suggested that this reflects a distinctive ideological base. Rhodri Morgan (2002) claims that 'The actions of the Welsh Assembly Government clearly owe more to the traditions of Titmuss, Tawney, Beveridge and Bevan rather than those of Hayek and Friedman'. As such, and returning to the issue of welfare retrenchment raised at the outset, commentators such as Stewart (2004) and Adams and Schmeuker (2005) among others make the somewhat controversial and problematic claims that it is increasingly 'the English', under the impact of more radical New Labour policies, that are divergent from the classic welfare state, not the devolved administrations in Wales or Scotland which are often uncritically constructed as 'defenders of the welfare state'. The coherence of the ideological differentiation is, of course, open to debate. Nevertheless, however limited in practice or whatever their rationale, the collectivist aspirations are a core feature of social policy rhetoric, if not policy and practice, in Scotland and Wales.

The issue for the discipline, as well as for the analysis of social policy in the devolved UK, then, is not simply one of competing perspectives of welfare (theoretical pluralism) but a trajectory that flags potentially diverse ways of doing and emerging 'ways of life' (Pfau-Effinger, 2005) organised around discourses of nation. This indicates an unsettling, though not entirely, of both the 'certainties' and assumed homogeneity of 'the British welfare state' in the light of competing 'welfarisms', even if this still strikes a salient chord with the national popular. The problem of values or the normative basis of interventionism can be presented as one axis in the decentring of mainstream social policy analysis.

Welfare subjectivities and territorial citizenship: does where you live matter?

Devolution was not intended to produce radically different citizenship rights across the nations, but by definition it has the potential to produce differing experiences of welfare as these interrelate with factors of place, history and ways of life, as well as differing popular imaginings of welfare. Arguably, 'place' has not significantly registered in the discussion of new welfare subjectivities other than perhaps in relation to the generic rural/ urban distinctions or more recently with regard to concerns with 'problem' places and 'problem' people. In the conceptual discussion framing the Care, Values and the Future of Welfare (CAVA 2000) research, Williams charts a number of fields of analysis aimed at exploring the dynamics between subjectivity, agency and identity and aspects of social structure, such as the discursive and institutional contexts at subnational, national and international levels. She identifies aspects of governance as one such contextual factor providing 'the social topography of enablement and constraint' in which individuals perform, negotiate, act upon and draw on welfare resources (2000: 13). It can be suggested that there is considerable potential within the devolutionary framework for new discursive/analytical trajectories as discourses, ideas and practices of nation, community, locality and place return to critically inform care giving and receiving, issues of crime prevention, managing 'disorder' and aspects of service delivery (for example, 'community planning' or 'community safety') within the context of national cultures.

The interrelationship between identity/culture and care is signalled more forcibly in the context of devolution, and sometimes in very practical ways, for example in the emerging literature around Welsh language provision and rights of access to welfare for Welsh language speakers. Similarly, the quality of citizenship involvement and the experiential nature of citizenship are, arguably, being transformed under devolution. The literature suggests that 'publics' (or perhaps more correctly, some of them) in the constituent nations have been engaged in more direct dialogue with government and that accordingly there is scope for a revitalisation of an ambiguous 'civil society' (Hodgson, 2004). All these trends speak to the contextual conditions for the (hoped *for*) democratisation of social policymaking. Thus, the idea of diversity in social policy is given spatial dimensions, and herein lays the potential for new methodologies that build in a territorial dimension to experiential welfare as the significance of place and more broadly nation in the meaning of welfare is reorganised and re-emphasised.

An associated dimension of spatial diversity is the issue of territorial justice and injustice. This issue takes us beyond imbalances in resourcing (note, for example, renewed debates in late 2007 about the Barnett funding formula (see Fraser, 2007) towards the idea of justified imbalances and public perceptions of these). Debates around the provision of personal care for the elderly in Scotland or free prescriptions in Wales are contemporary examples of such territorial politics. The 'postcode lottery' takes on new contours under devolution in that now it is not 'inadvertent' – as, for example, illustrated by Tudor Hart's inverse care law – but is seen as structured, has become more significant in the public mind and is seen as more amenable to change. Mooney argues devolution 'brings into sharp relief questions about social and territorial injustice, belongings, exclusions, mobilisations, inequalities and social divisions' that deserve greater examination (Mooney, 2006: 2). This reshaped interventionism inevitably implies a new role for the centre. Some devolutionists have argued for the limiting of policy divergence and suggest the role of the centre in 'holding the ring' particularly on inequities and inequalities (Jeffrey, 2002). However, again new and interesting questions are raised for analysis about the shifts and tensions *vis-`a-vis* the centre as issues of universalism/particularism and the issue of the distribution of power and resources come into view more acutely. Outcomes matter in social policy, and the philosophical basis on which differential outcomes are justified raises important questions for the discipline.

Social policy 'knowledges'

Part of the process of 'rethinking' social policy has been a call for the broadening of its concerns. Writers such as Cahill (1994) pointed to an expansion of the content of social policy to include aspects of environment and consumption. With devolution, new content pours into social policy fields. An example of this is Horgan's (2006) work on conflict in Northern Ireland and its interplay with social policy issues, in particular poverty and inequality. Such analysis might lead to the conceptual development of issues of conflict in mediating welfare need and welfare delivery more generally – at the interface with issues of war, 'ethnic' riots/asylum seeker hatred, class, religious and ethnic conflict. This will inevitably lead to new research priorities for the subject area emerging as relevant and legitimate. This idea of the devolved constituencies as national policy 'laboratories' is one that is featuring in the literature, and while this language speaks to the empiricist tradition, the implication is of insights gleaned from experimentation in one part of the UK enabling policy transfer. Notable examples here include the ban on smoking in enclosed public spaces introduced in Scotland in March 2006 and then in Wales in April 2007 and in England in July 2007, and the 'Fresh Talent' initiative in Scotland, the provision of extended permits to live and work in Scotland to non-EU graduates of Scottish universities, has led to similar policies being introduced for the rest of the UK at the end of 2005.

It is important to acknowledge here the way in which 'knowledges' emerge and are legitimated within mainstream social policy and how this in turn reflects wider power relations. Wales is a case in point. Day (2002: 3) cogently draws attention to the particular positioning of what he calls 'marginal' contexts in the wider sociological imagination. His argument is that nation theorists such as, for example, McCrone (2001) in the Scottish context and Rees and Rees (1980) in the Welsh context have not only lobbied to draw attention to a neglected field of sociological analysis (that is, Scotland/Wales) but have by definition prompted a *re/theorisation of the conventional model of society itself* through such juxtapositioning. That is to say, by theorising Wales we not only have to construct some conception of what 'Wales' (or Scotland or England or indeed the UK) 'is', but in doing so raise questions about the suggested 'national' norm of social policy accounts, thereby problematising dominant conceptions.

This process takes on a new force under devolution. Re-theorising the presumption of the 'national' – both UK multi-national and Scottish/ Welsh/ English national – also poses a challenge to the mainstream production of knowledge in social policy. The power to define what matters and what is deemed relevant is challenged. The power to define what appears in the mainstream journals and what should be the appropriate vantage point for considering issues comes under critical scrutiny. Day (2002: 5) notes in relation to sociological analysis, not only the marginalisation of work from Wales, which is often dismissed as parochial within the wider British social science community, but a dearth of a critical academic mass in Wales, resulting in a poverty of knowledge, with large and important topics under-explored.

[...]

The devolution debate *re-engages* with a number of established social policy issues: for example, territorial equity/justice, subsidiarity versus solidarity, liberty, equality and diversity, universalism, particularism, the questioning of the welfare settlement, and the old welfare state and new welfare state arguments and citizenship debates. It helps to ignite the discourse on the democratisation of welfare in very particular ways, and again draws our attention to the interrelationship between economic and social policy. It relates in new and differing ways with the recently emerging literature on transnational social policy/policies. However, it also raises new narratives in terms of the construction of 'social problems', their content and the social relations of welfare. It summons a new perspective; in particular, it offers a critical vantage point on centrist welfare policy analysis: a counter to the 'distortions' Mishra signalled. In addition, it brings into view the significance of *place* to welfare identifications, access and association and thus to other sources of wellbeing, such as the environment, rurality, 'civil society' and other infra-political involvements. It also signals a revisiting of issues of social divisions, social inequality and social justice; of class, ethnicity and race, gender (and other exclusionary positionings) at the interface with nation in the constituent parts of the UK. We suggest this is a major redrawing of the social policy map.

We are nonetheless faced with considering both the tensions and possibilities devolution portends for the discipline: to reflect it uncritically as an exercise in the technocratic pragmatism of the neo-liberal agenda is one possibility, or to engage with it as part of the 'expanding the social policy imaginary' approach (Lewis, 2000). We contend that devolution represents a potential paradigmatic shift for the discipline if we engage with it as a new dimension in the 'rethinking' story of contestation, conflicts and struggles over welfare arrangements, delivery and outcomes, through the forging of new arenas of analysis, new methodologies and concepts in a multi-nation, neo-liberal UK.

Acknowledgement

We are grateful to John Clarke, Gill Scott, Sharon Wright and Nicola Yeates for comments on an early draft of this article.

References

Adams, J. and Schmeuker, K. (eds) (2005) *Devolution in Practice 2006*, Newcastle: Institute of Public Policy Research North.

Cahill, M. (1994) *The New Social Policy*, Oxford: Blackwell.

Clarke, J. (2004) *Changing Welfare, Changing States: New Directions in Social Policy*, London: Sage.

Davies, S. (2003) *Inside the Laboratory: The New Politics of Public Services in Wales*, London: Catalyst.

Day, G. (2002) *Making Sense of Wales*, Cardiff: University of Wales Press.

Ditch, J. (1988) *Social Policy in Northern Ireland between 1939 and 1950*, Aldershot: Avebury.

Drakeford, M. (2007) 'Progressive universalism', *Agenda*, Winter, 4–7.

English, J. (1988) *Social Services in Scotland*, third edition, Edinburgh: Scottish Academic Press.

Fraser, D. (2007) 'Funding "will be the next step in UK devolution"', *The Herald*, 8 December.

Hodgson, L. (2004) 'Manufactured civil society', *Critical Social Policy*, 24: 2, 139–64.

Horgan, G. (2006) 'Devolution, direct rule and neo-liberal reconstruction in Northern Ireland', *Critical Social Policy*, 26: 3, 656–68.

Hudson, J. and Lowe, S. (2004) *Understanding the Policy Process: Analysing Welfare Policy and Practice*, Bristol: The Policy Press.

Jeffrey, C. (2002) 'Uniformity and diversity in policy provision: insights from the US, Germany and Canada', in J. Adams and P. Robinson (eds) *Devolution and Practice*, London: Institute for Public Policy Research.

Lewis, G. (2000) 'Expanding the social policy imaginary', in G. Lewis, S. Gewirtz and J. Clarke (eds) *Rethinking Social Policy*, London: Sage.

McCrone, D. (2001) *Understanding Scotland: The Sociology of a Nation*, second edition, London: Routledge.

Mishra, R. (1977) *Society and Social Policy: Theories and Practice of Welfare*, London: Macmillan.

Mooney, G. (2006) 'Social justice in the devolved Scotland: representation or reality?', ESRC Social Justice and Public Policy Seminar Series, Glasgow University Centre for Social Justice, 28 March.

Morgan, R. (2002) Speech to the University of Wales, Swansea National Centre for Public Policy Third Anniversary Lecture, 11 December.

Newman, J. (2001) *Modernising Governance: New Labour, Policy and Society*, London: Sage.

Pfau-Effinger, B. (2005) 'Culture and welfare state policies: reflections on a complex interrelation', *Journal of Social Policy*, 34: 1, 3–20.

Mooney, G. and Scott, G. (eds) (2005) *Exploring Social Policy in the 'New' Scotland*, Bristol: The Policy Press.

Rees, G. and Ress, T. (1980) *Poverty and Social Inequality in Wales*, London: Croom Helm.

Stewart, J. (2004) *Taking Stock: Scottish Social Welfare after Devolution*, Bristol: The Policy Press.

Welsh Assembly Government (WAG) (2007) *Fulfilled Lives, Supportive Communities: A Strategy for Social Services in Wales over the Next Decade*, WAG February 2007.

Williams, F. (1989) *Social Policy: A Critical Introduction*, Cambridge: Polity Press.

Williams, F. (2000) 'A conceptual chart for CAVA', ESRC research group on Care, Values and the Future of Welfare, Workshop paper no. 16, Methodologies for Researching Moral Agency. Workshop 4, 17 March, University of Leeds. www.leeds.ac.uk/cava/papers/ paper16fiona.htm (accessed 12 June 2007).

29

The intellectual origins of social capital

Andrew Gibson

Social capital and health inequalities

The links between social capital and health have come into increasing prominence in the literature on income inequality and health (Hawe and Shiell, 2000). The relationship between health and socioeconomic status (SES), using a wide range of measures, is well established (Whitehead, 1987; Townsend and Davidson, 1988; Independent Inquiry into Inequalities in Health, 1998).

In most developed countries, however, health inequalities have not decreased despite rising national wealth (as measured by increasing gross national product [GNP] per capita) and improvements in longevity. This has provoked discussion about the possible ways that social factors other than material deprivation may affect health outcomes. Some researchers (for example, Wilkinson, 1996; Kawachi et al, 1997; Kawachi and Kennedy, 1997; Wilkinson and Pickett, 2009) suggest that inequality is bad for health, independent of the impact on individuals of material factors such as income levels. This emphasises the negative impact on health of the *experience* of inequality. For example, Wilkinson has attempted to demonstrate a strong correlation between violent crime rates, income inequality and levels of ill health (Wilkinson et al, 1998; Wilkinson and Pickett, 2009). He has sought to explain these findings by arguing that living in a highly unequal society leads to feelings of humiliation, disrespect and shame among those who are lower down the social hierarchy. He argues, drawing on the work of Putnam (1993), that increased inequality erodes levels of social cohesion/social capital within society and increases the significance of differences in social status. These factors in turn lead to increases in psychosocial stress of various kinds, which translate into patterns of ill health and into violent crime. From this perspective psychosocial stress has an impact on health both directly, via the effects of stress on disease development, and indirectly, via its contribution to the incidence of health-damaging behaviours such as excessive alcohol consumption.

In support of Wilkinson's argument, Ichiro Kawachi et al (1997) report a strong correlation between group membership and social trust and both income inequality and total mortality. Kawachi, together with Kennedy

(1997), argue that a large gap between rich and poor people leads to higher mortality through the breakdown of social cohesion. This may have a direct effect on health via various psychosocial mechanisms, or an indirect effect through the experience of violence.

However, it is important to recognise that the value of social capital and its link to health and health inequalities has been contested. Navarro (2002) has criticised it as representing a neoliberalist approach to understanding social relations, while Hawe and Shiell (2000) suggest that social capital may merely represent a repackaging of what many public health practitioners have been doing for a long time.

Part of the dispute arises from ambiguity about what the concept of 'social capital' actually refers to. Despite a number of international meetings and conferences that have attempted to clarify the components of social capital, there is still a lack of theoretical clarity about the concept. Indeed, as Portes (1998) observes, social capital is being applied to so many events and different contexts that it is in danger of losing any distinct meaning.

This chapter begins by examining the work of Robert Putnam (1993, 1998, 2000) and the criticisms made of this work, since he has perhaps been most influential in bringing the concept of social capital to prominence. The parallel but independent development of the concept by the French social theorist Pierre Bourdieu (1986) is also discussed. It is suggested that Bourdieu's approach offers a potentially fruitful alternative theoretical approach to the study of health inequalities.

What is social capital?

It is generally acknowledged by both advocates and critics alike that Robert Putnam, an American political scientist, has done the most to bring the concept into prominence both within the social sciences and more broadly within social policy circles. In the UK setting Richard Wilkinson (1996) directly acknowledges Putnam's work as the inspiration for his own use of the concept. Although many researchers seem now to accept Putnam's definition of social capital, the subject area remains hotly debated (DeFilippis, 2001; Fine, 2001).

Putnam defines social capital as 'features of social life such as networks, norms, and social trust that facilitate co-ordination and co-operation for mutual benefit' (1995, p 67). He describes a number of beneficial effects that social capital has for society. He argues that high levels of social capital can improve economic performance and reduce corruption (Putnam, 1993). He also argues that it has positive effects on health, educational attainment, crime levels and political participation (Putnam, 2000). Putnam makes use of data on levels of voter turnout, involvement in political parties, trades unions and professional organisations, volunteering, church attendance, levels of trust in politicians and levels of 'neighbourliness' in order to support his argument empirically.

However, Putnam's work has been criticised on several grounds. For example, Skocpol (1996) has criticised the way that Putnam measures social capital. Putnam does this using a form of methodological individualism, that is, in his research on the US he uses the General Social Survey to measure the level of social involvement of individuals and simply aggregates up from this. The difficulty with this approach is that it ignores the way in which power relationships, both internal and external to a community, influence its development. As DeFilippis (2001) points out, communities or regions are not solely a product of the internal attributes of the individual people living and working within them. All communities have internal social structures and power relations that also interact with the rest of the world. It is not simply social networks that make people rich or poor. For DeFilippis what needs to be changed is not necessarily the level or number of connections, but the power relationships.

Putnam also tends to treat social capital and civil society as virtually synonymous. He argues, 'social capital refers to the norms and networks of civil society that lubricate co-operative action among both citizens and their institutions' (Putnam, 1998, p 5). He assumes that social capital and civil society are positive things necessary for democratic government and economic health. However, as DeFilippis notes, the nature of civil society is something that has been hotly debated. For Hegel, civil society was inherently conflictual (Hegel, 1965). This idea was developed by Marx, but reworked from a materialist perspective. The Italian revolutionary Gramsci viewed the associations of civil society as one of the principal means via which the ruling classes generate and sustain their 'hegemony' over labour and the peasantry (Gramsci, 1971). More recently some feminist authors have made similar arguments about how conceiving of civil society in terms of beneficial relationships and shared interests is inherently oppressive to those people who do not share in these interests or benefits (Benhabib and Cornell, 1987; Young, 1990).

Putnam's assumption that social capital is normatively good is also open to question. In order to illustrate the benefits of social capital Putnam quotes Coleman's (1988) example of the diamond industry in New York, and how market transactions involving large quantities of jewels are facilitated by the social networks of trust within the Jewish community that controls the industry. However, as DeFilippis (2001) points out, the description he offers ignores the reality of exploitation within ethnic enclave economies (see, for example, Waldinger, 1986). It also ignores the fact that anyone who is not a member of the ethnic enclave creating the market is excluded from that market, irrespective of their ability. One could argue in response that those who are excluded should develop their own connections to the relevant social networks in order to overcome this. However, as DeFilippis (2001) points out, if everyone is connected to the same networks and realises the same benefits, the advantages of network membership disappear. For DeFilippis, social capital must be premised on the ability of certain groups to realise it at the expense of others in order for it to operate as a form of capital.

Bridging and bonding social capital

Putnam has attempted to deal with some of these criticisms by introducing the concepts of bridging and bonding social capital, which he borrows from Gittell and Vidal (1998). 'Bonding social capital' refers to social networks designed to increase the bonds within a certain group. Putnam gives church-based women's reading groups, ethnic fraternal organisations and fashionable country clubs as examples. 'Bridging social capital' refers to social networks which attempts to build ties between groups. Putnam (2000) gives the civil rights movement, many youth service groups and ecumenical religious organisations as examples.

According to Putnam most groups have elements of both of these, but often they may be characterised by a predominance of one form of social capital or another. In particular he sees a lack of 'bridging social capital' as problematic since 'bonding social capital', along with holding a particular group together, can be used to exclude outsiders. Bonding capital can therefore be used to perpetuate inequality and exclusion.

However, Putnam's argument still leaves the issue at the level of the community and whether or not it has enough 'bridging social capital'. It fails to recognise the importance of the social and cultural systems in which relationships between groups are embedded. In particular, critics have stressed a lack of attention to class dynamics (Forbes and Wainwright, 2001; see also Muntaner et al, 2000; Navarro, 2002), although parallel arguments could be made about attention to issues of gender and 'race'.

Pierre Bourdieu and social capital

The criticisms of Putnam's work discussed above are not merely limited to questions about how variables have been measured, or about which variables have been omitted or included in his explanatory model. They also focus on the way in which the issues that Putnam is dealing with are conceptualised, and in particular the lack of analysis of the role of politics and the state. However, the work of Pierre Bourdieu (1986) provides an analysis that does consider these factors.

Bourdieu's account of social capital has been developed independently of Putnam's work described above. It is only one aspect of a more general account of how class divisions are produced and reproduced within societies.

In stark contrast to Putnam, Bourdieu sees the social structure of society as characterised by struggle and conflict over the appropriation of rare social goods and the legitimation of the power relationships that produce this distribution (Bourdieu, 1990).

Although the specific type of 'social goods' or resources at stake in this struggle may vary over time and place, Bourdieu argues that there is an underlying 'logic' involved, that is, the need to appropriate socially valued goods as efficiently as possible. He therefore attempts to elaborate 'a general theory of the economy of practices' of which 'the theory of strictly economic practices is a particular case' (Bourdieu, 1990, p 122). As Callinicos (1999) points out, this entails a generalisation of the concept of capital to embrace more than simply economic capital. Bourdieu suggests that four broad categories of capital commonly operate in contemporary, industrialised capitalist societies: economic, cultural, social and symbolic capital.

It is also clear from Bourdieu's work that he thinks that each one of these four broad types of capital can take on different specific forms in particular situations. Thus cultural capital can become institutionalised in the form of educational capital, that is, the formal and informal qualifications achieved by an individual can become objectified, for example, in the possession of objects of fine art, or embodied, as in the possession of a well-developed physique.

Bourdieu does not, however, consider that these differing forms of capital are equitably distributed between or within social classes. For example, university lecturers and schoolteachers may be well endowed with cultural capital, but relatively lacking in economic capital, whereas for employers and business people the reverse might be true. According to Bourdieu, it is the uneven distribution of these differing forms of capital that gives rise to a constant struggle in which the social actors involved take advantage of the resources in which they are relatively well endowed to defend their position within society.

Bourdieu goes on to suggest that, under certain circumstances, the differing forms of capital may be convertible. For example, economic capital may be converted into educational capital by investing in the acquisition of academic qualifications, which may in turn give greater access to better job opportunities and therefore to increased income.

Similarly he argues that symbolic capital can be used to legitimise one class's dominance of another. He argues that symbolic capital allows the economically dominant class to secure consent for its rule by fostering feelings of respect, and obligation among the dominated. It is therefore clear that for Bourdieu certain forms of capital play an important role in legitimising the existing distribution of wealth and power, giving it the appearance of being the product of talent or ability rather than the result of exploitation or privilege (Bourdieu, 1990).

It should be stressed that Bourdieu does not necessarily see the social actors involved in these processes as necessarily conscious of them. Instead he emphasises their implicit and pre-conscious nature.

Through his research Bourdieu develops a complex and dynamic analysis of the endless struggles involved in the accumulation, conservation and reconversion of different forms of capital that, according to him, constitute modern societies. However, while Bourdieu's work is undoubtedly original and represents perhaps the most theoretically sophisticated attempt to deal with the subject of social capital, it is not without its critics.

Fine (2001) finds Bourdieu's extremely broad and fluid conception of capital problematic. He points out that its various manifestations are not only open to projection across a variety of aspects of capitalist society, but also that Bourdieu applies them to pre-capitalist societies. Indeed his projection of the concept of capital across a number of societies and historical periods suggests that Bourdieu believes that his 'general theory of the economy of practices' possesses universal validity, with the meaning of all human behaviour seen as potentially explicable in terms of the need to accumulate and conserve various forms of capital.

Furthermore, as Lane (2000) points out, Bourdieu does not develop an adequate theory of the relationships between the differing social fields or markets within which these forms of capital operate. There is therefore a danger of slipping into a form of multi-causalism that is unable to distinguish between the relative significance of the various social fields or analyse how they interact.

A further problem arises from Bourdieu's focus on what may be termed the hegemonic or dominant forms of cultural, symbolic and social capital. In focusing on these Bourdieu seems to assume that the working class, and by extension other oppressed and exploited groups, lack the capacity to develop alternative social and cultural practices to those which dominate in capitalist society. Thus Bourdieu is critical of the notion of an independent popular working-class culture and has controversially claimed that 'there is no popular art' (1984, p 459).

Although Bourdieu's sympathies undoubtedly lie with the oppressed and marginalised, his focus on the processes via which certain cultural forms are either validated or denigrated lacks an analysis of how dominated social groups might resist these processes. As a result there is a tendency to portray oppressed people as nothing more than the victims of the powers that dominate them.

The politics of social capital

Bourdieu's work has received relatively little discussion in the British and US literature on social capital, despite the fact that it represents a theoretical and empirical advance over Putnam's use of the term. The explanation for this paradoxical situation appears to lie in the rhetorical power and political uses that these differing interpretations of social capital can (or cannot) be put to. Thus Hawe and Shiell (2000) note that Putnam's communitarian version of social capital has, like the closely related concept of community, attracted the interest of politicians from both the 'left' and 'right'. They suggest that this is because those on the centre 'left' see in Putnam's version of social capital a concept which can be mobilised to criticise the worst excesses of neoliberal individualism, while the 'right' see it as a concept capable of putting a human face on the economic rationalism of the market, without resorting to welfare expenditure.

In contrast Fine (2001) suggests that Bourdieu's political interventions in defence of the homeless, the unemployed and striking workers, together with his theoretical emphasis on the production and reproduction of class-based inequalities, make the appropriation of his work problematic for many mainstream political parties.

Conclusion

This chapter has contrasted two very differing approaches to the concept of social capital. It has been suggested that some of the weaknesses associated with Putnam's usage of the concept are not only weaknesses in substantive interpretation, but reflect significant problems within Putnam's conception of social capital, most notably the lack of any analysis of power dynamics and the accentuation of the positive aspects of social capital. Despite these difficulties, Bourdieu's work provides us with an understanding of the role played by differing forms of economic, social, cultural and symbolic capital in the reproduction of inequality and may be of considerable help in analysing the relationship between health, psychosocial and economic stress and social status.

Acknowledgements

The writing of this chapter was partially supported by funding from the National Institute for Health Research (NIHR). The views expressed in this publication are those of the authors and not necessarily those of the NHS, the NIHR or the Department of Health.

References

Benhabib, S. and Cornell, D. (eds) (1987) *Feminism as critique*, Minneapolis, MS: University of Minnesota Press.

Bourdieu, P. (1984) *Distinction: A social critique of the judgement of taste*, London: Routledge.

Bourdieu, P. (1986) 'The forms of capital', in J.G. Richards (ed) *Handbook of theory and research for the sociology of education*, New York: Greenwood, pp 241-58.

Bourdieu, P. (1990) *The logic of practice*, Cambridge: Polity Press.

Callinicos, A. (1999) *Social theory: A historical introduction*, Cambridge: Polity Press.

Coleman, J. (1988) 'Social capital in the creation of human capital', in P. Dasgupta and I. Serageldin (eds) *Social capital: A multifaceted perspective*, Washington, DC: The World Bank.

DeFilippis, J. (2001) 'The myth of social capital in community development', *Housing Policy Debate*, vol 12, no 4, pp 781-806.

Fine, B. (2001) *Social capital versus social theory*, London and New York: Routledge.

Forbes, A. and Wainwright, S.P. (2001) 'On the methodological, theoretical, and philosophical context of health inequalities research: a critique', *Social Science & Medicine*, vol 53, pp 801-16.

Gittell, R. and Vidal, A. (1998) *Community organising: Building social capital as a development strategy*, Thousand Oaks, CA: Sage Publications.

Gramsci, A. (1971) *Selections from the prison notebooks of Antonio Gramsci*, New York: International Publishers.

Hawe, P. and Shiell, A. (2000) 'Social capital and health promotion: a review', *Social Science & Medicine*, vol 51, pp 871-85.

Hegel, G.W.F. (1965) *Philosophy of right*, Oxford: Clarendon Press.

Independent Inquiry into Inequalities in Health (1998) *Independent Inquiry into Inequalities in Health* (Acheson Report), London: The Stationery Office.

Kawachi, I. and Kennedy, B.P. (1997) 'Health and social cohesion: why care about income inequality?', *British Medical Journal*, vol 314, pp 1037-40.

Kawachi, I. et al (1997) 'Social capital, income inequality, and mortality', *American Journal of Public Health*, vol 87, pp 1491-8.

Lane, J.F. (2000) *Pierre Bourdieu: A critical introduction*, London: Pluto.

Muntaner, C., Lynch, J. and Smith, G.D. (2000) 'Social capital and the third way in public health', *Critical Public Health*, vol 10, pp 107-24.

Navarro, V. (2002) 'A critique of social capital', *International Journal of Health Services*, vol 32, pp 423-32.

Portes, A. (1998) 'Social capital: its origins and applications in modern sociology', *Annual Review of Sociology*, vol 24, pp 1-24.

Putnam, R. (1993) 'The prosperous community: social capital and public life', *The American Prospect*, Spring, pp 35-42.

Putnam, R. (1995) 'Bowling alone: America's declining social capital', *Journal of Democracy*, vol 6, pp 65-78.

Putnam, R. (1998) 'Foreword', *Housing Policy Debate*, vol 9, no 1, pp v-viii.

Putnam, R. (2000) *Bowling alone: The collapse and revival of American community*, New York: Simon & Schuster.

Townsend, P. and Davidson, N. (1988) *Inequalities in health: The Black Report*, Harmondsworth: Penguin.

Skocpol, T. (1996) 'Unravelling from above', *The American Prospect*, March-April, pp 20-5.

Waldinger, R. (1986) *Through the eye of the needle: Immigrants and enterprise in New York's garment trades*, New York: New York University Press.

Whitehead, M. (1987) *The health divide: Inequalities in health in the 1980s*, London: Health Education Council.

Wilkinson, R. (1996) *Unhealthy societies: The afflictions of inequality*, London: Routledge.

Wilkinson, R. and Pickett, K. (2009) *The spirit level: Why more equal societies almost always do better*, London: Allen Lane.

Wilkinson, R., Kawachi, I. and Kennedy, B. (1998) 'Mortality, the social environment, crime and violence', *Sociology of Health and Illness*, vol 20, no 5, pp 578-97.

Young, I.M. (1990) *Justice and the politics of difference*, Chichester: Princeton University Press.

30

Social services for the aged in Cuba

Elizabeth M. Bertera

From E.M. Bertera, 'Social services for the aged in Cuba', *International Social Work*, vol. 46, no. 3, pp. 313–21, copyright © 2003 by Sage Publications, reprinted by permission of SAGE.

A group of 20-30 older adults are standing in the middle of Revolution Square in Havana, Cuba. It is around 8 o'clock on a sunny, radiant, morning. They all look well, strong and happy. A young woman in her early 30s arrives on a bicycle and begins gesturing to the group to form a line to sing the Cuban national anthem. She then leads the group in a set of exercises, strenuous enough for the young woman who leads them. However, this group of older individuals does the exercises with ease and enthusiasm. This scene repeats itself in neighborhood squares throughout Havana as part of a community wellness program for the elderly.

Through a series of meetings with Cuban social scientists, gerontologists and geriatricians, an analysis of the development and practices related to social services for the aged in Cuba was undertaken. Interviews were held at medical facilities, local community polyclinics, senior centers and the Center for the Third Age in Havana, Cuba. The interviews revealed a network of interrelationships between the health delivery system, where physicians, social workers and health educators play an active role in evaluating and modulating the system, and volunteer individuals and their neighborhoods, where local organizations are the mechanisms for community participation in social services, education and handing down traditional values. There is also a belief that the key to success of programs lies in required volunteerism, considered a duty among most Cubans.

There are limited reports on the elderly in Cuba. Oro Lau et al. (1989) reported the social problems of the elderly in Cuba and how improvement in their general health included the practice of physical exercise and ergotherapy, and how this has led to reduction of obesity and sedentariness. They concluded that 'the task of the nurse, together with that of the social worker and the ergotherapist is integral, since their work as a whole constitutes the essence of the Old People's Home' (Oro Lau et al, 1989).

In spite of the weakness of the Cuban economy, related to the US economic and political embargo, and the changes in the former Soviet

Union, the unbiased visitor might feel amazed that nobody is sleeping in the streets or begging. The economy may be deficient but Cubans receive proportionately better social benefits than many in developed economies (Halebsky and Kirk, 1990).

Following the Cuban revolution in 1959, the newly-formed government inherited a for-profit health-care system that was plagued by political corruption, poverty, illiteracy, economic inequality and social injustice. The system had neglected to develop human resources. Thirty-five years later the Cuban government had upheld its promise to provide free, high-quality health care for all Cuban citizens. The government made health care for all citizens an overarching national priority; major societal institutions made strong ideological, political and moral commitments to take medicine out of the marketplace. The Cuban constitution reflects these commitments in four policy principles:

1 Health care is a human right rather than a product for economic profit. Therefore, all Cubans have equal access to health services, and all services are free.
2 Health-care delivery is the responsibility of the state.
3 Prevention and curative services are integrated with national social and economic development.
4 The population participates in developing and maintaining the health-care system (Iatridis, 1990).

The Cuban revolution was nurtured on values of equality, commitment, service and a vision of unity or harmony. Thus, Cuba's social work knowledge base is informed by the nation's socialist politicoeconomic orientation, which blends well with the ideals of the social work profession. This article addresses social services for the older adult in Cuba separately from health services, but in reality these services are integrated.

The aging of the population in Cuba

The increase in the world's elderly population during the 1990s has had a powerful impact on the Caribbean island of Cuba. In 1950 there were 19 older people per 100 children and youth. By 1980 this number had doubled and it is estimated that by 1994 there were about 54 older people per each 100 children and youth. From a total of 304,100 older individuals in 1950, the number increased to 1.2 million in 1994, constituting 12 percent of the Cuban total population of 11 million. It is estimated that by the year 2025 the elderly in Cuba will be 20.1 percent of the total population (Prieto Ramos, 1994).

The life expectancy of Cubans is on a par with more developed countries as a result of universal access to high-quality health care.

According to United Nations statistics for 1992, Cuba's life expectancy was 76 years compared with Canada's 77, the US's 76, Italy's 76, Germany's 75.5, Finland's 76, the UK's 76. Cuba was significantly ahead of most developing countries: Mexico 70, Brazil 66, Egypt 62, India 60, Haiti 57, Bolivia 56, Cambodia 51, Angola 47 and Ethiopia 47.

Health services for the aged

Health care for the aged is considered a constitutional duty of the government and as such is accessible and free of charge. The health care system in Cuba has as its fundamental element the family physician *(et medica de familia)*, who operates out of the community health centers *(paticlinicas)* to provide comprehensive health care to the community. The Programa de Atencion al Anciano (Program to Care for the Elderly) includes the continuous follow-up of any elderly individual in each community where the *paliclinicas* are located. Once the *medica de familia* evaluates an elderly person, they are referred for geriatric consultation and treatment in an effort to treat serious health problems and prevent complications.

In anticipation of a sharp increase in its over-60 population, the Cuban government launched a fully fledged gerontology and geriatric program in 1980. The goals of the program were to train specialists to oversee the health and welfare of the elderly; to establish a national network of social and economic support systems; and to create a small scientific cadre to handle internal and international exchanges of ideas and research.

Cuba is proud of its 50 specialists, 142 physicians, 1212 nurses and 1605 auxiliaries dedicated to geriatric medicine. There are 434 hospital beds assigned to the elderly, plus 9750 beds distributed throughout 121 old people's homes for permanent live-ins and 43 grandparents' homes for day guests. Cuba also has 5214 grandparents' clubs around the country with 138,411 participants who prefer to live at home. Ancillary services provided for those residing at home draw on the help of some 10,720 public health personnel as well as dietitians and social workers (Prieto Ramos, 1994).

Other objectives outlined by the national gerontology and geriatric program call for an increase in the number of support systems as well as greater efficiency and streamlining. The regular retirement age is 60 for males and 55 for females. Elders are encouraged through delayed retirement benefits to remain part of the work force for as long as possible. For those who have retired, assistance is provided to organize their free time so as to make elders more productive by involvement in social action, education and transmitting cultural traditions. A campaign to inspire respect and consideration for elders in society is an important element of the program;

there also are special educational and briefing sessions for families with elderly members (Prieto Ramos, 1994).

The care of the aged in Cuba was limited during the 1950s to services through a small state budget. These limited resources were used to maintain 20 nursing homes operated by religious groups. There was no geriatric tradition and the only institution, called the 'Instituto del Viejo', was privately operated, serving a minority of older people mainly from the upper class. During the 1960s tremendous political and socioeconomic changes led to the creation of a national program to deliver medical and social services free of charge to all Cubans. During the 1960s and 1970s efforts went into the eradication of infectious diseases and improvements in maternal and child health care. The control of infectious diseases, massive immunization and preventive health programs caused a radical change in Cuba's morbidity and mortality rates. Morbidity rates are higher for non-infectious diseases such as heart and circulatory diseases, diabetes, cancer and accidents. Thus, life expectancy increased and infant mortality dropped. Cuba then embarked on developing programs for the aged (Prieto Ramos and Vega Garcia, 1994).

Health improvement programs for the aged in Cuba

A variety of program initiatives that have been developed since 1988 to improve the health of the population have an impact on the quality of life for older Cubans. They include the following.

1   Health promotion. The goal of this program is to give older people better control of their health and at the same time show them how to improve it. Included here are any programs aimed at improving the quality of life, such as physical fitness, social integration, substance abuse control, a healthier life and better use of leisure time.
2   Health maintenance and self-care. The term 'health' is a holistic one which encompasses not only the ability of older people to maintain their health but also the practice of self-care. Among the relevant programs are exercises aimed at maintaining the older individual's performance of ADL (activities of daily living) as well as health education classes.
3   Nutrition. As part of the health promotion programs, nutrition programs have been established to provide high-quality food to those older individuals who live alone and have limited resources. Even with the US embargo, which has had a great impact on food supplies for Cuba, older individuals do not go hungry. Food distribution gives priority to older adults through the local 'Circulos de Ancianos'.

4 Geriatric personnel. The development of geriatric educational programs to train personnel to work with the elderly to meet not only their medical but also their social and psychological needs.

5 Information. Covers three aspects: first, informing the elderly population about the various medical and social services available, so as to increase utilization; second, gathering data on the elderly population to ascertain gaps in services and increase utilization; thirdly, informing the medical profession about all aspects of aging through workshops and/or training.

6 Education. Upon retirement from the work force, individuals need to be re-educated to assume a different role in society, thus maintaining their self-esteem. One such role is that of grandparents as kin-keepers, in which elders take care of grandchildren and the children of other relatives, thus assisting in the education of the next generation, including teaching traditional values and culture.

Social services for the aged in Cuba

Cuba has 12,203 nursing-home beds run by state and religious organizations. Along with the increase in nursing homes, Cuba has developed other social institutions such as adult day care *(casas de abuelos)* and Grandparents' clubs *(circulo de abuelos)*, with the purpose of finding solutions to the challenges that an aging population presents. As of 1994, there were more than 4000 grandparents' clubs, with 225,000 participants. It is impossible to have solutions for all of the problems that are presented by an aging population. However, Cuba is experimenting with various innovative possibilities, as follows.

1 Economic aid *(ayuda economica)* includes assistance to those who retire and are in need of pensions.

2 Home care *(ayuda domiciliaria)*. Has the objective of maintaining older individuals in their community to assist in 'aging in place'. It may include housekeeping, preparation of food and laundry.

3 Eat-in-together *(comedores)*. The program is aimed at those older individuals living alone to ensure that their nutritional needs are met, taking into consideration any chronic illnesses.

4 Grandparents' clubs *(circulos de abuelos)*. Elderly individuals who sign up with the clubs participate in daily physical exercise, field trips, art workshops, movies and other social activities while staying with their families and grandchildren.

5 Adult day care *(casa de abuelos)*. Housing that has been adapted for about 40 people with facilities for cooking, day activities, medical care and

physical therapy, if needed. At 6.00 pm the adult goes back to his or her family.

6 Old people's homes *(hogares de ancianos)*. These are residences for elderly individuals who may be ill, handicapped or have a social problem, but for the most part can take care of themselves.

Many of these programs may be available in more developed countries with better economic resources than Cuba. The difference, however, is that these programs are integrated into the community and rely on broad community participation to sustain them.

The role of social workers in Cuba

Until now, social workers in Cuba have provided services at the state's request and based on the needs of the people. In addition social workers, health educators, physicians and other caregiving professionals work as teams to deliver these services. Social workers rely heavily on volunteers to assist in the delivery of services. However, Cuba's tradition of volunteer work by the average citizens is a different type of 'volunteerism'. In Cuba, volunteer work is not a charity but organized community action. It has overt and clear state support, being in fact one of the ideological pillars of the society. Volunteer work is considered a citizen's obligation and goes a long way to help in the allocation of prized commodities such as housing and cars. Volunteers and volunteer organizations, though not governmental agencies, have full state approval and support and provide the health services delivery system with much needed social, community and ancillary services. Thus, social workers have a range of human resources and community programs to provide the services necessary to meet human needs (Halebsky and Kirk, 1990). However, there is a need for professional training in the field of gerontological social work. More research is needed on the role of the elderly as transmitters of traditional values to the next generation, helping to build a. new society of justice, equity and solidarity. Research is also needed on how this role may help the elderly to develop their own sense of dignity, friendship and satisfaction as they age.

The goal of the government is to continue training in geriatrics and gerontology not only in Cuba but abroad. Social workers play an important role of making sure older adults receive all of the services they are entitled to. In addition, they act as a link between older Cubans and the various resources available to them. The main complaint of Cuban social workers was the isolation from their peers abroad. There is a need for social workers outside Cuba to extend a lending hand and help the profession grow and continue its much-needed help with older Cubans. Perhaps schools of social work abroad can organize study tours with students to learn more about the role of social workers in a socialist government and embark on what I call social work diplomacy. The recently played Elian Gonzalez drama showed US-based social workers helping Elian and his Cuban family grapple with the public debate, family turmoil and clashing values, suggesting the important role afforded to social workers in the Cuban society. Schools with international social work programs could offer opportunities for students to embark on social work diplomacy through the creation of links with social workers in Cuba. In addition, it is proposed that a large-scale exchange of Cuban social workers is needed with social workers from other countries in the region and around the world. We could learn much from their innovative approaches to dealing with an aging population. Exchange programs with universities that offer a concentration in international social work could be organized. The current geopolitical milieu suggests a warming in the US–Cuba relationship that would allow more intellectual interchange and communication in the future.

Discussion

Reports (1997) on Cuba suggest that the accomplishments in primary care include low- and high-technological developments that are pertinent to the US health-care system as well as to the delivery of social services. The accomplishments involve neighborhoodbased family medicine as the focus of primary care, and regional systems of hospital and social services. The innovative public health initiatives and epidemiological surveillance, universal access to services are all provided without substantial barriers related to race, social class, gender and age. Limited access to Cuban publications, impediments to presentations by Cuban healthcare professionals at professional meetings, all inhibit a better appraisal of Cuba's accomplishments. Cuba's isolation from the US clinical and research communities has prevented interchanges that would improve primary care and social services in both countries (Rojas Ochoa and Lopez Pardo, 1997).

Cuba continues to be unique in that its model seems to involve moral rather than material exchanges and reciprocities. Cuba moves forward a *su manera* (in its own way), one of the last states in which national goals remain specified by the regime as an expression of a socialist worldview. It still tends to regard the party as the sole repository of wisdom, with Fidel Castro as its agent.

However, regardless of the shortcomings of the regime, we cannot overlook the accomplishments in the areas of health and education. Public education and public health as powerful symbols of egalitarian values have been given the highest priority (Feinsilver, 1993). Social work as a profession is familiar with these values. Cuba has demonstrated resiliency against considerable odds. Older people in Cuba seem to have greater opportunities in terms of benefits and participation in programs. Their health care through the community physician seems to be the cornerstone of maintaining the health of the Cuban population, but especially the old. *Respeto,* or respect for older people, is taught early to children through intergenerational programs in schools, so that being *viejo* or old is nothing to be ashamed of. Their efforts at keeping older Cubans 'engaged' through a variety of programs in social action, education and culture are remarkable by US standards.

Cuba is an example of a developing country with a larger percentage of its population aging than others. The percentage of older people in Cuba is greater than that of many developed countries. Longevity in Cuba can be attributed to several factors: excellent health care and universal education and a concerted effort to keep older people involved in all aspects of Cuban society. The lessons that we can glean from Cuba can be instructive for other countries, including those from the developed world, that find themselves grappling with similar problems related to an aging population.

References

Feinsilver, J.M. (1993) *Healing the Masses.* Berkeley: University of California Press.

Halebsky, S. and J. Kirk (1990) *Transformation and Struggle: Cuba Faces the 1990s.* New York: Praeger Publishers.

Iatridis, D.S. (1990) 'Cuba's Health Care Policy: Prevention and Active Community Participation', *Social Work* 35(1): 29–35.

Ora Lau, N.F., M. Calzadilla Ramirez, M. Nocedo and A.Villavicencio (1989) 'Old Age: An Age for Respect and Enthusiastic Care', *Revista Cuhana Enfermedades* 5(1–2): 27–41.

Prieto Ramos, O. (1994) *Growing Old in Cuba: Profiles of Citizens in their Golden Years.* Havana, Cuba: CITED (Ibero–Latino American Center for the Third Age).

Prieto Ramos, O. and E.Vega Garcia (1994) *Atencion al Anciano en Cuba,* pp. 11–19. Havana, Cuba: CITED.

Rojas Ochoa, F. and C.M. Lopez Pardo (1997) 'Economy, Politics, and Health Status in Cuba', *International Journal of Health Services* 27(4): 79 J–807.

31

Perceptions of ageism: views of older people

Victor Minichiello, Jan Browne and Hal Kendig

Extract from V. Minichiello, J. Browne and H. Kendig, 'Perceptions and consequences of ageism', *Ageing and Society* (2000) vol. 20, pp. 253–78, © Cambridge University Press, reproduced with permission.

Introduction

Ageism is a set of social relations that discriminate against older people and set them apart as being different by defining and understanding them in an oversimplified, generalised way. Ageism is claimed to be very prevalent in Westernised societies [...] While Palmore (1988) shows that ageism is prevalent and widely experienced in the community, the literature does not widely report older people's stories of how this phenomenon impacts on their lives. Since the term 'ageism' was coined by Robert Butler in 1969, few studies have researched how older people may recognise and give meaning to the phenomenon of 'ageism'. [...]

Studies related to ageism have generally examined how the attitudes and beliefs of younger people contribute to denying older people opportunities and equitable treatment. For example, [...] Ryan and her colleagues (1995) show how younger people at an interactional level use patronising verbal and nonverbal communication towards older carers. Sawchuk (1995), who undertook an extensive analysis of advertisement campaigns and other marketing strategies, concludes that at a public level many marketing discourses perpetuate and reinforce negative stereotypes of old age. Studies which have focused on older workers have consistently found that they often face ageist stereotypes that define them as increasingly marginal in the workforce (Maule *et al.* 1996). The most significant barriers and deterrents are managerial biases that older workers are too costly, too inflexible and too difficult to train (Imel 1996). [...]

Health researchers have also examined how misconceptions about the ageing process can have a detrimental effect on healthy ageing (Grant 1996). Walker and his colleagues (1996) argue that ageist stereotypes underlie many of the services designed for older people with a disability, with the focus centred mostly on care and less on support of the older person to fulfil their potential. Numerous studies have also reported how therapists accept socially validated negative stereotypes of later life. For example, Woolfe and Biggs (1997) found that some counsellors were less likely to use a psychodynamic approach with older persons, and this decision could result in the underestimation of later–life potential. Social workers were reported to spend less time and had fewer contacts with older oncology patients than younger patients, with the result that social workers may not be effectively assisting older patients to cope with important health and social issues (Rohan *et al.* 1994). Examining audiotaped interactions between physicians and young and older patients, Greene and her colleagues (1996) found that there was greater disparity between the goals of the doctor and older patients, and less joint decision making with older patients. Doctors tended to be less egalitarian, patient, respectful, engaged and optimistic with the older patients. What these studies perhaps show is how easy it is for social arrangements in society to make it possible for ageism to be so prevalent, yet for the behaviour to be seen as obscure and non-intentional (Bytheway 1995). Yet as Bytheway and Johnson (1990) have argued ageism is about age and prejudice and has real consequences for older citizens.

[...]

Method

[...]

Qualitative interviews were conducted with 18 older people living in both urban and rural settings in Victoria and New South Wales, Australia. The informants were aged between 65 and 89.[...] Five of the informants are currently living with their husband or wife, eight are widow/widowers, one is single never married, four are divorced and live alone. Participants' involvement in the community ranged from heavily involved to not at all involved. [...] The majority of the informants are active and reported being able 'to do most of the things they want to do'. The informants have varied employment histories. Ten have retired from full-time employment, four have 'retired' from home duties, four retain some casual employment. Two informants were specifically recruited for their association with organisations that seek to achieve positive social perceptions of ageing.

[...] Due to financial constraints this sample did not include contrasts from different cultural groups and social classes. It is important to note that the sample is relatively well educated and includes more politically active older persons, which may mean that they are likely to have higher expectations with regard to their rights as citizens, and to be better positioned to recognise and react to 'ageism'.

[...]

The meaning of the word 'ageism'

When informants were asked to explain what they thought the term 'ageism' meant, their response ranged from 'no idea' and complete puzzlement, to complex conceptualisations of ageism as a socially constructed phenomenon based upon how society devalues older people. Initially, some of the informants' accounts gave the impression that they were indifferent to, or unfamiliar with, what was meant by or associated with ageism. Some responses to the question 'What does the word ageism mean to you?' included:

> Is that actually a word you'd find in the Oxford Dictionary? It's not a word at all in my book. I think it's one they've made up! You can understand ageing because we all age. But, no. I don't really get that word. I don't like it. I'll look it up in my dictionary. (Mrs Lock)

> I don't think I've come across it. I know of 'isms'. I have come across that in books. You'll know what you're reading in the context you're reading it, but I can't explain it. Of course, it would be something to do with your age if it's 'ageism'. (Mrs Dove)

What stands out in these answers is that some older people may lack the means or the vocabulary to talk about ageism because they do not recognise or understand the word. However, other interviewees possessed a clearer notion of what ageism meant to them:

> [...]

> Well, I suppose it's people's opinion of those who are not of economic value, who no longer contribute, and therefore are of no value – that seems to be how people are being measured now. I'm just trying to think of the people I had in mind when I didn't want to be one of them, because that was really ageism. I guess I used to get impatient with older people and think they didn't have anything to contribute, or what they had to contribute was so out of date and old fashioned that it wasn't worth listening to. They were slow and got in my way. They couldn't tell a story straight, they'd have to go off in various deviations to tell you why this happened and then eventually get back to the main theme. (Miss Phillips)

Despite understanding the general meaning behind the term and knowing how to use it, even these informants do not commonly use the word 'ageism'. However not using the term does not imply that informants cannot describe the fundamental principles associated with ageism. What the data reveal is that older people can talk about the experiences of ageism using a different terminology from that found in the gerontology literature.

Alternative ways of talking about ageism

The informants identified two social aspects of being an old person. The first of these is 'being seen as old' and the second is 'being treated as old'. The words 'stereotypes' and 'discrimination' are terms that they further used to describe some of their lived experience:

> I understand stereotypes and discriminating. Well, these things are bad, in my opinion, because I don't think age has got much to do with anything. I mean, why should you treat anyone differently because they're old? They're not a different person, and they probably don't feel old. A lot of people think, 'oh, you're old and silly'. (Mrs Lock)

This suggests that informants recognise that there is a common way of perceiving elders as a group who fit certain images and behave in particular ways. The accounts from informants incorporate stereotypical descriptive images of elders (*e.g.* frailty, being out of date, engaged in meaningless activity). These images also define older people as having specific needs (recipients of services and hand-outs from the government), and comprise a way of defining older people as a collective of similar people who occupy a particular (usually devalued) place in society (non-contributing, dependent). The informants acknowledge that older people may be treated in a certain way because of the labels that are given to them (*e.g.* being denigrated, being treated with impatience). Discriminatory treatment is, therefore, related to such predilections of who and what older people are, and their position in society.

The notion of 'oldness'

Although the *word* 'ageism' may have no immediate meaning to some older people, the *concept* of ageism and its characteristics has considerable relevance and meaning. However, in order more fully to comprehend how older people construct stereotyping of older people and discrimination against them, it is necessary to identify what being 'old' means to them, and how they identify, recognise, and can talk about such experiences.

According to Rodeheaver (1990) older people also exhibit ageist attitudes. Similarly, interviewees in this study reflected an internalisation and acceptance of ageist stereotypes and prejudices through their perceptions of what 'being old' was. The informants' descriptions of oldness consisted of an extensive list of negative terms including: not trying, withdrawn, isolated, irritating, self-oriented, living outside the mainstream, unattractive, uninteresting, frail, senile, silly, over the hill, narrow-minded, a burden, lonely, vulnerable, dowdy, and unproductive. Indeed, the word 'old' is used in a tautological way and it is assumed to 'speak for itself'; that is, no further explanation is needed when one says someone is old. Examples of how informants identified what they perceived to be an 'old' person include:

> If all those things that you enjoy are behind you and you're not enjoying the latter years of life because you're lonely, then I think you're old. My impression of getting old is physical frailty, of mental slow down, weighting those two factors against the continual factor of experience. (Mr King)

> I know friends of mine who are younger than me, and they're real old people. I just describe them as they feel sorry for themselves and getting real old you know, one of them particularly, he's had life, sort of thing. You know, they go into their shell and they won't talk to anyone unless they've got to. (Mr Hall)

These extracts show that older people embrace a notion of oldness which is not about chronological age, but about a state of being, that is about how one sees oneself. Once defined by the self or others as old, a person is then categorised as belonging to the negative stereotypical image of old age.

Being old to the informants, then, is about loneliness, loss of things that were meaningful, being unimportant and irrelevant, or having no role. Identifying that one has these feelings about oneself may be the primary condition under which a person categorises him or herself as old. Interestingly, informants made a definite distinction between 'ageing' and 'being old'. An examination of the texts shows that words used to describe themselves and other people as becoming *older* or *ageing* but not yet old, were positive and action-oriented, including being motivated, busy, interested, positive, useful, purposeful, adventurous, courageous, supportive and 'still trying':

> I know so many people in my age group that get out and do
> things all the time. They probably do things that are more
> daring and go out on their own more than when they were
> younger. (Mrs Smith)

Feeling old

There are a number of ways whereby the older person can dissociate
the self from the 'old' group. These include describing oneself as having
a positive attitude, not looking old, not acting old; portraying the self as
intellectually developing, while those who are 'old' are no longer trying to
be mentally challenged; being fit and active compared to 'old' people who
are sedentary; and not acting in ways that are perceived as 'old'. This finding
supports Cremmin's (1992) work on the process by which older people
may make a distinction between being old and feeling old. Although there
is a common assumption that older people must 'feel old', the informants
describe themselves as not old because they do not feel old. Statements like
the following examples are found in almost every transcript:

> I know I look older, but I don't feel old. I haven't arrived at the
> feeling of feeling old. (Mrs Smith)

> I know in my own mind I'm growing older but really I'm
> doing the same sort of thing as I've always wanted to do and
> I've never sort of considered myself to be growing old, I know
> by birth date and everything you are, but I don't feel that I'm
> getting old. (Mrs Rose)

[...]

Conclusion

This qualitative study [...] suggests that the words used within the
gerontological literature to talk about how older people are treated and
perceived are not the words that older people use to describe their own
experiences. Alternative language that older people use to talk about the
concept that gerontologists call 'ageism' includes being stereotyped or
being seen as old, being discriminated against or treated as old.

The results reveal that older people may be acutely aware of being
seen as 'old', but are often uncertain about making claims that they are
actively treated as old or discriminated against because they are old. This
can be partly explained by the way in which they construct the meaning

of oldness, and ways in which they dissociate themselves from the wider group of old people. The word ageing is associated with positive aspects of older people's lives that co-exist with external evidence of becoming older. The word 'old', however, has symbolic meaning which embodies the most common, negative stereotypical perceptions of older people.

[...] While ageism of all forms can be damaging, ageism in interpersonal relationships may have the greatest impact on the older person's self-perceptions and their feeling of safety in the community. The affronts of face-to-face discrimination can prompt an assessment of the self as old, with a subsequent move from a positive to a negative ageing experience.

[...] This study shows that although various forms of stereotyping and discrimination may impact on their lives, older people may not have the words or perceive the need to express these experiences as discrimination based on their age. Simultaneously, elders may be reluctant to classify those experiences as ageism for various reasons. Some of those reasons may be that they do not perceive older people as being markedly different from other marginalised groups. They do not classify themselves as old, so therefore seek ways in which to dissociate themselves from ageist stereotypes and behaviours. The study also shows that older people may internalise concepts of old age in which they believe that certain older people may deserve to be treated as old. [...]

The results reveal the importance for researchers to understand and articulate the real experiences of older people and to recognise that for older people to understand ageism is dependent upon them developing an awareness of being treated as old. This may explain why perhaps there has been a less visible social movement against ageism, and therefore older people's awareness of issues of discrimination around age may be less known. Some elders may firmly believe that it is best just to accept what happens and try to get on with their lives and not disrupt the status quo. Although they may encounter and recognise stereotyping of older people and witness or experience instances of discrimination, they accept these with resignation and a sense of powerlessness to act in those circumstances, or to prevent such situations from occurring. They may believe that older people do not have social power to change their situations so it is best simply to accept them and not make things worse for themselves by acting up.

In contrast, some older people work in both subtle and direct ways to change ageist stereotypes and discriminatory practices. They enact a 'new image of ageing people', challenge stereotypical notions of older people and educate others about positive images of ageing. They chip away at societal images of old people, which seem to others to be an insurmountable obstacle. By focusing on the struggle over ageism in their own lives, these older people are making a contribution to the transformation of older people's images, and to the creation of a climate in which ageism can be named and critically analysed in order to deconstruct it, identify its sources and causes, and determine ways in which it can be changed. Recent public commentators in the media both in Australia and elsewhere are predicting that the current activist groups of older people may be setting the scene for the baby boomers to create a politically correct agenda centred on the notion of ageism. Only time will show whether a similar study in the future will reveal that the word ageism is more widely recognised among older people, and that its consequences are neither acceptable nor to be accommodated.

References

Bytheway, B. 1995. *Ageism*. Open University Press, Buckingham.

Bytheway, B. and Johnson, J. 1990. On defining ageism. *Critical Social Policy*, **27**, 27–39.

Cremmin, M. 1992. Feeling old versus being old: views of troubled aging. *Social Sciences and Medicine*, **34**, 1305–15.

Grant, C. D. 1996. Effects of ageism on individual and health care providers' responses to healthy aging. *Health and Social Work*, **21**, 9–15.

Greene, M., Adelman, R. and Rizzo, C. 1996. Problems in communication between physicians and older patients. *Journal of Geriatric Psychiatry*, **29**, 13–32.

Imel, S. 1996. *Older Workers: Myths and Realities*. ERIC Clearinghouse on Adult, Career and Vocational Education, Columbus, Ohio.

Maule, A., Cliff, D. and Taylor, R. 1996. Early retirement decisions and how they affect later quality of life. *Ageing and Society*, **16**, 177–204.

Palmore, E. 1998. *The Facts on Aging Quiz: A Handbook of Uses and Results*. Springer, New York.

Rodeheaver, D. 1990. Ageism. In Parham, I., Poon, L. and Siegler, I. (eds), *Access: Aging Curriculum Content for Education in the Socio-behavioural Science*, Springer, New York.

Rohan, E. A., Berkman, B., Walker, S. and Holmes, W. 1994. The geriatric oncology patient: ageism in social work practice. *Journal of Gerontological Social Work*, **23**, 201–21.

Ryan, E. B., Hummert, M. L. and Boich, L. H. 1995. Communication predicaments of aging: patronizing behaviour towards older adults. *Journal of Language and Social Psychology*, **14**, 144–66.

Sawchuk, K. A. 1995. From gloom to boom: age, identity and target marketing. In Featherstone, M. and Wernick, A. (eds), *Images of Aging: Cultural Representations of Later Life*. Routledge, London.

Walker, A., Walker, C. and Ryan, T. 1996. Older people with learning difficulties leaving institutional care: a case of double jeopardy. *Ageing and Society*, **16**, 125–50.

Woolfe, R. and Briggs, S. 1997. Counselling older adults: issues and awareness. *Counselling Psychology Quarterly*, **10**, 189–94.

32

Mental health and mental disorder in a global context

David Pilgrim

Introduction

This chapter explores the conceptual and empirical complexities of discussing mental health and disorder in the world today. Attributions about madness and misery have been evident in all times and places. However, to date we have failed to develop a truly clear international consensus on that ubiquitous picture (Rogers and Pilgrim, 2010). This lack of clarity means that it is useful to examine the range of starting premises that operated about the 'nature' of mental health and disorder. Once these starting premises are understood, it frees us to examine what is agreed and what is not about our topic, from an international perspective. Most of the contention about mental health and mental disorder centres on these philosophical differences, which are still being played out on an international stage and are underpinned by a variety of professional and commercial interests.

Philosophical differences about conceptualisation and empirical claims

At the time of writing, mental health experts (so called because their role in society is largely about understanding and responding to *mental disorder*, not promoting mental health) tend to adopt one of three main philosophical stances in their work. They may or may not be aware of these starting premises, because practical knowledge is for the most part built on taken for granted assumptions about the world.

These assumptions are acquired particularly in professional training but they are also replayed and reinforced in the lay arena, for example, in the mass media, a process De Swaan (1991) calls 'protoprofessionalisation'. The latter term refers to the ways in which professional notions (such as 'clinical depression') are incorporated by lay people as 'facts'. This taken for granted character of working knowledge in particular cultural settings is called *doxa* by Bourdieu (1972). Given that mental health and disorder have been recurring sources of dispute in the past 50 years, and those disputes are far from resolved, it is particularly important that we examine the underlying assumptions operating within that ongoing contention.

The three main starting stances to consider are naive realism, critical realism and radical constructivism. The first of these is also discussed sometimes as 'psychiatric positivism' or 'medical naturalism'. The second and third have been associated with 'anti-psychiatric' and 'critical psychiatric' attacks on the first position. Because the first one remains dominant internationally, however (supported, for example by, among other bodies, the World Health Organization [WHO] and the World Psychiatric Association), it tends to be a form of *doxa*. By contrast, the other two positions more self-consciously make explicit their philosophical assumptions. Indeed, a good part of the writings and research from these camps of inquiry and action is about demonstrating why it is important to challenge the assumptions and conclusions of naive realism.

Medical naturalism

'Medical naturalism' is used by Hoff (1995) to describe the seminal contribution of Emil Kraepelin in German psychopathology in the second half of the 19th century. Kraepelin (1883) claimed three main scientific axioms:

1 Mental disorders are genetically determined diseases of the nervous system.
2 Mental disorders are separate, naturally occurring, categories.
3 Mental disorders are *fixed and deteriorating* conditions.

Our current dominant systems of classification still reflect the second of these, but aetiological assumptions have dropped away and the prospect of recovery is now assumed much of the time. But because axiom 2 is still assumed by most psychiatrists, the *Diagnostic and statistical manual* (DSM) of the American Psychiatric Association (APA) (1994), which is to be revised in 2013, and the International Classification of Diseases (ICD) from the WHO (1992), are still fairly called 'neo-Kraepelinian'. These systems of classification assume that mental disorders are naturally occurring categories that simply exist 'out there', awaiting verification by experts, who 'elicit' their symptoms from patients during 'mental state examinations'.

The global significance of medical naturalism can therefore be summarised in the following way. It was derived from one geographical and historical period: German psychopathology in the latter half of the

19th century. This dominant discourse has become the form of *doxa* noted earlier.

Critical realism and the biopsychosocial model

The above dominant position was criticised in a number of ways during the 20th century. For example, the inability of the Kraepelinians to persuade all psychiatrists (let alone other 'mental health professionals') about their bio-deterministic aetiological assumptions, especially in the face of a strong psychoanalytical lobby within the APA, meant that DSM could only retain the one, albeit important, trace of the tradition: categorical descriptions. Largely as a result of the influence of Adolf Meyer, Anglo-American psychiatry developed an important dissenting current from Kraepelinian bio-determinism.

Meyer was a Swiss psychiatrist who developed his ideas in the US in the first half of the 20th century. His work was influential in some parts of academic psychiatry, as well as clinical psychology and medical sociology, when it culminated in the latter part of that century in the 'biopsychosocial model' (Engel, 1980). That model invites a central question, which was also begged by Meyer's original 'psychobiology': 'why is this patient presenting with these particular problems in the light of their particular current and past personal circumstances?'. Meyer did not reject diagnosis in principle but saw symptom profiles as part of the person's unique psychological state derived from their particular lives, including their genetic make-up, features of their upbringing and their current social circumstances. If diagnosis was a crude starting point, the real business should be about unique and nuanced formulations.

Some critics took this approach further and argued that on scientific grounds categorical descriptions are invalid because of their implausible features. Functional psychiatric diagnoses are unreliable, they have weak predictive and conceptual validity and most mental disorders have no known or certain origins. Also they lack treatment specificity (a particular treatment is not restricted to a particular category). Taken together they are simply poor medical categorisations leading to incoherent and poor clinical and research practices (Bentall et al, 1988; Pilgrim and Bentall, 1999). For example, the diagnosis of 'schizophrenia' can include two patients with no symptoms in common. And its outcome ('prognosis') is never certain in any individual case. This means that a common diagnosis in psychiatric settings has poor concept validity and poor predictive validity.

These criticisms reflected a reaction against the naive realism of medical naturalism described above. For critical realists it is not reality that is socially constructed but the way that we *understand* reality (Bhaskar, 1998).

Our research and the knowledge we build up is always incomplete and highly saturated with assumptions and vested interests (Pilgrim, 2007). For example, the drug companies fund research into diagnostic categories in order to market 'anti-depressants' and 'anti-psychotics', and the psychiatric profession's status is bound up with expertly making diagnoses (in order to align itself with the respectability and reputation of general medicine).

To summarise the global relevance of the biopsychosocial model and critical realism, as a competing clinical model and philosophical current from Western Europe they have challenged the *doxa* of neo-Kraepelinian psychiatry in the past hundred years. They accept that there are multiple real forces that generate misery and madness, but the way we understand the latter requires a constant sceptical stance about analysing knowledge. Put simply, rather than accepting descriptions of mental health and mental disorder we should constantly think critically about them and avoid the error of reductionism. The latter refers to the reduction of complexity to simplicity. To make matters worse, in naive realism we encounter simplistic circular reasoning (see below).

Radical constructivism

The third position takes critique in a particular direction and is based on the premise that psychiatric categories are social constructs or by-products of psychiatric activity. At its most extreme this concludes that mental illness is simply a myth (Szasz, 1961). Other critics taking a radical constructivist position have drawn on French post-structuralist philosophy (Miller and Rose, 1986; Parker et al, 1997; Bracken and Thomas, 2006). The emphasis in this position is of situated or contingent accounts, which are representations of reality. This problematises reality in and of itself. As a consequence, this position limits itself to producing discourses on discourses. In other words, in this view, reality can only ever be known via the representations we create of it; reality is always socially constructed in particular circumstances (Brown, 2005).

Radical constructivism, like critical realism, warns against the epistemic fallacy. The latter refers to the tendency of naive realists to confuse reality with what they prefer to call reality (Bateson, 1972). Although the map is not the territory, medical naturalists mistakenly think that it is. The 'schizophrenic' patient in front of them is an obvious embodied example of a disease but this is a circular transaction of this type. Q: How does the psychiatrist know that this patient is suffering from schizophrenia? A: Because the patient hears voices and has rigid and odd ideas. Q: And why do they have these strange experiences? A: Because they suffer from schizophrenia.

The radical constructivist position has had a strong presence globally in what came to be called 'anti-psychiatry' (especially the work of Szasz and the early Foucault) and then 'critical psychiatry' (which also contains critical realists). Whereas medical naturalism was derived from German psychopathology and critical realism has been associated with one radicalised branch of British empiricism, radical constructivism has mainly been driven by postmodern French thinking. However, Szasz was a Hungarian émigré in the US and a psychoanalyst. This reminds us that psychoanalysis needs to be considered as a cross-cutting body of knowledge. It started in Central Europe, but was then carried by part of the Jewish diaspora in flight from Nazism in the 1930s and 1940s to England and the US, and so it shaped Anglo-American psychiatric thought. For example, psychoanalytical psychiatry put a brake on unbridled Kraepelinian thought in the revision of the DSM system, when the APA dropped assumptions about aetiology (Wilson, 1980).

Thus when we reflect on mental disorder as a global discourse we can observe a turbulent mix of currents of thought, drawn from naive realism, critical realism and radical constructivism, with the first of these, for now, constituting a form of *doxa* in the lives of most professionals, healthcare planners and many patients. These currents are the legacy of discussions in the professional world of the Northern hemisphere during the 19th and 20th century.

The integrity of a diagnostic approach, aligned to DSM and ICD, has been preserved by an acknowledgement of culturally specific forms of mental abnormality, so-called 'cross-cultural psychiatry'. This creates an immediate tension, however, between 'emic' and 'etic' accounts, with the first privileging the insider's culturally subjective view and the latter the objective view of expert outsiders, say, in our case, the global application of categories preferred by Western psychiatrists used in DSM and ICD (Shinobu and Cohen, 2007).

Take the example of the report of some people of South Asian origin, who when unhappy point to their chest and describe a 'falling heart' (Fenton and Sadiq-Sangster, 1996). Western psychiatrists consider that they are 'really' suffering from 'depression' and that their accounts reflect 'somatisation'. The latter refers to the presentation of psychological symptoms via physical symptoms (a sort of disguising of the 'true' underlying 'mental illness', according to naive realists). But why cannot people legitimately describe their distress as a 'falling heart'? Why is that an invalid description? For a longer discussion of the international challenge (or arguably impossibility) of retaining a single and simple objective medical view of 'depression', see Pilgrim and Bentall (1999) and Kokanovic (2010).

Cross-cultural psychiatry is therefore trying to 'have its cake and eat it'. On the one hand, it wants to preserve the idea of psychiatry as an objective medical specialty making universally valid claims about mental disorder. On the other hand, it tries to argue that there are culturally specific ways of experiencing misery, madness or personal dysfunction. If we really were to respect the latter sensitivity to diverse experiences over time and place, then the possibility of fixed and universal descriptions are fatally undermined.

Promoting mental health and the challenge of dualism

Turning away from mental disorder and to mental health, the latter has been the focus of increasing interest for healthcare planners in the developed world (especially in relation to the new discourse about 'well-being'). More generally the WHO has also taken an interest in the prevention of mental disorders. Mental health promotion is a population-wide concept, which includes those not deemed to have a mental health problem, whereas the prevention of mental disorder is defined by clinical populations and pathology.

The WHO emphasises that: mental health is intrinsic to health in general; it is more than the absence of mental disorder; and a close interdependence exists between physical and mental health (Herrman et al, 2005). The latter interdependence reflects, of course, a legacy of the dualism (of mind and body) associated with Western European thought in the past 300 years, and is even reflected in the Szaszian separation of physical and mental illness (see the previous section).

If the biopsychosocial model has played second fiddle to the neo-Kraepelinian *doxa* in clinical psychiatry, this is not the case when we examine psychiatric views about mental health promotion. Instead we find the strong presence of the Meyerian tradition. For example, within that tradition Herrman (2011) notes that mental health is:

> ... determined by social, psychological, and biological factors that interact with each other, just like health and illness in general. Poor mental health is associated with social disadvantage. Poverty, discrimination and violence, for instance, have a powerful influence on mental health in countries, whether they are high- or low-income (p 407).

Herrman goes on to note that positive mental health is inextricably bound up with social and economic development and so the concept resonates both at the individual and community level in any society. Certainly once a public health, rather than a clinical perspective is adopted, then it is impossible to see mental health any longer as simply a measurable psychological (that is, individual) variable, as it reflects inequalities defined using the *social* variables of class, 'race', age and gender (Rogers and Pilgrim, 2003). Reflecting this multi-factorial complexity, the Ottawa Charter for Health Promotion advocates five main public health strategies to improve the mental health of any society. These are:

- building healthy public policies;
- creating supportive environments;
- strengthening community action;
- developing personal skills;
- reorienting health services towards the prevention of problems and the promotion of well-being.

Moreover, longitudinal cross-national studies of happiness have been very revealing about the sources of mental health. For example, where absolute as well as relative poverty are present and democratic initiatives are thwarted, then the population will be notably distressed. Not surprisingly Zimbabwe is found to be the least happy country in these cross-national comparisons (Inglehart et al, 2008). However, these authors note that although the relationship between happiness and material wealth clearly exists, this is a curvilinear, not linear, relationship. That is, at the top of the curve there is not a neat co-relationship between being rich and being happy.

The happiest country in the world is not the US but Denmark. In the latter, 'post-materialist values' are evident. For example, boasting about wealth is criticised, relative wealth creates a sense of shame not pride and personal relationships are valued over social status. This value system fits poorly with the consumerism and individualism we now associate with late capitalism.

Thus, a final caution is that the more holistic and multi-factorial approach about mental health, linked to the biopsychosocial tradition noted earlier, and adopted by thinkers in the WHO, must still be placed in our postmodern context. In the latter we now find the following diverse beliefs, among others, in the general population:

- a rich life can be derived from non-rational-based activity (such as the creative arts and religion or spirituality) not just the pursuit of rationality;
- at times it is better to be out of the labour market than in it;
- accepting suffering may be more important than the pursuit of happiness;

- personal relationships are more important than impersonal technologies;
- evidence about what is acceptable and appropriate to people is more important than what is effective at changing them;
- those of us who do not fit neatly into the norms and role expectations of adult functioning (as workers and family members) should be tolerated and not required to change by others;
- serving God is more important than our individual homocentric interests.

The point here is not to prove or disprove any of these viewpoints, but to merely note that they exist. And *because* they exist, then we might want to proceed with caution when thinking about the desirability of 'mental health interventions' and the nature of terms such as 'mental disorder' and 'mental health' in our postmodern context. That context is now both globalised and locally diverse.

References

APA (American Psychological Association) (1994) *Diagnostic and statistical manual of mental disorders* (4th edn), Washington, DC: APA.

Bateson, G. (1972) *Steps to an ecology of mind*, New York: Chandler Press.

Bentall, R.P., Jackson, H. and Pilgrim, D. (1988) 'Abandoning the concept of schizophrenia: some implications of validity arguments for psychological research into psychotic phenomena', *British Journal of Clinical Psychology*, vol 27, pp 303-24.

Bhaskar, R. (1998) *The possibility of naturalism*, London: Routledge.

Bourdieu, P. (1972) *Outline of a theory of practice* (translated by R. Nice), Cambridge: Cambridge University Press.

Bracken, P. and Thomas, P. (2006) *Postpsychiatry: Mental health in a postmodern world*, Oxford: Oxford University Press.

Brown, P. (2005) 'Naming and framing: the social construction of diagnosis and illness', *Journal of Health and Social Behavior*, Extra issue, pp 34-52.

De Swaan, A. (1991) *The management of normality*, London: Routledge.

Engel, G.L. (1980) 'The clinical application of the biopsychosocial model', *American Journal of Psychiatry*, vol 137, pp 535-44.

Fenton, S. and Sadiq-Sangster, A. (1996) 'Culture, relativism and mental distress', *Sociology of Health and Illness*, vol 18, no 1, pp 66-85.

Herrman, H. (2011) 'Promoting mental health', in D. Pilgrim, A. Rogers and B. Pescosolido (eds) *SAGE handbook of mental health and illness*, London: Sage Publications.

Herrman, H., Saxena, S. and Moodie, R. (eds) (2005) *Promoting mental health: Concepts, emerging evidence, practice*, Geneva: World Health Organization.

Hoff, P. (1995) 'Kraepelin', in G. Berrios and R. Porter (eds) *A history of clinical psychiatry*, London: Athlone Press.

Inglehart, R., Foa, R., Peterson, C. and Weizel, C. (2008) 'Development, freedom, and rising happiness: a global perspective, 1981–2007', *Perspectives on Psychological Science*, vol 3, pp 264-85.

Kokanovic, R. (2010) 'The diagnosis of depression in an international context', in D. Pilgrim, A. Rogers and B. Pescosolido (eds) *SAGE handbook of mental health and illness*, London: Sage Publications.

Kraepelin, E. (1883) *Compendium der Psychiatrie*, Leipzig.

Miller, P. and Rose, N. (eds) (1986) *The power of psychiatry*, Cambridge: Polity Press.

Parker, I., Georgaca, E., Harper, D., McLaughlin, T. and Stowell-Smith, M. (1997) *Deconstructing psychopathology*, London: Sage Publications.

Pilgrim, D. (2007) 'The survival of psychiatric diagnosis', *Social Science & Medicine*, vol 65, no 3, pp 536-44.

Pilgrim, D. (2011) 'The hegemony of cognitive behavioural therapy in modern mental health policy', *Health Sociology Review*, vol 20, no 2, pp 120–32.

Pilgrim, D. and Bentall, R.P. (1999) 'The medicalisation of misery: a critical realist analysis of the concept of depression'. *Journal of Mental Health*, vol 8, no 3, pp 261-274.

Rogers, A. and Pilgrim, D. (2003) *Mental health and inequality*, Basingstoke: Palgrave Macmillan.

Rogers, A. and Pilgrim, D. (2010) *A sociology of mental health and illness* (4th edn), Buckingham: Open University Press.

Shinobu, K. and Cohen, D. (2007) *Handbook of cultural psychology*, New York: The Guilford Press.

Szasz, T.S. (1961) 'The use of naming and the origin of the myth of mental illness', *American Psychologist*, vol 16, pp 59-65.

WHO (World Health Organization) (1992) *The ICD-10 classification of mental and behavioural disorders*, Geneva: WHO.

Wilson, M. (1993) 'DSM-III and the transformation of American psychiatry: a history', *American Journal of Psychiatry*, vol 150, no 3, pp 399-410

The best it can be

Charis Uden

I'm watching a spider weave her web the other side of glass. I am transfixed and for the moment without my mind's incessant wittering. For the moment I am not even aware of the silence of no thought. For a moment I am nothing. I like being nothing.

Sometimes I feel I'm like the spider, creating life from thin strands, balancing on the edge, buffeted yet not broken. Sometimes I feel like prey, trapped and suffocated by a web, exhausted with the struggle to live in this world.

The sound of a doorbell and I am brought back to the terror of having to face whoever is on the other side.

In a spider's world mental illness has no meaning.

It has been 10 years. Now I no longer apologise for my dis-ease. Now I no longer wear it as a badge. Now I am not mental illness. It has been a challenging journey to come this far. Yet I know of people who think I have been travelling backwards. And I still need to enter their world of labels to explain my existence. I envy the spider for never having to explain.

"What if this is the best it can be for you?"

About 10 years ago my therapist asked me this question. At the time I was in hospital on close observation after a serious suicide attempt. To me she seemed to imply maybe nothing would change, and I wondered why I was bothering with therapy. Ten years later I still inhabit the same dark space of despair about the world, I still control my world through checking and cleaning, my difficult relationship with food continues. I am unable to work. I am still labelled mentally ill. Many might witness my life as meaningless and criticise my lack of contribution in the world. Yet inside me there are shifts in consciousness.

Back then I struggled more, clung to my identity as a therapist, argued against being mentally ill, felt ashamed and guilty about my 'lack of status' in the working world. I judged myself harshly and felt worse when I couldn't pull up the proverbial socks. After three years in mental institutions you get used to the water and the labels become as easy to swallow as the pills. In the wider world you are surprised at someone's silence when you tell them you have a mental illness.

To define a role for myself seemed so necessary. Yet I seldom questioned how far inhabiting a certain role took me from myself. I was just addicted to being seen as somebody instead of being nobody. Even in the most challenging circumstances I'd create a story where I was somebody – if only a victim, which can be the most powerful role of all.

At the beginning it was me, mentally ill? – inside still a therapist, able to listen tirelessly to others' tragic stories ... still able to contribute to others' lives ... smugly feeling I had more to offer, and so had more value, than those I lived among in hospital. Then me mentally ill – a victim of past abuse, and still within a system that abused. And then me mentally ill – able to disturb and challenge the comfortable out of complacency. And me mentally ill – the campaigner for other mentally ill people, aligning myself to the masses of mentally ill under an illusion we are an homogeneous group cemented by our outsider status. Yet with every role always aware of my non-being, and never really belonging anywhere.

My journey through the realms of mental illness has been about coming out of hiding.

Now I can seem more insane by belonging more to myself than anyone or anything else. I count aloud or sing mantras in the street like nursery rhymes to calm myself. I no longer engage with the stares. I talk to the sea and the moon to create a feeling of safe space. I ask an electrician dozens of repetitious questions until I understand exactly his work and trust he is qualified to carry it out for us. I then spend hours after worrying whether he has neglected some wire and I will be prosecuted for injuring people because the building burns down. I spend hours unpicking an innocent remark from a neighbour until I spiral into the darkest place, where suicide seems a welcome relief. I hear the doorbell or the phone ring and hide beneath the duvet until long after the threat of intrusion has gone. I analyse every word of our home insurance documents and question whether having cooking oil in our cupboard might invalidate the policy. I ring Transco in the middle of the night because I am terrified we have lead piping under our bed. I ask my husband to witness me go through my checklist many times before I leave the house. No matter where I am I don't hold back tears when I'm upset. I no longer pretend that living in this world is easy for me.

Yet I now also live with an observer me. One who compassionately witnesses my struggles and realises there is little wisdom in meeting my pain and panic with logic. One who weaves with skill the fine strands that hold me together, hoping one day I might for a second rest back into myself and take refuge from the torment in my head. One who knows there are people I can reach out to and trust. One who was brave enough to see I was worth the love of the man who is now my husband and best friend.

When I feel trapped I know it is my own web that traps me. Sometimes the rain and wind in my head tear my web apart. Yet over and over I painstakingly spin anew, knowing this is the best it can be.

Keep the change
David Uden

Imagine a life where everything from the past was stolen, destroyed, left behind. How would it feel? Liberating? Depleting? Would there be a need to rebuild or to let go? Could life be different from that moment on? Am I a product of the things I own, the experiences I have had, a present that relies exclusively on the past, or is it possible to let go and move forward? To shed the skin of a previously lived life, to emerge from the trappings and debris of old ideas and belief systems.

Several years ago my life seemed to disintegrate. A long-term relationship came to an end and I was made redundant, making it impossible for me to stay in my home. People slipped away from my life, friends from long ago. Although devastating it freed me to re-evaluate my life and challenge my views. It was at this time that I met the woman I have now married.

When my wife and I first corresponded, she told me she had spent some years in a psychiatric hospital and had attempted suicide. This was very early on, we had only met each other once and we had emailed maybe once or twice. I knew something serious had happened to her from the instant we met and I was, from that moment on, involved in a process of having the past revealed. This revelation of 'mental illness' triggered some interesting reactions. Almost simultaneously, I was aware of being attracted to the concept, like it somehow held a romantic notion of other-worldliness, a refreshing alternative to consensus reality. And I was also disconcerted, wondering how serious the 'illness' was. Was I getting involved with a psychopath, someone who might hurt or torment me in some way, maybe by being too 'needy'? These were instinctive knee-jerk reactions, and I was also, aware enough to realise that to judge in this manner, either positively or negatively, was not the way forward. I tried not to let any learned responses colour my reactions. What I did learn was the story of a woman who had suffered enormous hardships and cruelty, who had been abused in many different ways by family, partners and 'friends' and who had shown great strength and determination to remain true to herself. To find the light in the darkest places. It challenged me to do the same.

My initial reactions were based partly on cultural conditioning and partly on a morbid fear of mental illness that could be traced back to strange meetings with my Father's Mother, who was aggressively psychotic towards the end of her life, when I was about five or six. In retrospect maybe it was not so odd that I should have been fascinated by documentaries on mental illness as a teenager. It almost seems that I was preparing myself for the challenges that lay ahead. With that knowledge I was open to seeing that someone who had experienced 'mental illness' was not only less duplicitous and more honest than the so-called sane people in my life, but was actually more centred and wise.

As we became closer I realised that being a part of my wife's world meant living life in a very different way. We are vigilant over the smallest detail regarding locking doors and windows, making sure our space is safe, safe even from bacteria and dirt. Not only protecting our home from intrusion, but also our bodies. Time and dates have no meaning. My wife's insomnia can mean night and day are interchangeable. 'News' is consciously barred from my wife's life as much as possible as it causes too much distress. We spend our days finding creative ways through, especially in crises when chaos and disturbances trigger past trauma. We have a house full of our art as a result.

Strangely I feel more alive. My wife challenges me to be reflective on a daily basis, about attitudes and meaning. I have become an observer of myself and my own mental processes. My perspective on life has been transformed.

I used to work as a part of the advertising industry, designing for print and web for companies selling one product or another, cars, clothes, CDs etc. It mattered little what the product was, the important factor was that it sold, regardless of the subconscious manipulation and stress on those it targeted. My role in the world now is very different. It is mainly concerned with reducing the stresses and strains of modern life on my wife, and the by-product is a simpler more peaceful life.

My definition of the term 'work' has changed. I had a strict idea of work being within set boundaries of time and location. This I assume to be a rather usual model in our society and one for which I was rewarded with a mild sense of security and a comfortable feeling of fitting in to the status quo. I have had to redefine this model. Now my role is primarily a carer and I chose it at the expense of 'career opportunities', promotion and financial security. I am involved now in caring for another human being. And I am rewarded by the warmth and love this brings me.

I have struggled to tell people how my life has changed. I haven't been able to reveal to my brothers the reality of my everyday life. In social situations I still can't shrug off the stigma of not having a 'proper job'. It is often one of the first things people say when meeting: "So, what have you been up to?" "What are you doing now?" Or more explicitly: "Where are you working now?" "Are you still working at…?" etc, etc. More and more I am growing in confidence about what my role is and how it surpasses every other role I could imagine. And with this confidence I am finding my voice and know that some day soon I won't hesitate in answering with pride that I am a carer and an artist.

PART III

Understanding adulthood

Introduction

The very essence of adulthood is an understanding of real lives, however isolated, vulnerable, collaborative, confident or honest. In the final part of this reader the focus settles on issues that in many ways underpin the previous readings. Consideration is given first to ethical perspectives that test moral values and then to the ontological foundation, the basis of research that demonstrates not only the depth and complexity of the self but also how this holistic approach must be recognised in all social relationships between people wherever they may be.

George Giarchi begins Section Seven by examining the ethics of health and social care practice, reminding us of the classical origins. He demonstrates the centrality of 'doing good' and 'avoiding harm' that enables individuals to maintain their autonomy while recognising the balance between risk and responsibility. This exploration shows how virtues, values and professional codes of practice are inter-related. An example of a specific moral issue is demonstrated through **Jacques Thiroux**'s discussion of 'lying, cheating, breaking promises and stealing'. Here he looks at how 'lying' is defined and considers the arguments 'for' and 'against' this behaviour, showing through case examples the rationale used for such action and the potential consequences resulting in the acceptance of a more favourable moderate position. This example is challenging and encourages reflection.

To further extend ethical aspects of practice **Liz Lloyd** takes as her concern the policy development of 'personalisation' that seeks to develop a service response that meets individual need. By giving service users more choice and control over their own budgets and the management of their care, ethical issues related to maintaining personal control are discussed, and link back to Giarchi's chapter. For dependent older people these developments raise issues that Liz Lloyd addresses through applying the feminist ethics of care, a perspective that considers implications for all involved in caring relationships either as carers or care receivers.

Of course, the restricted or limited nature of service provision can always present ethical dilemmas, and in the last piece in this section **Ann Gallagher** and **Nigel Sykes** use the case study of Mrs M to consider the work of a clinical ethics committee in the health service. Here the decision over whether a terminally ill person should be moved from the scarce resource of a hospice to a nursing home is considered. The authors use Gallagher's ethics framework, a systematic process for considering reaching a decision, and discuss the ethical issues from different perspectives. In deciding 'what is right', the case reveals a balancing act that also refers to Giarchi's notion of 'virtue' and 'value' but within a particular code of practice.

Moving into the last section of the book, the crucial issue becomes the evidence base and the ongoing debate as to how specific types of research method are used to examine and foreground individual lives. From the late 20th century onwards the ever-present discussion concerning the interface between the individual and the social has nurtured recognition of subjectivity as a legitimate consideration. In addition, recognition of the importance of using the most appropriate method, either qualitative or quantitative, to address research questions has led to greater *innovation*. In her chapter sociologist **Jennifer Mason** says 'we need a methodology and methods that open our perspective to the multidimensionality of lived experience', showing us how real lives can be explored through a mixed methods approach to research originating through what she calls 'qualitative thinking', where different forms of data can be 'linked' or 'meshed'.

Mason's chapter provides a platform to which the work of **Julie McLeod and Rachel Thomson** adds further depth. Central to their discussion is how to explore the passage of time in everyday lives. By examining the methods of oral history and qualitative longitudinal research, the temporal process is considered through the past, the present and how meaning may 'transfer between generations'. Using examples from Australian research projects they identify the value of these methods and how empirical research has an impact on policy and practice. Recognising particular methods can also lead to questioning rigour and appropriateness and the views offered by healthcare practitioners and researchers, **Ayelet Kuper and colleagues**, can be seen as a pragmatic critique of the qualitative method. They pose six questions to be addressed when appraising qualitative research, from the sampling of participants to maintaining ongoing ethical justification.

The first three chapters in Section Eight provide an important introductory grounding for empirical research using a range of qualitative methods. The next three chapters illustrate the sensitivity needed both to address the research topics and to involve participants meaningfully. In the piece by **Rebecca Jones**, the research considers the lives of three bisexual women, Mel, Muriel and Anne, and how their lifestyles influence how they and their partners are perceived in health and welfare settings. Her case study approach is particularly interesting as the cases are composites based on a variety of research and real life situations that have been reviewed by others from the UK bisexual community. This is a way of working that gives a voice to an invisible group while providing useful material that can generate discussion and develop skills, thus having a practical outcome.

This challenge is also addressed in the next chapter by **Stephen Parkin** who uses diverse qualitative methods to capture both the context and experience of using 'public injection sites' from the perspectives of injecting drug users and agency employees, and whether this can inform practical service-relevant outcomes. Guided by a philosophy of harm reduction, the potential for practical application from research is seen as an important outcome. Research with drug users is also the focus of the final empirical study, where **Brenda Roe and colleagues** consider the growing number of older problematic drug users. Involving older participants through a voluntary sector drugs treatment service, they begin to show the implications for long-term, or more recent, drug use on health and well-being, social relationships and the experience of services. Once again this is a less visible group beginning to emerge through research.

To conclude this section it seems appropriate to reflect, through the views of **Catherine Pope** and **Nicholas Mays**, on the rise of qualitative research within health services research as seen in the fictionalised conversation between a research director and a sociologist who was a former colleague. They have not met for 15 years. Here, the director who previously had little time for qualitative research, talks enthusiastically about the need for mixed methods approaches. They talk earnestly about the need for quality and rigour in all research, focusing on issues relating to analysis, interviewing, focus groups, ethnography, ethics and the future development of mixed methods. This conversation allows us to reflect on Jennifer Mason's earlier call. Such research discussion also allows us to reconsider the real voices that are found throughout this text, where the biographical is essential to our understanding of adulthood, ageing and the life course.

SECTION SEVEN

Ethical considerations

33

The ethics triad: virtues, values and codes of practice

George Giarchi

Introduction

Ethics is not an esoteric subject. It affects everyday life, enabling people to decide what is the right way to act in particular circumstances. The derivation of 'ethics' in moral philosophy stems from the Greek word *ĕthikós*, meaning the 'good life', which was translated by the Roman philosophers into the 'good person' (Onions, 1966, p 329). Patients and service users expect professionals and carers to be people who have their best interests at heart and whom they can trust absolutely. This chapter considers the interlocking triad of virtues, values and codes of practice, proposing that integrity evidenced by virtues is at the heart of health and social care training and agency practice. Practice is no longer affected simply by western virtues, values and codes of conduct, but increasingly is also influenced and enriched by global perspectives.

The ethics of health and social care operate within a complex four-way set of normative 'pulls' that may sometimes be in tension. These interactive 'pulls' are dictated by:

- individual moral imperatives;
- government policy and legal requirements;
- professional codes of conduct;
- patents', service users' and carers' values.

They are presented in Figure 33.1 with further discussion guided by the following definitions:

Virtue ethics, value ethics and codes of conduct: definitions

- *Virtue ethics:* character traits that dispose a person to act for the good of others, and which guide what behaviour is preferable morally.
- *Value ethics:* what is held to be intrinsically valuable, and immutable, regardless of context.
- *Codes of practice:* ethical principles and binding rules of conduct for members of particular professions.

Figure 33.1: The four-way pull

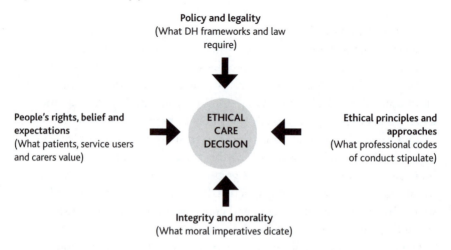

Policy and legality
(What DH frameworks and law require)

People's rights, belief and expectations
(What patients, service users and carers value)

ETHICAL CARE DECISION

Ethical principles and approaches
(What professional codes of conduct stipulate)

Integrity and morality
(What moral imperatives dicate)

Here the implications for practitioners are considered in relation to virtue ethics; value ethics; and professional codes of practice.

Virtue ethics: moral integrity as the basis of trust

'Virtue' is a term used by Greek philosopher Aristotle (384–322 BC) (1976, p 367). Aristotle's view was that virtuous people are 'dutiful, good, excellent and efficient' (1976, p 367). Virtue is another word for good character – people are judged to have a good character by how they act (Bowles et al, 2006, p 56).

Sprigge (2001) and Garcia (1999) stress that virtue ethics is about the 'moral subject', evidenced in the individual's way of life and manner of acting in delivering care. Fry and Johnstone (2002, p 26) simply refer to virtue ethics as 'character ethics' – 'By their deeds you shall know them'.

Ethics hinges on virtuous behaviour. The ethical perspective in western societies maintains that certain acts, such as torture, are always wrong, and this is backed by human rights legislation (for example, the Human Rights Act 1998).

Although a universal ethic is not possible, given differences of belief and cultures, there are some shared virtues across cultures. These include the 'Golden Rule': 'Do not do to others that which you would not wish them do to you' and conversely, 'Do to others that which you would wish them do to you' (Fasching and deChant, 2001; Hugman, 2005, p 131). This position is shared almost verbatim by the *Mahabharata* (Hinduism), *Udanavarga* (Buddhism), *Talmud* (Judaism), *Dadistan-i-Dinik* (Zoroasrtrianism), *Hadith* (Islam), *Gleanings* (Baha'i faith) and *Gospel of St Matthew* (Christianity) (Bok, 1995; Hugman, 2005).

Influential early virtue theorists such as Aristotle, Plato (429-347 BC) and Aquinas (1225-74 AD) refer to the growth and development of good character as 'human flourishing' (*oedemonia*) within the moral climate of a humane society. Virtue is a disposition to care about the quality of care relationships (Hugman, 2005). Virtuous behaviour stands between indifference at one end of a continuum, and vicious behaviour at the other.

> The Aristotelian virtues of courage, temperance, liberality, magnanimity, proper ambition, patience, truthfulness, wittiness, friendliness, modesty continue to be relevant for practitioners 2000 years later. Feminist ethicists have added empathy and feelings of compassion when caring (Gilligan, 1982). Being compassionate is to feel and show concern when communicating with those in distress, which is expressed by the "care voice" in feminist moral theory. (Heckman, 1995)

Comte-Sponville adds:

> 'Compassion allows us to pass from one realm to the other, from the emotional realm to the ethical realm, from what we feel to what we want, from what we are to what we must do.' (2003, p 116)

An ideal virtuous person is both compassionate and conscientious. Kant (1724-1804) introduced the notion of the 'categorical imperative', the operation of one's conscience (Kant, 1964; Gaarder, 1995, p 258), 'wishing to do one's work or duty well and thoroughly' (Onions, 1966, p 368). Heidegger (1889-1976) referred to the 'authentic person responding to the call of conscience, clear sighted and resolved' (cited by Blackham, 1991, p 98).

Conscience may act as a countercheck to unacceptable laws, hence the potential tension between legality and morality. Individual conscience can be in conflict with accepted good practice, for instance, the Jehovah's Witness objection to blood transfusion. The right of appeal to human conscience is central in a free society (Deigh, 2001). No one can be forced to act contrary to their conscience provided that acting out one's belief does not harm a third party (Hugman, 2005). Conscience can be caught in a moral stalemate where there is a tangle of ethical pulls and moral dilemmas that block moral action. This is where consultation is necessary. The practitioner is duty bound to get rid of the doubt.

In ethical decision making, the categorical imperative is the best interest of the vulnerable person informed by compassion. Seedhouse cites Kant's statement:

> To duty every other motive must give place, because duty is a condition good in itself, whose worth transcends everything. (2001, p 118)

There has been considerable debate about the most appropriate virtues for health and social care practitioners, but Beauchamp and Childress (2001, p 30) identify four virtuous obligations that are widely cited:

- *beneficence:* do what is good;
- *non-maleficence:* avoid causing harm;
- *respect for autonomy:* respect people's entitlement to make their own decisions;
- *justice:* fair distribution of benefits and risks.

Scenario One: Sam's dilemma

Friday evening at 6pm in the social work office. Sam was looking forward to a relaxing evening. He had put on his coat and packed his brief case. The phone rang. After hesitating, he picked it up. A mother in distress. Her 12-year-old daughter has not returned from school. He assures her he will be at her house after contacting the police and 'out of hours' team. Sam put the safety of the child first, his tiredness last.

In virtue ethics terms, Sam acted correctly, allowing his conscience to dictate that his duty prevailed over his comfort and convenience.

Value ethics: treating patients and service users as unique and special

Defining values is difficult. Timms (1983, p 107) identified 180 different definitions. Instead of entering into a moral debate about which is preferable, this section discusses the paramount overarching value of the individual and the prizing of the person's existence and uniqueness. It then contrasts a duty or conscience-led imperative approach with a pragmatic results–driven approach, described as consequentialism.

Focusing on the person was stressed originally by Kant as follows, a statement that has been cited by almost all ethicists ever since – his duty-led ethical orientation:

> 'To act as to treat humanity whether in your own person or that of any other, never solely as a means, but almost always as an end.' (1964, p 96)

In the ethics of care 'total regard' for the individual is imperative. Another influential philosopher, Martin Buber (1936), identified the importance of treating the individual ('thou') as singular. The danger is that 'thou' can be thought of as the plural 'you', reducing 'thou' to a category or object and not a unique individual.

Scenario Two: Total regard was lacking

A newly appointed public health officer, Dr Jay, accompanied a podiatrist on his rounds to familiarise himself with the delivery of the service. This podiatrist did not impress Dr Jay because he was stressing how many care visits he could 'clock up' in his morning round-up: "Care is on a tight budget. Time is of the essence." They came to a rundown apartment where the podiatrist attended to the feet of a 75-year-old man. When they got outside, Dr Jay turned to him saying, "You did a good job on that man's feet, but I am shocked because throughout the treatment you did not look at him. Had you done so you would have noticed he was trembling. We are going back to show concern and to see what must be done to help him. You are not delivering treatment on an assembly line".

Valuing the person is shared across major belief systems globally, as also basic standards of care and goodness are expected. The service user comes first. Although for example Hawley (2007), Tschudin (1994) and Downie and Calman (1994) point out, there are conflicts at times within values. In and between cultures the best interests of the patient/user ultimately matters. Ethicists see this as a question of duty and accountability. This is so, whatever the value ethics of Hinduism, Buddhism, certain forms of Judaism, Islam, evangelical and orthodox Christianity and Catholicism (WHO, 1995; Hadley, 1996; Hawley, 2007).

Diametrically opposed to values driven by duty and conscience is consequentialism or utilitarianism, as proposed by Jeremy Bentham (1748-1832) and John Stuart Mill (1806-73). The ethical goal for utilitarians is achieving happiness or attaining pleasure. Mill (1972) discussed the principle of utility as ensuring the greatest good of the greatest number. Utilitarians abide by the imperative of justice and that of best consequence for the greatest number of citizens, patients or service users, giving priority to justice, the fourth of Beauchamp and Childress's four obligations. However, the happiness of the majority may create the unhappiness of individuals and minorities (Parrott, 2007, p 51).

Scenario Three: Whose best interest?

Ahmed (age 65) needs a newly licensed drug treatment costing £50,000 per annum to extend his life expectancy by nine months. It would pay for two new community care posts to support 10 frail older people a week to stay in their own homes. Which decision is the ethical one?

Utilitarian decisions can become 'rule utilitarianism' dictated by policies, management requirements or protocols. There may be a tension between a policy requirement or legislation, because of the priority given to cost-effectiveness to the detriment of care effectiveness. A high position on the league table may be valued more than what is best for the individual patient or service user.

Ethical codes of practice: morally binding requirements

Each health and social care profession has its own codes of practice. Professional codes of practice consist of moral principles that form the basis of professional standards, and rules, such as the duty of confidentiality (Banks, 2006; Cuthbert and Qualington, 2008). Standards are backed by sanctions: serious breaches of codes (particularly the disclosure of confidential information, unless in the case of abuse) may result in being struck off the professional register (Hawley, 2007, p 143). The codes are upheld by regulatory bodies, such as the General Social Care Council (GSCC), Health Professions Council (HPC), Nursing and Midwifery Council (NMC), General Medical Council (GMC) and the British Medical Association (BMA).

Value conflicts have been considered earlier, but there are also codes that conflict when there are divergent views with regard to rules of conduct, depending on the philosophical angle adopted. First, the deontologist (derived from the Geek *deon*, meaning duty) will be 'duty bound' to obey the rules of conduct as a moral imperative; according to Kant, duty is 'the right thing to do' (Parrott, 2007, p 49). The basis of action is normative; it is not context specific. The teleologist (derived from the Greek '*telos*', meaning 'end' or 'purpose') will adopt the rules if on balance keeping the rules (as stated earlier) promotes the greatest good for the greatest number. The basis for action is calculative (Hope et al, 2003; Hugman, 2005; Banks, 2006).

The following scenarios illustrate these differences.

Scenario Four: Maintaining the duty of honesty in practice

Alice is a patient in a hospital ward, who appeared to be in the early stages of cardiovascular dementia. She became increasingly difficult and agitated in the evenings, refusing to take her medication. Matters came to a head when she slapped nurse Linda who was trying to persuade Alice to swallow her pills. Linda assumed that because Alice was often confused and showed signs that she lacked capacity, it was opportune to mix the medication with Alice's food. This she did for several days until her misconduct was detected by a senior nurse who reported Linda to the NMC because the test of capacity in the Mental Capacity Act (2005) (DCA, 2005) had not been carried out, and because of the dishonest way she had acted with the patient and towards the staff on the ward.

Here Linda had adopted a pragmatic stance, overriding her professional code *regarding her duty of honesty* and, indeed, her legal obligations.

Scenario Five: Should social workers go on strike?

The recession has led to sweeping cutbacks. On top of a 25 per cent drop in the budget, there is to be a 10 per cent reduction of staff and frozen vacancies in both child and adult care. Sickness rates are high. The UNISON steward proposed strike action. Staff are divided over taking action. Some take the view that it will be the service users who suffer. Lucy argued that the common good demanded action: "The people we serve are behind us. Results matter – if you support a strike it may be short-term loss for some, but long-term gain for all".

The two scenarios are about applying ethical codes of conduct in different contexts. The individual duty approach deals better with issues affecting the individual, whereas the utilitarian approach deals better with issues affecting the public good.

Discussion of ethical principles, conduct and rules may appear to be out of place in a fragmented, relativist society. The utilitarian position supports the view that the person is often a means to material ends in what Bauman (1994, 1995) describes as everyone for themselves in a more privatised world. But people in helping roles cannot afford to disregard the moral imperative to act according to conscience and duty. A value-free society is a dangerous place.

Conclusion

This chapter started by examining virtue ethics, and the need in heath and social care for moral integrity driven by conscientious compassion and a moral sense of duty, as the bases of trust and professionalism. People in care have the absolute right to be treated with respect and dignity, so value ethics were discussed, as well as total regard for the intrinsic potential and uniqueness of each person. Next, the ethical tension was considered between what is good for the individual and the greatest good for the greatest number. Finally, the chapter dealt with the inevitable conflicts that may arise when adhering to professional codes of practice.

Virtue is necessary because integrity upholds humanitarian values. Without virtue abuses must occur. Hence the importance of the inter-relationship in the ethics triad between virtues, values and codes of practice. As Figure 33.1 indicates, the triangulation is located within the four-way gravitational pull exercised between: what moral imperatives dictate; what professional codes of conduct stipulate; what Department of Health frameworks and law require; and what patients, service users and carers value.

References

Aristotle (1976 edn) *The ethics of Aristotle*, London: Penguin Books (translated by J.A.K Thomson).

Banks, S. (2006) *Ethics and values in social work* (3rd edn), Basingstoke: Palgrave Macmillan.

Bauman, Z. (1994) *Alone again: Ethics after certainty*, London: Demos.

Bauman, Z. (1995) *Postmodern ethics*, Oxford: Blackwell.

Beauchamp, T.L. and Childress, J.F. (2001) *Principles of biomedical ethics* (5th edn), Oxford and New York: Oxford University Press.

Blackham, H.J. (1991) *Six existential thinkers*, London: Routledge.

Bok, S. (1995) 'Golden rule', in T. Honderich (ed) *The Oxford companion to philosophy*, Oxford: Oxford University Press, p 321.

Bowles, W., Collingridge, M., Curry, S. and Valentine, B. (2006) *Ethical practice in social work*, Maidenhead: Open University Press.

Buber, M. (1936) *I and thou*, Edinburgh: Clark (translated by R. Gregory Smith).

Comte Sponville, A. (2001) *A short treatise on the great virtues*, London: Vintage.

Cuthbert, S. and Qualingron, J. (2008) *Values for care practice*, Exeter: Reflect Press.

DCA (Department for Constitutional Affairs) (2005) *Mental Capacity Act*, London: The Stationery Office.

Deigh, J. (2001) 'Ethics', in R. Audi (ed) *The Cambridge dictionary of philosophy*, Cambridge: Cambridge University Press, pp 284-9.

Downie, R.S. and Calman, K.C. (1994) *Healthy respect*, Oxford: Oxford University Press.

Fasching, D.J. and deChant, D. (2001) *Comparative religions: A normative approach*, Oxford: Blackwell.

Fry, S.T. and Johnstone, M.-J. (2002) *Ethics in nursing practice*, Oxford: Blackwell.

Fulford, K.W.M., Dickenson, D.L. and Murray, T.H. (eds) (2002) *Healthcare ethics and human values*, Oxford: Blackwell.

Gaarder, J. (1995) *Sophie's world*, London: Phoenix House.

Garcia, J.I.A. (1999) 'Virtue ethics', in R. Audi (ed) *The Cambridge dictionary of philosophy* (2nd edn), Cambridge: Cambridge University Press, pp 960-1.

Gilligan, C. (1982) *In a different voice: Psychological theory and women's development*, Cambridge: Polity Press.

Hadley, J. (1996) *Abortion: Between freedom and necessity*, London: Virago.

Hawley, G. (ed) (2007) *Ethics in clinical practice*, Harlow: Pearson.

Heckman, S.J. (1993) *Moral voices: Moral selves*, Cambridge: Polity Press.

Hope, T., Savulescu, J. and Hendrick, J. (2004) *Medical ethics and law*, Edinburgh: Churchill-Livingstone.

Hugman, R. (2005) *New approaches in ethics for the caring professions*, Basingstoke: Palgrave Macmillan.

Kant, I. [1785] (1964) *The moral law: Groundwork of the meta physics of morals* (translated by H.J. Paton), London: Routledge.

Mill, J.S. (1972) *Utilitarianism, on liberty and considerations on representative government*, London: Dent.

Onions, C.T. (ed) (1966) *The Oxford dictionary of English etymology*, Oxford: Oxford University Press.

Parrott, L. (2007) *Values and ethics in social work practice*, Exeter: Learning Matters.

Seedhouse, D. (2001) *Ethics: The heart of health care* (2nd edn), Chichester: Wiley.

Timms, N. (1983) *Social work ethics: An enquiry*, London: Routledge and Kegan Paul.

Tschudin, V. (1994) *Deciding ethically*, London: B. Tindall.

WHO (World Health Organization) (1995) *Complications of abortion*, Geneva: WHO.

34

Lying, cheating, breaking promises, and stealing

Jacques Thiroux

Extract from J.P. Thiroux, *Ethics, Theory and Practice* (6th edn), © 1998, pp. 290-301. Reprinted by permission of Pearson Education Inc., Upper Saddle River, NJ.

[...]

Introduction

Other than the taking of human life, the moral issues of lying, cheating, breaking promises, and stealing are usually considered the most important and the least acceptable moral violations humans can perform. These actions usually are not in direct violation of the Value of Life principle, ... but definitely constitute violations of the Principles of Truth Telling and Honesty, Justice and Fairness, and Goodness or Rightness. They also can be considered to be violations of the Principle of Individual Freedom, in that they tend to give unjustified freedom to the perpetrators but deny freedom to the victims of such violations.

   [...]

   The significance of the moral issues in this chapter cannot be overemphasized because violations and non–violations affect every level and activity of our daily lives.... [T]hey generally affect certain areas of our lives, but they come into play in all human relationships and therefore require careful scrutiny. In this chapter, I will state the issues as fully as I can, giving arguments for and against lying, for example, and citing cases for the application of these arguments. Further, I hope that both instructors and students will apply the arguments in these issues to their own experiences, bringing their own applicable cases for discussion and striving to reach some kind of resolution whenever possible.

Definition of key terms

Lying

General Definition. Lying, according to Sissella Bok in her book *Lying,* is "an intentionally deceptive message in the form of a statement"[1]. The dictionary defines a lie as a "piece of information deliberately presented as being true; anything meant to deceive or give a wrong impression."[2]

White Lie. According to Bok, a white lie is "a falsehood not meant to injure anyone, and of little moral import."[3] Bok presents this definition as how she understands most people to define a 'white lie,' but does not herself feel that white lies have little or no moral import.

Commission or Omission. I would like to add a further distinction to the definition of lying, which is that some lies are lies *of commission* or are direct statements that are outright lies. Other lies are lies *of omission,* which involve the not stating of certain information that is vital to a decision, relationship, or other important human activity. For example, to tell someone you are no longer taking drugs or drinking when you actually are, would be a lie of commission; on the other hand, to allow them to go on believing you have quit when you haven't, especially when the issue is vitally important to your relationship, would be a lie of omission.

Cheating

To cheat is "to deceive by trickery; swindle; to mislead; to act dishonestly or practice fraud."[4] As you can see by this definition, cheating and lying both fall under the general heading of deception.

Promise

According to the dictionary, a promise is "a declaration assuring that one will or will not do something; a vow." To break a promise, then, is to fail to conform to or to act contrary to or to violate the promise.[5]

Stealing

Again according to the dictionary, stealing is taking something without right or permission, generally in a surreptitious way.[6] ...

[...]

Lying

Arguments against lying

Dupes and Deprives Others. A major argument against lying is that it misinforms the people lied to and thus may frustrate them from reaching their own objectives. For example, [...]

Jane thinks she has a chance for a promotion at the company where she works because the present manager tells her so, though actually he has selected David for the job. Thus Jane may decide not to seek a better job elsewhere or may turn one down, hoping she will be promoted where she is. The manager, first of all, has led Jane to believe she has more alternatives than she really has, which is a violation of the Justice Principle - it's unfair to her. Second, though she would much rather stay with her present firm if she could move up, the manager's duplicity has caused her to lose confidence in what, for her, may have been the best alternative.

Causes Distrust in Human Relationships. Another major argument against lying is that it causes a breakdown in human relationships. If you think about it, human relationships are at their best when people can trust each other. Was Jane mistaken in trusting her boss? Most ethicists who do not support lying feel that we should be able to proceed on the positive assumption that we can trust, not on the negative one that we cannot. An entirely different atmosphere exists when human relationships are approached negatively rather than positively.

Lying not only causes distrust but also resentment disappointment, and suspicion in the deceived. [...]

Human relationships generally depend on the communication of thoughts, feelings, and information. Because lying essentially amounts to a failure to communicate honestly, human relationships are very hard to establish or maintain when their main foundation-honesty-is undermined or destroyed.

The Domino Argument. ... I have said that the domino argument in itself, without further evidence, will not influence people to refrain from performing certain acts. Nevertheless, we always should be aware that what we do may affect us and others by causing additional problems or reverberations beyond the initial action.

Those who are against lying feel that one lie tends to beget others in order to maintain the first one. As Sissela Bok states,

'It is easy, a wit observed, to tell a lie, but hard to tell only one. The first lie "must be thatched with another or it will rain through." More and more lies may come to be needed; the liar always has more mending to do. And the strains on him become greater each time–many have noted that it takes an excellent memory to keep one's untruths in good repair and disentangled. The sheer energy the liar has to devote to shoring them up is energy the honest man can dispose of freely.'[9]

For example, in refusing to tell dying patients the truth about their condition, a situation is set up in which many other lies must follow so as to back up the first. It might be argued that lying will make the patients try harder to recover (even though recovery may not be possible), and that knowing their true condition will only depress them and make communication with them harder and their last days terrible. The initial lie will seem reasonable in this setting. However, if the patients ask any serious questions about their condition, then more lies may have to be told. Precautions must be taken to prevent any information or even hints from leaking through to disrupt the growing web of lies that began innocently enough as a way of providing 'protection' for the dying patient.

Added to the difficulties of maintaining the initial lie (which was one of omission, not commission) is the fact that many people are involved in the care of such a patient. Thus, as the patient's situation worsens and more procedures (or fewer, when a doctor deems there is nothing more to be done) have to be done, the patient may ask questions of all these people, causing more lies to be told: "I don't know; you must ask your doctor. You're going to get better. There's no need to worry." The irony of all this, according to Dr. Elisabeth Kübler-Ross, who has worked with dying patients for many years, is that all those she dealt with knew the seriousness of their illnesses whether or not they had been told, and many even knew when they were going to die.[10] This means that the deception was not only painful and blocked communication, but it also was not really necessary because the truth was generally known to everyone involved–even those whom the lies were supposed to protect.

Additionally, once a lie has been told, further lying in other situations becomes easier, often to the point where liars no longer can distinguish between what is or is not the truth as they know it. And if a liar gets away with one lie that he has told in order to 'save his neck,' in no matter how trivial a situation, then future lying becomes easier and sometimes almost a way of life. Habitual lying, of course, increases the chance of discovery, leading to the breakdown of trust and the dilution if not destruction of vital human relationships. Therefore, although the domino argument may not in itself prohibit one from doing an act, in the case of lying, it is especially pertinent and should be carefully considered.

Unfair Advantage or Power for Liars. Another argument against lying is that because most liars do not themselves wish to be deceived, then to deceive others gives liars an unfair advantage. This is, of course, a violation of the Principle of Justice. [...]

Self-destructiveness of Lying. A major disadvantage in lying is that once liars are found out, their word is no longer trusted, their deceptions fall apart, and their power is de- creased or lost. The Watergate affair during President Nixon's administration exemplifies this loss of power. [...]

Another effect on the liars themselves, according to proponents of this argument, is that lying undermines one's own self-image. In other words, liars lose self-esteem be cause of their deceptions, and the more often these occur, the greater the loss.

Effect of Lying on Society. Bok assesses the general overall effect of lying on society as follows: "The veneer of social trust is often thin. As lies spread ... trust is damaged ... When it is damaged, the community as a whole suffers; and when it is destroyed, societies falter and collapse."[11] [...] Most people feel that a person's word is his or her bond and that it should be possible to trust everyone. Therefore, every breach of honesty destroys that belief, causes cynicism, condones lying, and destroys the thin "veneer of social trust". [...]

Arguments for lying

Most ethicists and others would not argue in favor of lying all the time, although some people might. Inveterate liars usually will *not* lie all the time because they can then be more strategically effective when they do. If one lies all of the time, one has a greater chance of being found out and of losing at least the semblance of trustworthiness, some thing a 'good' liar needs to maintain.

Most arguments for lying suggest that sometimes there are good reasons for telling lies. Therefore, to state unequivocally, as do Kant and others, that lying is never moral and should never be allowed, would be impractical and in some situations perhaps immoral. In some cases, they say, lying should be encouraged. For example, people ought to be able to lie when they need to or when lying could prevent the occurrence of a more serious moral infraction, such as killing.

Defense of the Innocent, Including Self-defense. According to Bok, "Deceit and violence ... are the two forms of deliberate assault on human beings. Both can coerce people into acting against their will."[12] In most instances, however, ethicists deem lying to be less harmful to human life than violence, especially when the latter terminates human life. With some exceptions, if killing or allowing innocent lives to be lost is wrong, and if one can save such lives by lying, most ethicists allow for lying in such instances. [...]

An ... example would be a wartime situation in which a member of the underground knows where other members are hiding. He would be justified in lying about their whereabouts rather than risking their capture and death.

... However, what about the president of a major corporation vital to national defense who is accused of embezzling funds and lies about it? When found out, she might argue that even though she was not protecting herself by her lie, as president of the company she felt a responsibility to lie to protect shareholders, workers, and also the 'innocent public' for whom her corporation manufactures defense products. Are her contentions justified? First, it might be seriously argued that for her crime to be covered up, only to surface at a later date, would cause even more problems in the future. Second, it's unlikely that her being found out and removed from the presidency would seriously affect the lives she is presumed to be 'protecting' by lying, because someone else could function as president.

National Security. Many ethicists argue for lying in order to maintain national security, an act that certainly may protect many innocent people. For example, if a woman spying for her country is caught, she may then lie about information she has in order to protect her country's security. Presidents and other members of the government sometimes state that they cannot reveal certain important information to the press or public because 'it would endanger national security.' Such people certainly should have some discretion in revealing information that would seriously affect national security, but they must be very careful not to abuse this right in order to protect their own self-interest.

[...] National security could be used as a valid reason for lying in certain circumstances only as long as it was not abused by members of the government or the military.

Trade Secrets in Business. Ethicists favoring lying might argue that business people may lie justifiably, either by omission or commission, rather than reveal vital trade secrets to their competitors. They aver that no business person has an obligation to tell competitors of his or her inventions or patents, which would give competitors unfair advantage. This permission to lie can also be extended to anything that would be in the business's self- interest, such as false and misleading advertising and lying for unfair advantage over other people or companies. Very often arguments sanctioning lying in business try to separate actions in the business world from those in life outside it, on the principle that in business anything goes, whereas one should never lie to loved ones or friends.

"Little White Lies". Many people, including some ethicists, allow for unimportant or harmless 'little white lies,' which are told to avoid hurting people's feelings or to protect those lying from embarrassment.

The arguments for these lies are that people need to have leeway in social intercourse and daily activities in order to keep things running smoothly. For example, if one woman asks another how an expensive new dress looks on her, the other woman might answer that the dress looks fine even if she doesn't think so because she doesn't want to hurt the asker's feelings. [...]

... [T]he liars usually feel that what they are lying about is unimportant, and that lying is a tactful way to avoid hurting people's feelings and save the liars some embarrassment. Further, they argue, in getting along in the world, lying sometimes can maintain the 'social veneer' rather than crack it, as is advocated by the people who argue against lying. In other words, rather than hurting someone or suffering embarrassment, and as long as no serious harm is done, it's all right to lie to prevent either from happening.

Moderate position

As with other topics ..., a moderate rather than a strict pro or con attitude to ward lying is the one most people probably favor. It advocates that, generally, one should avoid lying if possible and lie only as a last resort or clearly to save a life. This viewpoint is well expressed by the old saying 'Honesty is the best policy.' Moderates feel that lying is a serious matter, however little or white the lie. Moderates agree with those opposed to lying that the domino argument makes sense – that the more you lie, the easier it is to do so, and that one lie leads to another and another and another. They also agree that lying tends to break down the 'social veneer,' brings harm to those deceived, and destroys the integrity and human dignity of the liar whether or not he or she is caught.

Further, they believe that it's important to consider the consequences of any lie, however trivial. For instance, the woman who has lied to her friend about her dress may lose that friend if her lie is found out. Moreover, if by lying she encourages her friend to wear an unbecoming dress, then her lie has hurt, not helped, her friend. ... Thus, moderates argue, the consequences of even white lies may be worse than if one had told the truth.

One point moderates stress is that lying is not the only other alternative to giving someone truthful information that might hurt. As Elisabeth Kübler-Ross has stated, the important question is not whether I should tell the truth but *how* I should tell the truth, or how I should share information, important or not, with others who are asking me questions or who need to know what the truth is.[13] In other words, one does not have to be brutally frank. One can tell the truth, however terrible, but gently and with an intent to support and to give hope wherever possible. In the case of the women and the dress, for example, the friend could tell the one who asked, "Actually, I don't think that dress especially suits you, and I suggest you take it back and buy another. Since you thought enough of me to ask my opinion, may I help you return the dress and look for one that would be more flattering to you?" By replying in this way, the woman would not be lying, and she would be giving her friend some hope and encouragement about purchasing another dress that would be more becoming.

[...]

The basic thrust of the moderate position, then, is that one should generally try to tell the truth because telling lies often causes more problems than not doing so. Moderates also feel that

1 If people do choose to lie, they must try to make the consequences of their lying as harmless as possible.
2 People should try to avoid habitual lying and be aware of the risks of telling even one lie or a white lie.
3 People also should be aware that lying may have a deleterious effect not only upon the deceived but also upon them as the liars.
4 People should never lie about important matters that may affect the recipient of the lie significantly.
5 Lying is allowed when there is no other recourse and when innocent life is really at stake, such as in the cases cited earlier concerning the members of the underground during the wartime, and the captured spy. Every other type of situation must be fully justified and the consequences carefully weighed. People should favor telling the truth, however, remembering that *how* they tell it is as important as the telling.

Case for study ...

Jesusita, 80 years old and with a bad heart, is living in a convalescent hospital where she is visited regularly by her 50-year-old son, along with other members of the family. Her son dies suddenly one night of a heart attack. The remaining members of the family feel that she shouldn't be told of this because of her own weak heart, and in collusion with the hospital staff, no one tells her. After a week, Jesusita asks why her son hasn't visited her, and the family tells her he is on a business trip, hoping she will forget about him. But the next week she asks where he is and when he will return. She also wants to know why he hasn't called her or written a letter or postcard from where he is. The family tells her he is very busy but should be back soon. Another week passes and Jesusita becomes very restless and upset about her son not visiting her, she becomes harder and harder to care for, and she cries a lot. The staff and family gather to discuss what to do about the situation. They wonder whether they should tell her the truth now or think up some more excuses.

[...] Did they do the right thing in the beginning by lying to Jesusita?

Notes

[1] Sissela Bok, Lying: Moral Choice in Public and Private Life (New York: Vintage, 1979) 16.

[2] William Morris, ed, The American Heritage Dictionary in the English Language (Boston: Houghton-Mifflin, 1978) 754.

[3] Bok, Lying, 61.

[4] Morris, The American Heritage Dictionary, 229.

[5] ibid, 1047, 162.

[6] ibid, 1261.

[...]

[9] Bok, Lying, 26-27.

[10] Elizabeth Kübler-Ross, On Death and Dying (New York: Macmillan, 1969) 262.

[11] Bok, Lying, 28.

[12] ibid, 19.

[13] Kübler-Ross, On Death and Dying, 28.

35

The individual in social care: The ethics of care and the 'personalisation agenda' in services for older people in England

Liz Lloyd

Extract from L. Lloyd, 'The individual in social care: The ethics of care and the "personalisation agenda" in services for older people in England', *Ethics and Social Welfare* (2010) vol. 4, no. 2, pp. 188–200, reprinted by permission of the publisher (Taylor & Francis Group, http://www.informaworld.com).

The ethic of care provides not only a basis for understanding relationships of care at the micro level but also a potent form of political ethics, relevant to the development of welfare services. ... English social care services are currently in another period of change precipitated by the 'personalisation agenda'. This agenda is seen as having the potential to revolutionise social care, to create the conditions needed to tailor services to individual needs, and to give service users greater choice and control, including ... control over their own service budgets or direct possession and management of care funds. These developments are inextricably linked to broader economic and social trends, key amongst which are the ageing of the population and changing economic conditions affecting both the labour market and the market for care services. This article applies the feminist ethic of care to an analysis of the personalisation agenda in the context of care for dependent older people. ... It questions whether the personalisation agenda could potentially offer a more responsive form of care, by placing more power and control in older people's hands. ...

[...]

The ethic of care perspective

The ... discussion considers how an ethic of care approach contributes to an understanding of ... the need for care in old age and the personalisation agenda. Feminist ethicists (e.g. Held 2006; Kittay 2002; Sevenhuijsen 2000; Williams 2001; Tronto 1993) argue that it is because dependency and vulnerability are inherent within the human condition that the need for care arises. Kittay (2002), for example, refers to 'inevitable dependencies', which are a facet of human life and give rise to a need for care but which remain largely unacknowledged. Because this need for care is antithetical to the political aim of fostering independence and self-reliance as essential qualities of full citizenship, modern Western societies have devalued care and confined it to the private sphere. Feminist ethicists argue that the need to care is also inherent within the human condition. However, the interests of those who need and those who provide care are not always congruent and may in fact be in conflict. It is necessary therefore to give due consideration to the needs of all involved in caring relationships – either as care giver or receiver. Kittay's (2002) concept of 'nested dependencies' describes how care is also required by those who provide care.

Tronto's model for an ethic of care (1993) has influenced a number of subsequent critical analyses of social policies (see, for example, Sevenhuijsen 2000; Williams 2001). She conceptualises care as a process with four 'phases': attentiveness (caring about), responsibility (taking care of), competence (care giving) and responsiveness (care receiving). These are not to be regarded as neatly sequential, and Tronto argues that for an ethic of care to be realised, all of the above four stages must be integrated. Tronto's model has been criticised for being somewhat abstract (Fine 2007) and more relevant to micro-level caring relationships than to broader societal-level concerns about the politics of care (O'Neill 1996). However, it is arguably directly relevant to this discussion of personalisation. For example, responsibility is a fundamental element of the debate on social care set out in the British government's discussion document *Shaping the Future of Care Together* (DH 2009), which poses the question: what constitutes a fair balance of responsibility between the individual and the state for taking care of social care needs? Moreover, Tronto's concept of responsiveness is at the heart of the personalisation agenda, since enabling those using services to define their needs and how these should be met is, ostensibly, what personalisation is all about. The profound dissatisfaction expressed by many within the social care system is irrefutable, particularly the sense of being subjected to institutionalised regimes and unable to exercise choice and control. It is largely due to the advocacy work of service user groups that attention has been drawn to the need for system change.

The ethic of care is political (Sevenhuijsen 1998, 2000). If care is placed at the centre of public political discourses, Sevenhuijsen argues, it becomes possible to develop a clearer understanding of different interpretations of need and of conflicts of interest that exist between those in need of care and those who provide it. She defines care as a 'social practice', a human activity that is 'underpinned by formal or informal institutions, usually a combination of these' (Sevenhuijsen 1998, p. 21). Social and organisational contexts shape interpretations of need and actions taken to meet these. For Sevenhuijsen, universal ethical principles are required, not just as a framework for micro-level caring relationships but more broadly in public life. Once the principle is established that everybody needs care it follows that, in a democratic society, citizens should be enabled to both give and receive care. This means that the right to care and be cared for should be enshrined within the constitutional rights of citizens, which Sevenhuijsen argues could be achieved through a 'life-plan' approach that guarantees the right to take time for unpaid caring activities (see also Williams 2001).

In the context of social care, Tronto's (1993) observation that the moral agenda of rights and justice is usually conceptualised quite separately from the political agenda of resources also has particular resonance. Issues on the moral agenda, such as the promotion of service-user choice and control, frequently remain as unfulfilled aspirations because in the day-to-day reality of service organisation and provision the political agenda of resources always takes precedence. In many ways the personalisation agenda reasserts the aims of the community care reforms of the 1990s, when 'tailor-made' services were envisaged but never implemented in full because of a consistent shortage of resources (Means et al. 2003). With a projected 1.7 million more adults needing social care services by 2026 it is perhaps not surprising that the British government's concerns about resources and future funding options are dominant but they jeopardise the aims of service users for greater choice and control over services.

The ageing population and the personalisation agenda

The next part of the discussion will focus on the context of an ageing society ... Particular attention is given to key themes within the personalisation agenda: the individualisation of care and the focus on service-user control.

Demographic trends and needs over the life course

[T]he ageing of the population has generated a sense of urgency for policy makers. Currently, the emphasis is on finding ways to reduce the cost of providing care, with a number of strategies being followed including increasing preventive and re-ablement services and technological support that helps to maintain people in their own homes for as long as possible, as well as Direct Payments and Individual Budgets (DH 2008a).

However, demographic trends have another implication which is rarely considered in policies but which is highly relevant to a discussion of social care for older people. This concerns the connection between improved life expectancy and the concentration of death in old age. When the welfare of older people was being debated at the turn of the twentieth century just 24 per cent of deaths in the UK population were of people

aged over 65. By the turn of the twenty-first century this had grown to
84 per cent. The evidence demonstrates clearly that at whatever age we
die, it is in the period prior to our deaths that our claims on health and
care services are the greatest. Premature deaths are equally demanding on
resources and the costs associated with old age might therefore be more
accurately understood as the costs associated with dying (Lloyd 2010).
Increased life expectancy is also related to changes in the circumstances
of dying and the increase in chronic illnesses as causes of death. From an
ethic of care perspective chronic illness can be understood as increasing
the intensity of dependency in the period prior to death. Looked at from
this perspective care must necessarily encompass more than the restoration
of independence. Ultimately, what feminist ethicists refer to as inherent
human vulnerability is inextricably linked with mortality, and while
restoring or maintaining independence is crucially important for some
older people, the needs of others for whom this is no longer a possibility
should also be acknowledged in social care policies.

Age-related needs for care

The discussion document *Shaping the Future of Care Together* (DH 2009)
sets out the kinds of support that could be provided through personal
budgets. These include further or higher education, training to prepare for
a job, employment, bringing up children, caring for other family members,
volunteering, involvement in sport, leisure and social activities. There is
clearly little evidence here of *attentiveness* to older people's needs that arise
from events, such as a fall or stroke, or from growing frailty, degenerative
illness or cognitive impairment. On the contrary, policy aims such as these
represent a highly instrumental view of social care, portraying services as a
means of restoring people to their functions as active citizens.

   Waerness (2001) comments that there are separate and parallel discourses
on care for older people: the public management perspective of care
and the 'real world' practices of care. She argues that these two parallel
discourses should be brought together and that feminist ethicists should
seek to do this through the production of knowledge that is relevant
to policy makers (see also Twigg 2002). When policy makers speak of
social care for older people their focus is not on the daily activities
of helping them to wash and dress or to prepare and eat their meals
but on the economic challenge this need generates. Service providers
conceptualise care as a commodity and focus on its procurement, funding
and management. By contrast, an ethic of care would entail attentiveness
to the practicalities associated with dependencies that arise from frailty
and ill-health in old age. With its emphasis on human relationships and

connectedness, an ethic of care perspective would also consider how responsibility for taking care of older people's needs should be shared and would regard the question of resources not only in terms of how the costs of care should be managed and controlled but how they should be allocated to meet needs in a competent and responsive manner that does not exploit those who provide care.

Being 'in control'

In contemporary social care policies, placing service users in control is regarded as an unquestionable benefit for service users, ensuring that care is provided in a way that reflects their particular preferences and requirements. An ethic of care perspective raises a more complex picture by highlighting differences in needs and priorities between care providers and receivers.

Waerness (2001) distinguishes three basic forms of care: caring for dependants (where because of illness or disability one individual is dependent on another person to help them); caring for superiors (such as in employer/assistant relationships); and caring in symmetrical relationships in which balanced reciprocity is evident and the individuals involved in the relationship 'care for' each other. This last form reflects the experiences of many older people, whose giving and receiving of care reflects symmetry in the relationship and means it can be difficult to distinguish the carer from the cared for.

Waerness's typology is useful in demonstrating how in caring relationships power is not always in the hands of the carer but it is essential not to make assumptions about the quality of a relationship or to determine how control is exercised simply by looking at its form. For example, the provision of cash in lieu of services places service users in the position of employer, shifting them from the first to the second type, but the degree to which they are able to exercise control will vary significantly according to a wide range of factors. For example, the implementation of personalised budgets is a top–down process at the local level, with service providers determining the rates at which budgets are set. This will affect the rates at which care workers are paid and the local supply of care worker, thus impacting on the extent to which choice and control can be exercised. In addition, service users have widely differing capacities, which will impact on their caring relationships and their ability to exert control and manage their own care arrangements.

Kittay et al. (2005) argue that from an ethical standpoint independent living schemes should also be viewed from the perspective of the personal assistant, who is often invisible in debates concerning the provision of cash

in lieu of services. They point out how in the North American context
the supply of personal assistants depends on the migration of women from
developing nations whose pay and conditions of work are extremely poor.
From a UK context a related point is made by Yeandle and Steill (2007)
who identify both positive and negative experiences amongst personal
assistants employed through Direct Payments who found that their work
could be more satisfying because of the friendships that developed between
them and the people they supported but that these friendships could also
make it difficult to assert their rights as workers, for example, in keeping to
their contracted hours of work.

Control over caring arrangements also needs to be understood within
the wider power dynamics of the relationships. Kittay (2002) draws
attention to the relationship between dependency and power and the
potential for domination of vulnerable people by those with responsibility
for their care. This is a highly pertinent point to consider in relation to
the vulnerability of older people. Maintaining people in their own homes
can be a way of avoiding institutionalisation and can enhance reciprocal or
symmetrical family caring relationships. However, evidence on the nature
and extent of abuse of older people points to greater risks associated with
dependency for care on family, friends or neighbours (Manthorpe et al.
2008). According to a recent survey by the organisation Action on Elder
Abuse, 66 per cent of abusers were either family members or neighbours
and acquaintances. Arguably, safeguarding older people from abuse should
be at the heart of the implementation of the personalisation agenda, yet a
report by the Commission for Social Care Inspection in 2008 identified a
lack of awareness of the links between the two areas of practice and a lack
of involvement in the personalisation agenda by managers responsible for
safeguarding adults (CSCI 2008). An ethic of care would be attentive to the
potential for abuse within families and would minimise isolation in caring
relationships through appropriate support for both carer and cared for.

Individualism

With its focus on the individual, the personalisation agenda represents a
point around which different approaches to social care coalesce. Social
work traditions, consumerist values of individual choice and control and
the political aims of disabled people for non-institutionalised forms of
care all share an emphasis on individual self-determination and are open
to criticism from the perspective of the ethic of care. In social work, the
personalisation agenda is perceived to offer an opportunity to re-establish
core social work values by shedding the heavily bureaucratic administrative
approach that has dominated community care services. Carr and Dittrich

(2008), for example, argue that personalisation originated at least in part from social work values, which have always stressed respect for the individual and self-determination:

> Good social work practice has always involved putting the individual first; values such as respect for the individual and self-determination have long been at the heart of social work. In this sense the underlying philosophy of personalisation is familiar. (p. 8)

Carr and Dittrich's comments overlook long-standing debates in social work concerning its individualistic values. Jordan (2004), for example, argues that its individualistic focus allies social work with consumerist agendas of choice and independence and that this alliance runs the risk of creating an enforced form of independence for those who are poor and have little choice. Newman et al. (2008) make a similar point that the ideal of the consumer citizen within the personalisation agenda is vulnerable to neo-liberal political agendas in which the individual is expected to take greater responsibility for self-care, thus subverting the aims of enhanced choice and control.

A related point is made by Roulstone and Morgan (2009), who argue that personalisation runs the risk that enforced individualism and isolation will replace the enforced collectivities of old-style institutionalised services. This point calls into question the claims concerning the capacity of personalisation to enhance choice, since the chances of making a positive choice to move to a care home would be reduced, but it also directs attention to the conditions in which older people live in their own homes when they become more dependent. For example, the emphasis on maintaining people in their own homes has driven the development of telecare, which enables remote surveillance of older people's movements around their home and triggers rapid responses to unusual activities or alarms. From an ethic of care perspective, telecare is not undesirable if it is used in the context of supportive caring relationships, but it undoubtedly has significant potential to exacerbate isolation and loneliness. Where the aim is simply to enable an individual older person to remain in their own home, using telecare misses the point about the fundamental human need for social relationships.

From an ethic of care perspective, individuals are not already formed prior to engaging in relationships but it is through relationships with each other that individual identity is forged. Thus the older person should be seen in the context of their relationships, including those with carers. This perspective generates a different set of concerns. For those older people who lack supportive and caring relationships the aim of maintaining them in their own homes would need to be balanced against their need for social contact. Another concern is that older people's health status frequently fluctuates and changes and this poses a challenge to their identity as they experience a loss of self-reliance and growing dependency on others for help with everyday activities. In the context of a society that characterises them as a burden such challenges can be experienced in highly negative and damaging ways.

There are implications also for those who take on the identity of 'carer'. Kittay's concept of nested dependencies provides a constructive model for understanding the impact of caring on the identities of both carer and cared for, as it draws attention to the influence of wider relationships, including with health and social care professionals (Kittay 2002). In the UK context a question arises concerning the adequacy of support for carers in the context of increasing levels of care at home. The British government claims that the personalisation agenda will address pressures on family carers (DH 2008b) but the campaigning group Carers UK argues for a more holistic approach that understands carers not only within their caring role but in their lives more generally (Carers UK 2009).

[...]

References

Carers, UK (2009) *Policy Briefing: The National Strategy for Carers*, Carers UK, London.

Carr, S. & Dittrich, R. (2008) *Personalisation: A Rough Guide*, Social Care Institute for Excellence, London.

Commission for Social Care Inspection (CSCI) (2008) *Raising Voices: Views on Safeguarding Adults*, Commission for Social Care Inspection, London.

Department of Health (DH) (2008a) *Transforming Social Care*, Local Authority Circular DH (2008)1, Department of Health, London.

Department of Health (DH) (2008b) *Carers at the Heart of 21st Century Families and Communities: A Caring System on Your Side, a Life of Your Own*, Department of Health, London.

Department of Health (DH) (2009) *Shaping the Future of Care Together*, Cm7673, The Stationery Office, London.

Ferguson, I. (2007) 'Increasing User Choice or Privatizing Risk? The Antinomies of Personalization', *British Journal of Social Work*, Vol. 37, no. 3, pp. 387–403.

Fine, M. (2007) *A Caring Society? Care and the Dilemmas of Human Service in the 21st Century*, Palgrave Macmillan, Basingstoke.

Held, V. (2006) *The Ethics of Care: Personal, Political, and Global*, Oxford University Press, Oxford.

Jordan, B. (2004) 'Emancipatory social work? Opportunity or oxymoron', *British Journal of Social Work*, Vol. 34, no. 1, pp. 5–19.

Kittay, E. F. (1999) *Love's Labor: Essays on Women, Equality and Dependency*, Routledge, New York and London.

Kittay, E. F. (2002) 'When Caring is Just and Justice is Caring: Caring and Mental Retardation', in *The Subject of Care: Feminist Perspectives on Dependency*, eds E. F. Kittay & E. K. Feder, Rowman & Littlefield, Lanham, MD, pp. 257–76.

Kittay, E. F., Jennings, B. & Wasunna, A. A. (2005) 'Dependency, Difference and the Global Ethic of Long-term Care', *Journal of Political Philosophy*, Vol. 13, no. 4, pp. 443–69.

Lloyd, L. (2010) 'End of Life Issues', in *The Sage International Handbook of Ageing*, eds D. Dannefer & C. Phillipson, Sage, London and New York, pp. 618–29.

Manthorpe, J., Stevens, M., Rapaport, J., Harris, J., Jacobs, S., Challis, D., Netten, A., Knapp, M., Wilberforce, M. & Glendinning, C. (2008) 'Safeguarding and System Change: Early Perceptions of the Implications for Adult Protection Services of the English Individual Budgets Pilots – A Qualitative Study', *British Journal of Social Work*, Vol. 39, no. 8, pp. 1465–80.

Means, R., Richards, S. & Smith, R. (2003) *Community Care: Policy and Practice*, 3rd edn, Palgrave Macmillan, Basingstoke.

Meyers, P. A. (1998) 'The "Ethic of Care" and the Problem of Power', *Journal of Political Philosophy*, Vol. 6, no. 2, pp. 142–70.

Newman, J., Glendinning, C. & Hughes, M. (2008) 'Beyond Modernisation? Social Care and the Transformation of Welfare Governance', *Journal of Social Policy*, Vol. 37, no. 4, pp. 531–57.

O'Neill, O. (1996) *Towards Justice and Virtue: A Constructive Account of Practical Reasoning*, Cambridge University Press, Cambridge.

Roulstone, A. & Morgan, H. (2009) 'Neo-liberal Individualism or Self-directed Support: Are We All Speaking the Same Language on Modernization?', *Social Policy and Society*, Vol. 8, no. 3, pp. 333–45.

Sevenhuijsen, S. (1998) *Citizenship and the Ethics of Care: Feminist Considerations on Justice, Morality and Politics*, Routledge, London.

Sevenhuijsen, S. (2000) 'Caring in the Third Way: The Relation between Obligation, Responsibility and Care in Third Way Discourse', *Critical Social Policy*, Vol. 20, no. 1, pp. 73–80.

Tronto, J. (1993) *Moral Boundaries: A Political Argument for an Ethic of Care*, Routledge, London.

Twigg, J. (2002) 'The Body in Social Policy: Mapping a Territory', *Journal of Social Policy*, Vol. 31, no. 3, pp. 421–39.

Waerness, K. (2001) 'Social Research, Political Theory and the Ethics of Care', *Research Review*, Vol. NS 17, no. 1, pp. 5–16.

Williams, F. (2001) 'In and beyond New Labour: Towards a New Political Ethics of Care', *Critical Social Policy*, Vol. 21, no. 4, pp. 467–93.

Yeandle, S. & Steill, B. (2007) 'Issues in the Development of the Direct Payments Scheme for Older People in England', in *Cash for Care in Developed Welfare States*, eds C. Ungerson & S. Yeandle, Palgrave Macmillan, Basingstoke.

36

A little bit of heaven for a few?[1] A case analysis

Ann Gallagher and Nigel Sykes

Extract from A. Gallagher and N. Sykes, 'A little bit of heaven for a few? A case analysis', *Ethics and Social Welfare* (2008) vol. 2, no. 3, pp. 299–307, reprinted by permission of the publisher (Taylor & Francis Group, http://www.informaworld.com)

Introduction

... Clinical Ethics Committees (CECs) in health ... were first developed in ... the United Kingdom in the 1990s (Slowther et al. 2004). These committees engage with ethical issues that arise in care contexts and serve a number of functions, primarily ethics consultation, education and policy development. Committees meet regularly to analyse individual cases brought by clinicians and others. The role ... is to identify, analyse and attempt to resolve ethical problems that arise in practice (Singer et al. 2001). ... These committees also have a role in providing clinical ethics education to practitioners ... and in scrutinizing and developing institutional policies, for example, relating to resuscitation, ... or self-discharge.

Membership ... generally includes representation from professionals, lay membership ... and those with particular expertise in ethics and law. The membership at St Christopher's Hospice includes doctors, nurses, other health professionals, social workers and academics, thus bringing a wide-ranging inter-professional and inter-disciplinary approach to the cases discussed.

The case presented here was discussed at a recent CEC training day. It has been anonymized to preserve the confidentiality of the patient, family and professionals involved. We do not claim that this is a full discussion of the issues but we wish to suggest how the case might be approached more systematically by using a framework for ethical analysis. We conclude by pointing to some of the strengths and weaknesses of such frameworks in helping health and social care professionals to respond to ethical issues in the hospice setting.

The Case

Mrs M was a 77-year-old woman, diagnosed with pancreatic cancer, who was admitted to the hospice for symptom control. Her main symptoms were nausea and abdominal pain. ... For a period Mrs M was put on the Liverpool Care of the Dying Pathway[2] as she appeared to be deteriorating. However, her condition stabilized and she was taken off the pathway.

Mrs M had periods of anxiety but once her pain and nausea had been controlled she was considered mainly to need nursing rather than specialist palliative care. She repeatedly expressed a wish to die. However, when plans for transfer to a nursing home were discussed, she said that if this happened she would die more quickly. She asked if this was the intention of the hospice staff. Mrs M's daughter understood the reason for the transfer but was concerned that a nursing home would not provide the standard of care delivered by a hospice.

The ETHICS Framework

The ETHICS framework used in this paper was developed for the Open University Course A181 by Gallagher (2008). The approach requires the practitioner or CEC to:

> Enquire about the facts of the case
> Think through the options available to those involved
> Hear the views of those involved
> Identify relevant principles and other values
> Clarify the meaning and implications of the key values
> Select a course of action and present ethical arguments to support this

Enquire about the facts of the case

The clinicians ... confirmed that she had a diagnosis of pancreatic cancer. Pancreatic cancer accounts for about 2 per cent of all cancers and is most common in older people. Overall, there is a poor prognosis and patients may be told they have less than a year to live.[3] Mrs M was in the terminal phase with a limited life expectancy, thought to be a number of weeks, although her fluctuating condition made estimation of prognosis difficult as she had already outlived the expectation at the time of her hospice admission. ...

When the decision for transfer to a nursing home was taken Mrs M's pain was controlled by a subcutaneous infusion of a modest dose of morphine ... combined with medication that satisfactorily controlled her nausea. There were no further anti-cancer treatments available and once her key symptoms were relieved her main need was regular nursing care because of her general frailty.

... It was noted that Mrs M had already been in the hospice over twice as long as the average length of stay. A key question for the CEC was whether the nursing home would be able to offer ... an adequate range of treatment and care options and, if it could, whether there were any morally determinative reason why she should not be transferred there. The level of care and specialist expertise in a nursing home is not the same as in a hospice. The hospice team concluded that it was nonetheless adequate for Mrs M's needs. ... [A] hospice bed costs at least three times as much as a nursing home bed. The CEC also considered evidence relating to the impact of transfer from a hospice to a nursing home. ... [T]ransfers may be unsatisfactory for patients and relatives and that there may be 'a shortfall' in meeting their needs (Maccabee 1994). Patients may experience ... anxiety, apprehension, loneliness and depression and a move may result in higher mortality and morbidity (Porock et al. 1997). ... Reith and Lucas (2006) have argued that the evidence base for discharging patients to nursing homes is weak and conclude 'if in doubt, don't'. Although inconclusive, such perspectives from research have an important role in CEC deliberations.

Think through the options available to those involved

The two most obvious options were that Mrs M remained in the hospice or she was transferred to a nursing home. There were, perhaps, other options that might have been ... discussed with Mrs M and her family. Was, for example, discharge home possible or desirable? Might support at home have been available? ... Given Mrs M's condition, discharge home did not seem possible or desirable.

Hear the views of those involved

The professionals involved ... need to consider whose views are relevant ... It was important to hear the views of Mrs M and, with her consent, the views of her daughter. Professionals needed also to consider which team members were best placed to provide opportunities for Mrs M and her daughter to discuss their needs and preferences. Was there, for example, someone with whom Mrs M had a particularly good relationship? ... Mrs M had, potentially, conflicting views: on the one hand, expressing a wish to die and, on the other, objecting to a transfer to a nursing home as it would hasten her death. If a member of the hospice spiritual care team had met with Mrs M it might have been possible to have had more clarification regarding these seemingly conflicting views. Wanting to die does not, of course, mean that Mrs M would have wished positive steps to be taken to end her life.

Hospice staff may have had a range of divergent views: the nurses who worked closely with Mrs M may have been challenged by her wish to die, upset at her reluctance to be transferred and, perhaps, concerned that a move might indeed hasten her death. The palliative medicine consultant took the view that Mrs M no longer required the specialist services of the hospice and that her palliative care needs would [be] adequately met in the nursing home. The consultant was also ... aware of the number of people on the hospice waiting list and was keen that beds were made available.

Identify relevant principles and other values

The four-principles approach (Beauchamp & Childress 2009) is the most common framework of principles in biomedical ethics. All ... four principles (respect for autonomy, beneficence, non-maleficence and justice) were relevant to Mrs M's situation. ... Professional codes provide guidance regarding relevant professional values. Neither codes nor ... framework of principles make explicit which principle or value is paramount. If it was established that Mrs M was able to engage in autonomous decision making then should ... she have been permitted to remain in the hospice?

The CEC had to weigh up the benefits (beneficence) and harms (non-maleficence) to Mrs M of her remaining in the hospice versus her move to a nursing home. Might she be harmed by the move, as some of the evidence suggests, and as she had said? Was this a sufficient reason for her to continue to have a bed in the hospice ...? The CEC would ... also consider the impact of a decision on other patients ...

... [T]he principle of justice or fairness. If Mrs M's need for specialist hospice services was less than the need of others ... was it just that she should have been permitted to continue to remain in the hospice? ... It can also be argued that palliative care is more about a philosophy and a particular approach, and can be provided effectively in any care context provided adequate specialist expertise is available ... This ... must be balanced against the recognition that nursing home care is, by definition, less specialized than hospice care.

... The virtue of professional wisdom requires that professionals and members of the CEC are able to identify the salient features of the situation and understand the different perspectives of those involved. ... [P]rofessionals require courage, compassion and integrity to respond to what might be considered a dilemma – if Mrs M's autonomy was to be respected then another patient(s) would be deprived of a valued end-of-life opportunity ...; if Mrs M was transferred to the nursing home she might have become distressed and her life might, indeed, have been shortened. ... In both scenarios professionals might have felt callous and, perhaps, in a no-win situation. However, it is relevant to consider the ethos and purpose of hospice care and to acknowledge that although respect for autonomy is important, it was not necessarily the most important principle ... in this situation.

... Mrs M's daughter was involved in discussions and understood the need for the move to a nursing home. She was reassured that a community specialist palliative care team would follow up her mother in the nursing home. Mrs M's claim regarding the intention of the hospice staff may have had a negative impact on individual team members. They may, for example, have felt guilty and concerned that the move might indeed shorten her life or been offended or hurt that she could think this. They may have considered that she would benefit more (beneficence) from remaining in the hospice and might be harmed (maleficence) if she was moved to the nursing home. They might have felt a conflict between respect for the autonomous wishes of Mrs M and an awareness that other patients are in need of, and have a right to, a hospice bed – a conflict, therefore, between autonomy and justice or fairness.

Clarify the meaning and implications of the key values

...Two conditions are required for autonomy, that is, that an individual has agency (capacity to act intentionally) and liberty (freedom from influences that control or coerce) (Beauchamp & Childress 2009). [...]

It did seem that Mrs M had both agency and liberty although, arguably, her care options were limited. Respect for the autonomy of patients supports rules such as respect for privacy and confidentiality, telling the truth, obtaining consent and providing information that helps people to make decisions. [...]

Beneficence (do good) and non-maleficence (avoid or minimize harm) are generally considered together in relation to the question: will this action or omission result in more benefit than harm? The rules that emerge from the principle of beneficence include protecting and defending rights, preventing harm to others, removing conditions what would cause harm, helping and rescuing people (Beauchamp & Childress 2009). The rules that are said to emerge from the principle of non-maleficence include not killing, not causing pain, suffering, incapacity or offence and not depriving 'others of the goods of life'. The principle of justice is one of the most challenging principles. In simple terms, it can be thought of as relating to the fair distribution of benefits and burdens. Context is, however, all important. It is not uncommon to hear people speak of the situation in health and social care services as one of 'infinite demand and finite resources'. There is, therefore, not always enough to go around. Decisions have to be made about the allocation of resources (such as, in this case, a scarce hospice bed) and there is a need to underpin these decisions with criteria and arguments that are ethical. Beauchamp and Childress (2009) outline a range of principles relevant to the principle of distributive justice; for example, people should receive resources according to need, effort, contribution, merit, on the basis of a free-market exchange, or everyone should get an equal share. It is the first of these principles of justice – need – that seems most relevant to the situation of Mrs M and to other patients who are waiting for a hospice bed.

Select a course of action and present ethical arguments to support this

The CEC and the professionals involved concluded that it was appropriate that Mrs M be transferred to the nursing home with the support of hospice staff. It was also agreed that the approach of staff to Mrs M should continue to be sensitive and compassionate but also honest. The four ethical principles (autonomy, beneficence, non-maleficence and justice) were relevant to this case but, it seemed, that the key conflict was between respect for autonomy (if it was determined that Mrs M did not wish to be transferred) and justice. The case of Mrs M suggests that patients' expectations of hospice care need to be addressed prior to admission. Hospice stays are now shorter (a mean of two weeks) and interventions much more focused and often community based. Dying is not a reason per se for hospice admission unless it is accompanied by symptoms or psychosocial distress that cannot be managed in the community. It was acknowledged that responding to Mrs M was challenging and that staff may have an emotional reaction, for example feeling anxious and guilty lest her transfer resulted in negative consequences. It was acknowledged also that staff required courage to confront the issue and to inform Mrs M that once her level of need had been reduced to what could be catered for elsewhere it was appropriate that the hospice enabled other patients to access what is a scarce, valued and helpful resource. The End of Life Care Strategy (Help the Hospices 2008) supports the role of hospices in helping the NHS and ... nursing homes, to deliver high-quality palliative care.

What happened?

The hospice consultant explained the rationale for the move to Mrs M and reassured her that the nursing home could meet her needs with the assistance of the community palliative care team, and that readmission to the hospice would be possible should her needs change.

After a prolonged admission to the hospice (over five weeks, ... more than twice the length of the average stay), she was eventually transferred to a nursing home. Within a week there was a complaint from Mrs M's daughter about care in the nursing home. A meeting between the home care Clinical Nurse Specialist, the daughter and her husband and the nursing home manager resulted in some resolution. Mrs M spent two months at the nursing home before she died and after her initial difficulties was reported to have settled well there.

Discussion

We have considered how a CEC might approach the case of Mrs M using a framework for analysis. [...]

... [T]here are advantages in using a more structured approach in that there is the opportunity to work systematically through the issues and for CEC members to deepen their understanding of ethical concepts and arguments.

... [T]hey are facilitated to consider and articulate the key factual and ethical considerations.

[...]

Acknowledgements
The authors would like to thank members of the St Christopher's Clinical Ethics Committee and colleagues from Kingston Hospital Clinical Ethics Committees and from Princess Alice Hospice Clinical Ethics Committee who contributed to the case discussion at the CEC training day. We would also like to thank Professors Malcolm Payne, Paul Wainwright and Penney Lewis who provided comments that contributed to the development of this paper. Ann Gallagher would also like to acknowledge the support of the National Research Ethics Service who provided funding to attend the Imperial College applied clinical ethics course.

Notes

[1] Title from Clark et al (2005).

[2] The Liverpool Care of the Dying Pathway is a quality improvement framework for those who are dying. See www.liv.ac.uk/mcpil/liverpool_care_pathway (accessed 21 July 2011).

[3] See www.cancerhelp.org.uk/help/default.asp?page=7519 (accessed 3 June 2008).

References

Beauchamp, T. & Childress, J. F. (2009) *Principles of Biomedical Ethics*, 6th edn, Oxford University Press, Oxford.

Clark, D., Small, N., Wright, M., Winslow, M. and Hughes, N. (2005) *A Little Bit of Heaven For a Few: An Oral History of the Modern Hospice Movement in the United KIngdom*, Observatory Publications, Lancaster.

Gallagher, A. (2008) *Block 3: Introducing Ethics in Health and Social Care in A181 Ethics in Real Life*, Open University, Milton Keynes.

Help the Hospices (2008) *End of Life Care in England: How the Government could Change the Way We Die – Report on End of Life Care from the Hospice Movement*, Help the Hospices, London.

Maccabee, J. (1994) 'The Effect of Transfer from a Palliative Care Unit to Nursing Homes – Are Patients' and Relatives' Needs Met?', *Palliative Medicine*, Vol. 8, pp. 211–14.

Porock, D., Martin, K., Oldham, L. & Underwood, R. (1997) 'Relocation Stress Syndrome: The Case of Palliative Care Patients', *Palliative Medicine*, Vol. 11, pp. 444–50.

Reith, M. & Lucas, C. (2006) 'Transferring Patients from Hospices to Nursing Homes', *European Journal of Palliative Care*, Vol. 13, no. 6, pp. 241–43.

Singer, P. A., Pellegrino, E. D. & Siegler, M. (2001) 'Clinical Ethics Revisited', *BMC Medical Ethics*, Vol. 2, no. 1, available at: www.biomedcentral.com/1472-6939/2/1 (accessed 9th October 2008).

Slowther, A., Johnston, C., Goodall, J. & Hope, T. (2004) 'Development of Clinical Ethics Committees', *British Medical Journal*, Vol. 328, pp. 950–52.

SECTION EIGHT

The complexity of real lives

37

Mixing methods in a qualitatively driven way

Jennifer Mason

[...]

In this article I shall argue that mixing methods can be a very good thing indeed, but is not inevitably or by definition so (see also Bryman, 2004). The value of such approaches must be judged in relation to their theoretical logic, and the kinds of questions about the social world they enable us to ask and answer. I focus here on the value of mixed-methods approaches for researching questions about social experience and lived realities. [...]

[...]

Why mix methods?

There is a range of well-rehearsed arguments about the value of mixing methods, many of which centre on the concept of triangulation and its value in validating data or analysis, or in gaining a fuller picture of the phenomenon under study (Bryman, 1998, 2004; Fielding and Schreier, 2001; Kelle, 2001; Mason, 2002a). However, I want to put a rather different set of arguments for mixing methods. I start from two basic premises.

The first is that social experience and lived realities are multi-dimensional and that our understandings are impoverished and may be inadequate if we view these phenomena only along a single dimension. Let us consider an example from my own sphere of research interest – family and interpersonal relationships ...Viewed multi-dimensionally, these relationships are likely to involve elements and practices that are, in varying combination: emotional, sentient, imaginary, spiritual, habitual, routinized, accidental, sensory, temporal, spatial, locational, physical/bodily/corporeal, bio-genetic, kinaesthetic, virtual and probably more.

So, for example, my relationship with my mother may be characterized for me by the kinaesthetic and physical actions of manoeuvring her in her wheelchair, of her bodily presence and scent when we hug, of the touch and grasp of those once capable and grown-up hands that comforted me through childhood sicknesses, smacked my legs and 'knew better' than I did. Our relationship may be infused with the scent of her house – my childhood home, with a child's remembered secret places now transformed by the presence of mechanically utilitarian and aesthetically vile disability apparatus which my mother finds impossible to operate, and the growing untidiness and dustiness which she finds difficult to endure and which no-one but she would be able to put right. I may be haunted by the enduring sense of missing her when we are apart so that I telephone her daily or feel bad when I do not, and worry about her for hours at a time at work or during the night when I should be sleeping, yet I also experience the difficult tensions when we are physically together or when we speak on the phone, and our struggle to negotiate her increasing dependence. Everything between us may feel like it is shaped by the spatial and geographical distance between us and for me the complex, time-consuming, tiring and costly transport connections I must negotiate to visit her with all that time spent on the train, trying to work, failing to concentrate. Or the different socio-cultural world into which I feel transported when I visit her in her leafy home counties neighbourhood that feels simultaneously so much the past I have left behind yet the present that we are now creating, and of the shared regret and sometimes denial that she will never again be capable of visiting my distant home and experiencing its noise and chaos, its smells and secrets. My time with her may be dominated by my profound sense of homesickness for my own place and people, for their hugs and closeness and daily gripes and preoccupations. My mother and I may be frustrated by the tensions and disagreements between us about how lives should be lived, how food should be prepared and eaten, about religious faith, about what will happen to her things, keepsakes and treasures, her home, when she dies.

... [T]o understand how relationships work and are done, what they mean, how and why they endure or do not, how they are remembered, emulated or reacted against and in general what matters in and about them, we need a methodology and methods that open our perspective to the multi-dimensionality of lived experience. To do that ... we need to think creatively and multi-dimensionally about methods, and about our research questions themselves.... [S]imply to measure the frequency of visits between mothers and daughters, or even what they do together and their views of the quality of their shared time, will not capture the 'heart and soul' – the essence or the multi-dimensional reality – of what is taking place.

The second basic premise ... is that social (and multi-dimensional) lives are lived, experienced and enacted simultaneously on macro and micro scales. [...] In my earlier example, the 'macro' organization of transport systems, the 'socio-cultural' regulation of disability and impairment, and 'cultural' or 'public' narratives or collective organization of kinship and of dependence and independence, of region, class and identity, are all part of the frame along with the more apparently 'micro', 'subjective', 'individual', 'relational' or 'interpersonal' elements. Lived experience is about connections between these multi-dimensional domains.

Although my example relates to family and interpersonal relationships, it is important to note that these points about multi-dimensionality in experience and the transcendence of micro-macro divides are not confined to those substantive spheres. In her fascinating study of car culture and 'automotive emotions', Mimi Sheller puts a similar argument ... :

> Cars elicit a wide range of feelings: the pleasures of driving, the outburst of 'road rage', the thrill of speed, the security engendered by driving a 'safe' car and so on. They also generate intensely emotional politics in which some people passionately mobilize to 'stop the traffic' and 'reclaim the streets', while others vociferously defend their right to cheap petrol. ...
> Car consumption is never simply about rational economic choices, but is as much about aesthetic, emotional and sensory responses to driving, as well as patterns of kinship, sociability, habitation and work. Insofar as there are 'car cultures' vested in an 'intimate relationship between cars and people' [Miller, 2001: 17], we can ask how feelings for, of and within cars occur as embodied sensibilities that are socially and culturally embedded in familial and sociable practices of car use, and the circulations and displacements performed by cars, roads and driver. (Sheller, 2004)

Social science research methods need to match up to this complexity of multidimensional experience, and I ... suggest ... three sets of reasons why mixing methods can help ... inspired by a qualitative logic ...

1. MIXING METHODS ENCOURAGES US TO THINK 'OUTSIDE THE BOX'

I fully endorse the view that research strategies should be driven by the research questions we seek to answer, and part of this must involve choosing methods that are appropriate to the questions being addressed. Research questions themselves give expression to, but are also bounded by, the particular ontological and epistemological perspectives that frame the research. [...]

[A]lthough it is fairly widely accepted that our theoretical orientations inform our methodological practice, it is perhaps less readily recognized that this process works in reverse too (Skeggs, 2001) ... because the way we see shapes what we can see, and what we think we can ask. ... [V]ery few individuals are conversant or competent with a wide palette of interdisciplinary methods, or those spanning quantitative and qualitative demarcations. This means that research questions may tend towards conservatism, and social scientists may repeatedly miss whole dimensions of social experience because their methodological repertoire or tradition limits their view.

Mixing methods therefore offers enormous potential for exploring new dimensions of experience in social life, and intersections between these. It can encourage researchers to see differently, or to think 'outside the box', if they are willing to approach research problems with an innovative and creative palette of methods of data generation. This palette could certainly include, for example, the 'qualitative standards' of semi-structured interviewing, observation and textual analysis, and the 'quantitative standards' of social surveys, demographic or economic data collection and analysis. However, if we are to think outside the box, then methodological creativity should extend into other dimensions – for example, with visual or sensory methods which are grounded in and interested in dimensions other than talk or text (visual, aesthetic, material, aural, bodily, kinaesthetic), experimental as well as naturalistic methods, psycho-dynamic methods, bio-genetic methods, participatory methods, and so on. Of course, many of these methods are not easily or usefully defined as either quantitative or qualitative.

In proposing a palette of methods, I am not making an argument for eclecticism or for non-strategic proliferation of techniques, as though ... variety is an inherently good thing ... the logic for choosing which methods to select from the palette should as always continue to be governed by the questions that drive the research. However, ... the relationship between the questions and the palette of methods is ... an iterative one, and there is a will to think creatively and multi-dimensionally.

2. MIXING METHODS CAN ENHANCE OUR CAPACITY FOR THEORIZING BEYOND THE MACRO AND MICRO

Social theory and empirical research have what is sometimes an uneasy relationship, with some of the most significant strands of theorizing in recent times – for example, in relation to de-traditionalization, globalization, risk and postmodernity – drawing on little if any empirical 'evidence' (for example, Bauman, 1998; Giddens, 1999). On the other hand, there is a wealth of theoretically informed empirical research, particularly of a qualitative nature, that speaks to (and sometimes refutes) these 'big' theories, without necessarily crafting new theories on the same scale....

Partly, the problem may be that although these macro-scale theories make claims about far-reaching, sometimes global phenomena, these are manifested in the everyday lives and cultures of people and populations. In this sense, they are wanting to be macro and micro, global and local, socio-cultural and individual, all at the same time, and it is something of a challenge to conceptualize what form of empirical 'evidence' might be required to support this. ...

Some qualitative researchers have engaged effectively with the micro/macro question, starting apparently at the other end from the 'big' theorists. There is for example a long qualitative tradition that sees everyday or interpersonal interactions, life experiences, narratives, histories, and so on, as informing us not only about personal or 'micro' experience, but crucially also about the changing social and economic conditions, cultures and institutional frameworks through which ordinary lives are lived. In this sense, the macro is known through the lens of the micro – social change is charted in how it is lived and experienced in the everyday (Chamberlayne et al., 2000; Crow, 2002; Lawler, 2002).

[...] If the 'macro' cannot be fully explained without speaking *through* (not simply in opposition to) the 'micro', then micro and macro cannot stand in direct opposition to each other.

However, ... there is a tendency for social scientists to locate their research activities and orientations on one side or the other of a micro-macro (or similar) boundary, and this is not always helpful. For the 'big' theorists, their interest in primarily macro explanation and commentary appears to give licence to an unsystematic and idiosyncratic use of micro examples. For micro qualitative researchers, there is a bigger picture that their methods may not always enable them to see. [...]

The micro/macro boundary ... arguably ... hinders the development of meaningful social theory and explanation. Mixed-method research has a major contribution to make here, because it can help us to move beyond what is a rather unhelpful micro/macro impasse, using theoretically driven empirical research. This is particularly the case if we view mixed methods multi-dimensionally, rather than simply in qualitative-plus-quantitative terms, which risk mimicking and reinforcing the micro/macro distinction.

Instead, using mixed-method and multi-dimensional approaches, we can frame questions whose aim is precisely to focus on how different dimensions and scales of social existence intersect or relate. We can explore ... how it is that what we might think of as primarily micro or macro domains are shifting and fluid categories, and are in perpetual interplay. This allows the focus of the research (rather than its by-product or background) to be upon how social experience and 'real lives' are simultaneously or connectedly 'big and little', global and local, public and private, and so on. Using creatively mixed methods we can begin to assemble data and argument that can be woven into meaningful and empirically well-founded social theory.

3. MIXING METHODS CAN ENHANCE AND EXTEND THE LOGIC OF QUALITATIVE EXPLANATION

The particular strengths of qualitative research lie in the knowledge it provides of the dynamics of social processes, change and social context, and in its ability to answer 'how' and 'why' questions in these domains. ... I am drawing loosely here on a broadly inductive logic that informs a great deal of qualitative thinking. This involves exploring as fully as possible the situational contours and contexts of social processes, and then making strategic and theoretically driven comparisons with similar processes in other contexts, or similar contexts where different processes occur, to generate explanations. Conversely, quantitative research charts and sometimes aims to predict wide patterns and changes in social phenomena, and can say a great deal about trends, commonalities and averages. However, its emphasis on variable analysis and correlation mean that, although it can identify associations between variables, its capacity to explain what these mean and to understand the mechanics of the processes of association, is ultimately more limited.

... [Q]ualitative research has the explanatory edge precisely because it is concerned with *explanation* in a wider sense than measurement or causation.... [T]wo core elements in the logic of qualitative explanation ... are particularly important, and that can be extended and enhanced in mixed-methods work.

(a) A qualitative logic of comparison ... be it between cases, situations, contexts, over time and so on. Instead of seeking to compare by using standardized measures or comparators applied to all the cases, a qualitative comparative logic works by seeking to understand the distinctive dynamics, mechanics and particularity of each case *holistically*, and then to make comparisons at the level of analysis (Platt, 1988). As a consequence, qualitative research is not fixated on how to standardize units of measurement for cross-sectional analysis. This is important because, although standardization may be useful for some comparative purposes, it can have a stultifying effect on our capacity for understanding and interpreting social change. This becomes very clear in quantitative longitudinal surveys, where a concern for standardizing measures and

comparators over long time frames and over sequential sweeps of a survey, can result in a failure to spot changes that fall outside the measurement criteria. Similarly, in some quantitative cross–national comparative research, an approach that compares using the 'lowest common denominator' set of variables can miss crucial culturally specific explanatory factors (Ackers, 1999; Hantrais, 1999). Part of the problem ... is that change does not occur in standardized or predictable ways, so we need fluid and flexible ways of understanding it. That issue is compounded if we see social existence as multi-dimensional, with change occurring potentially on a range of dimensions that cannot be compared 'like with like'.

A qualitative logic of making comparisons at the level of analysis should therefore be at the core of a mixed-methods, multi-dimensional approach to explanation. Within that broad approach, ... some forms of comparison based on standardized measures, and indeed qualitative and multi-dimensional approaches can contribute creatively to the development of such measures. [...]

(b) Cross-contextual and contextual explanations The second core element in the logic of qualitative explanation ... is the significance of *context*....These situated and contextual understandings are at the centre of qualitative explanation and argument. Indeed, sometimes qualitative explanations are dismissed because they are seen as 'too local' or 'too contextual' to be able to underpin generalization or theorization. ... [U]nderstanding how social processes and phenomena are contingent upon or embedded within specific contexts is a vital part of meaningful social explanation. Going on to understand how they are played out across a range of different contexts makes possible the development of cross-contextual generalizations.

If we examine how social lives are lived in different contexts, and understand the relationship of the specifics of contexts to processes and practices, then we can begin to move between different contexts to develop the principles for cross-contextual explanation of the particular issues and concerns under scrutiny. There are two elements to this process. The first involves 'contextural' ... explanation, where the emphasis is upon explicating how different dimensions of context weave together in relation to the processes or questions driving the study – in other words, what particular constellations and groupings of (multi-dimensional) relevancies have meaning for a specific research problem or process under scrutiny? The second involves using a comparative logic to move across different contexts or settings, to enhance the scope and generalizability of the explanation. The logic of this approach, which draws on elements of case study and comparative case analysis, is that it factors contexts into explanation, rather than attempting to control for them or edit them out (Platt, 1988; Ragin, 1987).

[...]

... [W]e need sensitive and dynamic ways of understanding contexts, and creative thinking about what the relevant contexts might actually be. [...] We need an extensive repertoire of creative and mixed methods to be able to explore these elements.

The list of possible forms of context, of course, is endless, but context is not about lists ... Context means *associated surroundings* and the concept of 'association' is crucial here. The analysis needs to be able to show how these elements are connected to the issues and concerns of the study, and hence in what way they are *contextual* rather than coincidental. Mixed methods can help us to explore these relationships, and being able to do that can significantly increase the power of our explanations.

What we identify the relevant context to be depends upon the focus and nature of our enquiry, what processes or puzzles we are trying to explain, and of course our theoretical orientation. However, often, when context is invoked in a research report (either quantitatively or qualitatively) it is not even clear that there is a connection with the issues being researched, let alone an examination of how that connection operates. [...]

There cannot be one singular, universally applicable and unvarying 'context' whose salience can be known through a definitive specification of, for example, local area statistics and demographics, distributions of socio-economic characteristics (seen as variables), or attitudinal or behavioural patterns. Moreover, different social science disciplines and sub-groupings, and different research philosophies and methodologies, paint context in different ways across a micro–macro canvas. ... [E]xploring context in the sense of 'associated surroundings' means mediating between and conceptualizing beyond aggregate or individual, micro or macro. It also means allowing some fluidity between theoretical approaches. [...] My argument is that, if we are going to improve our capacity to explain and to ask and answer rigorous and useful questions in our complex social environment, we need to understand how contexts relate to social life, and factor this understanding into our explanations.

Dialogic explanations and creative tensions

... I have emphasized the importance of a qualitatively informed logic of explanation for theoretically driven mixed–methods research.

However, the construction of explanations based on mixed and multidimensional methods research poses its own challenges. How is it possible to reconcile different epistemologies and ontologies, which may result in vastly differing world views and may depend upon contrasting explanatory logics? How can we integrate different forms of data and knowledge?

... If we are seeking to use mixed methods to triangulate, or to corroborate each other, then this suggests an integrated framework, where we use each method and form of data to tell us about a specific part of 'the picture', or to provide views of 'the picture' from specified angles. [...]

...[W]e need to factor into rather than out of our mixed-method approaches the capacity to see and think about things differently and creatively. This suggests that, instead of seeking to 'integrate' methods and data, we should think in terms of looser formulations like 'linking data' (Fielding and Fielding, 1986), or 'meshing' methods?[1] But how can this be done without sinking into a relativist mire, where we have many different and fragmented descriptions of social experience, but no real explanation of anything? On the face of it, mixed-methods approaches are trapped between the devil and the deep blue sea.

I think the answer lies in how we construct our explanations and what we expect them to do. Explanations do not have to be internally consensual and neatly consistent to have meaning and to have the capacity to explain. Indeed, if the social world is multi-dimensional, then surely our explanations need to be likewise? I want to suggest that we should develop 'dialogic' explanations which are 'multi-nodal'. By 'multi-nodal' I mean that the explaining that is done involves different axes and dimensions of social experience. By 'dialogic' I mean that the ways in which these axes and dimensions are conceptualized and seen to relate or intersect can be explained in more than one way, depending upon the questions that are being asked and the theoretical orientations underlying those questions. ... [F]or 'multinodal' and 'dialogic' explanations, multiple relevancies and questions can be held together in creative tension and dynamic relation within the explanation itself. This involves factoring the different ways of asking questions, as well as the 'answers' into the explanatory process. Of course, this position develops from a constructivist epistemology (because it recognizes that explanations themselves are constructions, and that more than one version is possible) and hence represents a qualitatively driven approach to mixed-method explanation. But it moves beyond a qualitative solution to the problem.

The practice of dialogic explanation is particularly well suited to interdisciplinary collaborative or team-based mixed-methods research. ...This dialogic process, and the capacity of the team and its willingness to engage in ongoing constructive dialogue, are likely to be highly influential in the quality and scope of the explanations developed.

Conclusion: some qualitatively derived principles for mixing methods

Finally, ... there are a number of principles that inform the qualitatively driven approach to mixing methods ... put forward, and that can usefully guide practice. Each of these derives from qualitative thinking, but also each suggests a need to push against the boundaries of a purely qualitative paradigm.

1. A questioning, reflexive and non-accepting approach to research design and practice
[...]
2. Recognizing the validity of more than one approach
[...]
3. A flexible, creative approach
[...]
4. Celebrating richness, depth, complexity and nuance
[...]
5. A reflexive approach to what it is that data represent and how they constitute knowledge
[...]

In conclusion, the case ... for mixing methods in a qualitatively driven way says that such approaches should involve theoretically driven empirical research, and should push beyond the boundaries of a qualitative paradigm while retaining some key qualities and principles of qualitative approaches. Underpinning my discussion is a commitment to moving beyond paradigm wars and theoretical stalemates to find 'effective ways of proceeding' and of facilitating creative and innovatory research that transforms our ways of seeing, and enhances our capacities for asking compelling questions about the social world.

Notes
[1]The Leeds Social Sciences Institute team chose the term 'meshing methods' for its project because it was felt to be more flexible and therefore potentially would allow a range of strategies to flourish.

References

Ackers, L. (1999) 'Context, Culture and Values in Migration Research on Children with the European Union', *International Journal of Social Research Methodology* 2(2): 171–81.

Bauman, Z. (1998) *Globalization: The Human Consequences*. Cambridge: Polity Press.

Bryman, A. (1998) 'Quantitative and Qualitative Research Strategies in Knowing the Social World', in T. May and M. Williams (eds) *Knowing the Social World*, pp. 138–57. Buckingham: Open University Press.

Bryman, A. (2004) *Social Research Methods* (2nd edition). Oxford: Oxford University Press.

Chamberlayne, P., Bornat, J. and Wengraf, T. (2000) *The Turn to Biographical Methods in Social Science*. London: Routledge.

Coffey, A. and Atkinson, P. (1996) *Making Sense of Qualitative Data: Complementary Research Strategies*. London: Sage.

Crow, G. (2002) *Social Solidarities: Theories, Identities and Social Change*. Buckingham: Open University Press.

Fielding, N. and Fielding, J.L. (1986) *Linking Data*. London: Sage.

Fielding, N. and Schreier, M. (2001) 'Introduction: On the Compatibility between Qualitative and Quantitative Research Methods', *Forum Qualitative Sozialforschung/Forum Qualitative Social Research* (On-Line Journal) 2(1), URL (consulted 17 October 2005): http://www.qualitative-research.net/fqs-texte/1–01/1–01hrsg-e.htm

Finch, J. and Mason, J. (1993) *Negotiating Family Responsibilities*. London: Routledge.

Giddens, A. (1999) *Runaway World: How Globalization is Reshaping our Lives*. London: Profile.

Gillies, V. and Edwards, R. (2005) 'Secondary Analysis in Exploring Family and Social Change: Addressing the Issue of Context', *Forum Qualitative Sozialforschung/Forum Qualitative Social Research* 6(1), URL (consulted 17 October 2005): http://www.qualitative-research.net/fqs-texte/1–05/05–1–44-e.htm

Hammersley, M. (2004) 'Causality as Conundrum', Paper presented to ESRC Methods Programme Methods Festival, University of Oxford. URL (consulted 17 October 2005): http://www.ccsr.ac.uk/methods/festival/programme/Fri/am/D/documents/ hammersley.doc

Hantrais, L. (1999) 'Contextualisation in Cross-National Comparative Research', *International Journal of Social Research Methodology* 2(2): 93–108.

Kelle, U. (2001) 'Sociological Explanations Between Micro and Macro and the Integration of Qualitative and Quantitative Methods', *Forum Qualitative Sozialforschung/Forum Qualitative Social Research* 2(1), URL (consulted 17 October 2005): http://www.qualitative-research.net/fqs-texte/1–01/1–01 kelle-e.htm

Lawler, S. (2002) 'Narrative in Social Research', in T. May (ed.) *Qualitative Research in Action*, pp. 242–58. London: Sage.

Layder, D. (1993) *New Strategies in Social Research*. Cambridge: Polity Press.

Mason, J. (2002a) *Qualitative Researching* (2nd edition). London: Sage.

Mason, J. (2002b) 'Qualitative Interviewing: Asking, Listening and Interpreting', in T. May (ed.) *Qualitative Research in Action*, pp. 225–41. London: Sage.

Mouzelis, N. (1995) *Sociological Theory: What Went Wrong?* London: Routledge.

Mouzelis, N. (2000) 'The Subjectivist-Objectivist Divide: Against Transcendence', *Sociology* 34(4): 741–62.

Platt, J. (1988) 'What Can Case Studies Do?', in R.G. Burgess (ed.) *Studies in Qualitative Methodology,* Vol. 1, pp. 1–23. Greenwood, CT: JAI Press.

Ragin, C.C. (1987) *The Comparative Method: Moving Beyond Qualitative and Quantitative Strategies*. Berkeley, CA, and London: University of California Press.

Sheller, M. (2004) 'Automotive Emotions: Feeling the Car', *Theory, Culture & Society* 21(4/5): 221–42.

Skeggs, B. (2001) 'Feminist Ethnography', in P. Atkinson, A. Coffey, S. Delamont, J. Lofland and L. Lofland (eds) *Handbook of Ethnography*, pp. 426–42. London: Sage.

Smith, D.E. (1987) *The Everyday World as Problematic: A Feminist Sociology*. Boston, MA: North Eastern University Press.

Smith, D.E. (2002) 'Institutional Ethnography', in T. May (ed.) *Qualitative Research in Action*, pp. 17–52. London: Sage.

38

Researching social change

Julie McLeod and Rachel Thomson

In this chapter we draw on our book *Researching social change* (McLeod and Thomson, 2009) to provide an introduction to ways of researching temporal processes, that is, the passage of time and the ways in which personal biographies form part of broader historical trajectories, and vice versa. The book itself considers six methodological approaches, divided into three temporal registers: remembering (methods that deal with the past and how the past is apprehended in the present), being with (methods that involve researching in the present) and inheriting (methods that involve some form of exchange or transfer between generations). This chapter focuses on two examples of these methods. The first focuses on oral history as a research method, and the second on qualitative longitudinal research. In outlining these two approaches, we hope to show how research methods generate representations of the world, or data, that capture aspects of human and social experience. These data cannot be treated as simply producing the 'truth', but rather they constitute a form of knowledge that is partial (that is, reveals some things while obscuring others) and situated (is shaped by the conditions of its production). In sharing these examples we also hope to share our enthusiasm for the potential of empirical research to make a contribution to the world, enabling voices to be heard and demanding recognition of experiences and lives that may be marginal or difficult to hear.

Myths about time in social research

In 1984 the social psychologist Kenneth Gergen identified three underlying myths about time that circumscribe social research. The first of these is the privileging of synchronic over diachronic analysis, that is, the coincidence of events rather than the unfolding of events. This is reflected in the way that social science focuses on static entities (such as social class) rather than states across a temporal period (such as social mobility). The second is an adherence to research methods which truncate temporal patterns rather than allowing for periods/flows of time. Gergen points to how familiar features of everyday life require extended time horizons: whether this be phenomena at the micro level ('such as holding a conversation, playing games, teaching a lesson, having a fight, making love' [1984, p 8]), or phenomena that take place against a wider time horizon ('getting an education, developing friendships, carrying out a romance, raising a child, getting ahead occupationally' (Gergen, 1984, p 6), or even those macro-phenomena that qualify as historical and social changes. The third romance about time is what he terms 'the privileging of immutability over contingency' (1984, p 8), which translates as the search for laws that hold irrespective of time and place rather than situated meanings which recognise that the research itself is part of the data that it generates. More than 20 years after the publication of this book we feel that we are at last witnessing a turn towards time in social research which goes some way towards overturning these myths.

Research methods are the products of times and places. They have histories and the forms of knowledge that they produce are in turn productive of power–knowledge relations (Alastalo, 2008). The 'invention' of questionnaire-based survey methods and ethnographic fieldwork at the end of the 19th century enabled representations of the present, replacing a reliance on narrative and library-based approaches, which Peter Burke (1992) describes as an expression of a new moment in modernity and a shift in influence from the old Europe to the new world. The rise of biographical and narrative methods in the 1980s and 1990s spoke to the rise in influence of new social movements and a turn to subjectivity within western cultures and across academic disciplines. More recent talk of a 'crisis in empirical sociology', including anxieties about the lack of purchase of survey and interview methods in the face of commercial information technologies and 'real life' documentary genres, can be seen as yet another moment in this history of social research methods (Savage and Burrows, 2006). To illustrate these arguments, we turn now to our two examples, beginning with oral history, to show how research methods are products of particular historical contexts and can also help effect cultural and political change.

Oral history

Oral and life history take personal narratives and memories as a route into exploring social and historical processes. A focus on individual stories and 'subjective experience' (Chamberlayne et al, 2000) is accompanied by an interest in how histories and memories are constructed in the present. As a movement and a method, oral history gained ground during the 1970s amid a flourishing of social, labour and women's history (Thomson, 2007). These histories sought to understand the experiences of people whose lives were typically neglected or subordinated in the historical record – women, labourers, the illiterate – and oral and life history methods helped realise these ambitions (Perks and Thomson, 2006). This was a time in many parts of the world when political and social changes, such as the women's movement, permeated universities and challenged traditional forms of knowledge. Concurrently, a radical critique of historical methods from the 1960s onwards (Munslow, 1997) challenged the selection and construction of sources, the role of the archive, the privileging of written documents and the topics deemed worthy of historical investigation: whose past and what kind of experiences and events became recorded as history? Whether motivated by the concerns of socialist or feminist history, oral historians were united by a common desire to create a different kind of history. By excavating stories of oppression, they sought to transform understandings of the past and to build movements and invent counter traditions, which in turn would reshape the present, and the future.

Working with interviews and personal narratives, oral and life histories gave expression to experiences not necessarily or easily available through traditional archival and written sources. 'Our present *is* history', declared Daniel Bertaux (1981, p 35). Oral and life historians saw the past not as a distinct temporal domain, cut off from the present, but as indissolubly connected to the present. What we see in the past, the things remembered or forgotten, are shaped by what is happening in the present. Cultural studies researchers similarly explored 'the social production of memory', which describes all the ways in which memories and a 'sense of the past are constructed' (Popular Memory Group, 1982, p 207). The cultural and collective nature of memory was explored, and the Popular Memory Group saw the relationship between public representations and private memories as crucial. Oral history, the Group argued, is not about the past, but the 'past–present relationship' (1982, p 240), and such histories are 'profoundly influenced by discourses and experiences in the present' (1982, p 243). Memories are social and collective, but are manifested, apprehended and sustained in particular life stories. Individual memories, while idiosyncratically interesting, have the potential to illuminate cultural myths, dominant memories and public histories. Oral histories involve individuals in a process of making their own history, speaking back to and co-constructing public or collective histories.

The powerful social effects of oral histories are evident in recent Australian race relations, notably in responses to the forced removal of Aboriginal and Torres Strait Islander children from their families and the placing of them with white families or in orphanages and children's homes – forcibly removed children and their families are known as 'the stolen generations' (Haebich, 2002). In some Australian states, this continued from 1910 until the 1970s, and the devastating effects of these practices were documented in the commissioned report *Bringing them home* (HREOC, 1997). The National Inquiry received submissions from many Aboriginal organisations and Indigenous people, many in the form of an oral or life history, and these convey the impact of child removal on individuals, families and communities.[1] These oral histories show how experiences in the past continue to shape lives in the present, and have ongoing effects on future generations. Simultaneously, the circumstances of the time shaped how these stories and memories about the past were told, and received. These memories were held by families and communities prior to the Inquiry, but its establishment gave some formal, if overdue, sanction to these memories, recognising them as evidence, and saw the telling – and listening to – them as central to the political process of redressing injustice.

Since the report, these histories have been instrumental in driving calls for the Australian government to say 'sorry', to formally apologise for past acts of child removal. The former conservative Primer Minister, John Howard, refused to do so, arguing that the current generation could not be responsible for, nor feel guilty about, acts committed in the past. Following the election of a Labor government in Australia in late 2007, the new Prime Minister, Kevin Rudd, in the opening of Parliament in February 2008, formally apologised to Indigenous people. In his speech, the Prime Minister retold the recorded story of an Aboriginal woman, Nungala Fejo, who had been taken away as a child. In preparing his speech the Prime Minister met with Nungala Fejo and asked her permission to use her story; this also represented a symbolically important protocol. The stories contained painful memories; they belonged to people and should be used respectfully. The use of life histories was integral to how the government framed its apology; the stories showed in personal and direct ways how previous policies had affected individual lives, giving an immediacy to arguments about the need to acknowledge past wrongs in order to look towards a future politics.

Research methods are not decontextualised techniques: they have histories, they develop and become popular in particular times and places, and, as this example suggests, can be the means to provoke powerful emotional and political responses. The formal apology to Indigenous Australians – delivered with widespread public support – suggested not only that the politics of the present had changed, but also pointed to the power of testimony and oral histories to effect that political and cultural change. In the next section we consider another methodological approach to researching social change which works somewhat differently to oral history, although relying again largely on interviews and testimonies.

Qualitative longitudinal research

Social research that follows the temporal rhythms of lived lives is rare. Studies tend either to rely on retrospective accounts of the past (for example, life history approaches) or they seek to capture trends by repeating a survey with different groups of people. It is much less common for research to follow the same individuals or groups over extended periods using qualitative methods. Qualitative longitudinal studies aim to 'walk alongside' individuals or groups over time in such a way that privileges the present in which they are encountered (Leisering and Walker, 1998; Corsaro and Molinari, 2000). It is an approach that sits somewhere between the reflexive documentary approach of the Seven Up[2] series and the large-scale academic enterprises of long-term ethnographies and cohort studies. Bren Neale and Jennifer Flowerdew (2003) develop a cinematic metaphor to distinguish the value of quantitative and qualitative approaches to longitudinal research, within which the former is portrayed as producing a series of still pictures, frozen moments in time, offering 'a bird's eye view of social life that is panoramic in scope but lacking in any detail' (p 192). Developing the metaphor they argue that although quantitative longitudinal data has the capacity to sketch a 'grand narrative [...] it is a movie in which the intricacies of the plot and the fluid twists and turns of the individual story lines are hidden from view' (Neale and Flowerdew, 2003, p 192). In contrast, a qualitative approach to longitudinal research is able to provide the 'close-up' shot of real lives, with a focus on plot, story line, turning points and defining moments.

An example: the 12–18 project

The 12–18 project was a study of subjectivity, schooling and social change funded by the Australian Research Council and carried out by Julie McLeod and Lyn Yates. Over a seven-year period (1993-2000) the researchers interviewed and videotaped 26 young Australians (14 girls and 12 boys) as they aged from 12 to 18. The young people came from diverse backgrounds, and attended four different types of schools. Interviews were undertaken twice annually over the high school years, and twice in the year afterwards. In the researchers' words, 'we listened to these students talk about their sense of self, their values, attitudes to the future, and their experiences of school. Their individual narratives illuminate the uneven and differentiated impact of contemporary social and gender change, and the profound influence of school community and culture on the shaping of subjectivity' (McLeod and Yates, 2006, p 2).

Central to the research design of the study was a focus on *school culture*, and the sample of 26 was carefully constructed to include young people from similar class backgrounds going to different schools, as well as those from a different class background in the same school. So although the study followed individuals over time, it was also a *comparative* study of institutional culture and the way that institutions shape subjectivities.

McLeod and Yates locate their study at a crucial moment in the history of equity policy within Australian education. In terms of social inequalities, education policy had shifted away from the 'disadvantaged schools programme' of the 1970s through which resources were targeted at schools in poorer areas towards a focus on 'effective schooling' in the 1990s and the 'Schools of the Future' programme which economically rewarded 'schools who were seen to be winners' (McLeod and Yates, 2006, p 30). Discourses around gender inequality were also on the move, with the attempts of feminists in the 1970s to identify sexism within the curriculum, giving way to a mainstreaming of gender reform in the 1990s and a growing concern with the under-achievement of boys. McLeod and Yates were intrigued both to understand how these changes in policy and discourse were manifest in different kinds of educational institutions, but also in the kinds of subjectivities of the young people growing up in these contexts.

The 12-18 project was designed carefully to enable the researchers to engage with questions about school type, education policy and social divisions as well as providing biographical portraits of how individuals are formed and transform over time. McLeod and Yates explain that they attempted to build two forms of temporality into the study: historical specificity (what they call 'contemporary times') and the timescape of the adolescent or high school years (what they call 'biographical life stage') (2006, p 39). Through a qualitative longitudinal design they sought to bridge these two temporalities, showing the ways in which history is manifest in lives as well as demonstrating that the abstract and normative 'ages and stages' approach of developmental psychology is challenged by a recognition that nothing is inevitable in concrete times and places.

The 12–18 project is an example of an 'intense' research design, with relatively few cases over many waves. Lyn Yates has written about how their study was simultaneously very small (based on only 26 cases) and very large (350 interviews collected over eight years), and the consequences of this for methodological and substantive significance (Yates, 2003). The decision that the two principal researchers would also do all interviews as well as analytic work was also consequential, for the quality of the research and for the speed and duration of the project. The intensity of this kind of research means that the biographical time of the researchers (always in play in any form of knowledge production) becomes explicit, as they acknowledge in the preface to their book:

> During the eight years of interviews we saw the participants change and grow, and we thought often about our own children and the world and the situations they face. Our project was concerned with schooling and identity, and with retrospective and prospective visions of that. Doing this research evoked emotions and memories for us of our own growing up, our own schooling, and the support we had from teachers (in country high schools) our families, and especially our parents. (McLeod and Yates, 2006, p xi)

The interviews themselves were recorded on video, allowing the researchers to capture the changing bodies and demeanours of the research subjects as well as the interpersonal dynamics of the interview encounters. In each interview participants were asked to describe themselves as well as imagine themselves in the future or recollect themselves when younger. In the final year the researchers created compilation videos for each young person, drawing on excerpts from all their interviews, to be viewed in advance of the final research encounter.

The experience of conducting and living a qualitative longitudinal study results in a heightened awareness of the impossibility of separating the researcher from the researched, and of stepping outside the temporal flow that encompasses the whole research enterprise – from the power relations that shape policy agendas and funding decisions, and the ebbs and flows of fashion for social theory, through the biographies of researchers and their subjects through to the sequences of labour that constitute the research process. The method proceeds by capturing fragments of the 'present', in this case in the form of videoed interview encounters. These fragments are then brought together within new contexts, and interpretations and accounts are forged. These accounts are themselves fixed in times and places and may be revisited with hindsight. The nature of qualitative longitudinal research processes demand that we understand the endeavour as socially and temporally located *and* as mobile, and this has consequences for our claims about the kind of knowledge that we produce. This kind of insight can be very productive; as McLeod and Yates observe, 'refusing the possibility of full truth does not cancel meaning, does not remove the possibility of learning something new, of gaining insight while being mindful of the construction and limits of the research encounter' (McLeod and Yates, 2006, p 83).

We illustrate how qualitative longitudinal methodologies can capture the changes, continuities, motifs, repetitions and reiterations that are part and parcel of the process of becoming, by presenting McLeod and Yates's story of Brett, whose self-description remained consistent yet 'resonated differently in changing circumstances' (2006, p 81):

> When Brett was in grade 6 [end of elementary school], he looked directly at us, smiled, and told us that he sees himself as a good friend, kind and cheerful boy. This remains a vivid memory for us, one somewhat poignant in retrospect. He was sweet-faced, and slightly serious, excited about going to secondary school, which was one that had a poor reputation in the town and was known by other students as "Tip Tech", a "dirty school", where there were lots of fights. In the middle years of secondary school, he tells us again that he hopes his friends know that "I'd do anything for them". In his final year he is impatient with school and longs for the adult world of work, where he can be with his mates and be treated by others as an adult. At each of these stages, being close to his friends is important for Brett, and central to how he sees himself. But "having mates" takes on different meanings as Brett gets older, and he becomes more obviously embittered with the rest of the world around him. As he moves through high school, the commitment to his friends is no longer voiced as a gentle expression of concern for them, which we had found quite touching. Soon it becomes part of a litany of grievances he voices about the school and the uncaring teachers and about bullies and his readiness to fight. The relationships with friends are a refuge rather than a more intense reflection of how he relates to others, as it appeared in the earlier interview. Brett leaves school without completing his year 12 qualification, hoping to get work in the manufacturing and construction industries: it is likely that he will have limited opportunities for full-time work in the future. Doing things with his mates, being seen as a good friend becomes particularly important; signifying entry to adulthood against the child's world of school and providing a focus for activity against, simultaneously, the dull routine of school where he is labelled as a bad boy/a poor student and unreliable, and the likely prospect of unemployment. (McLeod and Yates, 2006, p 81)

A dynamic approach?

Research methods, the data they generate and the interpretations that we make from them are characterised by a dynamic relationship between temporal registers. While it can be necessary for analytic and everyday purposes to distinguish the past, present and future, they are inseparable, constitutive of the temporal flow (Elias, 1992). Philosophers of time have conceptualised this in different ways, for example, distinguishing between an objective measurable 'clock time' and an understanding of time as experienced subjectively. The notion that the past and the future are apprehended in the present has not always found its ways into empirical paradigms. Although different methodological strategies may emphasise particular temporal registers (for example, oral history may appear to be about the past), the interrelating dimensions of past–present–future are always in operation. So accounts of the past are created in relation to the demands of the present and in their telling evoke a possible future.

Another element of this dynamism concerns the dual aspect of continuity and change. Traditionally social theory has been schematised as either explaining continuity or explaining change (for example, via distinctions drawn between conflict and consensus theories). Yet empirical research regularly confronts us with the paradoxical nature of phenomena that express aspects of both (Crow, 2008). For example, the idea of the 'invented tradition', a term coined by historians Hobsbawm and Ranger, helps us see how the creation of national celebrations, which appear to establish continuity with the past, are in fact highly modern phenomena speaking to the future. As Paul Connerton (1989) observes, beginnings demand recollection and we tend to hear the 'echo of tradition at the moment of its de-authorisation' (Connerton, 1989, p 6). Such understandings offer a way of thinking about change where the past and present co-exist and where social reproduction is a situated and emergent accomplishment.

In this chapter we have attempted to show some of the ways in which methods for researching social change are themselves situated in particular social contexts and wider intellectual histories. This argument stands in some tension with traditional academic approaches in which research methods are seen to exist in isolation from people, times and places. Questions of timing and synchronisation tend to be glossed over when researchers report their methodologies. Temporality is even more invisible in accounts of analysis, with styles of academic writing tending to occupy an extended present within which claims to generalisation and validity appear to make sense. Making temporality visible also brings certain ethical dilemmas to the fore. In the case of projects conducted over time, such as qualitative longitudinal research, ethical complexity is amplified due to the long-term engagement of the researcher, and the changing demands of consent, perspective and representation. In the case of oral histories, eliciting difficult, painful or traumatic memories poses profound political and ethical challenges, particularly when harnessed to an agenda to provoke cultural change. And finally, across many qualitative methods for researching social change, the close relation between researcher and researched, developed in and over time, carries with it particular ethical challenges for how we interpret, represent and write about 'informants'.

Notes

[1] A selection of these stories can be found on the website of the Australian Human Rights and Equal Opportunity Commission: www.humanrights.gov. au/social_justice/bth_report/about/personal_stories.html.

[2] Seven Up is a series of documentary films produced by Granada Television and directed by Michael Aptred, following the lives of 14 British children since 1964 when they were aged 7. The documentary has seven episodes spanning 49 years.

References

Alastalo, M. (2008) 'The history of social research methods', in P. Alasuutari, L. Bickman and J. Brannen (eds) *The Sage handbook of social research methods*, London: Sage Publications, pp 36–41.

Bertaux, D. (1981) 'From the life historical approach to the transformation of sociological practice', in D. Bertaux (ed) *Biography and society: The life historical approach in the social sciences*, London: Sage Publications, pp 29–45.

Burke, P. (1992) *History and social theory*, Ithaca, NY: Cornell University Press.

Chamberlayne, P., Bornat, J. and Wengraf, T. (eds) (2000) *The turn to biographical methods: Comparative issues and examples*, London: Routledge.

Connerton, P. (1989) *How societies remember*, Cambridge: Cambridge University Press.

Corsaro, W.A. and Molinari, L. (2000) 'Entering and observing children's worlds: a reflection on longitudinal ethnography of early education in Italy', in P. Christensen and A. James (eds) *Research with children: Perspectives and practices*, London: Sage Publications, pp 179–200.

Crow, G. (2008) 'Thinking about families and communities over time', in R. Edwards (ed) *Researching families and communities: Social and generational change*, London: Routledge, pp 11–24.

Elias, N. (1992) 'Time: an essay', in N. Elias, S. Mennell and J. Goudsblom (eds) (1998) *On civilization, power, and knowledge: Selected writings*, Chicago, IL: University of Chicago Press.

Gergen, K.J. (1984) 'An introduction to historical social psychology', in K.J. Gergen and M.M. Gergen (eds) *Historical social psychology*, Mahwah, NJ: Lawrence Erlbaum Associates, pp 3-36.

Haebich, A. (2002) '"Between knowing and not knowing": public knowledge of the stolen generations', *Aboriginal History*, vol 25, pp 70-90.

HREOC (Human Rights and Equal Opportunity Commission) Australia (1997) *Bringing them home: Report of the National Inquiry into the separation of Aboriginal and Torres Strait Islander children from their families*, Commissioned by the Commonwealth Government of Australia (www.humanrights.gov. au/social_justice/bth_report/index.html).

Leisering, L. and Walker, R. (eds) (1998) *The dynamics of modern society: Poverty, policy and welfare*, Bristol: The Policy Press.

McLeod, J. and Thomson, R. (2009) *Researching social change: Qualitative approaches*, London: Sage Publications.

McLeod, J. and Yates, L. (2006) *Making modern lives: Subjectivity, schooling and social change*, Albany, NY: State University of New York Press.

Munslow, A. (1997) *Deconstructing history*, London: Routledge.

Neale, B. and Flowerdew, J. (2003) 'Time, texture and childhood: the contours of longitudinal qualitative research', *International Journal of Social Research Methodology*, vol 6, no 3, pp 189-99.

Perks, R. and Thomson, A. (eds) (2006) *The oral history reader* (2nd edn), Abingdon: Routledge.

Popular Memory Group (1982) 'Popular memory: theory, politics, method', in R. Johnson, G. McLennan, B. Schwarz and D. Sutton (eds) *Making history: Studies in history-writing and politics*, London: Hutchison, in association with the Centre for Contemporary Cultural Studies, University of Birmingham, pp 205-52.

Savage, M. and Burrows, R. (2007) 'The coming crisis of empirical sociology', *Sociology*, vol 41, no 5, pp 885-9.

Thomson, A. (2007) 'Four paradigm transformations in oral history', *The Oral History Review*, vol 34, no 1, pp 49-71.

Yates, L. (2003) 'Interpretive claims and methodological warrant in small-number qualitative longitudinal research', *International Journal of Social Research Methodology*, vol 6, no 3, pp 223-32.

39

Critically appraising qualitative research

Ayelet Kuper, Lorelei Lingard and Wendy Levinson

Extract from *BMJ* (2008) vol. 337, pp. 687-9.

Six key questions will help readers to assess qualitative research

[...]

In this article we offer guidance for readers on how to assess a study that uses qualitative research methods by providing six key questions to ask when reading qualitative research (box 1). However, the thorough assessment of qualitative research is an interpretive act and requires informed reflective thought rather than the simple application of a scoring system.

> **Box 1** Key questions to ask when reading qualitative research studies
> ▸ Was the sample used in the study appropriate to its research question?
> ▸ Were the data collected appropriately?
> ▸ Were the data analysed appropriately?
> ▸ Can I transfer the results of this study to my own setting?
> ▸ Does the study adequately address potential ethical issues, including reflexivity?
> ▸ Overall: is what the researchers did clear?

Was the sample used in the study appropriate to its research question?

One of the critical decisions in a qualitative study is whom or what to include in the sample – whom to interview, whom to observe, what texts to analyse. An understanding that qualitative research is based in experience and in the construction of meaning, combined with the specific research question, should guide the sampling process. For example, a study of the experience of survivors of domestic violence that examined their reasons for not seeking help from healthcare providers might focus on interviewing a sample of such survivors (rather than, for example, healthcare providers,

426

social services workers, or academics in the field). The sample should be broad enough to capture the many facets of a phenomenon, and limitations to the sample should be clearly justified. Since the answers to questions of experience and meaning also relate to people's social affiliations (culture, religion, socioeconomic group, profession, etc), it is also important that the researcher acknowledges these contexts in the selection of a study sample.

In contrast with quantitative approaches, qualitative studies do not usually have predetermined sample sizes. Sampling stops when a thorough understanding of the phenomenon under study has been reached, an end point that is often called saturation. Researchers consider samples to be saturated when encounters (interviews, observations, etc) with new participants no longer elicit trends or themes not already raised by previous participants. Thus, to sample to saturation, data analysis has to happen while new data are still being collected. Multiple sampling methods may be used to broaden the understanding achieved in a study. These sampling issues should be clearly articulated in the methods section.

Were the data collected appropriately?

It is important that a qualitative study carefully describes the methods used in collecting data. The appropriateness of the method(s) selected to use for the specific research question should be justified, ideally with reference to the research literature. It should be clear that methods were used systematically and in an organised manner. Attention should be paid to specific methodological challenges such as the Hawthorne effect,[1] whereby the presence of an observer may influence participants' behaviours. By using a technique called thick description, qualitative studies often aim to include enough contextual information to provide readers with a sense of what it was like to have been in the research setting.

Another technique that is often used is triangulation, with which a researcher uses multiple methods or perspectives to help produce a more comprehensive set of findings. A study can triangulate data, using different sources of data to examine a phenomenon in different contexts (for example, interviewing palliative patients who are at home, those who are in acute care hospitals, and those who are in specialist palliative care units); it can also triangulate methods, collecting different types of data (for example, interviews, focus groups, observations) to increase insight into a phenomenon.

Another common technique is the use of an iterative process, whereby concurrent data analysis is used to inform data collection. For example, concurrent analysis of an interview study about lack of adherence to medications among a particular social group might show that early participants seem to be dismissive of the efforts of their local pharmacists; the interview script might then be changed to include an exploration of this phenomenon. The iterative process constitutes a distinctive qualitative tradition, in contrast to the tradition of stable processes and measures in quantitative studies. Iterations should be explicit and justified with reference to the research question and sampling techniques so that the reader understands how data collection shaped the resulting insights.

Were the data analysed appropriately?

Qualitative studies should include a clear description of a systematic form of data analysis. Many legitimate analytical approaches exist; regardless of which is used, the study should report what was done, how, and by whom. If an iterative process was used, it should be clearly delineated. If more than one researcher analysed the data (which depends on the methodology used) it should be clear how differences between analyses were negotiated. Many studies make reference to a technique called member checking, wherein the researcher shows all or part of the study's findings to participants to determine if they are in accord with their experiences.[2] Studies may also describe an audit trail, which might include researchers' analysis notes, minutes of researchers' meetings, and other materials that could be used to follow the research process.

Can I transfer the results of this study to my own setting?

The contextual nature of qualitative research means that careful thought must be given to the potential transferability of its results to other sociocultural settings. Though the study should discuss the extent of the findings' resonance with the published literature,[3] much of the onus of assessing transferability is left to readers, who must decide if the setting of the study is sufficiently similar for its results to be transferable to their own context. In doing so, the reader looks for resonance – the extent that research findings have meaning for the reader.

Transferability may be helped by the study's discussion of how its results advance theoretical understandings that are relevant to multiple situations. For example, a study of patients' preferences in palliative care may contribute to theories of ethics and humanity in medicine, thus suggesting relevance to other clinical situations such as the informed consent exchange before treatment. ...There are many who believe that a key indicator of quality in qualitative research is its contribution to advancing theoretical understanding as well as useful knowledge. This debate continues in the literature,[4] but from a pragmatic perspective most qualitative studies in health professions journals emphasise results that relate to practice; theoretical discussions tend to be published elsewhere.

Does the study adequately address potential ethical issues, including reflexivity?

Reflexivity is particularly important within the qualitative paradigm. Reflexivity refers to recognition of the influence a researcher brings to the research process. It highlights potential power relationships between the researcher and research participants that might shape the data being collected, particularly when the researcher is a healthcare professional or educator and the participant is a patient, client, or student.[5] It also acknowledges how a researcher's gender, ethnic background, profession, and social status influence the choices made within the study, such as the research question itself and the methods of data collection.[6,7]

Research articles written in the qualitative paradigm should show evidence both of reflexive practice and of consideration of other relevant ethical issues. Ethics in qualitative research should extend beyond prescriptive guidelines and research ethics boards into a thorough exploration of the ethical consequences of collecting personal experiences and opening those experiences to public scrutiny (a detailed discussion of this problem within a research report may, however, be limited by the practicalities of word count limitations).[8] Issues of confidentiality and anonymity can become quite complex when data constitute personal reports of experience or perception; the need to minimise harm may involve not only protection from external scrutiny but also mechanisms to mitigate potential distress to participants from sharing their personal stories.

In conclusion: is what the researchers did clear?

The qualitative paradigm includes a wide range of theoretical and methodological options, and qualitative studies must include clear descriptions of how they were conducted, including the selection of the study sample, the data collection methods, and the analysis process. The list of key questions for beginning readers to ask when reading qualitative research articles (see box 1) is intended not as a finite checklist, but rather as a beginner's guide to a complex topic. Critical appraisal of particular qualitative articles may differ according to the theories and methodologies used, and achieving a nuanced understanding in this area is fairly complex.

Notes

[1] Holden JD. Hawthorne effects and research into professional practice. *J Evaluation Clin Pract* 2001;7:65-70.

[2] Hammersley M, Atkinson P. *Ethnography: principles in practice.* 2nd ed. London: Routledge, 1995.

[3] Silverman D. *Doing qualitative research.* Thousand Oaks, CA: Sage, 2000.

[4] Mays N, Pope C. Qualitative research in health care: assessing quality in qualitative research. *BMJ* 2000;320:50-2.

[5] Lingard L, Kennedy TJ. *Qualitative research in medical education.* Edinburgh: Association for the Study of Medical Education, 2007.

[6] Seale C. *The quality of qualitative research.* London: Sage, 1999.

[7] Wallerstein, N. Power between evaluator and community: research relationships within New Mexico's healthier communities. *Soc Sci Med* 1999;49:39-54.

[8] Mauthner M, Birch M, Jessop J, Miller T, eds. *Ethics in qualitative research.* Thousand Oaks, CA: Sage, 2002.

40

Learning about bisexuality: a case study approach

Rebecca L. Jones

Extract from R. Jones and R. Ward, *LGBT Issues: Looking beyond categories* (2010) Edinburgh: Dunedin Academic Press, reproduced with permission.

Bisexual people use and work in health and social care services but are often even less visible than lesbian and gay people (1). In this chapter, I … illustrate some of the ways in which bisexuality matters and can be relevant in health and social care settings.

[…]

These issues are examined through … case studies involving people who either identify as bisexual or who might be categorised by other people as bisexual.

[…]

Case studies

In the case studies that follow, I focus on three ways in which common features of bisexuality can complicate notions of the nature of sexual identities, and how this can have implications for health and social care. These are that, firstly, bisexuality is a particularly 'invisible' sexual identity – it is often overlooked as a possible sexual orientation and people are assumed to be really homosexual or heterosexual. Secondly, people who have attractions to or relationships with people of the same and different genders than themselves, either at the same time or over the course of their lives, may not describe themselves as bisexual. Thirdly, non-mainstream relationship patterns are more common among bisexual people and this can have implications when they use health and social care services.

First, a word about the provenance of these case studies. They are not based on particular individuals who took part in research studies. Rather, they are composites, based on the findings of a variety of research studies and also on real life situations known to members of the UK bisexual community. All the case studies have been reviewed by at least 25 people who are active in the UK bisexual community and by UK academics doing research into bisexuality. This review process took place partly online and partly during a workshop at BiReCon 2008 – a conference for academics and practitioners held as part of the annual national bisexual gathering, BiCon 2008 (www.bicon.org.uk/). These reviewers helped refine the case studies and agreed that they are plausible, authentic, realistic and, in some instances, common.

> **Mel** works in a care home for adults with severe physical and learning difficulties. She likes her job even though it is often extremely challenging and very tiring. She gets on well with most of her colleagues and they help each other to cope with the difficult bits of the work. She has been living with her partner, Cleo, since before she started this job. Her colleagues seem to deal okay with her having a female partner and Cleo even went along to a few work socials with some of the other partners. After a difficult few months, Cleo and Mel split up and Cleo moved out. Mel was quite upset but some of her colleagues were supportive and helped her to come to terms with the break up. Mel's colleagues had assumed that she is a lesbian but she actually identifies as bisexual. She has never mentioned this because it didn't seem immediately relevant when she was seeing Cleo, and she was worried about how they would react. After a few months she started seeing someone else, Martin. Eventually her colleagues find out about her new partner. She picks up that there is a lot of gossip about her going around and a few people make jokey comments to her about her 'coming back to join us' and that all she needed was the love of a good man. One colleague says that she always thought Mel was really straight and it must have just been a phase she was going through. Mel starts to feel really uncomfortable at work and no longer feels supported by her colleagues when service users behave challengingly. In the end this leads to her leaving the job because she can't cope with its stresses when she is not feeling supported by her colleagues.

This case study exemplifies how people's lack of awareness of the possibility that someone might be bisexual can create difficulties for individuals. Bisexuality could be described as an invisible identity, in this sense. Mel's colleagues have assumed that she is a lesbian because she had a female partner and, when this relationship ends and her new partner is a man, they assume that she is now, or indeed always really was, heterosexual. Such assumptions are perhaps not surprising, given the prevalence of the idea that people are either heterosexual or homosexual and the consequent tendency to equate someone's sexual identity with their current relationship, if they are monogamous. As Ochs argues:

A quiet bisexual will be assumed to be either heterosexual or homosexual. To avoid being mislabelled, a bisexual woman must declare her bisexuality and risk being seen as aggressively and inappropriately flaunting her orientation. (Ochs, 2007: p. 76)

It is perhaps because she does not want to be seen to be making an unnecessary fuss about her sexual identity that Mel has let her colleagues assume that she is a lesbian.

The comments her colleagues make about Mel 'coming back to join *us*', just needing to meet the right man, and positioning same-sex relationships as a phase, also highlight the latent homophobia of even workplaces that are apparently accepting of non-heterosexual relationships. The nature of Mel's work means that supportive and friendly relationships with colleagues are particularly important. These comments contribute to Mel's feeling that she is not accepted by her colleagues and her subsequent inability to cope with the challenges of her demanding job.

[...]

Muriel is 78. When she was a girl she had a series of intense 'crushes' on older girls but she met her husband-to-be when she was 18 and quickly fell in love with him. They got married and had three children. When Muriel was in her early-30s, her husband divorced her.

When she was in her late-30s Muriel joined a women's consciousness-raising group. In the group she came across the idea of lesbianism, which she had never heard discussed before and she met a woman, Pat, who already identified as a lesbian. Muriel was strongly attracted to her and before long they had started a relationship. After Muriel's children had left home, they lived together for several years, and became a familiar couple on the local lesbian scene. Pat developed breast cancer and, after many difficult months, she died. Muriel got a lot of support from her circle of lesbian friends and from a local voluntary organisation which supported lesbians and gay men who had been bereaved.

Some months later, to her astonishment, she fell in love with a man, Colin. Her friends were very disapproving of her new relationship and gradually cut contact with her. The new relationship flourished, although Muriel recognised that she was still attracted to women too and missed her old circle of friends, especially as she was still grieving for Pat. She didn't feel able to keep using the bereavement service because she no longer seemed to count as a lesbian.

In the mid 1980s, Muriel came across the idea of 'bisexuality' and started calling herself bisexual. After some years, the relationship with Colin ended

> amicably and Muriel met another woman, Joan, and went back to thinking of herself as lesbian because that was Joan's identity and she expected this to be the final relationship of her life.
>
> Last year Joan died and Muriel experienced some major health problems. She started receiving home care. She gets on well with one of her regular carers who asked her about the photos she had up around the house of her former partners. Muriel answers honestly but is horrified to discover later that her carer has spread malicious gossip among her colleagues about her past, saying that Muriel had been sexually predatory and promiscuous.

Over the course of a relatively long life, Muriel had relationships with both men and women. She identified variously as heterosexual, lesbian and bisexual. Such movements between identity labels are relatively common among women who have been sexually attracted to people of more than one gender (George, 1993; Ochs, 2007; Rust, 1995). Which identity she drew on at a particular time depended not only on who she was in a relationship with, but also on the social circles she was moving in, the wider political climate and the ideas about sexuality to which she had access. Like Mel, Muriel found that the support available to her to help her cope with traumatic life events depended on her displaying an 'acceptable' sexual identity. When Pat died she needed a bereavement support service that understood the additional issues of having lost a same-sex partner, but she did not feel able to continue to use the lesbian and gay bereavement service because she was now in a relationship with a man. Since she did not have a social group who identified as bisexual or who were sympathetic to her bisexual identity, she only experienced support when she identified as lesbian or heterosexual.

Once Muriel started receiving health and social care services in her own home, her past relationships with both men and women became the source of unpleasant gossip among her carers, a problem also experienced by some of the participants in Dobinson, MacDonnell et al.'s (2005) study. People who behave bisexually are often seen as greedy, promiscuous and predatory, a phenomenon which is claimed to be part of a wider biphobia (George, 1993; Mulick and Wright, 2002; Ochs, 1996, 2007).

> **Anne**'s first child, Luca, has been born six weeks early. Luca is in Special Care because of breathing difficulties and low birth weight. Anne has three partners, all of whom think of themselves as having a parental role – she is married to Jonti, Mark is the baby's biological father and Lara is also going to be extensively involved in bringing up the child. Lara was present at the birth but Mark and Jonti were not because the labour was very quick and they could not get to the hospital in time. The Special Care Baby Unit has a policy that

only parents can visit their children while they are on the Unit. The hospital has assumed that Jonti is Luca's father because he is Anne's husband. Anne is terrified about whether Luca is going to be alright and wants all her partners to see him so they will feel involved in his care and she will feel supported by their involvement. Lara was very moved by the experience of supporting Anne in labour and seeing Luca being born. She is now feeling bereft at him being taken away to somewhere she cannot see him. Mark is feeling angry about not being allowed to see his son, and is thinking of storming up to a nurse and shouting 'I am the father', but doesn't want to upset Anne by creating a scene. Jonti is longing to see Luca too, but feels a bit guilty that he should be the one allowed to visit when he is neither the biological father nor the person who was present at the birth.

Anne is in what is often described as a 'polyamorous' or 'poly' relationship – negotiated, consensual non-monogamy. Many bisexual people are monogamous, but poly relationships are more often found among people who identify as bisexual than among other groups (for further discussion, see Anderlini D Onofrio, 2004; Weitzman, 2007 and the special issue of the journal *Sexualities* (Haritaworn et al., 2006), so it can be an important issue for bisexual people using health and social care services. In this case, the hospital's definitions of who counts as a parent does not map onto the family's ideas and this creates unnecessary distress at what is already a stressful time.

Using case studies to explore bisexuality

In this chapter I have illustrated some of the ways in which bisexuality matters in health and social care settings. The case studies I have presented have emphasised some of the difficulties that may be experienced by bisexual service users and care workers due to others' lack of knowledge or unhelpful conceptualisations of what is meant by bisexuality. Change is needed at many different levels, from the strategic and organisational to the personal and emotional, if health and social care services are to be made accessible and acceptable to all people who have some relationship to the identity 'bisexual'. One important way in which care can be improved is by providing training and education to front-line care workers and their managers. Within a training and education programme, case studies such as these can provide a useful resource.

Summaries of people's experiences, based on real life, and presented in the form of a story can be a particularly effective way of presenting unfamiliar issues (Northedge, 2002). They can introduce a complex topic in a way that it unthreatening because it appears to be 'just about people'. They can provide concrete examples of apparently abstract issues which are grounded in everyday practice. They can provide a way of moving beyond fixed categories and thinking critically about them.

Case studies such as these can form the basis of discussion by asking participants to relate the stories to their personal experience and practice. Participants could address such questions as:

- Do you think the person in this case study would describe themselves as bisexual?
  - In what circumstances might it be helpful to use the word 'bisexual' to describe their identity?
  - In what circumstances might it be unhelpful to use the word 'bisexual' to describe their identity?
- How could things have worked out better for the person in the case study?
  - What could the care worker involved have done to help?
  - What could the care organisation do to make a better outcome more likely?
- Have you ever met someone like the person in this case study?
  - In what ways was their situation similar or different to the case study?
  - What happened for them?
  - What did you do?
  - Is there anything you wish you could have done?
  - Are there any ways you could help there to be a better outcome next time you meet someone in this situation?

Conclusions

There are, of course, many situations in which bisexuality is non-problematic or beneficial in health and social care. In particular, care workers who identify as bisexual, such as Mel, may constitute a valuable resource within organisations, since they may have the skills and experience both to raise awareness generally of bisexual issues and to work sensitively with bisexual service users. They may also be well placed to work with both heterosexual and homosexual service users, since they may have a good understanding of a range of different social networks.

There are, nonetheless, situations in which bisexual practitioners experience problems in health and care settings due to a lack of understanding of bisexuality. Given the relative invisibility of bisexual identities, colleagues are likely to have wrongly assumed that an individual is either heterosexual or lesbian/gay, on the basis of a current partner. Such an assumption may be especially problematic given the emotional demands made on many front-line care workers in the course of their day-to-day work, which makes the support of colleagues particularly important.

Bisexuality is also relevant when service users either identify as bisexual (like Anne and her partners, and Muriel at some points of her life) or have some relationship to bisexuality without so identifying (like [...] Muriel at other points in her life). Service providers' lack of understanding of bisexuality can create real difficulties in making services accessible and appropriate for bisexual people.

While some of these difficulties can be at least partially addressed by training and general awareness-raising activities (for specific suggestions in relation to health, see Dobinson et al., 2005). I have also argued ...that the relative complexity of bisexuality as an identity category makes this a more challenging task. How bisexuality is theorised affects how the categories work – at the most straightforward level, practitioners need to ask: are we talking about behaviour, identity or feelings here? The difference between these different theorisations of bisexuality can have major implications for service users and care providers. Someone who behaves bisexually but does not use that label to describe themselves is unlikely to use a service aimed at LGBT people, for example.

However, the relative complexity of the category 'bisexual' also carries benefits for care providers aiming to improve the accessibility and effectiveness of services. Since many bisexual people have changed the sexual identity label they use, and since bisexuality carries such various meanings, remembering the 'B' in LGBT can help care providers to remain aware of the provisional and fluid nature of all sexual identity categories.

Note
[1] The issue for Trans people is less often one of invisibility: see Firestein, B. (ed.) (2007) for a discussion of bisexual invisibility

Bibliography
Anderlini D Onofrio, S. (2004) *Plural Loves: Designs for Bi and Poly Living* Binghamton: Harrington Park Press.
Dobinson, C., MacDonnell, J., Hampson, E., Clipsham, J. and Chow, K. (2005) 'Improving the access and quality of public health services for bisexuals', *Journal of Bisexuality*, Vol. 5, No. 1, pp. 41-78.
Firestein, B. (ed) (2007) *Becoming Visible: Counseling Bisexuals Across the Lifespan*, New York: Columbia University Press.
George, S. (1993) *Women and Bisexuality*, London: Scarlet Press.

Hickson, F., Nutland, W., Doyle, T., Burbidge, N., Burnell, C., Cadette, M., Henderson, L., Ward, M., Woolls, C. and Weatherburn, P. (2000) 'Making it count: A collaborative planning framework to reduce the incidence of HIV infection during sex between men', CHAPS partnership, see www.chapsonline.org.uk/who-we-are, accessed 22 July 2011.

Mulick, P.S. and Wright, L.W. (2002) 'Examining the existence of biphobia in the heterosexual and homosexual populations', *Journal of Bisexuality*, Vol. 2, No. 4, pp. 47–64.

Northedge, A. (2002) 'Organising excursions into specialist discourse communities: A sociocultural account of university teaching' in Wells, G. and Claxton, G. (eds.) (2002), *Learning for life in the 21st century: Sociocultural perspectives on the future of education,* Oxford: Blackwell.

Ochs, R. (1996) 'Biphobia: It Goes More Than Two Ways', in Firestein, B.A. (ed) (1996), *Bisexuality: The psychology and politics of an invisible minority,* Thousand Oaks: Sage.

Ochs, R. (2007) 'What's in a name? Why women embrace or resist bisexual identity', in Firestein, B.A. (ed) (2007), *Becoming visible: Counseling bisexuals across the lifespan*, New York: Columbia University Press.

Rust, P.C. (1995) *Bisexuality and the challenge to lesbian politics*, New York: New York University Press.

Weitzman, G. (2007) 'Counseling bisexuals in polyamorous relationships', in Firestein, B.A. (ed) (2007), *Becoming visible: Counseling bisexuals across the lifespan*, New York: Columbia University Press.

41

Identifying and predicting drug-related harm with applied qualitative research

Stephen Parkin

Introduction

This chapter concerns a qualitative inquiry of public injecting drug use and aims to provide a summary of the way applied research may generate service-relevant findings in addition to meaningful contributions to the academic literature. More specifically, attention is paid to how data from semi-structured interviewing, ethnographic observation and visual methods (photography and video) may be 'triangulated' to establish more nuanced understandings and appreciations of the way in which illicit substances are prepared and injected in public/semi-public environments. A further section summarises how the analysis of qualitative datasets established a framework for predicting social behaviour and drug-related harm in specific environmental settings used for injecting illicit drugs.

Public injecting drug use

The term 'public injecting' is a self-defining expression that involves the injection of illicit drugs (for example, heroin, crack cocaine, amphetamine sulphate) in places frequented by a wider (non drug-using) population. 'Public injecting sites' (PIS), in contrast, are those shared community spaces that are temporarily frequented by injecting drug users (IDUs) for the purposes of preparing and injecting drugs. PIS can be further categorised into 'public' and 'semi-public', with the former including public toilets, parks, transport termini, telephone boxes, fast-food restaurants and shopping centres, in contrast to the carparks, derelict buildings, alleyways, abandoned vehicles and stairwells that comprise the latter. Dovey et al (2001) define PIS as occupying a 'liminal zone' that exists between public and private space, a place that is essentially 'out of the public gaze' (Dovey et al, 2001, p 324). Accordingly, the extent of public injecting in Britain is largely unknown (Rhodes et al, 2007) and is likely to remain this way due to the transient and secretive nature of both the act and those who participate in it.

Although public injecting may not be an openly visible phenomenon, it is possible to identify a particular 'risk profile' of those who may engage in such drug use. Namely, a frequent public injector would typically be male, homeless, unemployed and more likely to have spent time in prison, he will have injected a wider range of substances into more places in his body, will be more likely to have overdosed in the previous six months and more likely to report a greater range of dependency-related problems (Klee and Morris, 1995; Darke et al, 2001; Green et al, 2003; Fitzgerald et al, 2004; Navarro and Leonard, 2006; McKnight et al, 2007). Similarly, those consistent with such a profile are more likely to engage in a wider range of risk behaviours (for example, sex work, sharing drugs and injecting equipment within wider social networks) and report a greater range of physical harms associated with injecting (Klee and Morris, 1995; Darke et al, 2001; Dovey et al, 2001; Fitzgerald et al, 2004; Taylor et al, 2004, 2006; Small et al, 2006).

Research framework

It was within this area of knowledge that a study of public injecting took place in the city of Plymouth (Devon, UK) during 2006-09 (Parkin and Coomber, 2009a). This qualitative study of drug-injecting environments aimed to identify the effect of place on health risk, with a specific remit of informing local practitioners of drug-related harm associated with such settings.

An epistemological framework that prioritised 'harm reduction' informed the research. This is a philosophy and practice that has continued to inform international drug policy since the emergence of HIV/AIDS in the early 1980s. Harm reduction is also an established aspect of UK-wide local and national policy agendas due to various public health concerns associated with injecting drug use (principally relating to the management of blood borne viruses).

Methods and data analysis

A variety of qualitative methods were utilised. These included generic methods typically employed within social sciences research, such as semi-structured interviews, ethnographic and participant observation. Other 'less traditional' methods included the use of visual methods (photography and video) that were employed during 'environmental visual assessments' (EVAs) of injecting sites throughout the city environs. EVAs are essentially 'walk and talk tours' (see Pink, 2004, 2007, 2008; Rhodes and Fitzgerald, 2006) that involve key respondents guiding the researcher through a particular physical setting, with explanations of how place/space is affected by an issue (such as public injecting) by those with first-hand knowledge acquired via direct experience. These EVAs were initially conducted with a sample of agency representatives and involved visits to 41 PIS recognised by local authority employees (public toilets, car parks, shopping centres and other 'street-based' settings). While attending such settings, the relevant employees were interviewed regarding their experiences (including concerns and criticisms) of public injecting/injectors. In addition, photographs of PIS were taken in situ to establish a visual database of known injecting environments. More significantly, these images were used to inform semi-structured interview schedules designed for application among the second sample of research respondents, namely, local IDUs with recent experience of public injecting.

A total of 31 IDUs were recruited into the study from a number of drug-related services and interviewed in confidential rooms within appropriate settings.[1] The sample consisted of 24 male and 7 female respondents and most (23/31) were homeless or resided in non-secure housing (with friends, on the street or in hostels). Their average age was 33 and the average injecting career was 14 years. Almost all had served prison sentences for drug-related offences and some female respondents currently participated in sex work. In short, the respondent group was characterised by social and economic exclusion and reflected the risk profile of public injectors outlined above.

Twelve IDUs were invited to take part in a second phase of EVA, in which priority was to be given to injectors' perspectives of PIS. However, due to various drug-related issues, only seven of those invited actually completed the study (and perhaps this reflects the attrition rate when conducting research among vulnerable groups involving sensitive issues). These EVAs were considered integral to the study as they provided opportunities for the author to gain a more informed appreciation of a further 36 public environments used for illicit drug use throughout Plymouth (that is, a total of 77 different PIS were therefore assessed during the study). Such data (from IDUs) provided starkly contrasting views, explanations and accounts regarding the 'use' of public space to those obtained from the agency sample. In short, whereas the latter dataset provided an 'etic' (outsider) account of public injecting, the former provided an 'emic' (insider) evaluation.

These oppositional perspectives were consolidated by the use of video equipment during EVAs with IDUs while attending Public Injecting Sites (PIS). Whereas only photographs were taken of PIS with agency employees, the initial images served to substantiate the 'outsider view' of PIS, as they were essentially taken from the perspective of *'outside-*

looking-in'. However, the use of video provided opportunities to invert this perspective and to obtain a view of '*inside-looking-out*'. Namely, IDUs were asked to demonstrate how they accessed and exited the PIS concerned and to 'recreate' all injecting procedures (without actually using any drugs and/or injecting paraphernalia) associated with particular settings (such as carparks, stairwells, city centre toilet cubicles and/or railway sidings). Following this explanation, the author then repeated the process described by the IDU participant and used a video camera to record this account of emulated drug preparation/injection. In this manner, 'a bird's eye view' of PIS was obtained via the 'skilled vision' (Grasseni, 2004) of IDUs and further enhanced by the author's attempts to visually record the immediate 'injecting environment' in a 360^0 'sweep'.[2]

In employing these assorted methods, a broad range of qualitative data was generated for subsequent analysis. These datasets consisted of a comprehensive field journal, audio-recorded interviews with 31 IDUs and 37 agency employees, 400+ digital photographs and over an hour of video material collected from 77 PIS. Similarly, the range of data included experiences and opinions of public injecting from drug users and agency representatives/employees.

The data was principally analysed using a qualitative software package (NVivo 7 and 8), in which accounts, images and responses were coded into 'themes' such as 'injecting behaviour', 'perceptions of place', 'dirt', 'hygiene' and 'harm'. All analysis was epistemologically framed by the philosophy of harm reduction and safer injecting techniques associated with cleanliness and hygiene (see Preston and Derricot, 2006). Accordingly all data were considered from the harm reduction ideal of 'safer injecting facilities' (that operate in many cities throughout Europe, North America and Australia). These 'drug consumption rooms' aim to reduce drug-related harm by providing regulated, hygienic, sterile, supervised settings of injecting drug use. Although such facilities do not currently exist in the UK, these premises inadvertently provide a qualitative 'benchmark' for PIS comparison. As such, textual and visual data were evaluated alongside such applied harm reduction intervention in which analyses noted how environmentally *similar*, or how environmentally *distant*, each of the 77 PIS were to this ideal standard.

The analytical process of comparing and contrasting data obtained from varied qualitative methods alongside the experiences of PIS described by IDUs, agency employees and the author's own reflexive accounts served to totalise understandings of public injecting in the local setting. This was facilitated by a process of triangulation, described by Quine and Taylor (1998), that seeks completeness (not confirmation) of understanding by means of contrastive interpretation.

Findings: hazardous health places

One of the most significant, service-relevant, findings to emerge from this study was a framework for classifying PIS within an urban environment. This framework prioritises harm reduction (and therefore does not consider the use of public settings for injecting purposes in terms of criminality, morality or other sanction) and is known as the 'continuum of descending safety' (Parkin, 2009a; Parkin and Coomber, 2009b; Pearson et al, 2011).

Within this model, PIS are organised into three different environmental categories: namely, 'controlled', 'semi-controlled' and 'uncontrolled'. In this framework, 'control' refers to the 'naturally occurring' level of amenity available to IDUs within PIS that may facilitate safer practice/harm reduction. As such, 'controlled' environments (typically public toilets) provide varying degrees of sanitation: access to running water, relatively clean surfaces for preparation, the co-presence of others (in the event of drug-related harm) and limited levels of privacy. However, regardless of the range of amenity within 'controlled' environments, any harm reduction function is perhaps reduced due to a tendency for injecting to occur behind locked cubicle doors in which practice is typically rushed and drugs inappropriately administered.

Similarly, 'semi-controlled' environments are typically places within public settings that are frequented almost exclusively by IDUs for injecting purposes. Such 'hidden' places may include derelict buildings, wasteland and/or settings associated with street-based sex work. IDUs attending these settings are, in general, aware that they are places known within the local injecting fraternity. For this reason, 'semi-controlled' settings provide a harm reduction function due to the social orientation associated with such places (networking, co-presence of others and the sharing of resources including unused injecting paraphernalia).

Finally, 'uncontrolled' PIS are those associated with 'individual' IDUs and more related to 'opportunistic' settings of injecting episodes. Due to the spontaneous nature of behaviour within such settings, those within this category are less static, more transient and subsequently more difficult to monitor and observe (from a harm reduction perspective). Indeed, such PIS were more associated with rough sleeping, sex work and rushed/hurried injecting practice. Furthermore, those settings in this category offered the least opportunity for harm reduction to occur.

However, each PIS category was found to be equally associated with numerous injecting-related hazards. More significantly, it was noted that the relationship between environmental setting and particular behaviour both produced and reproduced injecting-related harm *in an amplified manner*.

This is perhaps made apparent in the following account of attempted overdose/resuscitation in a public toilet:

'... one of my mates (overdosed here) once an' me an' my other mate had one leg an' one arm each side of him. An' we had to carry him out the toilet (up two flights of stairs to street level), an' all the way up to the top of town (approximately 500 metres) an' leave him there where he was out of view of everyone till he came round a bit.' (Respondent V6, outside city centre toilets)

Furthermore, those settings considered to be 'semi-controlled' and 'uncontrolled' emerged as the most hazardous of all PIS. This may be substantiated with the following IDU comments recorded during EVA-related fieldwork.

'No (it's not a safe place). Not with the trains and things. If you are off your head, or if you fall asleep, or gouch-out and roll down the bank, *you're dead* ... it's a low risk place for getting caught *with* your drugs but it's a high risk 'cos you've got more chance of killing yourself here (with a train).' (Respondent V2, describing semi-controlled injecting site near railway embankment)

Similarly, the following account of injecting in an isolated stairwell further typifies an IDU acceptance of risk associated with drug use within uncontrolled settings:

'I think it's quite out the way; it's quite deep down there and don't think people would realise as they're going past that there is anyone down there. That's one of the reasons why (IDU) use it ... and people aren't gonna notice you lying on the floor unconscious there are they? I think the only way someone would have found you would be when the security guard locked up at night and checked the premises. So you'd probably be found within 24 hours. If you're lucky!' (Respondent V1, describing basement stairwell)

The hazardous health–place nexus was further confirmed in a retrospective analysis of newspaper reports concerning local drug-related deaths in public settings (*The Herald*, 2006, 2007a, 2007b, 2007c, 2007d, 2007e, 2008a, 2008b). During the period 2006-09, 10 deaths were noted throughout

Plymouth, in PIS that were known to the study. Of these, two occurred in public toilets, two in 'semi-controlled' settings and six within 'uncontrolled' environments of injecting drug use. More specifically, 80 per cent of drug-related deaths occurred in 'semi/un-controlled' settings, environments that are characterised by limited opportunities for the application of harm reduction. As such these tragic statistics serve to confirm the model as one of 'descending safety' and as a model that may be used as a tool to predict harm and hazard within outdoor injecting environments.

Discussion: informing policy and practice

Although this study was primarily an academic exercise that aimed to provide contributions to knowledge of a particular health concern (injecting drug use in public settings), it was also designed to inform local service development and practitioner intervention. Indeed, throughout/ subsequent to the study, local services and agencies were able to respond to findings that emerged from analysis. For example, the visual data gathered during fieldwork initiated local service responses to address 'semi-controlled' and 'uncontrolled' injecting environments, existing services were reconsidered (and redesigned) to accommodate public injecting (including hostel arrangements), local policing was reviewed and 'sharps' bins in public settings was further considered. Indeed, the value of the study may be noted in the following personal communication sent to the author from a local service provider that stated:

> (The study) allows services to target IDUs most at risk into treatment through outreach schemes; it provides feedback to services on the effectiveness of their needle exchange services, enabling better harm reduction interventions through a process of service review. It also tells you where risky people are so you can "go and find them" and offer them fast-track treatment.... (Wallace, 2010)

Additionally, study findings have been considered and disseminated at a national level. For example, the 'typology' model has been presented at numerous hepatology conferences attended by practitioners (such as consultants, general practitioners, nurses and drugs workers) as a means of further explicating the *social* and *environmental* routes of viral transmission (Parkin, 2009b, 2009c, 2010). Similarly, various visual aspects of the study have been considered by a national organisation as a means of providing 'safer injecting' information to IDUs (in the media of video, leaflets and posters).

However, the most ambitious service-relevant outcome of the study was the formation of the Public Injecting Rapid Appraisal Service (PIRAS) at the University of Plymouth (Parkin et al, 2010). The aim of PIRAS (as commissioned research) is to inform localised policy debates on how drug services, practitioners and community members may play a jointly constructive role in addressing public injecting drug use. Similarly, PIRAS-related findings aim to prioritise community safety/public health development with a particular focus on sustainable harm reduction. Accordingly, this harm reduction remit aims to prioritise the health concerns of IDUs and the *safety* of community residents as part of a programme of qualitative health research that has been (and continues to be) *applied* in local settings beyond the original study site.

Acknowledgement

The research was core funded by an Economic and Social Research Council (ESRC) Collaborative Award in Science and Engineering (CASE) studentship with co-funding provided by Plymouth Drug and Alcohol Action Team.

Notes

[1] Further details of all ethically approved recruitment procedures can be found in Parkin and Coomber (2009a, 2009b, 2009c, 2010a).

[2] A more comprehensive account of the visual methods attached to this study can be found in Parkin and Coomber (2009c).

References

Darke, S., Kaye, S. and Ross, J. (2001) 'Geographical injecting locations among injecting drug users in Sydney, Australia', *Addiction*, vol 96, pp 241-6.

Dovey, K., Fitzgerald, J. and Choi, Y. (2001) 'Safety becomes danger: dilemmas of drug-use in public space', *Health & Place*, vol 7, pp 319-31.

Fitzgerald, J., Dovey, K., Dietze, P. and Rumbold, G. (2004) 'Health outcomes and quasi-supervised settings for street injecting drug use', *International Journal on Drug Policy*, vol 15, pp 247-57.

Grasseni, C. (2004) 'Video and ethnographic knowledge: skilled vision in the practice of breeding', in S. Pink, L. Kurti and A.I. Afonso (eds) *Working images: Visual research and representation in ethnography*, London: Routledge, pp 15-30.

Green, T., Hankins, C., Palmer, D., Boivin, J.-F. and Platt, R. (2003) 'Ascertaining the need for a safer injecting facility (SIF): the burden of public injecting in Montreal, Canada', *Journal of Drug Issues*, pp 713-32.

Herald, The (2006) 'Police probe heroin deaths', *The Herald*, Plymouth, p 2.

Herald, The (2007a) 'Dead man in park is identified', *The Herald*, Plymouth, p 7.

Herald, The (2007b) 'Final hours of Czech friends killed by drugs', *The Herald*, Plymouth, p 4.

Herald, The (2007c) 'Jamie, 5 pricked by dirty needle', *The Herald*, Plymouth, p 1.

Herald, The (2007d) 'Man found dead in public toilets', *The Herald*, Plymouth, p 9.

Herald, The (2007e) 'Man's body found in city toilets', *The Herald*, Plymouth, p 5.

Herald, The (2008a) 'Another body in Mutley Park', *The Herald*, Plymouth, p 2.

Herald, The (2008b) 'Drugs scourge killed our son', *The Herald*, Plymouth, p 1.

Klee, H. and Morris, J. (1995) 'Factors that characterize street injectors', *Addiction*, vol 90, pp 837-41.

McKnight, I., Maas, B., Wood, E., Tyndall, M.W., Small, W., Lai, C., Montaner, J.S.G. and Kerr, T. (2007) 'Factors associated with public injecting among users of Vancouver's Supervised Injecting Facility', *American Journal of Drug and Alcohol Abuse*, vol 33, pp 319-26.

Navarro, C. and Leonard, L. (2004) 'Prevalence and factors related to public injecting in Ottawa, Canada: implications for the development of a trial safer injecting facility', *International Journal of Drug Policy*, vol 15, pp 275-84.

Parkin, S. (2009a) 'The effects of place on health risk: a qualitative study of micro-injecting environments', PhD thesis, Faculty of Health, University of Plymouth, Plymouth.

Parkin, S. (2009b) 'Places of risk, places of harm: visualising public injecting drug use in Plymouth', South West Hepatology Nurses' Group Meeting, Exeter, Buckerell Lodge, 20 November.

Parkin, S. (2009c) 'Places of risk, places of harm: visualising public injecting drug use in Plymouth', South West Hepatology Nurses' Group Meeting, Plymouth, Future Inn, 27 November.

Parkin, S. (2010) 'Risk, harm and opportunities for blood borne virus transmission in public settings: findings from a qualitative study of injecting drug use in Plymouth (UK)', British Association for the Study of the Liver: Nurses Forum, Royal College of Physicians, Edinburgh, 8-10 September.

Parkin, S. and Coomber, R. (2009a) '"Informal sorter houses": a qualitative insight of the "shooting gallery" phenomenon in a UK setting', *Health & Place*, vol 15, pp 981-9.

Parkin, S. and Coomber, R. (2009b) 'Public injecting and symbolic violence', *Addiction Research and Theory*, vol 17, pp 390-405.

Parkin, S. and Coomber, R. (2009c) 'Value in the visual: on public injecting, visual methods and their potential for informing policy (and change)', *Methodological Innovation Online*, vol 4, pp 21-36.

Parkin, S. and Coomber, R. (2010a) 'Fluorescent blue lights, injecting drug use and related health risk: findings from a qualitative study of micro-injecting environments', *Health & Place*, vol 16, pp 629-37.

Parkin, S. and Coomber, R. (2010b) *A rapid appraisal of public injecting and drug related litter in the London Borough of Barking and Dagenham*, Barking: Barking and Dagenham Drug and Alcohol Action Team.

Parkin, S., Coomber, R. and Wallace, G. (2010) 'Going public', *Drink and Drug News*, London, pp 14-15.

Pearson, M., Parkin, S. and Coomber, R. (2011) 'Generalizing applied qualitative research on harm reduction: the example of a public injecting typology', *Contemporary Drug Problems*, vol 38, no 1, pp 61-91.

Pink, S. (2004) *Home truths: Gender, domestic objects and everyday life*, Berg: Oxford.

Pink, S. (2007) 'Walking with video', *Visual Studies*, vol 22, pp 240-52.

Pink, S. (2008) 'Mobilising visual ethnography: making routes, making place and making images', *Forum Qualitative Sozialforschung/Forum: Qualitative Social Research*, vol 9, no 3, accessed 21 July at www.qualitative-research. net/index.php/fqs/article/viewArticle/1166/2575

Preston, A. and Derricot, J. (2006) *The safer injecting handbook* (6th edn), Dorchester: Exchange Supplies.

Quine, S. and Taylor, R. (1998) 'Methodological strategies', in C. Kerr (ed) *Handbook of public health methods*, Sydney, McGraw-Hill, pp 17-23.

Rhodes, T. and Fitzgerald, J. (2006) 'Visual data in addictions research: seeing comes before words?', *Addiction Research and Theory*, vol 14, pp 349-63.

Rhodes, T., Watts, L., Davies, S., Martin, A., Smith, J., Clark, D., Craine, N. and Lyons, M. (2007) 'Risk, shame and the public injector: a qualitative study of drug injecting in South Wales', *Social Science & Medicine*, vol 65, pp 572-85.

Small, W., Kerr, T., Charette, T., Schechter, M.T. and Spittal, P.M. (2006) 'Impacts of intensified police activity on injection drug users: evidence from an ethnographic investigation', *International Journal of Drug Policy*, vol 17, pp 85-95.

Taylor, A., Fleming, A., Rutherford, J. and Goldberg, D. (2004) *Examining the injecting practices of injecting drug users in Scotland*, Edinburgh: Effective Interventions Unit, Scottish Office.

Taylor, A., Cusick, L., Kimber, J., Rutherford, J., Hickman, M. and Rhodes, T. (2006) *The social impact of public injecting (Independent Working Group on Drug Consumption Rooms)*, York: Joseph Rowntree Foundation, Paper D.

Wallace, G. (2010) 'Reducing Injecting Drug Use', Personal communication via email, 14 June.

42

Experiences of drug use and ageing: health, quality of life, relationship and service implications

Brenda Roe, Caryl Beynon, Lucy Pickering and Paul Duffy

Extract from *Journal of Advanced Nursing* (2010) vol. 66, no. 9, pp 1968–79.

Introduction

With populations ageing, it is estimated that people aged 50 years and over requiring treatment for drug or alcohol problems will also increase. In the United States of America (USA) this number is projected to rise from 1.7 million people in 2000 to 4.4 million by 2020 (Gfroerer et al. 2003), and in Europe it has been suggested that people aged 65 years and over requiring treatment will double between 2001 and 2020 (EMCDDA 2008). In the United Kingdom (UK), the proportion of problematic drug users aged 50 and above in contact with drug treatment services in Cheshire and Merseyside has increased statistically significantly from 1998 to 2005 from 1.5% to 3.6% for men and from 1.9% to 3.2% for women (P < 0.001; Beynon et al. 2007). Problematic drug use is defined in the UK as use of opiates and/or crack cocaine (Home Office 2008). However, recent reviews suggest that services specifically for older people misusing drugs in the UK are not widely available or accessed by them, and that diagnosis of drug and substance misuse among this population is missed and access to services and treatment not provided (Crome & Bloor 2005a, 2005b, 2006).

[...]

The study

Aim

The aim of the study was to explore older people's experiences of substance use in the context of ageing, and its impact on health, quality of life, relationships and service use.

Design

An exploratory qualitative study was undertaken using semi-structured interviews with prompts.

Participants

A convenience sample was recruited from a voluntary sector drugs treatment service in the North West of England. Staff informed clients aged 50 years and above who currently used drugs about the study, and if they were interested gave them an information sheet. The names and contact details of clients willing to participate were passed on to the research team. Contact was made with potential participants and a convenient time and location that assured privacy and safety for the interview was arranged. Prior to interview participants were re-issued with the project information sheet and consent form, and received an oral explanation of the project followed by time for questions. The final sample size recruited was determined by thematic saturation of the data, with no new themes being identified (Morse 1995).

[...]

Findings

Interviews were conducted with a sample of 11 participants aged 49 years and over (nine men and two women; mean age 57 years, range 49–61 years). All participants were single, with five having been previously married but now divorced and eight living alone. Two lived with a male friend who acted as a carer, one lived next door to a friend/male carer, and another shared accommodation with other drug using 'mates'. Their accommodation varied, with some living in a hostel, their own homes (council house, flat or housing association bedsit), a care home or caravan. Interviews took place in a general practice surgery (n = 2), at home (n = 2), in the care home (n = 1) or at the drug service facility (n = 6).

[...]

Drug careers: past and present

Participants were categorized into two types of user: 'early onset' or 'later onset' problematic drug use. Early onset drug use commenced for most of those interviewed during adolescence or early adulthood as a consequence of recreational use, experimentation, escape or part of the 'hippie era', or was triggered by child abuse and/or a parent dying, as this typical quote indicates:

> Just bush (cannabis) (17 years) and then from there it went on to other things, y' know, until I got on to the hard stuff. I was about 21. (Man, 61 years)

'*Late onset*' problematic use of illicit drugs began later in the life course for some due to stressful life events such as divorce or death, or because of close personal relationships with a 'drug user', evidenced by this man talking about his partner:

> She's been using for another 6 months, so I was absolutely devastated. So I took them, thinking that the shock of how much she loved me, seeing me take drugs would stop her taking them. Y'know, that was how naive I was. And subsequently I ended up with a habit. (Man, 54 years), started using 6 years previously.

[...]

Consequently, a variety drugs was used first, such as amphetamines, cannabis, lysergic acid diethylamide (LSD), 'magic mushrooms' (containing psilocybin), morphine, heroin, speedballs (heroin plus, usually, cocaine), and people used drugs according to availability and personal choice based on their effects. Alcohol use and tobacco smoking also featured in their drug use repertoires ...

Characteristic features of drug taking patterns across their lives included drug/s of choice; periods of reduction, cessation and abstinence or cycles of relapse, maintenance and substitution of drugs and alcohol; and near continuous and even escalating consumption, for example of heroin as well as methadone and other drugs ... A characteristic of participants' ageing, and perhaps the influence of drug treatment services, was that all were trying to 'use' responsibly and to maintain their personal safety based on previous experiences. Such experiences included their own and others' overdoses, accidental and intentional deaths of 'drug-using mates', hospitalization, ill-health and unsafe personal situations in which they found themselves:

> [...]

So I've got to be very careful – my body's not what it was. Occasionally I can get carried away and I'll be feeling, because I'm feeling young inside, I'll be feeling young outside, which is just not so. These days I've got a handle on that. If I've been drinking a lot, I won't smoke. Even if I'm not feeling too good, I'll leave it until the alcohol's worn off some to make sure that I'm not going to go asleep and not wake up. (Man, 61 years)

Health and quality of life

Participants generally recognized that their drug use was having detrimental effects on their health. It had resulted in a range of chronic and life-threatening conditions which related to their physical and mental health, resulting in hospitalization and the need for ongoing treatment. Their health conditions included circulatory problems, such as deep vein thrombosis, injection site ulcers, stroke, respiratory problems, pneumonia, breathlessness, and conditions such as diabetes, hepatitis and liver cirrhosis. Malnutrition, weight loss, obesity and impaired mobility were also consequences. Impacts on their mental health included memory loss, paranoia and changed mood states, with anxiety and anger being common. Accidental injury due to falls and drug overdose also featured.

Changes in health status seemed cumulative consequences of drug use. One man aged 61 years said that his health had 'dramatically deteriorated' and, despite their survival and resilience, there did seem to be an accelerated experience of health changes with ageing. Some put these down to ageing and others to drug use or a combination of the two ...

Participants reflected on their lives and drug use over time. This life review made them remark on their survival, despite so many friends and acquaintances having died prematurely, and their own resilience. Death and dying was a common feature for all participants confronting their own or other people's situations, and seemed to be a specific accelerated feature of ageing for them. A man described using drugs and its associated lifestyle and culture as 'disgusting and squalid' (61 years). ...

All wished they had not started to use drugs, and some would advise younger contemporaries not to start or to quit, but commented that they did not seem to listen to their wisdom of experience. Drug addiction is powerful and hard to quit, with one man reporting that he did not want to grow old but knew that he would never give up drugs as this is too difficult. A small minority of participants aspired to abstain from drug use, and were abstinent or were reducing their drug use in order to become eligible for a detoxification programme and abstinence supported by drug treatment services. They expressed goals and life plans for the future. A majority were continuing to use drugs and were maintained by methadone replacement provided by primary health care or voluntary drug treatment services. Only a few reported that their drug use had increased despite their advancing age, and involved heroin as well as methadone, and they put this down to their living accommodation, living with fellow drug users, relationships and consequent lifestyles. They did, however, try to 'use' drugs safely and not put themselves at undue risk, which they might not have considered when they were younger.

Relationships and social networks

All participants were single or divorced, and loss of relationships with family members, spouses or partners and with their children due to divorce, death or drug use was a common feature. For a majority, drug use coincided with chaotic and non-sustaining relationships and lifestyles, with some also experiencing repeated imprisonment. Three men now relied on male carers who were also drug users for help and support with daily living. For others, pets provided key relationships which gave structure to their days, responsibility and companionship.

Loss of key relationships and social networks may have been an amplified and accelerated feature of ageing for participants as a consequence of their drug use over the life course. Confronting death and dying of oneself and others is a feature of ageing, but for this group of people earlier and accelerated experiences of loss, death and dying and their magnitude were marked. Loss of access to children and deaths of friends were described as heartbreaking. This was illustrated by a man who had experienced the early death of his father, which precipitated his drug career (at aged 14 years), the death of a baby son, and deaths of other drug-using friends and acquaintances:

> But there were people I would not sell to 'cos I knew they'd end up dead. Y'know, guys who'd just hit up and hit up and hit up until there's nothing left of them. Yeah. I found a few dead bodies as well (friends)…I went to theirs and (he) was in the chair. I just walked in the door and it was open. Oh stink, y'know, the smell in there was terrible, and I kicked a chair – he had this weird chair…And it went… he were dead, stone cold dead. (She) was upstairs full of maggots, she was a terrible state. I just called the police and they got rid of the bodies, but I had to go to a coroner's court just say that I found them. The downside to drugs is bad…One of my brothers was murdered and my other brother, he's got a family and I sometimes wonder what

it would have been like if I'd had…I have kids but don't now where they are. I mean, that's the way life is. (Man, 61 years)

This man attributed his own survival to frequently being in prison and the resulting enforced abstinence from drugs. He appreciated the close support of his remaining siblings and believed that his mother would have been proud that he has survived. He reflected that he would not want to be a burden on his family and would rather die. … [F]or many the loss of relationships with parents, siblings, partners, spouses and children was a feature, for a few, like the man above, family support was vital and enduring. One woman (aged 61 years) reported that her family did not want to know her while she was using heroin, but now that she was clean her family 'are all around me' and 'I feel more happier'. She was not depressed: 'Now I am off the two of them (alcohol and heroin) I am happy as a lark' and 'I feel better now than when I was younger'.

Chaotic relationships were a feature and related to past and current drug use. Some participants described other users as 'drug buddies', 'part of a fraternity' and said that 'users mix with users'; however, they described them as not 'true friends'. Some stated that they did not have any friends … Loss of supportive relationships, whether familial or friendship, deteriorating health and quality of life and living circumstances made them increasingly vulnerable and potentially socially isolated.

Service use

All participants were in contact with voluntary sector drug services, which reflected how the sample was recruited. They were generally positive about the care and support they received from drug treatment services, which largely met their needs. They also described other formal services they had received, such as primary health care, general practice or dental care, hospital and social services. In contrast, their experiences of these were mixed, with examples of less–than–favourable care due to their being drug users and stigma or prejudice of healthcare professionals, but with some instances of compassionate care and acknowledgement of their drug–using status.

The age range of the sample was 49–61 years, with some having been in contact with drug treatment services for over 20 years. A few participants revealed that they knew of contemporaries aged in their late 60s and early 70s who continued to smoke or inject heroin. It is unknown whether they were receiving drug treatment services. Therefore health and drug services are providing care to an increasing population of ageing drug users, although there may be cohorts of older users who are not receiving services and have unmet needs.

The majority of participants were having methadone replacement/ maintenance treatment, with a minority now abstinent or aiming for abstinence. They were generally positive about the specific drug treatment services and care provided, staff attitudes and relationships, and reported benefits. One woman described how bereavement counselling had been particularly helpful, from which this specific population could particularly benefit. In contrast, there were mixed reports of their own or friends' experiences of hospital and primary health care, which made some fearful of going into hospital:

> I won't go into hospital – my doctor goes mad. I went in and, 'cos you tell them you're on methadone, they come in one night…and they put it in one of them big syringes and squirted into my mouth in front of everybody. Makes you feel that big. You know, they shouldn't do that, they shouldn't do that at all. (Man, aged 58 years).

Others described instances of care and compassion by nurses which helped them recover and regain weight with improved nutrition. Services with tailored treatments based on compassion and care are required and feasible. There were some reported difficulties in accessing residential detoxification programmes, and preferences for individual as opposed to group-based treatment sessions, which illustrates the need for individualized and targeted care. Participants acknowledged that drug services were more widely available and accessible compared with when they were younger, and this was seen not only as positive but might have made a difference if they had been available earlier in their lives. It was thought that younger users, if they accessed services now, could avoid a lifetime of drug abuse and detrimental consequences ...

Their advice to younger people would be to 'keep off and not use drugs'. Ageing drug users and former drug users may have a role to play in service provision and prevention, based on their life experiences.

A further consideration for service provision is that older drug users may have different requirements and needs compared to younger users, and more specific tailored services are required:

> It's made me extremely depressed, in as much as the few that were left are people I could talk to, and at least there's consolation in company if it's good company. And the way it is at the moment the only company I could find if I wanted

to, apart from the likes of (D), who's an exception to the rule…would be people who are younger and on that totally different scene, and, like I say, I have nothing in common with them. I don't want to sit round a room talking about who sells the biggest bags, I don't want to sit round rooms talking about who sells the best crack, and that's the sum total of their conversations. And who stole off who, who didn't pay the fiver back the other day for the heroin he took from so and so.' (Man, aged 61 years)

Discussion

Study limitations

This was an exploratory qualitative study with a convenience sample of ageing predominantly male illicit drug users, and has provided information on issues of drug career, health status, quality of life, relationships, social networks and service use related to ageing within one geographical area of the UK and can help to inform future research and service development. This is an emerging area of investigation as an increasing number of drug users are surviving into older age (Levy & Anderson 2005, Beynon et al. 2007, Gossop & Moos 2008) and require the use of public and voluntary services to remain supported and living in the community. However, the study had a small sample, reflecting the lower prevalence in this ageing cohort and the difficulty of access and recruitment, and did not include affluent ageing drug users who could afford private treatment. Their experiences of ageing, drug career, needs and service use could differ. The study did not include older drug users who did not access support from drug treatment services, and they may also have different experiences and needs. A larger, longitudinal study with ageing cohorts representative of drug career, gender and social status from wider geographical areas is warranted.

Drug career and ageing

Ageing drug users could be classified into *early* and *later onset users* and a variety of drugs served as a gateway to drug use, as opposed to the general public perception that a particular drug or drugs or a pattern of drug-taking is responsible. Public health initiatives in the UK have largely targeted younger users (*early onset users*), focusing on preventing younger people starting drugs, harm reduction for individuals and communities, crime reduction, improved access to treatment and reduction of drug supply (..., National Institute on Drug Abuse 2003, ..., Home Office 2008). The common belief that drug use discontinues in middle age due to illness, death, voluntary cessation or for other reasons is simplistic and may not reflect real ageing and cohort effects (Gilhooly 2005, ...). Our findings concur with those in other studies that some people are *late onset users* as a result of life events and relationships, rather than early youthful escapism or experimentation (... Johnson & Sterk 2003, Levy & Anderson 2005). There is emerging evidence that drug use continues in old age and research is needed to understand the issues and consequences for older people and their families, and the implications for public services (Phillips & Katz 2001, Crome & Bloor 2005a, 2005b, 2006, Beynon et al. 2007, ... Gossop & Moos 2008).

[...]

References

Beynon, C.M., McVeigh, J. and Roe, B. (2007) 'Problematic drug use, ageing and older people: trends in the age of drug users in northwest England',. *Ageing and Society* vol. 27, pp. 799–810.

Crome I. and Bloor R. (2005a) 'Older substance misusers still deserve better services – an update (Part 1)', *Reviews in Clinical Gerontology*, vol. 15, pp. 125–133.

Crome I. and Bloor R. (2005b) 'Older substance misusers still deserve better services – an update (Part 2)', *Reviews in Clinical Gerontology*, vol.15, pp. 255–262.

Crome I. and Bloor R. (2006) 'Older substance misusers still deserve better services – an update (Part 3)', *Reviews in Clinical Gerontology* vol. 16, pp. 45–57.

EMCDDA (2008) *Substance use among older adults: A neglected problem.* Lisbon: European Monitoring Centre for Drugs and Drug Addiction, p. 4.

Gilhooly, M.L.M. (2005) 'Reduced drinking with age: is it normal?', *Addiction Research and Therapy*, vol. 13, no. 3, pp. 267–280.

Gfroerer, J., Penne, M., Pemberton, M. and Folsom, R. (2003) 'Substance abuse treatment need among older adults in 2020: the impact of the aging baby-boom cohort', *Drug and Alcohol Dependence* vol. 69, no. 2, pp. 127–135.

Home Office (2008) *Drugs: Protecting families and communities. The 2008 Drug Strategy*, London: Home Office.

Johnson, W.A. and Sterk, C.E. (2003) 'Late-onset crack users: an emergent HIV risk group', *Journal of Acquired Immune Deficiency Syndromes* vol. 33 (Suppl. 2), pp. S229–S232.

Levy, J.A. and Anderson, T. (2005) 'The drug career of the older injector.' *Addiction Research and Theory* vol. 13, no. 3, pp. 245–258.

National Institute on Drug Abuse (2003) *Preventing drug use among children and adolescents: A research-based guide for parents, educators and community leaders,* 2nd edn, Bethesda, MD: National Institute on Drug Abuse.

Phillips, P. and Katz, A. (2001) 'Substance misuse in older adults: an emerging policy priority', *NT Research* vol. 6, no. 6, pp. 898–905.

43

Critical reflections on the rise of qualitative research

Catherine Pope and Nicholas Mays

Extract from *BMJ* (2009) vol. 339, pp. 737-9

In 1993 the *BMJ* published an unusual article about qualitative research in which we reported a fictitious encounter in the corridors of health services research.[1] The article was a socratic dialogue between a quantitatively trained director of a health services research unit and a more junior qualitative sociologist. The dialogue was designed to stimulate debate about the dominance of quantitative research and, in particular, the randomised controlled trial in health related research. It went on to suggest that qualitative methods should be taken more seriously. Since then qualitative research methods have become far more widely accepted in health services research and many areas of medical and nursing research.[2-8]

Although it seems that qualitative research is established in healthcare settings, we are not convinced that it is always conducted appropriately. This article critically evaluates how far qualitative research has come and asks some searching questions about whether researchers are using its full potential to inform and improve health service organisation and the delivery of care.

...The scene is the retirement party in honour of the director of the research unit in the 1993 dialogue. We join him just as he concludes his speech of thanks.

DIRECTOR: And so, the unit has grown, both in terms of the number of people and the range of disciplines they draw on. We use diverse research methods, notably much more qualitative research. This is something I am proud of, and something I look forward to my successor taking forward. I wish her and all my former colleagues the very best of fortune. But I've talked long enough. There is food and drink waiting for us, so let's enjoy ourselves.

[The director sees someone he recognises approaching him]

DIR: So it is you. I didn't think you'd respond to my invitation considering our differences of opinion. How long has it been?

SOCIOLOGIST: 15 years.

DIR: You must be amused to hear me talking about qualitative research with such enthusiasm. But I have come round to your view. There is such a range of qualitative research going on and it's making a huge contribution. We even have qualitative work embedded in randomised controlled trials, helping to improve trial design and shape the outcome measures we use.[9] Most of the researchers here are using interviews and focus groups in their research. You'll have noticed that there was barely a regression equation in sight all afternoon during the scientific meeting in my honour.

SOC: You sound like me 15 years ago. What's happened?

DIR: Well, I have to admit, you really made me think. And after you left the unit I hired more social scientists, and we've come a long way since then.

SOC: I'm delighted that qualitative research is so much more mainstream. For one thing, I don't have to have to revisit those tired old arguments about small samples and "soft" science. But don't you think it's all got a bit out of hand?

DIR: I thought this was what you wanted.

Quality of qualitative research

SOC: Yes, but I do worry about the quality of some of the qualitative research out there.[10] Everyone thinks they can do qualitative research now, and I'm not always convinced we do justice to what we were trying to achieve when I started doing health research.

DIR: What do you mean?

SOC: Oh, you know, those papers that report thematic analyses. The kind that report six themes and don't explain what the relationship is between the themes and so don't really go anywhere in terms of trying to explain the data. Sometimes the problem is the word limits set by journals, but sometimes it's just superficial work.

DIR: But wasn't I reviewing one of your reports the other day? It had exactly that kind of analysis if I remember correctly.

SOC: Well, yes, you've caught me out there. But we had a tight deadline and were already late starting our next project. I just didn't have time to get beyond a basic analysis.

DIR: But haven't you got software like ATLAS.ti and NVIVO now? It must speed things up from the old days when you had to use sheets of paper and marker pens.

SOC: I still analyse my data like that, I'm afraid. The trouble with software packages is that you can actually get quite a long way without having to make sense of what you've found.

DIR: Now you sound as disapproving as me. That is how those of us with a proper statistical training feel about today's user friendly SPSS software.

SOC: Yes, I agree, though I suppose qualitative analysis software has helped make qualitative research acceptable. It certainly makes it look technical, which is quite appealing in health research. Software is useful, but it doesn't produce the interpretation for you; all too often that creative turn is missing.

DIR: Some of our researchers use something called framework for their research.[11] What do you think of that approach?

SOC: It's seductive because it looks systematic. But you have to use it with care and remember it was designed for tightly framed, commissioned policy research. It can sometimes be very deductive, which is odd for qualitative analysis. A real strength of qualitative research is induction – interpreting the data. That's where you find the unexpected. I sometimes worry that we don't push qualitative research far enough. I'd like it to be less descriptive and for us to try harder to explain things.

Ubiquity of interviews

DIR: Finally, you're talking like a real scientist. But, to be fair, qualitative researchers have changed the way the rest of us do research. We wouldn't design a study these days without incorporating people's views – talking to patients in depth – it's so important to get the users' as well as the professionals' perspectives.

SOC: But there are so many studies that are just based on "one shot" interviews. You end up with 20 minutes of talk, no private accounts, just surface description. Researchers short change themselves by taking talk at face value. I'm particularly concerned about interviews with health professionals, service managers, and policy makers. They're well educated and experienced at presenting themselves in public. It makes them hard to interview, but few people seem to try to get behind their façades. When you do, of course, things can seem very different. Checkland and colleagues highlighted this in their study of the implementation of clinical best practice guidelines in general practices.[12] The GPs they interviewed listed commonsense implementation barriers such as lack of time. However, their accounts could not be understood literally; instead, they related to the GPs' underlying beliefs about how work should be allocated in a general practice and what it meant to be a GP. The things that stopped GPs implementing guidelines actually had little to do with information management and shortage of time, the main reasons they gave to the interviewer.

DIR: I can see that one to one interviews taken at face value might be problematic. But maybe focus groups are less superficial, because people in a group talk to each other in a less self conscious way, don't they?

SOC: But focus groups are often only used to get hold of a bigger sample, which misses the point. People think that three focus groups of six people equates to 18 face to face interviews, but ideally you would use the group dynamics of a focus group to get more interesting data.[13] [14] I know I shouldn't say this, but I'm fed up with interviews. I'd really like to get back to doing more observation, or ethnography, so we can see what people really do, not just what they say they do.

DIR: But ethnography takes far too long and is difficult to get funded. It's just not efficient. It's also sometimes difficult to get permission to do observations from research ethics committees or healthcare organisations. Even if you do obtain funding, ethics approval and access to sites, you spend days hanging around and can't guarantee you'll see anything important. You also have to rely on an individual researcher to collect good data. With interview studies, I can send a team of less experienced researchers out with a topic guide and a tape recorder and they usually come back with useable data if they've been briefed properly. I'm not sure that ethnography is predictable enough in that way.

SOC: I think your enthusiasm for interviews is getting the better of you. I can see the practical constraints of ethnography, but, in fact, these are as much the result of assumptions from quantitative research about the appropriate length of time for research projects as inherent weaknesses in ethnography. As it happens, ethnographers are adapting to new time requirements. Health researchers are using ethnographic methods successfully and in the timescales of conventional research projects.[15]

DIR: But what about the more fundamental ethical issues with observation? How can you get consent from people when you don't know in advance who you're going to observe and what you might see or overhear? That book you gave me once about psychiatric hospitals and their effect on their patients was great,[16] but I can't see it getting through research ethics these days, what with the author pretending to be a physical education instructor on the hospital staff and collecting data covertly.

SOC: Don't get me started on the problems of ethics in qualitative research. I admit it's difficult, especially explaining to research ethics committees how it's possible for an observer to behave ethically without obtaining written consent from all the people she is going to observe.[17]

Mixed up methods?

DIR: Despite all these difficulties, more and more qualitative research is being done, and many studies use mixed qualitative and quantitative methods these days.[18]

SOC: I call it "mixed up" methods.

DIR: But you were always pushing us to consider qualitative methods alongside quantitative research.[1]

SOC: Mixed method approaches have made researchers take qualitative methods more seriously, but we are not really making as much of mixed methods as we could. Many studies use parallel methods, keeping qualitative and quantitative methods separate in the same study. And qualitative research still tends to be in a supporting role.[19] Researchers seldom think about how to integrate methods and findings[20] or take notice of the fact that different methods give you a different picture of what's going on (Box 1). You can't just add everything together. What happened to the idea that we could learn more from the fact that qualitative research looks at things in a different way?

Box 1: Qualitative and quantitative methods can be integrated at different stages in a research project

Design – eg, using qualitative interviews to develop a quantitative measure

Sampling – eg, using an initial survey to determine or provide a sampling frame for qualitative interviews

Analysis – eg, using qualitative research to inform priors for bayesian statistical analysis

Interpretation – eg, integrating the findings in chapter, papers, reports

O'Cathain suggests that health services research tends to be weakest at integrating at the analysis stage.[20]

DIR: So we don't always make the best of all the data in a study, but how do you square different accounts of the same thing, especially when you're up against a deadline?

SOC: I agree it makes things more complicated, but the creative tension between methods can be positive – it can lead to better, more complex explanations. The challenge is to provide an account that is dialectical –

that uses the different insights from different methods to tell us something new (Box 2).

> **Box 2:** Three examples of integrating mixed methods
>
> Turnbull et al examined geographical variation in use of general practice out of hours services using statistical analysis of routine data.[21] This generated hypotheses for qualitative research and prompted a choice of two very different locations to explore the role of place in determining service use.[22] The quantitative results also showed that the greatest variation in service use between urban and rural areas was in children aged 0-4 years (compared with other age groups), so the qualitative study focused on the experiences of parents of young children. Using mixed methods this research showed the importance of place in addition to distance or rurality in access to care
>
> Mannion et al used semistructured interviews and documentary analysis in six English NHS acute hospital trusts to look at the relation between culture and performance (in terms of the government's star rating system).[23] This was followed by a large quantitative study to see if the findings from the case studies were replicated nationally.[24] The research established that organisational culture varied across hospitals and that some of this variation was associated, in predictable ways, with organisational characteristics and performance
>
> Murtagh et al did a qualitative process evaluation alongside a randomised controlled trial.[25] As a result of observation and semistructured interviews the researchers decided to discontinue one arm of the trial because "the intervention in that arm, a standard gamble values elicitation exercise, was causing confusion and was unlikely to produce valid data on participant values"

DIR: That sounds ambitious in a typical two year, commissioned study. You sound so negative about most qualitative health research – isn't there anything positive?

Possibilities of synthesis

SOC: Well, I have been excited by the development of methods for qualitative synthesis.[26] For a long time, qualitative research has been criticised because it produces lots of seemingly unique and small scale case studies. Qualitative synthesis provides ways of integrating qualitative studies to build a cumulative knowledge base, and potentially for combining qualitative reviews with quantitative systematic reviews and meta-analyses. Of course, it won't be much good if the original studies were under-analysed. Then you just end up with an assembly of reports of people's views on a subject.

DIR: Well I am glad to hear you positive about at least one aspect of qualitative health research. It has been fascinating talking to you again.

[...]

Notes

[1] Pope C, Mays N. Opening the black box: an encounter in the corridors of health services research. *BMJ* 1993; 306: 315-8.

[2] Britten N. Making sense of qualitative research: a new series. *Med Educ* 2005; 39: 5-6.

[3] Kuper A, Reeves S, Levinson W. An introduction to reading and appraising qualitative research. *BMJ* 2008; 337: a288.

[4] Lingard L, Albert M, Levinson W. Grounded theory, mixed methods, and action research. *BMJ* 2008; 337: a567.

[5] Hodges BD, Kuper A, Reeves S. Discourse analysis. *BMJ* 2008; 337: a879.

[6] Reeves S, Albert M, Kuper A, Hodges BD. Why use theories in qualitative research? *BMJ* 2008; 337: a949.

[7] Reeves S, Kuper A, Hodges BD. Qualitative research methodologies: ethnography. *BMJ* 2008; 337: a1020.

[8] Pope C, Mays N. Reaching the parts other methods cannot reach. An introduction to qualitative methods in health and health services research. *BMJ* 1995; 311: 42-5.

[9] Medical Research Council. *A framework for development and evaluation of RCTs for complex interventions to improve health*. London: MRC, 2000.

[10] Seale CF. *The quality of qualitative research*. London: Sage, 1999.

[11] Ritchie J, Lewis J. *Qualitative research practice: a guide for social science students and researchers*. London: Sage, 2003.

[12] Checkland K, Harrison S, Marshall M. Is the metaphor of "barriers to change" useful in understanding implementation? Evidence from general medical practice. *J Health Serv Res Policy* 2007; 12: 95-100.

[13] Barbour R, Kitzinger J. *Developing focus group research: politics, theory and practice*. London: Sage, 1998.

[14] Dingwall R. Do focus groups provide all the answers? *J Health Serv Res Policy* 1999; 4:191.

[15] McDonald R, Harrison S, Checkland K, Campbell SM, Roland M. Impact of financial incentives on clinical autonomy and internal motivation in primary care: ethnographic study. *BMJ* 2007; 334: 1357-9.

[16] Goffman E. *Asylums: essays on the social situation of mental patients and other inmates*. New York: Doubleday, 1961.

[17] Murphy E, Dingwall R. Informed consent, anticipatory regulation and ethnographic practice. *Soc Sci Med* 2007; 65: 2223-34.

[18] O'Cathain A. Exploiting the potential of mixed methods studies in health services research. [PhD thesis.] University of Sheffield, 2006.

[19] Barbour RS. The case for combining qualitative and quantitative methods in health services research. *J Health Serv Res Policy* 1999; 4: 39-43.

[20] O'Cathain A, Murphy E, Nicholl J. The quality of mixed methods studies in health services research. *J Health Serv Res Policy* 2008; 13: 92-8.

[21] Turnbull J, Martin D, Lattimer V, Pope C, Culliford D. Does distance matter? Geographical variation in GP out-of-hours service use: an observational study. *Br J Gen Pract* 2008; 58: 471-7.

[22] Turnbull J. Out of hours general practice: an investigation of patients use and experience of access to services. [PhD thesis.] University of Southampton, 2008.

[23] Mannion R, Davies HTO, Marshall MN. Cultural characteristics of "high" and "low" performing hospitals. *J Health Organ Manag* 2005; 19: 431-9.

[24] Davies HTO, Mannion R, Jacobs R, Powell AE, Marshall MN. Exploring the relationship between senior management team culture and hospital performance. *Med Care Res Rev* 2007; 64: 46-65.

[25] Murtagh MJ, Thomson RG, May CR, Rapley T, Heaven BR, Graham RH, et al. Qualitative methods in a randomised controlled trial: the role of an integrated qualitative process evaluation in providing evidence to discontinue the intervention in one arm of a trial of a decision support tool. *Qual. Saf. Health Care* 2007; 16: 224-9.

[26] Pope C, Mays N, Popay J. *Synthesizing qualitative and quantitative health evidence: a guide to methods*. Buckingham: Open University Press, 2007.

Keeper
Andrea Gillies

Extract from *Keeper* (2009) London: Short Books.

"This book turned out to be as much about the unravelling of a carer as it is about the person cared for, but its starting point was wanting to write about Alzheimer's and about life with an Alzheimer's sufferer, my mother-in-law Nancy. We spent many years looking after Nancy at one remove, a responsibility made more stressful by distance, and then until recently, at a big Victorian house in a remote part of Scotland: Nancy and her disabled husband Morris, living with us and our three children"

[...]

"Morris has grown dangerously unsteady on his feet. His aides have doubled the number so that the twosomes can cooperate on the heavy lifting. The consequences of this prove far-reaching. He can't any longer manage his bathroom visits alone. He's too unsteady to manage the pulling up and down of trousers and knickers. He has to keep his hands on the Zimmer frame or he will fall. This puts the poor man in a very tricky situation. What makes it especially tricky is that Nancy stops cooperating. The manner of his demanding that she help, and her refusing, becomes an explosive part of every day. Chris helps Morris when he can, but often Chris is on the phone at the crucial moment. Morris would, in any case, far prefer that Nancy help him. He certainly doesn't want me in there, a scruple for which I'm grateful.

"Nancy! Nancy!" we hear, urgently from the sitting room. "No! Not that ! I need the Zimmer. The Zimmer frame . The Zimmer frame, there. The silver thing with the..... the frame, Nancy, the frame! The bars, the rack, the frame thing, there. There!" His conversations with her have become thesaurus-like. "The Zimmer. Right there, right in front of you. The thing right in front of you, the big silver thing, the Zimmer. No! Not the biscuit tin!" He takes a sharp breath inward, and bellows. "THE ZIMMER!".

Nothing I say to Morris can make him understand that Zimmer is part of the English that's become a foreign language to Nancy. She relies on cues now, cues and context, a "now you're hot, now you're cold again" kind of verbal directing, an impersonal in-car sat-nav approach. He may as well use the word zangle.

Unfortunately, by the time I get Morris into the bathroom, Nancy has had enough of being yelled at, and is marching off in the other direction. I leave him standing, balancing precariously while I run after her, taking her hands in mine and imploring.

Her reaction is predictable.

"Why on earth should I help anybody? It's got nothing to do with me."

This is the crux of it. Nothing has anything to do with Nancy any more. She floats free of connections to the world. Alzheimer's has invaded her empathy and placed its flag.

"That's your husband, though, Nancy," I tell her.

"No it is not. It most certainly isn't."

"Yes it is. Yes. Yes. You have to come and give him a hand."

"I never heard of anything so ridiculous."

"He needs help with the loo. And you are his wife. You need to go and help."

I'm wasting my breath giving her the back story. All she is listening to, responding to, is my authority over her, my determination that she should act. That alone will save the day. Her respect for my presumption of power is all that drives her acceptance of my orders.

Afterwards, she retreats to her bedroom, and that's where I find her, sitting on the side of her single bed, hands in her lap, staring downwards and utterly dejected. The conversation that we have now, the daily conversation about her living here with us her family, and her 47 years of marriage is becoming grindingly repetitive. As the saying (often attributed to Einstein) goes, the definitions of madness is doing the same thing over and over again and expecting different results, and from that point of view my explaining things is a mad enterprise.

Except on one occasion. On that day, instead of staring at the floor, she turns to look at me as I come in.

"I'm so glad it's you," she says with feeling.

"What's up, Nancy? What's up dear?" I ask, sitting by her. "It was only poor Morris having to go to the loo. He has to go to the loo every day in the afternoon and every day you help him. It isn't worth getting this upset about."

She fumbles with a tissue, twisting and untwisting it.

"I don't understand it," she says, looking into my face, her eyes wet with tears.

"What don't you understand?"

"I don't understand at all what is going on here."

I put my arm round her shoulders. She rests her head on my shoulder and cries, abjectly and with abandon.

"None of it makes sense," she says when she's able to talk. "What's happening here? How did I get here? What's happening? Please. Please."

What will validation do for us now? There's no cosy pretend world to slip into, averting our eyes from the present, taking refuge in dementia-fantasy, stepping through into dementia-time. What else is there to tell her but the truth? If it were me, that's what I'd want.

"Here's the thing," I tell her. "You have a condition. Your memory doesn't work properly. You don't remember things. That might seem like something quite trivial but actually, it undermines your whole life. It means that you don't really know who you are."

She snuffles through the tissue and tells me her maiden name.

"That used to be your name, but when you were about 30, a little over 30, you got engaged to a nice chap called Morris. You got married to him and you adopted two babies."

"But I don't remember that. I don't remember any of it," she says.

"That's because you have this illness and —"

"I am not ill. I am absolutely fine."

"You have a condition that lots of old people get. You're in great health otherwise, fit as a fiddle, but your memory is almost gone. Lots of old people get it."

"Am I old?"

"You're 79. nearly 80."

"Am I? Am I? I'm not. I'm not 80. Am I?"

"Yes. Nearly."

"Oh my God. That's right , is it? I'm 80." She laughs nervously. I consider taking her to the mirror but then think better of it.

Index